# Gandhi

# Gandhi

## A Political and Spiritual Life

*Kathryn Tidrick*

I.B. TAURIS
LONDON · NEW YORK

Published in 2006 by
I.B.Tauris & Co. Ltd
6 Salem Rd, London W2 4BU
175 Fifth Avenue, New York NY 10010
www.ibtauris.com

In the United States and Canada distributed by Palgrave Macmillan,
a division of St. Martin's Press, 175 Fifth Avenue, New York, NY 10010

ISBN 10    1 84511 166 4
ISBN 13    978 1 84511 166 3

A full CIP record for this book is available from the British Library
A full CIP record for this book is available from the Library of Congress
Library of Congress catalog card: available

Typeset in Monotype Ehrhardt by illuminati, Grosmont,
www.illuminatibooks.co.uk
Printed and bound in India by Replika Press Pvt. Ltd

# Contents

# List of Illustrations

*All illustrations courtesy of Hulton Archive/Getty Images*

# Acknowledgements

I would like to thank the friends and acquaintances in India who took an interest in my work, talked to me about Gandhi, and in various ways smoothed my path.

I would also like to thank the following institutions for their courteous assistance: the Gandhi Memorial Museum and Library, New Delhi; the Gandhi Library, Sabarmati Ashram, Ahmedabad; the Navajivan Publishing House, Ahmedabad; the Gujarat Vidyapith, Ahmedabad; the Nehru Memorial Museum and Library, New Delhi; the National Archives of India, New Delhi; the India International Centre Library, New Delhi; the British Library; the Library of the Vegetarian Society, Altrincham, Cheshire; the Library of the Mahatma Gandhi Memorial Foundation, Washington, DC; the Library of the American University, Washington, DC; the Center for Research Libraries, Chicago. In addition, I take with pleasure the opportunity presented by the publication of this book to record my indebtedness to the Library of Congress, which over the years in connection with this and other projects has been my principal resource. Its staff's dedication is beyond praise.

Lead, Kindly Light, amid the encircling gloom,
    Lead thou me on;
The night is dark, and I am far from home,
    Lead thou me on.
Keep thou my feet; I do not ask to see
The distant scene; one step enough for me.

*To Rachel and Sabino*

# Prologue

This is the story of the greatest Indian godman of them all. Known to the world as the leader of the Indian nationalist movement, Mohandas Gandhi entered politics, not to liberate his country in the sense understood by other Indian leaders and the western public which followed his career with such fascinated attention, but to establish the Kingdom of Heaven on earth. The Indian masses, who revered him, grasped this, up to a point. They knew that a mahatma walked among them, poured out their devotion, and awaited results. But the adoring masses possessed as little conception as anyone else outside Gandhi's inner circle of the complex system of religious ideas, refined through years of self-scrutiny and reflection on events, which guided his every action. These ideas, though clothed in Hindu terminology, were not Hindu in origin. They owed their existence to Gandhi's precipitation in his youth into the atmosphere of experimentation with esoteric and occult forms of religion which flourished in the London of the 1880s, where he went to qualify as a barrister. An innocent vegetarian, seeking out first wholesome food and then the company of reformers who ate through preference what he ate through obedience to custom, the young Gandhi stumbled into a world of theosophists, esoteric Christians, vital food enthusiasts, and exponents of the simple life, which proved utterly formative. Later influences – Tolstoy, Ruskin, the American 'New Thought' movement which spawned Christian

Science and other forms of positive thinking – were absorbed into a system of belief whose essential features were already in place.

The principal article of this belief system has to be stated as clearly as possible at the outset. It was that he, Gandhi, was the pre-ordained and potentially divine world saviour whose coming was logically implicit in the 'ancient', and especially 'Eastern', religious writings to which so many of his English acquaintances had turned in their search for a new revelation of god's purpose in the world.

How this came about will be related at length later on. It need only be said here that it was not a process which took place overnight. The awkward and barely educated young man who flitted like a ghost through the furnished rooms and lecture halls of late-Victorian London had much to learn, about his own as well as other religions, before he could begin to entertain such thoughts about himself. The process of learning began during the three years he spent in London. It continued during the two years he spent in India trying unsuccessfully to practise law, and it came to its extraordinary fruition in South Africa in 1893 or 1894.

From then on, events as a rule conspired to confirm in Gandhi the suspicion awakened in him by his reading and deliberations that it was his destiny to lead a troubled world along the path to salvation.

When he first began to apply his new idea of himself to the practical business of life and politics (his 'experiments with Truth') the results perhaps at first exceeded his expectations. But after a while they simply confirmed him in the kind of expectations he should have. He had an aptitude for politics which was evident from the start, and he employed it then and later in the service of his larger aims. His rise to prominence in South African Indian politics was rapid, and his consolidation of his position remarkable. When he returned to India in 1915, it was because he believed that the next act of the drama must unfold on an Indian stage. He would set the world to rights by setting India right first.

The career that followed was by any standard an amazing one. Within five years of his return Gandhi had captured the Indian National Congress and got it into a position of beholdment to him from which it was never, before 1947, completely to shake itself free. His power over the masses, his genuine if equivocal standing with the British, his usefulness as a conciliator and focus of unity, his worldwide reputation as an elevated personality, all worked together to bring about his long ascendancy in Indian politics. Taking care not to tie himself down to a mere official position within the Congress, Gandhi used it as his instrument, and seemed to come and go from it mostly as he pleased. At times he took an astonishingly long view, and was prepared to detach himself for years if necessary from its public activities, while he waited for conditions once again to become ripe for his intervention. These waiting games were not always played serenely. Though Gandhi strove for detachment he did not always achieve it. Sometimes the dark nights of the soul were so long that he felt doubtful whether his ends would ever, after all, be accomplished, and at such times he consoled himself with the expectation of reincarnation. Might it not be that God would require from him one more lifetime of celibacy and suffering before he was pure enough to shine forth as the invincible instrument of his will? These preoccupations did not reside in some mental compartment which can be labelled 'Gandhi's religious ideas'. They had a profound and practical influence on his political career.

Clearly, the secular saint of popular renown is not the Gandhi we will be discussing here.

The Gandhi I now feel I know well enough to write this book revealed himself slowly, and only after the point in my studies had been reached when I wondered whether I should give up the attempt to write anything about him. I had known from work done for an earlier book that much about Gandhi remained to be understood. Indeed it was the sense of an enigma at the heart of the millions of words written by and about him which inspired me to begin work on the present book. My experience had been that the writings of a historical personality provided a key to his mind and it was in the confident expectation of enlightenment that I embarked on the long and often tedious task of reading in chronological order the 97 volumes of Gandhi's *Collected Works*. At the end he seemed more of an enigma than ever. The problem was not one of obscurity of expression. Gandhi was a master of plain and simple English. Yet the ideas he expounded over and over again, in a manner which clearly implied their interconnectedness, seemed to possess no fundamental coherence. It was at this point that I decided to look more closely at some of Gandhi's early reading which Gandhi himself, it appeared from the historical record, had at the time taken far more seriously than his biographers – with the interesting exception of his devoted secretary, Pyarelal – had ever seemed inclined to do. I soon realized I had been floating about on a vast sea of words without a compass. What I found convinced me that,

without a knowledge of the crucial early influences to which he was exposed, much of Gandhi's writing and many of his actions make little sense. With that knowledge, much makes sense which otherwise seems obscure. I decided not to be deterred by the obvious danger of overinterpretation and settled down to read the 97 volumes over again. The reader must judge whether the results were worth the trouble. (The reader must also bear with me while I lay out at some length, in Chapters 1 and 2, the long-forgotten ideas which gripped Gandhi's youthful mind.) I do not intend to argue every point. I mean to present forthrightly what I now believe to be the likely interpretations of Gandhi's words and actions, proceeding chronologically so that his political career is seen at every stage in its religious context. Gandhi's life was a tremendous drama, and I would like the reader to see it unfold as it unfolded to me. I leave to others the task of determining its significance.

Gandhi never acknowledged the importance of these early experiences except to a few intimates. With the shrewdness about matters of tone, style and comportment that distinguished his career after he returned to India, he would have known that to associate himself with figures, not exactly on the fringe of English society but connected with activities which even in their own day invited ridicule, would compromise the world role that he set out to play. References to the 'cranks' he had known in youth, though indulgent, were few.

This was not the only consideration inspiring the discretion which gives Gandhi's writing for public consumption (which was almost all his writing, including much of his supposedly private correspondence – he liked to say his life was an open book) its peculiarly disorientating character. Gandhi believed that his life, not his speaking and writing, constituted his message. This was not a logical position to take for a man who wrote and spoke so much. Nevertheless, for doctrinal reasons, it was important to Gandhi that the effect of his personality should be allowed to operate without the distortion of special pleading for the authority of what he might say or do. He could not proclaim himself. This was at the root of his ambivalence towards the mass devotion he inspired.

Discretion may seem a strange word to associate with someone who announced his wet dreams to the world and kept millions informed of the state of his digestive apparatus. How could such a man have anything to hide? The answer is that these revelations were part of the exemplary life Gandhi strove to lead. He aimed to achieve complete purity of body and soul – but not for himself alone. He wanted others to follow him along the thorny path, and thought their progress would be faster if they could learn from his mistakes. Therefore these had to be made public. Not all of them in fact were. Gandhi was only human.

It took a long time to reach the point where I was ready to write this book – not only because of the amount and complexity of the material, but because it was necessary for me to work out where I stood in relation to its subject. I found much in Gandhi's life that surprised me, and quite a lot that disgusted me. There was a strong temptation to write a gleeful book about the many ways in which he disappointed me. But I kept putting off writing it. For anything worthwhile to be written about a human personality, the desire to understand has to secure precedence over the urge to revile. I now realize that the time required to arrive at that state of mind was part of the preparation for writing this book.

The reader perhaps has wondered, what was this Kingdom of Heaven which Gandhi felt called on to deliver? What form would it take? Ultimately, it would take no form at all, for Gandhi aimed at the universal transcendence of the body and the absorption of all souls into the divine essence. His target in this life, the preliminary stage, was *swaraj* – self-rule in a sense not limited to political independence, which would eventually create the conditions necessary for the deathless flight of every soul from its prison, the body. At times he spoke of *Ramarajya*, customarily understood in India as a golden age, but understood literally by Gandhi as God's rule on earth, the rule of spirit over flesh. Only towards the end of his life, during a period of political retirement, did he really focus on working out a practical vision of the social arrangements it would be desirable to bring about. Before this he was 'delightfully vague', in Nehru's words, when it came to defining *swaraj* – or as he himself, believing that the journey and the destination were intimately conjoined, simply put it, in words from his favourite hymn: 'One step enough for me.'

# ONE

# Kathiawar and London

The future mahatma was born on 2 October 1869 in the Kathiawar region of western India, the son of the *diwan* of the little princely state of Porbandar. A *diwan* was the right-hand man of an Indian ruler, a combination of administrator and politician who relieved his prince of as much of the business of government as he wished to be relieved of. The office normally passed down through a family. The Gandhis were people of standing.

We know little of Gandhi's parents. Karamchand, the father, appears in his son's *Autobiography* as a model administrator and paterfamilias, his character spotted only by a weakness for 'carnal pleasures'; he married four times. Putlibai, the mother, the last of Karamchand's four wives, is described as 'saintly', which seems to mean extreme scrupulousness in religious observance.[1] Privately, Gandhi confessed that 'Ours is a notorious family, that is, we are known to belong to a band of robbers.' He meant that the Gandhis, like other similarly placed families in the petty principalities of Kathiawar, had never let public service get in the way of family advancement.[2]

Schooldays seem not to have been happy days, though the record shows a creditable level of achievement. Considering the difficulties and distractions he had to contend with – English-medium instruction, marriage at the age of 12 or 13 (Gandhi's own accounts differ[3]), his father's long illness and eventual death during his next to last year in high school – Gandhi did well, finishing school tenth in his class of forty boys. Along the way there were minor acts of adolescent rebellion – meat-eating, smoking (cigarettes and *bhang*), and an unconsummated visit to a brothel. Some of these were instigated by a fascinating friend, a bold Muslim boy, Sheikh Mehtab. At the age of 18 Gandhi entered Samaldas College in the town of Bhavnagar. He found himself unprepared for the level of instruction and withdrew after the first term. All the same, having got further up the educational ladder than his brothers, he was the repository of his family's hopes.

A plan was concocted, less unrealistic than it sounds, to send him to England to qualify as a barrister. This could be achieved, as a number of Indians were discovering, by a short and relatively easy course of study, combined with a few formal appearances at one of the Inns of Court. Gandhi leapt at the opportunity. The money was scraped together, Putlibai's reservations were overcome, and opposition from the Gandhis' Modh Bania subcaste – extending to formal exclusion for incurring the pollution of a journey across the sea – was ignored. On 4 September 1888 Gandhi took ship for London, his self-confessed motives being, 'In a word, ambition', and a desire to see England, 'which completely possessed me'.[4]

When Gandhi shook the dust of Kathiawar off his feet, he left behind a young wife and a son. He may not have expected to live with his wife again. The marriage had by then collapsed under the strain of his persistent suspicions regarding her fidelity. The *Autobiography* refers to a 'bitter quarrel', but what happened was more serious. Recalling the events after many years, Gandhi described how he 'broke her [his wife Kasturbai's] bangles, refused to have anything to do with her and sent her away to her parents. The hatchet was buried only after my return from England.' He blamed the insinuations of Sheikh Mehtab, but the *Autobiography* reveals that from the start Gandhi was both passionately attached to and jealously possessive of his little wife.[5] An Adrian Mole-ish picture emerges of a sexually awakened adolescent boy (the marriage was consummated right away) sitting at his desk in school gripped by painful thoughts of what his wife was up to at home. While he was in England he kept quiet about Kasturbai and did not write to her. 'You will perhaps be astonished to learn', he told an interviewer for *The Vegetarian* magazine shortly before his return to India, 'that I am married.'[6]

Gandhi later repudiated his sexual passion for his wife and embraced total mental and physical chastity. In the *Autobiography* he described how this process of renunciation began.[7] The occasion was the night of his father's death, when the actual moment of passing found Gandhi not at his father's side, but in bed having intercourse with his pregnant wife. 'It was a blot', he says, 'which I have never been able to efface or forget, and I have always thought that, although my devotion to my parents knew no bounds and I would have given up anything for it, yet it was weighed and found unpardonably wanting because my mind was at the same moment in the grip of lust.' The baby which was born shortly afterwards lived for only a few days – a misfortune which Gandhi viewed in years to come as no more than the appropriate karmic consequence.

One can see how the connection between sexual desire and moral inadequacy could have formed itself in Gandhi's mind as he reflected on this experience. The question is when the connection was formed. His behaviour suggests that it was not right away. Kasturbai was soon pregnant again, and he was obsessing himself with thoughts not of his unchastity but of her infidelity. His devotion to his surviving parent seems not to have prevented his leaving for London in the face of her objections. And there seems to have been no reason, according to his own account, to suppose that his father's death was imminent on the night in question. 'No one had dreamt', he says, 'that this was to be the fateful night. The danger of course was there.' Gandhi retired to bed at the normal hour after an evening spent in attendance on his father, leaving his uncle to sleep, as he had been doing, by the invalid's side. Putlibai and a family servant were also in regular attendance. On the basis of this account, there seems no justification for the feeling of guilt which Gandhi says possessed him.

That said, anyone who has kept watch at a bedside knows the fear of not being there when the climactic moment comes. Absence seems at best a misjudgement, at worst a crime. When he was writing the *Autobiography* 35 years later Gandhi was in no doubt that lust had kept him from his sacred duty and demonstrated his need of redemption. By then his awakened religious consciousness had long since taken the flesh-hating form which it did.

The suddenness and completeness of his escape from life as a college dropout and estranged teenage husband in an Indian backwater liberated Gandhi to acknowledge the 'ambition' he seems not to have known he had until the opportunity to satisfy it arrived. From the moment he stepped on to the Tilbury docks wearing the white flannel suit he had reserved for the occasion he showed his determination to get everything right.

His first efforts were directed towards transforming himself into 'an English gentleman'. Lessons in dancing, French, elocution and playing the violin were undertaken. Disappointed with the results, he decided that 'character' would have to make a gentlemen of him.[8] These undertakings were unusual for an Indian student of limited means. They do not seem to fit in either with Gandhi's much-mentioned shyness. In fact, though quiet and nervous about public speaking, Gandhi went about a good deal in his London years, and through the societies he joined formed the habit of meeting notable people.

He took his studies seriously and sat for the London University matriculation examinations as well as the examinations for the bar, preparing for these by working his way through the prescribed texts, rather than using notes which were available or employing a crammer. He read the Roman law textbook in Latin with the help of a crib, and passed sixth in the examination in a field of 46. He acquired a taste for jurisprudence and displayed ever after a relish for arguing things out from what he took to be first principles. Some of what he later claimed to be 'scientific' reasoning about ethical and religious matters owed more to the legal reasoning he encountered in such texts as Snell's *Equity*. He passed all his examinations and on the day before he left London was called to the bar.

But he understood by then that he was not thereby qualified to practise law. A course of legal study was merely the gateway to a profession in which acumen, initiative and accumulation of experience would be the factors deciding success.

Through his studies he learned, and never forgot, the importance of methodical application. His attempts to become a gentleman, though at first misdirected, were not a waste of time. He acquired by what appears to have been a natural gift of observation a degree of social polish in his relations with the English. His shyness proved to be the self-consciousness of inexperience.

Before he left India, Gandhi's mother had made him promise not to stray from the family's strict vegetarian diet. He kept his promise, but soon tired of the jam and bread and boiled cabbage on which he seemed compelled to subsist in his London lodgings. Roaming the streets in search of sustenance he found a vegetarian restaurant. He began to frequent it, found other such restaurants, and in this way established contact with London's lively and even fashionable world of 'reform'.[9] It happened that in 1888 a young man arriving in London could hardly have found a more direct route into that stimulating and surprising world. 'Dietary reform', embracing possibilities from pure veganism to occasional abstention from flesh, was a preoccupation of dissenters of almost

Student in London, 1888

every stripe. This was not a coincidence but reflected the nature of the critique of the established order to which he was now to be exposed.

Few of the people Gandhi met were revolutionists or even members of the working class. Some were socialists. Mostly they were middle-class men and women who wanted to see 'brotherhood' replace economic exploitation, and a vital connection with the natural world, nourishing both body and spirit, restored to the world of the machine. Like the evangelical Christians of the early part of the century, whose heirs they were, they sought to create a better society by creating better people, starting with themselves. They were rarely orthodox Christians: the rise of evolutionary biology and German biblical scholarship had seen to that. But the evangelical concern with the state of the human soul lived on in them, as did the evangelicals' love of the purposeful society of friends. They were the characters who populated the plays of Bernard Shaw – their official satirist and fellow campaigner.

Gandhi did not join the London Vegetarian Society right away. He was intrigued by *The Vegetarian*, which had begun publication early in 1888, and impressed by Henry Salt's *A Plea for Vegetarianism*. But he found vegetarians in person hard to take. They were always talking about their ailments and seemed obsessed with food.[10] It was not until the summer of 1890 that he joined the society at the invitation of *The Vegetarian*'s youthful editor, Josiah Oldfield, who seems to have known of Gandhi from a mutual friend. Oldfield was the opposite in every way of the valetudinarians to whom Gandhi had taken exception: hardworking, humorous, self-denying, an Oxford graduate and a practising barrister, a reformer and a gentleman. It was not long before he had Gandhi at work on the executive committee. A few months later Gandhi moved into digs with him.

The London Vegetarian Society at that time was dominated by the extremely Shavian A.F. Hills, its founder, president and chief financial backer. Hills is said to have been the inspiration for Andrew Undershaft in *Major Barbara*. He owned the Thames Iron Works, which built battleships, and his employees worked an eight-hour day and had a profit-sharing contract. He took a kindly interest in Gandhi and encouraged him to write articles on Indian food and customs for *The Vegetarian*. Hills had a whole system of ideas about food's significance in the cosmos which he expounded in *The Vegetarian* and then published as *Essays on Vegetarianism*. Gandhi later observed that Hills's 'reasoning used to appeal to me in those days. I do not know whether it would now if I read all his writings afresh.'[11]

Vegetarianism has long been associated with renunciatory and purificatory forms of religion which seek to unite the divine spirit residing in the
individual man with the divine spirit immanent in and ordering the universe.
Hills was a representative of this type of vegetarianism. Though he seemed
unaware of it, the ideas he disclosed in weekly instalments to readers of *The
Vegetarian* had deep roots in the history of religious consciousness. In the
West they have appeared in systems of thought which the Christian Church,
recognizing their implicit threat to its authority as the intermediary between
man and God, has condemned as 'heresy'. In the East they have tended to
be accepted as part of the normal texture of religious belief and experience.
The essential point has been that the avoidance of meat, allied usually with
sexual continence, etherealizes the flesh and provides the means of achieving direct spiritual union with God. So central to unorthodox systems of
Christianity, from the gnostics and Manicheans of the early Christian era to
the Cathars and Bogomils of the Middle Ages, has vegetarianism been that
known abstinence from meat has at times been considered a sign of spiritual
subversion. 'I have a wife whom I love,' said a man under interrogation by
the Papal Inquisition in Toulouse in the thirteenth century, 'I have children,
I eat meat, I lie and I take oaths, I am a good Christian.'[12]

Hills proclaimed a 'Gospel of Vitality' in which vegetarianism was the
means by which men would become like gods, through cultivating the 'vital
force' within.

The Gospel of Vitality was professedly Christian. Hills preached a doctrine
of 'Sonship', which taught that Jesus was not the only son of God: all men
could become sons of God if they followed Jesus' commandment, 'Be ye
therefore perfect, even as your Father which is in heaven is perfect.' Perfection
is achieved through obedience to the 'Laws of God', the chief among which
is the 'Law of Love', which vegetarians observe when they refrain from killing their fellow creatures for food; and the state of perfection is the state of
'At-one-ment' with God, whereby man himself becomes divine. Sin is wilful
disobedience to God's laws. The orthodox Christian view that Jesus died to
wash away our sins is rejected as barbaric – on a level with the propitiatory
sacrifice of animals, a practice particularly offensive to vegetarians; and the
notion of original sin, with its implication that man unaided by divine intervention can never rise above his evil nature, is also rejected, as a remnant
of the priest-ridden past. Sinfulness is conceived as a consequence of man's
submission, during 'the Fall', to his bodily state and its unruly appetites, and

redemption is the process of controlling these appetites and becoming 'purer', as God's laws are first discovered and then voluntarily obeyed. 'Here, in the body,' Hills declared, 'is the beginning of Sonship – here, in the physical life, is based the Divinity of Man.'[13] With divinity comes divine power, and everlasting life. 'What is power,' Hills asked, 'but determined vital force?' And what is disease but an 'abnormal vital defect'? The Gospel of Vitality was 'the reign of Life overmastering the dominion of death'.[14]

Hills wished to reconcile his self-divinizing religion with the laws of science by which he made his living. From the fact that force can only be deduced not seen he reasoned that forces of one kind and another proliferate in nature, and all of them operate according to the discoverable laws of God, which include the known laws of science. 'Muscular force produces muscular phenomena; nervous force produces nervous phenomena; psychical force produces psychical phenomena; spiritual force produces spiritual phenomena.'[15] The sum of God's laws constitutes 'absolute Truth';[16] these laws and this truth can be discovered, as the laws of science have hitherto been discovered, through experiment.

With the final collation and universal observance of God's laws the Kingdom of Heaven will have arrived on earth. Then divinized beings will work together for the good of all. Strikes, trades unions and socialists will disappear, as all captains of industry will operate their businesses like the enlightened Hills. Government will be carried out not by corrupt political parties locked in everlasting battle, but by 'the best': even in the Kingdom of Heaven, apparently, nature distributes her gifts. But Hills was genuinely agitated by a yearning for 'brotherhood', even if in practice he only meant the elimination of strife. 'The common brotherhood of humanity', he wrote, 'is founded in the eternal Godhead of man.'[17]

Vital food – uncooked fruit, vegetables, nuts, pulses and grains – was an essential part of Hills's programme, producing both purity and vigour: 'Vital Vegetarianism alone marks the road to Paradise-regained.'[18] Such food, 'suffused with the storage of the sunshine', contained 'the vital spark of heavenly flame', destroyed by cooking, which was 'the Elixir of Life'.[19] Had God not meant this to be the human diet, he would not have so instructed Adam and Eve in their innocence in the garden (Genesis 1:29). The consumption of vital food was thus a law of God and only through obedience to it could man achieve 'At-one-ment' and be restored to his prelapsarian, deathless state.

Gandhi made several attempts during his life to live on vital food. The first was in Bombay in 1892. After a week his heavy social engagements made it impractical to continue; otherwise he was pleased with the results. In Pretoria in August 1893 he tried it again, with the idea of adopting it permanently. But he soon felt hungry, weak and unwell, and abandoned it after ten days. 'Rose up with a heavy stomach', he recorded on the fourth day. 'For breakfast I had half a tablespoonful of peas, half of rice, half of wheat, two and a half of sultanas, ten walnuts, and one orange. The mouth did not taste well throughout the day. Did not feel well either.' Nevertheless, in his report to *The Vegetarian*, he felt unable on the basis of a short experiment undertaken in unfavourable circumstances – he was living in a boarding house – to rule out the value of a vital food diet. It might be, he concluded, that the regime was too strenuous for the ordinary vegetarian and was best left to 'adepts'.[20] Other experiments in vital food took place in 1929 when Gandhi was touring India to rouse the country to civil disobedience, and in 1934 when he resigned from Congress and set out to run the nationalist movement without it.

Considering it self-evident that sex for any purpose other than procreation was equivalent to breaking training, Hills as a matter of course advocated celibacy. Sex for pleasure was an offence against purity – 'the dominion of the animal over the spiritual' – and a waste of 'the reserves of vital force' whose conservation leads man 'to sovereign power'.[21] Birth control was thus anathema, and he sought to purge the Vegetarian Society of its advocates. At the fateful committee meeting, Gandhi put on record the view that it was not the Society's business to suppress opinions which were sincerely held. He seems to have felt some attraction to the idea of contraception. But, if its advocacy 'had some temporary effect on me, Mr. Hill's (*sic*) opposition to those methods and his advocacy of internal efforts as opposed to outward means, in a word, of self-control, had a far greater effect, which in due time came to be abiding.'[22]

It was through vegetarianism that Gandhi met Edwin Arnold, the translator of the *Bhagavad Gita* and the author of *The Light of Asia*, a verse biography of the Buddha which made him famous after its publication in 1879. *The Light of Asia* went through many editions and is estimated to have sold between half a million and a million copies. It became a cantata, an opera (*La Luce dell'Asia*) and a play, and in 1928 a German company made a film of it. It was a book which struck a chord. The Christianized Buddha who emerged from its pages appealed to many who could not have coped with the unconsoling doctrines of the real Gautama.

*The Song Celestial*, Arnold's translation of the *Bhagavad Gita*, followed in 1885. This was the form in which Gandhi first encountered the *Gita*, the book which in his maturity he was to consider his sacred text.

He was introduced to both books by some English acquaintances in 1889. They were probably his first encounter with 'Oriental' ideas filtered through the Western Christian imagination. *The Song Celestial* struck him as profound, but, knowing how little he knew about philosophical Hinduism, he seems to have put it aside pending further study. He did not begin to clarify his thoughts on the *Gita* till later on. *The Light of Asia* he read 'with even greater interest'.[23] It presented the Indian Gautama as the equal if not the superior of Jesus in his life and moral teaching. Gandhi was stirred by the experience of encountering such views in the heart of Christendom. He accepted Arnold's account as authoritative. Much later he learned that one of his favourite images from the poem, of Gautama carrying a sick lamb while the mother trots beside him, was one Arnold had made up. Until he made this discovery, he cited the passage as an example of Gautama's superior compassion, which included all living things and not just humans as did that of Jesus.[24]

Arnold's religious ideas were similar to those of A.F. Hills, stripped of their heroic vitalism. They were summed up in another long poem, *The Light of the World*, a verse biography of Jesus published in 1891. The Jesus of *The Light of the World* was not a god come to earth but a man who achieved perfection through renunciation and selfless love and thus became divine. He redeemed, not vicariously by self-immolation, but by showing other men the way. Sin is imperfection and disappears as man become perfect. The Kingdom of Heaven is the full application on earth of Jesus' teaching.

Some of these doctrines were prefigured in *The Light of Asia*, in the context of Buddha's teaching – the doctrine of vicarious atonement discreetly deprecated, salvation presented as the result of human striving. Arnold was nominally a Christian, but whether his religion can better be described as Buddhistic Christianity or Christianized Buddhism is hard to say. In *The Light of Asia* nirvana is given a happiness content reminiscent of the Christian heaven, if the Christian heaven were populated by divinized human beings. It was Arnold's 'firm conviction that a third of mankind [the world's Buddhists] would never have been brought to believe in blank abstractions, or in Nothingness as the issue and crown of Being'.[25]

Hills was an admirer of *The Light of Asia* and quoted at length from it in his essay on 'Sonship'. The Buddha's rejection of asceticism (not an invention of Arnold's but an important part of Buddhist doctrine) was taken as corroboration of his belief that it was only through the body that man could expect to make progress towards perfection.[26]

Gandhi met Arnold in the spring of 1891, when he and Oldfield founded the West London Food Reform Society and persuaded Arnold, who lived nearby, to be vice-president. Presumably Gandhi saw something of him during his remaining months in London. But he left no account of the acquaintance and does not say if he read *The Light of the World*.

The same acquaintances who introduced Gandhi to Arnold's works were also responsible for introducing him to the Theosophical Society. Gandhi does not give their names but they may have been Archibald and Bertram Keightley, uncle and nephew, who edited Madame Blavatsky's *The Secret Doctrine* for publication in 1888. Whoever they were, they took Gandhi to meet Blavatsky and invited him to join the Society. He declined, but then took out a six-month membership a few months before leaving London. He read Blavatsky's *The Key to Theosophy* and, according to Pyarelal, *The Secret Doctrine*.[27] He also met Annie Besant (the original of another of Shaw's characters, Raina in *Arms and the Man*), whose conversion from freethinking socialism to theosophy had just taken place. He read her *Why I Became a Theosophist*, and was present on one of the occasions when the pamphlet was delivered as a lecture.

Theosophy preached the self-divinizing perfectionism Gandhi was encountering through Edwin Arnold and A.F. Hills, but with a distinctly 'Hindu' slant. When she arrived in London in 1887 Madame Blavatsky had just spent eight years in India and had formed the habit of using Hindu terminology to get her ideas across. Her early work had a more Buddhist tinge.

Gandhi in the *Autobiography* recalled *The Key to Theosophy* as stimulating his interest in Hinduism and dispelling 'the notion fostered by the missionaries that Hinduism was rife with superstition'. *Why I Became a Theosophist* was recalled as confirming his aversion to atheism and his assent to theism. These recollections give no sense at all of the distinctive flavour of these publications, or their essential point.[28]

Madame Blavatsky[29] arrived in London towards the end of a career which by her own account took her from Russia, where she was born into the minor nobility in 1831, across the United States in a covered wagon, to Italy where she fought for Garibaldi, to Serbia where she pursued a career as a concert pianist, to Greece where she survived a shipwreck, to Egypt where she learned the secrets of the Kabbala, and to Central Asia where she spent seven years in Tibet. Here she received instruction in esoteric and occult knowledge from certain 'Himalayan Masters', or 'Mahatmas', immortal beings of extraordinary goodness, wisdom and power who, though principally resident in Tibet, materialized here and there and were the authors of Madame Blavatsky's books.

Despite spending much time in communion of an extra-sensory nature with these exalted personages, Madame Blavatsky was not the ethereal type. Coarse, humorous, unscrupulous, appallingly frank, a chain-smoker and a glutton, she was an ironically self-created magus who yet had something to say.

Her religious philosophy appeared principally as massive multi-volume works touted as the product of spiritual 'precipitations' from the Masters, but in reality they were put together from the works of nineteenth-century occultists and students of esoteric religious traditions, with liberal additions of invented material. They are anything but dull. The stamp of Madame Blavatsky's restless and inventive mind appears on every page, and she had a purpose which may still be considered outrageous but was certainly serious. This was the destruction of established Christianity and its replacement by a world religion which recognized no barrier but ignorance between man and God. Blavatsky thought it was time for the bloody intolerance and neurotic self-abasement of historical Christianity to be set aside, and the foundations laid for something better. She set her sights higher than the search for the historical Jesus, or the return to 'primitive' Christianity, which preoccupied the more conventionally unorthodox. She saw that the fantastic growth of knowledge which was taking place about the history and thought not only of other societies but of Europe itself provided the material out of which a universal religion might plausibly be constructed. She founded a sizeable movement. It displayed little of its creator's mental energy or audacity and soon became a form of ritualized eclecticism with local variations.

The Theosophical Society was founded in New York in 1875 by Blavatsky and her associate Colonel Henry Olcott, at a time when Blavatsky was struggling to develop a career as a medium. Its aim was to discover the secret laws that govern the universe. It did not prosper, and Olcott and Blavatsky decided in 1878 to move to India. Here the laws of the universe began to take on a more Hindu complexion as the Society surprisingly began to flourish among occult-minded Anglo-Indian civilians, and officials of the Raj. Among the latter was A.O. Hume, the founder of the Indian National Congress. In masterly fashion, Blavatsky secured her position by controlling access to communication with the spiritual masters in Tibet, principally the Masters Morya and Koot Hoomi. Members were soon vying for contact with the spirits or the spiritual elite, or hoping to learn that they were reincarnations of Julius Caesar or Marie Antoinette. Perhaps it is not so surprising that the Society throve in surroundings as hierarchical and snobbish as British India.

By 1885 the Society had taken off and was on its way to becoming an international movement. But by then Blavatsky was involved in a scandal which forced her to leave India and look for somewhere else to settle down. Letters sold by her housekeeper to a Christian missionary revealed that the occult phenomena produced at the Society's headquarters in Madras were fraudulent. Most notoriously, objects which had magically materialized in a 'shrine room' next to Blavatsky's bedroom were revealed to have done so by the use of a hidden panel – which embarrassingly flew open as one of the Society's trustees, in an attempt to refute the accusations, struck the wall with his hand and said, 'You see, it is quite solid.' In 1887 Blavatsky moved her base of operations to London. Bold in adversity, she enlivened the local Society and reasserted her spiritual authority by founding an Esoteric section, which offered qualified candidates advanced tuition in the occult. This was the state of her fortunes when Gandhi met her in 1889.

*The Secret Doctrine* (1888) presents the 'Wisdom Religion' as it has been esoterically preserved from ancient times – kept alive by initiates, of whom Blavatsky is the most recent. It takes the form of an explication, with many discursions into comparative religion and mythology, of stanzas from *The Book of Dzyan*, an ancient text in the unknown language of Senzar, presented in English translation. *The Key to Theosophy*, a work of relative sobriety, adapts the Wisdom Religion to the present day. It includes Blavatsky's social gospel. An earlier book, *Isis Unveiled* (1877), was chiefly about magic and the supernatural, but also contained Blavatsky's earliest polemics against Christianity and materialist science. (It is not known if Gandhi read *Isis Unveiled*.[30])

Volume One of *The Secret Doctrine* presents Blavatsky's cosmogony; Volume Two deals with the history of the earth and the human race. Briefly, in an immensely long and complex process, involving a descent of spirit into matter, the universe's divine primordial essence breaks up into a multitude of conscious beings. In an equally long and complex process, over aeons, these beings recover their divine nature. This is broadly consistent with the emanationist doctrines of both Hinduism and Western esoteric systems such as Neoplatonism. The details, however, are pure Blavatsky. There are seven 'root-races' of humanity, appearing in sequence on different planets and in different parts of the earth. The third root-race, the 'Lemurian', is the first to possess bodies and reproduce sexually, and also the first to have a choice between doing good and doing evil. Adam and Eve were members of this race, and negroes are a remnant of it. As further races appear, each one more advanced, a capacity for reproduction by 'spiritual means' re-emerges. Eventually, 'the inner and divine man adjusts his outer terrestrial self to his own spiritual nature', and the flesh becomes the mere integument of the soul.[31] A final entrance into a realm of pure spirit is contemplated but not much considered, its nature being beyond the capacity of human intelligence to discover. The human race as it exists at present is the fifth of seven sub-races of the fifth ('Aryan') root-race, and has begun its return to divinity. The beginnings of the sixth sub-race are discernible on the west coast of America.

This mighty drama is propelled by the 'laws of evolution'. Open to any notion offering support for the proposition that the whole of mankind could eventually become perfect, Blavatsky embraced the idea that the human species experienced evolutionary change. But she rejected the amoral process of natural selection through which it was argued by Darwin to occur. Mere biological survival could be of no interest. The purpose of evolution being the soul's emancipation from material existence, progress could only be according to 'laws' which were 'spiritual' not material in nature.

Science involved the operation of 'reason', the defining quality of both the human and the divine mind, which held the key to human progress. It was therefore held in high esteem by Madame Blavatsky. No thinking person alive in the West at that time could ignore the glamour of scientific achievement, and Blavatsky was no exception. She dabbled in chemistry and physics and deduced from them the nature of the 'spiritual' laws governing the cosmos. Large parts of *The Secret Doctrine* were given over to such speculations. The principal conclusions were that the underlying mechanism of evolution was reincarnation, and the law according to which it progressed was the law of karma.

The Mahatmas did not reveal the existence of reincarnation to Blavatsky until she went to live in India. The concept is absent from *Isis Unveiled*. But according to *The Secret Doctrine* the soul must pass through many incarnations to acquire the moral experience which makes possible spiritual progress, and the rate of progress is determined by performance. The law of karma, which links cause and effect, binds humans to the consequences of their actions and determines the form of each rebirth. The souls that progress fastest are the spiritual vanguard of humankind and lead the way to godhead for all. This looks like Hinduism. But it is Hinduism so infused with active regard for human potential that it is transformed into something else. A Hindu looks forward to eventual absorption into the divine essence and an end to rebirth. But reincarnation is more accepted as a necessity than embraced as an opportunity.

The implications for Christianity of Blavatsky's view of man's spiritual nature were clear. It permitted no belief in either original sin or vicarious atonement. Divine forgiveness was also out of the question. Man progressed by his own efforts, and these were rewarded according to the impersonal operation of karmic law. But Jesus was neither disregarded by Blavatsky nor conceived solely according to the usual formula of liberal Christianity as a 'great teacher'. He occupies an important place in theosophical doctrine as one of the spiritual masters whose performance in past lives puts them on the cusp of divinity, who perhaps achieves it.

Jesus was argued by Blavatsky to be one of many Christs – full embodiments of the 'Christ' principle, which is the inner spark of divinity in man – who have appeared in history, most of them unknown. Gautama Buddha and the Hindu *avatar* Krishna were others. Jesus' teachings were esoteric and theosophical and have been either misunderstood or deliberately distorted by the Church. The key text is the Sermon on the Mount, whose esoteric meaning is that without renunciation of the world and of the ego reunion with the divine cannot be contemplated. Blavatsky would have been delighted by the discoveries at Nag Hammadi which are currently revising our understanding of Christianity's beginnings. Audaciously, she included Jesus among the Mahatmas resident in Tibet, though not among those with whom she was in direct communication.

*The Key to Theosophy*, a short book, gives the highlights of theosophical doctrine, emphasizing that all religions, being in origin local developments of the quintessential Wisdom Religion, contain the same truths in different form: hence the motto of the Theosophical Society, 'There is no religion higher then truth'. Something of a practical handbook to theosophy, it gives information on the organization and aims of the Society. There are no excursions into numerology, no vampire stories, few references to the Kabbala. But nothing of doctrinal significance is left out, and some points are expanded.

The concept of theurgy ('divine work') is given prominence – the idea (not new but ancient) that adepts and spiritual masters can acquire knowledge of the laws of the universe which gives them superhuman powers and enables God to do his work through them. This work is that of mankind's spiritual evolution. Theurgy is distinguished from magic, which also relies on knowledge of the hidden laws of nature but may not be benign, by the fact that its practitioners are always men of 'almost superhuman purity and holiness of life'.[32]

Blavatsky suggests certain refinements in the doctrine of karma.

Karma rewards moral effort and punishes moral laziness. It is both 'the highest reason for reconcilement to one's lot in life, and the very strongest incentive towards effort to better the succeeding re-birth'. But, recognizing that no one can make spiritual progress while physical wretchedness preoccupies him, the theosophist is duty-bound to assist 'every wise and well-considered social effort which has for its object the amelioration of the condition of the poor'. The operation of 'Distributive Karma' (a felicitously mathematical term) meanwhile ensures that individual moral effort directly benefits all humanity, for the spiritual unity of mankind means that 'no man can rise superior to his individual failings, without lifting, be it ever so little, the whole body of which he is an integral part'. Conversely, 'no one can sin, nor suffer the effects of sin, alone'. Hurting one man, we hurt humanity. This means that not even revenge for injury is permissible, for the fresh injury caused cannot be confined. It also disrupts the law of karma, which, left to itself, ensures that everyone receives his just reward. The theosophist must therefore follow the precepts 'Resist not evil' and 'Render good for evil'. A special case of Distributive Karma is 'National Karma'. Nations are spiritual units making distinct contributions to the karma 'of the World'. At times, 'heroic souls, the Saviours of our Race and Nation', arise in them, not only to restore the National Karma to a healthy state, but to ensure that everyone has the opportunity to make a positive contribution.

Theosophy is, then, necessarily a religion of brotherhood. Like Jesus, it preaches the 'law of love'; like Jesus, it enjoins men to love their enemies and not just their friends, because theosophists know, as Jesus did, that all men are 'of one and the same essence', and that to forget self and serve others is to embrace the divine.

The book's sections on the organization of the Society deal mostly with the Esoteric Section, whose members are to be trained in the occult sciences. These are 'real, actual, and very dangerous sciences' which develop 'the hidden powers "latent in man"'. Private study, while possible, is disparaged. Without guidance the student lapses into 'unconscious black magic or the most helpless mediumship'. Spiritualism is strongly deprecated: it was vital for Madame Blavatsky to dissociate herself from the world of seedy parlour mediumship of which she had once been part. Mediums are pronounced not necessarily fraudulent but deluded, the phenomena of the seance room – voices, apparitions, automatic writing – resulting from the manipulation of a sensitive personality (the medium) by his or her own 'astral' (ghostly) self, or that of another (alive or dead). To ensure that the secret knowledge divulged is used only for the 'Real divine theurgy', aspirants to the Esoteric Section are required to show evidence of a high character, and particularly of a capacity for abstinence, altruism and self-denial. Madame Blavatsky was not inclined to go overboard regarding abstinence. Vegetarianism is given a rather tepid endorsement. So is celibacy. The thing is '*moral* asceticism', which involves 'self-sacrifice'. While recognizing that only through 'pain and suffering' is spiritual progress made, theosophy condemns self-sacrifice which is 'rash and useless'.

The supernormal powers of the adept include control of the behaviour of others, even at a great distance, through his or her own thought processes, which are directly connected to God's. Hypnosis gives a crude indication of such powers which the 'World of Science' will one day take seriously and explain. Prayer is necessarily part of the adept's spiritual discipline – not supplicatory prayer, which Blavatsky despised, but prayer as 'an occult process bringing about physical results': 'Will-Power' which becomes 'a living power'.[33]

The aim of the Theosophical Society is not just to move the human race in the right direction, but to prepare the ground for the arrival at a not too distant date of 'the new torch-bearer of Truth'. Through the work of the Society he 'will find the minds of men prepared for his message, a language ready for him in which to clothe the new truths he brings, an organization awaiting his arrival which will remove the merely mechanical, material obstacles and difficulties from his path'. It was to be the life work of Madame Blavatsky's distinguished convert, Annie Besant, to attempt to complete this process of preparation.

For Annie Besant the brotherhood of man was no mere argument.[34] It was felt and lived, and only when pessimism about human nature briefly gained the upper hand did she go looking for proof. Theosophy provided it. A vicar's wife who had lost her faith but not her hope for a better world, and left her husband, Besant was for fifteen years a heroine of the left. With Charles Bradlaugh she edited the *National Reformer*. She was a stalwart of the Fabian Society and the National Secular Society. She was the organizer of the London matchgirls' strike. An orator of national repute, when she spoke she filled the hall.

In 1888 Besant was feeling discouraged with the progress of socialism. The socialists were strong on class war, weak on constructive effort. She began to wonder if there was something yet to be discovered in human nature which was the key to future progress. She began to dabble, sceptically at first, in spiritualism. Then one day W.T. Stead, the editor of the *Pall Mall Gazette*, gave her *The Secret Doctrine* to review, because he could not bear to read it himself. Bowled over, she sought out its author. Madame Blavatsky welcomed her: she had already, she intimated, identified Besant as the person who would take her message to the world.

*Why I Became a Theosophist* was written in July 1889, after a holiday with Blavatsky during which a nocturnal visit was arranged from one of the Mahatmas, the Mahatma Morya. He appeared, a 'radiant astral figure', at the foot of the bed. After that, Besant laboured for theosophy, first in London, then in India, for forty years, becoming president of the Society in 1907.

*Why I Became a Theosophist* set out to show, first, why the author had exchanged atheism for theosophy; second, why she thought theosophy rather than socialism was the road to reform. The principal argument against atheism was that materialism was 'unable' to explain 'the phenomena of clairvoyance, clairaudience, and thought-transference'. Hypnosis, too, appeared to be beyond material explanation. It seemed there was a power which lay dormant in human nature – not 'supernatural', for it must lie within 'the realm of law', but 'superhuman' – which might be trained up and used for humanity's good. The Theosophical Society, to whose founder the Mahatmas had imparted their secrets, was equipped to perform the task.

Besant anticipated the gradual development in the human race, as new 'laws' were discovered and applied, of enormous mental power over matter – power which 'may be, so to speak, "forced" by any who choose to take the requisite means'. These included certain ascetic practices, of which celibacy was one.

Theosophy's assertion of the spiritual unity of mankind revived Besant's flagging belief in the brotherhood of man. She was joining the Theosophical Society, she said, because there was 'sore need ... in our unbrotherly, anti-social civilization, of this distinct affirmation of a brotherhood as broad as Humanity itself'. She found in the Society's doctrines of karma and reincarnation the solution to the problem of suffering – both why it existed and how it might be ended. 'It may well be', she wrote, 'that the present poverty, misery and disease spring inevitably from past evil'; but that was 'no reason why we should not start forces of wisdom and love to change them, and create good karma for the future instead of continuing to create bad'. Karma was indeed an unalterable 'law of nature' – but 'it no more prevents us from aiding our fellow-men than "the law of gravitation" prevents us from walking upstairs'.

Blavatsky's *The Key to Theosophy* and Besant's *Why I Became a Theosophist* were both produced in 1889, a time when the two women, after their instant rapport, were inseparable. Conversion was probably experienced on both sides, with Besant discovering in theosophy a rationale for human progress, and Blavatsky inspired to consider theosophy's relevance to social justice.

Another product of the period was Blavatsky's *The Voice of the Silence*, written while Besant was staying with her at Fontainebleau in the summer of 1889. A collection of aphorisms translated from the Senzar, *The Voice of the Silence* elaborated the doctrine of liberation through service to others, and introduced into theosophy the Buddhist concept of the *bodhisattva* – the enlightened being who postpones indefinitely his entry into nirvana, in order to serve others. The voice of the silence is the inner voice heard by the sufficiently pure, the voice of 'thy inner GOD', 'The Higher SELF'. It leads the hearer 'unto the realm of *Sat*, the true'.[35] Gandhi does not say if he read the book in London, but he knew and admired it in South Africa.

Gandhi did not forget how, 'as a lad', he had gone to the Queen's Hall to hear the famous Mrs Besant speak. The 'utter sincerity' of the declaration with which 'she wound up her great speech which held her audience spell-bound' left a lasting impression. It would have been the peroration of *Why I Became a Theosophist* – Besant's riposte to her old friends of the Fabian Society and the Secular Society who were lamenting their lost comrade. She must, she said, 'keep stainless' her 'loyalty to Truth'. 'She may lead me into the wilderness, yet I must follow her; she may strip me of all love, yet I must pursue her; though she slay me, yet will I trust in her; and I ask no other epitaph on my tomb but SHE TRIED TO FOLLOW TRUTH.'[36]

I have tried to present all these ideas in the form in which Gandhi was exposed to them, rather than as exemplifying 'movements' of which he would not have been aware. I have not attempted analysis: Gandhi was no metaphysician; neither am I. What he made of them at the time we really do not know, except for his brief comments in the *Autobiography*,[37] and a few later remarks, which add little to our direct knowledge.

The books and magazines Gandhi read, the ideas he heard discussed, represented the life work of passionately unorthodox people. There was nothing tentative about them. They did not permit a tepid response. Yet the response he describes, even allowing for the decades which separate the mahatma from the ignorant youth, seems tepid. A.F. Hills was not just writing about vegetables, Madame Blavatsky was not just writing about Hinduism, and Annie Besant wanted to tell the world that she had abandoned atheism, not for 'theism' but for theosophy. Gandhi acknowledges none of this, yet he grants these people some influence on his youthful mind.

Gandhi came on the scene just at the moment when the 'Wisdom Religion' – representing principally the wisdom of the East – and the evangelical conscience briefly converged. Clearly, he had a thorough exposure to a sacralized idea of politics which combined social reform with personal spiritual growth. Equally clearly, he was exposed to the idea that, through a process of correct alignment with the great laws that govern the universe – laws which are discoverable through the 'experiments' of the spiritual elite – mankind can be made perfect. Acknowledged or not, these were ideas that came to dominate Gandhi's thinking and repeatedly revivify his hope. In time, also, he came to accept and apply to himself some of Madame Blavatsky's and Annie Besant's ideas about the extraordinary powers of the spiritually superior man. He distinguished his thinking on this subject from the traditional Indian belief in the acquisition of special powers through yoga, though at times he turned to yoga for inspiration.

When Gandhi arrived in London, he possessed little formal knowledge of his religion. 'I knew of Hinduism what my parents taught me, not directly but indirectly, that is, by their practice, and I knew a little more of it from a Brahmin to whom they sent me in order to learn *Rama Raksha* [a Sanskrit prayer]. That was the stock with which I sailed for England.'[38] An important part of his response to encountering European writings besprinkled with 'Hindu' terminology was the pleasure to which he alluded in the *Autobiography*, of finding that there were Westerners who did not share the views of missionaries and found in Hinduism inspiration for progressive ideas. Hinduism has its own traditions of righteousness. The *Ramayana* and the *Mahabharata* are meditations on the nature and difficulty of *dharma* – virtuous conduct. In Gujarat, when Gandhi was growing up, there were forms of Vaishnavite piety strongly marked by a spirit of loving kindness; he was often to quote Shamal Batt's 'For a bowl of water, give a goodly meal.' But in Hinduism there had never been a cult of self-sacrifice for the good of others, let alone a tradition of service as the route to perfectionment of oneself and society. It was what Gandhi heard and read in London that set his mind moving in this direction.

His reading in London was not confined to the works of vegetarians and theosophists. He was interested in Christianity and attended church services, remembering particularly Dr Joseph Parker's Thursday lunchtime services at the City Temple. These he went to 'again and again', intrigued by Parker's appeal to the young men who came to the services to model their behaviour on that of Jesus Christ.[39] He was taken by his friend Narayan Hemchandra to call on the Catholic prelate Cardinal Manning, who was celebrated for his austere life and advocacy of the rights of labour. He set out to read the Bible, starting with Genesis. Exodus sent him to sleep, but he carried on and, arriving at the New Testament, was captivated by the Sermon on the Mount. In the *Autobiography* he recalled comparing it with the *Gita*, not an obvious comparison for someone unschooled in both Hinduism and Christianity to make, but common in theosophical circles where Krishna – whose words addressed to the prince Arjuna on the eve of battle constitute the *Gita* – was considered the Hindu Christ. 'My young mind', Gandhi wrote, 'tried to unify the teachings of the *Gita*, *The Light of Asia* and the Sermon on the Mount. That renunciation was the highest form of religion appealed to me greatly.'[40] The teaching of renunciation was what he assumed the *Gita*, *The Light of Asia* and the Sermon on the Mount had in common. Gandhi was sometimes to chastise Christians for not living up to the Sermon on the Mount, but he also suggested that his understanding of the Sermon was not the orthodox one.[41]

A final influence in this period which must be given its due is Thomas Carlyle. A friend recommended *On Heroes and Hero-Worship* and Gandhi read the chapter on Mohammed, from which he 'learnt of the Prophet's greatness and bravery and austere living'.[42] Carlyle had been dead for seven years when Gandhi reached London, and *On Heroes and Hero-Worship* had been published fifty years before. But Carlyle's strange and powerful influence was still making itself felt and was felt by Gandhi. In 1908 and 1909 Carlyle's works formed part of Gandhi's reading programme in Pretoria jail, and Carlyle was one of those writers to whom he referred with approval throughout his life. It was no doubt the essentially religious nature of Carlyle's historical imagination which struck a chord.

*On Heroes and Hero-Worship* was a reflection on the heroic in history, built up from Carlyle's view that 'A man is right and invincible, virtuous and on the road towards sure conquest, precisely while he joins himself to the great deep Law of the World'.[43] Carlyle believed that the material world was 'at bottom, in very deed, Nothing; is a visual and tactual Manifestation of God's power and presence, – a shadow hung out by Him on the bosom of the void Infinite', and that 'Nature', conceived thus, was divine 'Truth' organized as an interconnected whole according to divine 'Law'. The hero was he who was 'in harmony with the Decrees of the Author of this World'; who was, in a strong sense of the word referring to his alignment with cosmic 'Truth', 'sincere'. Islam prospered because 'It was a Reality direct from the great Heart of Nature', and its prophet was a man who accepted 'the Infinite Nature of Duty' and understood Duty's identity with denial of self and total submission to the will of God.[44] This was language and these were ideas with which Gandhi would have felt at home by the time he left London.

Carlyle's inspirations were his youthful study of the writers of the German Romantic movement and his friendship with the American Transcendentalist Ralph Waldo Emerson. These were writers who, like Blavatsky, had drunk at the well of 'Eastern mysticism' and found in it not a chilly denial of the significance of individual human life but an affirmation of individual human potentiality. From the immanence of a divine principle in the world they deduced that the more the individual lost himself in the collectivity of life – the more he became, in Carlyle's words, 'portion of the primal reality of things'[45] – the more powerfully individual, paradoxically, he became.

Carlyle did not practise magic. Nor would he have been found in the same room as Madame Blavatsky had he lived long enough to meet her. He saw himself as a rough-hewn, large-minded Christian man with his feet firmly planted on the stony ground of Craigenputtock. But what he believed in was nevertheless a kind of magic, and Madame Blavatsky would have descried in him a kindred spirit.

# TWO

# South Africa:
# Beginnings

G ANDHI returned to India and for two years experienced the humilia-
tions of the England-returned unemployed barrister. He sought work in
Kathiawar and Bombay and found little, even after agreeing to pay touts for
business. His first attempt to argue before the Bombay courts ended when
words deserted him. His family awaited returns on its investment. None came.
To add to his woes, despite the resumption of married life with Kasturbai
relations were no better. But another child arrived and had to be provided
for. Had Gandhi stayed in India he might have settled down and earned a
living in his calling. Two years was not a long time for a lawyer to establish
himself. But rescue came in the form of a job in South Africa. Before then,
he had two experiences which marked him.

The first was his acquaintance, beginning the day he set foot on Indian
soil, with a young Jain, Raychandbhai. Raychandbhai was something of a
celebrity in Kathiawar. A businessman with a flourishing international trade
in diamond and pearls, he was also a poet, a Shatavadhani (literally, someone
who could attend to a hundred things at once; practically, someone who
performed extraordinary feats of memory), and a religious philosopher and
teacher. In Gujarat this was not an improbable combination. The Jains had
long ago gravitated as a community into the pursuit of commerce, deeming
it non-violent, and it was a pursuit at which they excelled. Their religious
regard for simplicity discouraged the translation of wealth into luxury. Money

in the bank was thus no bar to religious authority, since austerity of life was assumed.

Gandhi was fascinated by this man not much older than himself who combined with apparent ease worldly success and spiritual equipoise. For almost two years he observed him closely. There were spiritual conversations: apparently Gandhi was advised to read the *Gita*. Hinduism enjoins a spiritual preceptor, a *guru*, and Raychandbhai would have been a natural choice. But Gandhi held back. Later he said that Raychandbhai's early death denoted spiritual imperfections.[1] There was evidently tension in the relationship; but distance and the dignity of employment reduced it, and when Gandhi was in the throes of religious perplexity in South Africa he wrote to Raychandbai for advice.

The other experience was a distressing one. Gandhi's brother Lakshmidas had been secretary to the ruler of Rajkot, Rana Bhavsingh. The Rana was alleged to have removed some jewels from the state Treasury without author- ity, an act in which Lakshmidas was said to have been complicit. The family asked Gandhi to put in a good word for his brother with the British political agent in Rajkot, an officer whom, as it happened, he had met in England. He could not refuse, and went to make his representations.

By his own account, disaster happened. As soon as the small talk was over, he came to the purpose of his visit. The political agent warned him off the subject. He pressed on and was asked to go. He pressed on further and the agent asked his servant to show him out. He was reluctant to leave. The servant gripped him by the shoulders and propelled him through the door.

There was nothing he could have done to retrieve his dignity. But he did the worst possible thing and sent a note to the agent threatening to sue. As you like, came back the reply. The eminent lawyer and politician Sir Pherozeshah Mehta happened to be in Rajkot and was consulted. He told Gandhi to swallow the insult and learn from the experience. The advice was 'as bitter as poison' but he accepted it.

He had humiliated himself in every possible way. He had involved himself in a family matter of dubious propriety and thus associated himself, in the eyes of a powerful English official, in whose court he would have to argue if he ever got a brief, with the corrupt intrigues of the traditional ruling class. He had blundered on when asked to desist and been ejected. He had then made himself entirely risible by threatening to sue. In the eyes of his family he had failed to further their cause and made a mess of a delicate mission. Finally, he had come to the notice of the immensely influential Sir Pherozeshah Mehta, a man of notorious hauteur, in a manner which guaranteed a dismissive response. We can believe him when he says simply, 'This shock changed the course of my life.'[2]

The humiliation was all the more dreadful for its contrast with the family's efforts to anglicize itself. On Gandhi's return Lakshmidas had fixed up the house and bought in European crockery. Gandhi had introduced knives and forks and European dress, and directed cocoa and porridge to be served for breakfast. The family had set itself up for a fall, and fallen.

Even so, Gandhi jibbed at first when the offer came not long after from South Africa. It was not a job for a barrister but for someone a cut above a clerk. A big Kathiawari firm in Durban needed help with a civil suit going on in Pretoria. The job would be for one year. After some hesitation, Gandhi took it.

Gandhi spent 21 years in South Africa and left with an international reputation which he was eager to put to work in India. This was his plan at least from 1901. But its fulfilment was delayed by his inability before 1914 to use his South African experience as a springboard into Indian politics.

It is not clear that there was ever a time when Gandhi's political ambitions were confined to South Africa. He recalled that in 1893, when he was first in South Africa, 'I dreamt about the Congress'.[3] When the Natal Indian Congress was founded in 1894, the name was chosen, Gandhi says, because he wanted to evoke the Indian Congress, 'the very life of India'.[4] He said more than once in South Africa (and many times later on) that he had gone into politics for the purpose of spiritual self-realization.[5] But his political ambitions appear to have slightly antedated his religious ones.

Gandhi's first call to passive resistance came in 1904, and his first *satyagraha* campaign began in 1906. The decade from 1894 to 1904 was occupied in political activity of a purely conventional kind – meetings, petitions, letters to the editor, and 'memorials' submitted to the British and South African governments. This was Gandhi's apprenticeship in politics. In those years he learned the skills of organization and persuasion, tactical manoeuvre and negotiation.

Gandhi's way of life also remained relatively conventional until 1904, when the agricultural settlement at Phoenix, the prototype of his Indian ashrams, was founded. Even then, there was little outward change. For the most part he lived the life of a lawyer–politician in Durban or Johannesburg, visiting Phoenix when he could. The visits rarely lasted more than a month and were usually much shorter.[6] The same was true of Tolstoy Farm, which Gandhi and Herman Kallenbach founded in 1910. Except for the latter half of 1911, when he was biding his time after reaching his 'provisional agreement' with Smuts, Gandhi was rarely in residence there. He chafed at this, and frustration at not being able to reconcile the demands of politics with the austere and laborious life dictated by his religious and social convictions appears to have increased his anxiety to get to India.[7] In South Africa he had to choose between being a spiritual leader and being a politician. He could neither credibly nor practically be both. In India politics and holiness might be combined.

Except when he was at Phoenix or Tolstoy Farm, Gandhi was to all outward appearance part of a flourishing subculture of mildly nonconforming idealists, of which a surprising number seem to have found their way to South Africa in the 1890s and early 1900s. At various times he baked his own bread, cut his own hair and laundered his own shirts. He took up nature cure, experimenting first on himself and then, with increasing boldness, on others. None of this would have marked him off in any striking way from the people with whom he associated. What did distinguish him from them was that he was brown and they were white. Despite his involvement in the Indian community through his legal and political work, and after 1896 his life as a family man, his closest friends in South Africa were European. Of the original eight settlers at Phoenix, four were drawn from his European acquaintance.

As in London, it was Gandhi's contact with Europeans that was the crucial influence on his development, and as in London he made friends through his interests in vegetarianism and religion. In South Africa Gandhi was not the religious tourist he had been in London but an active seeker after truth. The years 1893 and 1894 saw the emergence of most of the ideas which were to guide him through life, though he did not see all their implications at once; this was a process which had to wait on experience and events. During this period he worked out the basic religious rationale for *satyagraha*, which he also termed 'soul-force' and defined as power through suffering.

Gandhi arrived in Durban some time towards the end of May 1893. As with his arrival in London, he had taken thought for his appearance, and stepped on to the dock dressed in a frock coat and a turban of his own design.[8] His employer, Dada Abdullah Sheth, was there to meet him. The turban was to be the cause of his first act of resistance to South African authority.

At the time of Gandhi's arrival, Dada Abdullah was probably the richest Indian in South Africa. His assets included a shipping line which plied between India and Natal, as well as commercial interests scattered through Natal, the Transvaal and Mozambique. Like most other Indian businessmen in South Africa he was a Muslim from a long-established trading community in Gujarat. These men had gone to South Africa initially to trade with the large number of Indian indentured labourers employed on the sugar estates. Profits from supplying their simple wants – ghee, rice, cloth – were invested in land, property and other concerns and soon South Africa had a prosperous Indian business class. It attracted the resentful attention of the white population; by 1891 Indian traders had been expelled from the Orange Free State and were uncertain about their future in Natal and the Transvaal.

The social divisions within the Indian community went deep. The indentured or freed labourers, who were the vast majority, were either north Indian Muslims, or Tamil- or Telegu-speaking Hindus from the south, driven by extreme poverty into indentured servitude in South Africa. The business class had no social relations with them: as it would have been in India, so it was in South Africa. The whites, however, generally despised all Indians impartially. The merchants responded by emphasizing their apartness from the labouring majority. They called themselves 'Arabs' and adopted flowing robes. Other Indian groups also tried to indicate their distinctness. The merchants' Parsi clerks called themselves 'Persians' and wore traditional Parsi costume. The labourers' colonial-born children, who were often Christian, wore European dress.

The merchants' clothes reflected their politics, which were designed to convince the whites that disabilities attached to being Indian need not apply to them. Gandhi was to become the political representative of this group in its struggle against discriminatory legislation. But first he had to convince Dada Abdullah that he was worth his hire. He had no experience of business and little knowledge of commercial law. He had no knowledge of bookkeeping. Yet he set to work with the same thoroughness he had shown in studying for his bar exams to learn the fundamentals of his job. After a week or so Dada Abdullah felt confident enough to send him to Pretoria to work on his lawsuit.

Before leaving he was taken on a visit to the Durban magistrates' court and was asked by the presiding magistrate to remove his turban. It was not a completely unreasonable request. Europeans removed their hats in court, and apart from his turban Gandhi was wearing European dress. Nevertheless, he refused and left. It was a bold thing to do for someone in his position – young, untried, newly arrived – and he instantly thought better of it. He decided to switch to the English hat which would normally accompany a frock coat and remove it when custom required. But Dada Abdullah told him if he wore a hat he would look like a waiter (the colonial-born sons of indentured labourers were often waiters), and abandoning his turban was allowing himself to be insulted. The turban was reinstated and apparently worn with impunity to subsequent appearances in the magistrates' court.[9]

He set off on the journey from Durban to Pretoria with a first-class ticket that covered the train journey to Charlestown on the Transvaal border, and then the coach journey from Charlestown to Johannesburg and then Pretoria. Normally the entire journey took three days.

At Pietermaritzburg, about 70 miles from Durban, Gandhi attracted the attention of a white passenger who objected to a brown man's presence in a first-class compartment. A railway official ordered him to move to the baggage van, and when he refused he was manhandled off the train by a policeman. He spent the night in the waiting room of the Pietermaritzburg station. The next day he telegraphed a complaint to the railway management, received a conciliatory reply, and boarded the evening train. At Charlestown the stagecoach agent was obstructive, but allowed him to get on the coach providing he sat outside with the driver on a seat normally occupied by a company employee known as the 'leader', while the leader sat inside with the passengers. When the leader felt like a smoke and came outside, he motioned Gandhi to go and sit on a piece of sacking draped over the footboard. The indignity was too much and Gandhi refused, clinging on as the man set about him and tried to drag him off the seat, until some of the other passengers intervened and rescued him. At Standerton Gandhi complained to the coach company and was assured of a seat with the other passengers for the journey the next day. In Johannesburg he was turned away from the Grand National Hotel and found shelter in the home of an Indian merchant. His troubles were not over. There was a struggle to purchase a first-class ticket for the train journey to Pretoria, and then in Pretoria he again faced the difficulty of finding a hotel. A chance encounter led him to an American-owned establishment where he was eventually, once the permission of the other guests had been obtained, allowed to eat in the dining room.

According to the *Autobiography*, a political intention formed itself during that long night in Pietermaritzburg.

> I began to think of my duty. Should I fight for my rights or go back to India, or should I go on to Pretoria without minding the insults, and return to India after finishing the case? It would be cowardice to run back to India without fulfilling my obligation. The hardship to which I was subjected was superficial – only a symptom of the deep disease of colour prejudice. I should try, if possible, to root out the disease and suffer hardships in the process. Redress for wrongs I should seek only to the extent that would be necessary for the removal of colour prejudice.[10]

A week after arriving in Pretoria Gandhi held a meeting at the house of one of the merchants 'to present to them a picture of their condition in the Transvaal'.[11] He also addressed them on their responsibility to be truthful in business and sanitary in their habits – a preview of many future addresses on these topics. He proposed the formation of a representative association and offered to give English classes. These initiatives petered out. It was only in July 1894, when legislation was introduced to deprive Indians in Natal of the franchise, that his political career really began.

There was little work to do in Pretoria and Gandhi occupied his time with religion.

Dada Abdullah's attorney in Pretoria was A.W. Baker. Baker was a director of the South Africa General Mission, a keenly evangelical Christian group established in 1889 to take the word of God to whites and blacks alike in benighted South Africa. Baker set out to save Gandhi's heathen soul. But he was prepared in the process to treat him as a man and a brother, and on one occasion he shared with him not only a hotel room but a double bed. He was the first European Gandhi knew in South Africa who provided an example of a consciously lived Christian life which ignored the existence of race.[12]

Baker's associates in the South Africa General Mission took up Gandhi and he responded to their friendly interest. He was far from home and had just experienced in concentrated form the racial hatred which envenomed South African society. Soon he was attending daily prayer meetings and Sunday teas. He made no commitment, but did not hide the fact that he was a searcher, and open to religious ideas other than orthodox Hinduism. His new friends gave him books to read. They did not convince him that Jesus Christ was his saviour. Nevertheless, for six months or so he was intimately involved with the South Africa General Mission, and remained on terms of mutual respect and friendship with some of its members for a long time.

The high point of Gandhi's connection with the Mission was his attendance in October 1893 at the 'Wellington Conference for the Deepening of the Spiritual Life', held at Wellington near Cape Town, and modelled on the evangelical religious conferences held at Keswick in the Lake District since 1875. The South Africa General Mission had originated as an offshoot of what had become known as the Keswick movement.

In their scale and organization and spirit the Keswick conferences owed much to the open-air revival meetings of early Methodism, though they were more decorous. Each summer the faithful gathered in large numbers at Keswick to make public affirmation of their belief, and to celebrate the personal spiritual rebirth which they were convinced would not only carry a man forward through life and into heaven, but give him an inner light which would shine irresistibly on the unconverted. Keswick was in the forefront of the 'Holiness' movement then arising in the Protestant churches of Europe and North America.

The leaders of the Keswick movement laid out 'seven steps' to be taken on the road to holiness and the grant of 'power from on high' to save souls. They were:

1.  Immediate abandonment of every known sin and doubtful indulgence.
2.  Surrender of the whole being to Jesus Christ as not only Saviour, but Master and Lord.
3.  Appropriation by faith of God's promise and power for holy living.
4.  Voluntary mortification of the self-life, that God may be all in all.
5.  Gracious renewal or transformation of the inmost temper and disposition.
6.  Separation unto God for sanctification and service.
7.  Enduement with power and filling with the Holy Spirit.[13]

It was a curious accident that Gandhi's encounter with a group of Christians at this time should have been with people fascinated by the power of holiness. This may have been why he allowed himself to be prayed over for so long before deciding that his involvement should cease. Open yourself fully to the Holy Spirit, a prominent Keswick preacher said, and 'not you, but the power of God through you, will repeat the marvels of Pentecost'.[14] (Pentecostalism in fact grew out of the Holiness movement.) The Keswick doctrine was a form of Christian theurgy.

The Wellington convention's theme that year was 'Perfect Love', it being the hope of its convenor, the Rev. Andrew Murray, who was president of the South Africa General Mission, that 'Our relation to the Christians, with whom we are in contact, to the world around us, to the perishing millions of Heathendom, will all be made new in the light and the strength of Perfect Love.' Though he resisted the delegates' theology, Gandhi was impressed by their fervour. 'I was delighted', he later wrote, 'at their faith.'[15]

During the period of Gandhi's connection with the Mission it was divided by controversy. On the one side there were the perfectionists, who believed that 'Holiness without sin is attainable in this life'.[16] On the other side were those who shrank from the pridefulness of belief in the perfectibility of man. It is clear from the *Autobiography* that Gandhi's sympathies were with the perfectionists.[17] Among the perfectionists there was a further division, between those who believed that sinlessness could be achieved through faith in Jesus alone, and those who thought that reaching the sinless state involved a process of self-purification. Gandhi naturally sided with the latter.

Gandhi said in his *Autobiography* that he parted company with the South Africa General Mission because it was 'impossible for me to believe that I could go to heaven or attain salvation only by becoming a Christian'.[18] But his difficulties, he wrote, 'lay deeper'.

> It was more than I could believe that Jesus was the only incarnate son of God, and that only he who believed in him would have everlasting life. If God could have sons, all of us were His sons. If Jesus was like God, or God Himself, then all men were like God and could be God Himself. My reason was not ready to believe literally that Jesus by his death and by his blood redeemed the sins of the world. Metaphorically there might be some truth in it. Again, according to Christianity only human beings had souls, and not other living beings, for whom death meant complete extinction; while I held a contrary belief. I could accept Jesus as a martyr, an embodiment of sacrifice, and a divine teacher, but not as the most perfect man ever born. His death on the Cross was a great example to the world, but that there was anything like a mysterious or miraculous virtue in it my heart could not accept. The pious lives of Christians did not give me anything that the lives of men of other faiths had failed to give. I had seen in other lives just the same reformation that I had heard of among Christians. Philosophically, there was nothing extraordinary in Christian principles. From the point of view of sacrifice, it seemed to me that the Hindus greatly surpassed the Christians. It was impossible for me to regard Christianity as a perfect religion or the greatest of all religions.

These words summarize Gandhi's mature position with respect to the Christian Church and Christian missionary activity.

Gandhi remained, he said, 'for ever indebted' to his Mission friends 'for the religious quest that they awakened in me'.[19] But even during his period of involvement with the Mission he was pursuing other lines of spiritual inquiry.

It seems he acquainted Josiah Oldfield with his religious concerns, for Oldfield put him in touch some time in 1893 with Edward Maitland, a vegetarian and mystic who had founded the Esoteric Christian Union in 1891.[20] Gandhi corresponded with Maitland until the latter's death in 1897, and in November 1894 became active as the Esoteric Christian Union's agent in South Africa. The correspondence has not survived.[21]

At some point Gandhi also entered into correspondence with Raychandbhai. The correspondence continued until 1901, but only one of Raychandbhai's letters, in which he answered questions posed by Gandhi, has survived. This letter is dated 20 October 1894 and responds to a letter from Gandhi written 'Before June 1894'.[22] Gandhi's questions to Raychandbhai reflected his familiarity with Maitland's ideas.

Edward Maitland and his collaborator Anna Kingsford were part of the world of religious and social reform which impinged on Gandhi during his stay in London. They were prominent in the vegetarian and anti-vivisectionist movements, and Maitland was a founder, with Henry Salt and Edward Carpenter, of the Humanitarian League.[23] Anna Kingsford died in February 1888, and it is not known if Gandhi met Maitland while in London.

In 1882 Kingsford and Maitland jointly published *The Perfect Way; or, the Finding of Christ*, an unorthodox interpretation of Christianity for which they claimed divine inspiration in the form of revelations vouchsafed to them at intervals during the past five years.[24] These revelations were sufficiently similar to theosophy for Kingsford and Maitland to be made president and vice-president respectively of the London Lodge of the Theosophical Society in 1883, but they were forced out a year later after a public quarrel which briefly divided the Society. After Kingsford's death Maitland published *Clothed with the Sun* (1889), a collection of Kingsford's mystical 'illuminations', and *The Story of the New Gospel of Interpretation* (1894), an account of his partnership with Kingsford, giving as it were the inside story of the production of *The Perfect Way*. Shortly before his death he published a two-volume biography of Kingsford. *The Perfect Way*, *Clothed with the Sun* and *The New Gospel of Interpretation* were offered for sale by Gandhi in his capacity as South African agent of the Esoteric Christian Union, a tiny organization which collapsed on the death of its founder.[25]

Gandhi's biographers have not taken seriously his connection with the Esoteric Christian Union, and its doctrines have received little attention from Gandhi scholars. It is true that Gandhi himself never made public reference to the Esoteric Christian Union after 1895. But it is also true that Edward Maitland and Anna Kingsford were not the kind of people whose influence an admirer of Gandhi can easily accept. 'It is most unlikely', writes one of Gandhi's biographers of Anna Kingsford, 'that ... Gandhi would have recognized any spiritual authority in her'.[26] In *The Story of the New Gospel of Interpretation* spiritual truths are revealed via table-tilting or the planchette (an automatic writing device consisting of a board on castors attached to a pencil); battles take place with 'astrals', spirits close to the earth and hence allied with matter, who send false messages and thereby work to abort the birth of Esoteric Christianity; claims are made to distinguished past incarnations, among them St Mary Magdalen (Kingsford) and St. John the Evangelist (Maitland). The authors of *The Perfect Way* are revealed to have been a pair of comically vainglorious spiritualists with a rich fantasy life fuelled by mutual obsession.

Yet Gandhi's secretary, Pyarelal, who knew him intimately, told the Gandhi scholar James Hunt in 1978 that Esoteric Christianity had a 'specific and lasting influence' on Gandhi's thought, and 'gave a very distinct colouring to his thoughts on some very vital aspects e.g. Brahmacharya [continence], the doctrine of absolution through Christ's suffering, allegorical interpretations of the scriptures etc.' Pyarelal added that, 'Whatever [Gandhi] absorbed in this extremely impressionable and formative phase of his development abode with him for life.'[27] These very explicit statements suggest that the doctrines of Esoteric Christianity, however dubious their origin, merit close examination.

There is in fact no reason to think that Gandhi would have been put off by the origins of Esoteric Christianity. He was at the time, and remained, a believer in the possibility of communication with spirits and in mediumship.[28] He even believed in the planchette as a means of communication with the spirit world, but disapproved of it because it tended to be employed for vulgar and impure purposes and thus ruin its user for serious spiritual striving.[29] (Maitland and Kingsford also developed reservations about the planchette, an instrument whose use, it gradually dawned on them, was beneath their spiritual dignity.)

Indeed, Gandhi's interest in the spirit world at the time he became involved with the Esoteric Christian Union was pronounced. An entry in his diary for 18 August 1894 reads: 'Wrote to Mrs. Mary Alling Aber subscribing to a copy of *Spirit* and making a few remarks on *Souls*.'[30] This can only refer to Aber's *Souls* ... , published in Chicago in 1893. (*Spirit* was presumably a journal; if so, it has vanished without trace.)

Aber was an American admirer of Anna Kingsford. She considered Kingsford's revelations superseded by the one granted to her, that by 1901 the planet Earth would have been destroyed for its sins, and the good souls on it removed to Jupiter. Her specialty was the genealogy of souls, to which she was privy through her power of 'separating soul from body at will'.[31] We learn from her book that the reincarnated twelve disciples of Jesus are

> with one exception [Edward Maitland?] in the United States. One is a railroad magnate, another a college president, another a teacher who is widely known and loved, and two are women. The mother of Jesus lives near the upper head waters of the Hudson River; and John the Baptist is in Russia – a second time, 'A voice crying in the wilderness.'[32]

Gandhi's opinion of Aber's book appears in a letter to a Mrs Lewis, a member of the Esoteric Christian Union, on 3 August 1894.

> If you do not think much of the *Souls*, what position is the book to occupy in respectable literature? If the author has written what is absolutely true from personal observation, the book cannot be lightly treated. If it is an attempt to delude the people into a belief in real truths by fascinating falsehoods, the book deserves the highest condemnation possible. For we will not learn truth by means of falsehoods. Of course I write this without meaning the slightest dis-respect to the author of whom I know nothing. She may be a lady of the highest probity and truth. I only repeat that to appreciate the *Souls*, acquaintance with the author's character is absolutely necessary.[33]

He felt, in other words, that the value of the book depended on whether the author was lying or telling the truth as she saw it.

The Maitland–Kingsford partnership began in 1874, after Anna Kingsford, then living quietly in Shropshire, wrote to Maitland with praise for his novel *By and By*, a work of science fiction in which some early ideas of Maitland about the power of the perfected soul find expression.

In 1874, after an adventurous life in the goldfields of California and the Australian outback, with many solitary hours passed in the company of his favourite authors, Emerson and Carlyle, Maitland was back in England, trying to earn money from writing and looking for a soulmate to replace his wife, who had died in Australia. He found the soulmate in Anna Kingsford, whose husband, the Rev. Algernon Kingsford, was content to let her spend long periods travelling for her health, and pursuing medical studies in Paris and London, under Maitland's chaperonage. Plainly, Maitland was in love with the beautiful Anna, but their relationship appears not to have been physical.

Maitland discovered on his first visit to Kingsford that she possessed a gift. Words came to her during sleep which when written down proved to be spiritual revelations of a high order. They addressed the Christian doctrines about which Maitland happened to be particularly concerned – original sin and vicarious atonement – and suggested that Christianity could manage without them. Maitland resolved to join forces with Kingsford, perceiving that she could be the seer and he the systematizer in the project which now took shape. This was to launch a new form of Christianity to replace the priest-ridden and terrifying religion in which he had grown up.

The relationship, and Kingsford's spiritual gifts, developed apace. Soon Kingsford was experiencing the trance-like state of 'illumination', and intoning while awake the words which were reproduced in *The Perfect Way* and *Clothed with the Sun* – words which the friends at length concluded were a recovery of spiritual knowledge acquired in Kingsford's past lives. Being in her present incarnation almost but not quite perfect, she possessed the power to summon up what she had previously experienced and known. Visions began to appear, culminating in the 'Vision of Adonai' – the Lord God manifest – described in *The Perfect Way* and Maitland's *The Story of the New Gospel of Interpretation.*

The messenger god Hermes, the angel Gabriel, and the spirit of Swedenborg helped to interpret the revelations received. Maitland himself began to hear voices. They sometimes directed him to correct the feminist tendencies appearing in Kingsford's dicta, and reconcile them with his own more old-fashioned conception of the 'noble' woman who delights and completes the intellectual man. Occasionally God himself spoke to Maitland, in a voice which appeared to come from within. Eventually a doctrine took shape which was no more absurd then that of official Christianity, and possessed in certain respects more coherence.

The authors of *The Perfect Way* believed that the world was in a state of spiritual crisis. Science, in itself morally neutral and intellectually admirable, had undermined religious belief and encouraged a devotion to the material. The church, morally bankrupt and intellectually exhausted, could neither withstand the onslaught of scientific and textual criticism of its traditional beliefs, nor reverse the advance of materialism. It was time for a new revelation which would satisfy both the claims of reason and the longings of the soul.

Vivisection was singled out as the most compelling evidence of man's degraded state. It showed that the preservation of men's bodies – the aim of medical science – was now so important that the vilest cruelties could be tolerated for its sake. (In nineteenth-century medical schools, live dogs were nailed to boards and dissected for the benefit of students.) In such a material age, Kingsford and Maitland believed, men must be recalled to the truths which were central to all religions. These were that man's attachment to his material nature was the root of all evil, and that nurturance of the divine spirit within offered the only possibility of transcending the body and thus evil itself.

Esoteric Christianity rejected the Christian version of creation found in Genesis, in which God creates the universe out of nothing and man is thus other than God, in favour of the emanationist conception (common to Hinduism and theosophy), in which a primordial divine substance manifests itself as matter and all matter is thus in a sense divine. Matter 'itself is, whatever its kind, a mode of Substance, of which the nature is spiritual', and matter is also 'Substance in its dynamic condition'. But God is also more than the aggregation of all manifest substance, for 'the Manifest does not exhaust the Unmanifest'.[34]

On to this cosmogony is grafted the idea of 'the Fall' – a concept central to Christianity though not exclusively Christian. Matter in itself is not re-garded as evil but simply as the inevitable 'limitation of good' which defines the fact of creation.[35] An Edenic state is postulated in which human beings were not attached to their bodies but were governed by pure impulses of the soul. Sinfulness arrived in the form of attachment to the flesh. When men began to lose control over their senses 'the Fall' took place: it is 'the general tendency towards Matter and Sense, that constitutes the Fall'.[36] Esoteric Christianity allows for the existence of the Devil. He is 'that which gives to Matter the pre-eminence over Spirit'; and as God is love, the Devil is 'before all else, Hate'.[37]

Working against the tendency towards matter and sense is the almost inde-structible aspiration of the individual soul to reunite itself with the universal divine soul which is God. This aspiration makes possible the processes of 'regeneration' and 'redemption' (not always clearly distinguished) in which control of the senses is regained over many lifetimes of effort. Souls progress at different rates, but it is a journey which all may undertake – for, 'of the doctrine we seek to restore, the basis is the Pre-existence and Perfectibility of the Soul'.[38] The doctrine of karma is acknowledged.

At some point in his journey the man who is on his way to regeneration 'sees God', in the sense of becoming truly cognizant of the divine principle within himself and others. At the moment when perfection is attained he 'sees God face to face', as his individuality merges into God's universality. 'True, the *man* cannot see God. But the divine in man sees God.... and beholds God *with the eyes of God*.'[39]

Perfection is complete non-attachment to the bodily state. It means liberation from the power of the senses – though not, at first, from the body. When the state of non-attachment is reached, a process takes place of 'complete withdrawal of the man into his own interior and celestial region'.[40] His soul is now united with the divine soul (the 'At-one-ment'), his will is now consonant with the divine will, and he is filled with the power of God working through him. He who experiences this condition is 'a Christ'.

A Christ is not born perfect but becomes perfect in the course of his final lifetime, and at the end of this life he returns to the spiritual state and is not born again. A realized Christ is free of all disease and has miraculous powers 'on all planes' physical and spiritual,[41] which, having accomplished his own redemption, he directs to the redemption of others, though he can do no more than kindle in them the desire to be redeemed. Ultimately, each must be responsible for his own salvation. Yet the appearance of a Christ – or even the fully revealed doctrine of the Christs, without the physical presence of a Redeemer – significantly hastens the spiritual progress of mankind. In the presence of revelation, 'Materialism, with all its foul brood, [flees] discomfited, like Python, the Mighty Serpent of Darkness, before the darts of Phoibos.'[42]

The anticipated end of this process of redemption is that the whole of humanity will return to the state of spirit whence it came. First, however, it will pass through an intermediate stage – a Golden Age, the New Jerusalem, Paradise regained, the Kingdom of God. This stage will arrive when matter has come generally under the control of spirit, and – consequently – modern civilization, which is the expression of materialism, has been destroyed.

Kingsford and Maitland set out to show, through a true interpretation of Christian scripture, how by following Jesus' example the individual could achieve At-one-ment of his soul with the divine soul. They argued that the New Testament, like other scriptures, was meant to be understood allegorically and 'mystically' (meaning the interpretation of allegory under divine inspiration). Correctly understood, it preached the doctrines of the universal immanence of the divine soul and the 'Pre-existence and Perfectibility' of the human soul. It then revealed itself to be a variant of the quintessential religion, the ancient and long-lost 'Gnosis' (secret spiritual knowledge) which 'constituted the basic and secret doctrine of all the great religions of antiquity, including Christianity'.[43]

But an allegorical approach to Christian scripture calls into question the historical existence of Jesus, and this presented as big a problem for Kingsford and Maitland as for more conventional Christians. Was the reality of Jesus to be discarded with so much else? No, was the eventual answer. Personal devotion to Jesus, and the desire to show that Christianity was distinct enough to compel allegiance in itself, held them back. Nevertheless, the biblical narrative of Jesus' life is often treated as allegory in *The Perfect Way*. The historical existence of other 'Men Regenerate', particularly the Buddha, is acknowledged. But Jesus is supreme in the perfection of his life and teaching.

In practice, Kingsford and Maitland's interpretation of the New Testament was constructed on the foundation of Christian esotericism.

Once their collaboration had begun in earnest they began to frequent the Reading Room of the British Museum, immersing themselves with increasing excitement in the works of Christian Neoplatonists and other professedly Christian exponents of implicitly self-divinizing religious traditions. The Kabbala also provided inspiration. *The Perfect Way* in the end contained little direct exegesis of scripture. Its authors knew by then that they were not original religious thinkers but heirs to a long tradition of unorthodox Christian speculation. Hence the importance they came to attach to the notion of 'recovery' of spiritual knowledge. It was not just from previous lives that knowledge was recovered, but from the unrivalled resources of the British Museum.

As their researches progressed, they were drawn into the study of ancient and not so ancient works of 'divine science' – essentially theurgical works, deeply contaminated with magic. They were led to the writings of contemporary magians such as 'Eliphas Lévi' (the Abbé Constant), who made occultism fashionable in France in the 1850s and preached a universal religion similar to theosophy. The publication of *The Perfect Way* brought them into contact with Lévi's 'heirs', Baron Spedalieri of Marseilles and Dr Ernest Gryzanowsky of Berlin, who gave *The Perfect Way* their blessing. Kingsford did not resist the occult implications of her doctrines and in 1886 began taking instruction in 'practical occultism'.[44]

How, then, does one become a Christ? According to *The Perfect Way*, *Clothed with the Sun* and *The Story of the New Gospel of Interpretation*, through self-purification, suffering, renunciation and love. Self-purification is the foundation.

Like A.F. Hills, Kingsford and Maitland believed that it is our existence in material form that renders possible the purificatory experiences that make us perfect. (Hills's writings are full of echoes, terminological and doctrinal, of *The Perfect Way*.) Not neglect of the body but its rational subjection to discipline is the route to Christhood and to God. Abstention from meat is both part of the discipline of self-purification and a means of creating a body sensitized to receive God's instructions.

To understand what it is that has to be held in check, an individual must first experience his material nature. This is the beginning, over many earth lives, of his or her spiritual education. With understanding comes the conscious desire for progress. Further aeons of reincarnated existence are then passed in subduing the demands of the flesh, and even in the lifetime of a Christ there will be opportunities for restraint.

The presumption is the greater the sinner the greater the saint. Abandonment to sin in the earliest incarnations denotes a capacity for self-surrender which will be fruitful later in the cause of virtue, as the soul learns from experience. This is the reason for 'the leniency and even tenderness exhibited by the typical Man Regenerate' towards the woman of loose morals, as shown by Jesus to Mary Magdalen. He sees in her the potential repetition of his own spiritual trajectory.[45]

The aspirant to Christhood must cultivate detachment in every sphere of life, forsaking family and friends and concentrating on his spiritual quest, which will benefit all mankind. He must avoid cities and live 'in unfrequented places, or in lands such as those of the East, in parts where the abominations of Babylon are unknown, and where the magnetic chain between earth and heaven is strong'.[46]

There are higher spiritual natures already in existence. They have 'crucified in themselves the flesh', and thereby made their bodies instruments not masters of their souls; means of expression, not sources of limitation, for their spirits.

The crucifixion of the flesh, meaning the death of the body in the sense of its complete subjection to the divine will, is a central concept.[47]

The idea of suffering, as befits a Christian work, is pervasive in *The Perfect Way*. Suffering has merit, whether passively – in bearing life's unavoidable afflictions – or actively undergone. But the latter has more merit. Active suffering can take the form of self-discipline or self-sacrifice. Most meritorious of all is to experience in oneself the suffering of others – for the process of becoming at one with God involves becoming at one with all of suffering humanity, in which God is. Thus, 'that the Christ is said to suffer and die for others is because through his abounding sympathy he suffers even to death in and with them.'[48] These ideas appear to have found their way, in diluted form, into *The Key to Theosophy*.

Renunciation of the material world is both a process and the climactic experience of the life of a Christ. In the life of Jesus the climactic moment arrives when he accepts that he must die on the cross, and in the lives of all Christs there is an equivalent test of resolution. At the moment when the potential Christ accepts his fate, he decisively renounces his 'lower nature' and becomes defined by his 'higher nature'; he rejects the flesh and rises at last above it. He then becomes 'the Man Regenerate with Power', a state identified allegorically with the Christian 'Resurrection'. (It is never clear whether Kingsford and Maitland believe the historical Jesus died on the cross.) The At-one-ment having taken place, when the Christ speaks it is God speaking through him. Still in the body, he is beyond the operation of karma and cannot sin. He has attained 'immunity, not merely ... from the consequences of sin, but from the liability to sin'.[49] An exchange is implied: the Christ has rejected the demands of the flesh; his reward is power. Only he who 'accounts the Resurrection worth the Passion, the Power worth the Suffering' should aspire to Christhood; and only he 'does not hesitate' when his 'time has come'.[50]

It is love which distinguishes the Christ from the mere 'adept'. 'The "Adept" covets power in order to save himself only; and knowledge is for him a thing apart from love. Love saves others as well as oneself.'[51] Love of others makes the Christ embrace the final renunciation, and he accepts for others' sake the suffering which unites him with God: only by example can he show others the way. 'The Christ gives and dies in giving, because Love constrains him and no fear witholds.'[52] When he fully unites with God, the Christ is filled with love – for God is love.

In Esoteric Christianity the capacities to suffer and to love are regarded as feminine. Kingsford and Maitland revived an ancient conception of the divine principle as having a dual nature – the 'spirit' being masculine and active, the 'soul' feminine and passive. To complete himself in the image of God the male must become female, the active masculine spirit become one with the loving and suffering female soul. It is above all love which the Christ learns through identification with 'the Soul, or Essential Woman'.[53] Even to learn the soul's lessons he must first have identified to some extent with the feminine principle. For the 'intuition' (as opposed to the intellect) is also the preserve of the female sensibility, and to those without intuition spiritual knowledge is denied. At the time of his birth Jesus was spiritually a woman, but he had a man's body to fit him for his wandering life and 'mission of poverty and labour'.[54]

The supreme manifestation of the Christ principle will come through the spiritual fertilization of the West by the East, followed by the consequent spiritual revivification of the East by the West. In the East 'the oldest souls are wont to congregate', vegetarianism is practised, and science was born; the 'soil and astral fluid there are charged with power as a vast battery of many piles'.[55] India above all will have a role to play. The home of great contributions to religious thought and the representative in the world today of spirituality in its 'feminine' aspect (this seems to refer to the goddess cults of India), India's spiritual potential will be fulfilled once she has absorbed the lessons of Christianity. The agent of this will be the British Empire, which has already brought Christian texts to India. Now it can take the true revelation in the form of Esoteric Christianity. Then England and India, 'as representative Man and Woman of Humanity, will in due time constitute one Man, made in the image of God, regenerate and having power'. It is thus necessary that Britain remain, for now, in charge of India: 'All ... that tends to bind England to the Orient is of Christ, and all that tends to sever them is of Antichrist'.[56]

Islam, too, 'the one really monotheistic and non-idolatrous religion now existing', will have its part to play, once it has achieved 'the practical recognition in "Allah" of Mother as well as of Father, by the exaltation of the woman to her rightful station on all planes of man's manifold nature'.[57]

Their election as president and vice-president of the London Lodge of the Theosophical Society confirmed for Kingsford and Maitland that the 'unsealing of the World's Bibles' was at hand. Madame Blavatsky had been given the task of recovering the gnosis of the East, while they had been assigned the recovery of the gnosis of the West.[58]

But people did not join the Theosophical Society to rediscover Christianity, and the pair soon found themselves in a vaguely heretical position. Kingsford's intimations that there was too much occultism and not enough religion in the London Lodge were not well received. Nor was her claim to a direct line to the ancient gnosis, which was bound to unsettle anyone who took seriously Madame Blavatsky, her Mahatmas, and the nascent hierarchy of the Theosophical Society. Perceiving a rival, Blavatsky moved to squash her, taking ship from India for the purpose. Kingsford was pronounced a *'mediumistic creature'*,[59] and she and Maitland forced out. But when Annie Besant took over the Society she made an attempt to reconcile Hindu philosophy with Christian theology. Some of Kingsford's and Maitland's ideas lived on, though they themselves were forgotten.

Gandhi observed in 1894, as he was launching himself as an agent of the Esoteric Christian Union, that 'there is little difference between Theosophy and Esoteric Christianity'.[60] Why, then, did he choose publicly to identify himself with the latter, when as a Hindu he might have been expected to choose (if either) the former?

First, Gandhi had just felt the full force of the 'Holiness' movement emerging in contemporary Christianity, and while attracted by its spiritual vigour had been put off by its fundamentalist crudeness. Kingsford's and Maitland's doctrine could be seen as an elaboration of the idea of Christian holiness, without the exclusivist and literalist taints of organized Christianity. Second, Gandhi may have preferred the social activism of the founders of the Esoteric Christian Union to the indolence of Madame Blavatsky. Third, the vegetarian connection was important. It was Oldfield who had connected Gandhi with Maitland. The letter of 4 August 1894 to Mrs Lewis, the one letter which survives from Gandhi to a known member of the Esoteric Christian Union, reveals that Oldfield was a mutual friend. A.F. Hills seems to have been propagating his own brand of esoteric Christianity. Gandhi's closest English acquaintances then were allied in spirit, and perhaps in practice, with Edward Maitland rather than Madame Blavatsky.[61] In Durban Gandhi presented himself as agent for the Esoteric Christian Union *and* the Vegetarian Society.

But before he committed himself to the Esoteric Christian Union, he had first to hear what Raychandbhai had to say.

Gandhi's first set of questions to Raychandbhai – 'What is the Soul? Does it perform actions? Do past actions impede its progress or not?' – suggests that by 1894 he and his Indian friend were speaking different languages.[62] Raychandbhai replies that the *atman* (the soul – though the terms are not precisely equivalent) is imperishable and its essence is knowledge. It does not perform actions and can be said to be the author only of its own self-realization. Its 'progress' in the sense Gandhi would have had in mind is not considered: Raychandbhai writes of the state of ignorance 'from which the soul must withdraw itself'. Gandhi's second question is, 'What is God? Is He the creator of the universe?' Raychandbhai replies that the liberated soul is God, and vice versa; God is no greater and no less than this. He is not the creator of the universe. But Raychandbhai seems agnostic on what the exact relation between matter and spirit might be. Gandhi's third question is, 'What is *moksha*?' *Moksha* is understood in India to be the final liberation from rebirth, and Raychandbhai's reply to what may have seemed an odd question is rather dismissive, but he does say that *moksha* involves deliverance from the 'bondage' of the body (and, in answer to a later question, from 'attachment'). Gandhi's next question is, 'Is it possible for a person to know for certain, while he is still living, whether or not he will attain *moksha*?' Raychandbhai's answer is a definite 'yes', and, going further, he says that the *atman*, while 'still dwelling in this body', can become 'conscious of its pure essence and of its absolute otherness and freedom from all relations. In other words, it is possible to experience the state of *moksha* even while living.' So Raychandbhai allows for the possibility of full liberation of the soul while in the body. But he does not see this liberation as involving absorption into the godhead; indeed, quite the contrary. In reply to a question about whether Rama and Krishna were incarnations of God, he says that he does 'not think that any [embodied] soul can be a portion of God'.

Gandhi asked Raychandbhai how it was possible to know if a particular religion was 'the best'. The reply was 'That religion alone is the best and is truly strong, which is most helpful in destroying the bondage of worldly life and can establish us in the state which is our essence.' To the question whether Jesus was God's son, Raychandbhai replied that this 'may perhaps be acceptable if we interpret the belief as an allegory'; to the question whether the Old Testament prophecies were fulfilled in Christ, he replied obscurely. He confirmed that one 'whose knowledge has become pure' may be able to remember past lives. He denied that the entire world could either be destroyed materially or merge into God.

A month after this letter was written Gandhi set up shop as agent in South Africa for the Esoteric Christian Union. He seems to have interpreted Raychandbhai's replies as a dispensation to embrace Esoteric Christianity without feeling he was betraying Hinduism. The lesson he learned from the correspondence, he said later, was that the man 'whose one aim in life is to attain *moksha* need not give exclusive devotion to a particular faith'.[63]

Gandhi announced his association with the Esoteric Christian Union in a letter in *The Natal Mercury* on 26 November 1894.[64] In his enthusiasm for the synthesis attempted in *The Perfect Way* he ignored its Christian supremacism. 'The system of thought expounded', he wrote

> ... is not, by any means, a new system but a recovery of the old, presented in a form acceptable to the modern mind. It is, moreover, a system of religion which teaches universality, and is based on eternal verities and not on phenomena or historical facts merely. In that system, there is no reviling Mahomed or Buddha in order to prove the superiority of Jesus. On the other hand, it reconciles the other religions with Christianity which, in the opinion of the authors, is nothing but one mode (among many) of presentation of the same eternal truth.

It also, he added, provided a solution to the 'many puzzles of the Old Testament'. He recommended the books offered for sale to anyone who was disillusioned with the materialism of modern civilization and offered himself for 'a quiet interchange of views' with interested persons. He concluded with the endorsement of 'the late Abbe Constant': ' "Humanity has always and everywhere asked itself these three supreme questions: Whence come we? What are we? Whither go we? Now these questions at length find an answer complete, satisfactory, and consolatory in *The Perfect Way*." '[65]

Gandhi's innocent proclamation of the new dawn of human understanding provoked a rude reply from a reader of the *Mercury*, who observed that 'we skim over the marvellous news ... and pass on to the share market report as if nothing had happened!'[66] In his next letter on the subject, to *The Natal Advertiser* on 21 January 1895, he tried to show that serious people who took a stand against materialism were thinking along the lines of *The Perfect Way*.[67] He cited the rise of the Theosophical Society, 'the gradual acceptance by the clergy of the doctrine of holiness', the writings of the Indologist Max Müller, and 'the publication of *The Unknown Life of Jesus Christ*'. The last is an account (of which Gandhi had read a review) by a Russian, Nicolai

Notovitch, of his discovery in a Tibetan lamasery of manuscripts showing that Jesus was a Buddhist missionary from Tibet. Once again, an endorsement was included, this time from an English clergyman, the Rev. John Pulsford, D.D., who did not see how it was possible ' "for a spiritually intelligent reader to doubt that these teachings were received from within the astral veil" '. The advertisement accompanying the letter quoted the view of 'Gnostic (U.S.A.)' that *The Perfect Way* was 'the most illumined and useful book published in the nineteenth century', and that of the 'late Sir F.H. Doyle' that reading *The Perfect Way* was 'like listening to the utterances of God or archangel. I know nothing in literature to equal it.'

These letters and advertisements are Gandhi's only significant references in print to the Esoteric Christian Union, to Edward Maitland, and to Anna Kingsford. In his *Autobiography* he said of *The Perfect Way* and *The Story or the New Gospel of Interpretation* only that: 'I liked both. They seemed to support Hinduism.'[68] Though he sent an encouraging report to London of his activities on behalf of the Union in 1894, nothing in the way of organization is known to have transpired.[69] What happened to Gandhi's enthusiasm? One would expect some hint of repudiation of a position once so strongly maintained. But if he changed his mind about Esoteric Christianity, he never said so. He could have been concerned, as his political activity on behalf of South African Indians increased in 1895, about his credibility as a leader. The merchant elite which launched him into public life considered Indian Christians their social inferiors.[70] To the average European, an Indian who embraced an exotic variety of Christianity was *ipso facto* ridiculous. His continuing correspondence with Raychandbhai may have swung him back towards Hinduism. He said in 1926 that he had felt 'reassured' by it that Hinduism 'could give me what I wanted'. If so, it was a Hinduism of his own design.

There are reasons to think that Gandhi not only remained a convert to the basic doctrines of the Esoteric Christian Union but began to apply them to himself, as a Christ in the making. His writings are saturated in the ideology of Esoteric Christianity, and he used its terminology to express some of his most distinctive ideas and most personal aspirations. He never said outright that he hoped to become a Christ. But on many occasions, using the language of Esoteric Christianity, he said it as clearly as made no difference.

Much of this will become apparent as we follow Gandhi's spiritual and political career, and will be left to the reader to note for himself. Certain aspects of Gandhi's thinking will come under scrutiny at the moments in his life when they seemed to become of special importance to him. Meanwhile some general points can be made.

Indians who have written seriously about Gandhi have found it difficult to come to grips with the 'Hinduism' he professed in his maturity. Even allowing for Hinduism's capaciousness, it was clearly not orthodox, but what was unorthodox about it was also not always clear.[71] Gandhi rarely took on orthodoxy directly. He ignored it and concentrated on Hinduism as he understood it. In his writings 'Hindu' terms with an accepted meaning regularly metamorphosed into something else, and 'Hindu' concepts for which there was not an exact term expanded or contracted to meet his requirements. The term *ahimsa* (non-violence) – to take an important example of the first process – originally meant avoidance of injury and was a rather moribund notion when Gandhi appeared on the scene. In his hands it came to mean active, suffering love, and was singled out as Hinduism's special contribution to the moral and religious guidance of the world.

Some at least of Gandhi's unorthodox – or just off-key – renderings of traditional Hindu beliefs can be understood in the context of Esoteric Christianity (and theosophy, where the two systems overlap). Such unorthodoxies include Gandhi's very positive notion of rebirth as an opportunity to strive for spiritual improvement; his version of the Hindu concept of *avatar*, which he expounded particularly in his writings on the *Gita*, as a mortal man who achieves perfection, rather than as a flawless incarnation of God; his polite but persistent refusal to find a *guru*, and insistence that each individual is responsible for his own spiritual development; his claim that he, who was not even a Brahmin, was entitled to interpret the Hindu scriptures with only his purified conscience for a guide, and treatment of the *Mahabharata* and *Ramayana* as inspired allegory; his substitution (with varying emphasis at various times) of the notions of service, sympathetic suffering and renunciation for the traditional Hindu notion of *yajna* (sacrifice in the sense of an offering to God); his conflation of Indian ascetic practices (*tapascharya*) with an un-Indian aspiration to condition the body for spiritual effort; his repeated and very non-traditional assertion that 'control of the palate' was the essential first step on the road to liberation.

Bhikhu Parekh has observed that Gandhi 'cherished the Hindu ideal of *moksha*, but his anxiety about his success, his search for proof, and his paradoxical desire to become desireless were profoundly un-Hindu'.[72] Gandhi often spoke of his desire to achieve *moksha* in this life, and even at times of his expectation of achieving it. In a period of despondency in 1918, he told his friend Millie Polak that he feared he would not 'finish the wheel of rebirth in this incarnation', and would have to come back one more time.[73] Either of these ambitions would have seemed amazing, to most Hindus, in a Bania in the prime of life, a family man, who had been earning a living as a lawyer and pursuing a career as a politician. But there was nothing in the Esoteric concept of a Christ which prevented Gandhi from aspiring to release from rebirth in his present incarnation.

Gandhi regularly proclaimed his ambition to 'see God', preferably 'face to face' in this life. His use of the term was Esoterically Christian. 'Seeing God', he wrote, 'means realization of the fact that God abides in one's heart.'[74] The man 'who sees God in the whole universe', he also wrote, 'should be accepted as an incarnation of God'.[75] For Gandhi, 'seeing God' was both the critical experience on the way to becoming one with God, and also, in its final fullness, the end point of that journey, when God would take over for the time he remained on earth.

Reconciling this Esoterically Christian concept with the Hindu pursuit of *moksha* was a lifelong project for Gandhi, the principal question in his mind being whether the state of *moksha* could or could not be experienced while still alive and active. Indian traditions which allow for the living experience of *moksha* usually associate it with a rather passively joyful state. Gandhi never arrived at a final answer to this question. At times he seemed to identify martyrdom – the most decisive repudiation conceivable of the demands of the flesh – with *moksha*.[76] But to a Hindu martyrdom and *moksha* would normally seem distinct. Gandhi's greatest uncertainties were related to *moksha*.

Becoming 'perfect' was another way in which Gandhi expressed his hope to become one with God. 'When I am a perfect being', he said, 'I have simply to say the word, and the nation will listen'; and 'There is no point in trying to know the difference between a perfect man and God.'[77] The simple earnestness of Gandhi's many statements of his personal quest for perfection finds no echo in the Hindu tradition.

Gandhi was much concerned, in a way that was not conventionally Hindu, with 'sin'. *Dharma*, right behaviour, has been the reigning concept in India embracing ideas of wrongdoing, and it is a concept which receives only passing attention in Gandhi's writings. He no doubt received a good dose of the theology of sin from his friends at the South Africa General Mission. We know that they implored him to wash away his sins through faith in Jesus. But that idea, as Gandhi would have put it, had in the end no appeal to him. The Esoteric Christian Union held out a more attractive prospect – that of purging oneself for ever, through one's own efforts, of sin's ugly taint. While in Pretoria Gandhi met a Plymouth Brother of extreme antinomian views, who argued that faith freed Christians to sin as much as they liked. According to the *Autobiography*, Gandhi told the Brother that he did not seek 'redemption from the consequences of my sin' but sought 'to be redeemed from sin itself, or rather from the very thought of sin'. This echoes closely *The Perfect Way*'s conception of the fully realized Christ as having attained 'immunity, not merely ... from the consequences of sin, but from the liability to sin'.[78] (If Gandhi really used such words at the time, it suggests that an aspiration to Christhood had already formed itself. 'Until I have attained that end', Gandhi recalls saying to the Plymouth Brother, 'I shall be content to be restless.')

Gandhi made no secret of his belief that sin was rooted in subservience to the bodily state. The remedy he advocated was 'crucifixion of the flesh'. He classed himself with 'those who seek liberation of the soul through crucifixion of the flesh, a practice general to mankind and indispensable for the subjection of the body to the soul'. 'It is not possible', he wrote, 'to see God face to face unless you crucify the flesh.'[79] This is pure Esoteric Christianity.

Gandhi's famously unpredictable 'inner voice', on which he relied for instructions, appears to have come principally from Esoteric Christianity. Many devout Christians of course strain to hear the 'still, small voice', but what was distinctive about Gandhi's conception was that he claimed authority for his inner voice because of his 'fitness' – the result of self-purificatory practices, including a stringent diet – to hear it. There is much concern in *The Story of the New Gospel of Interpretation* about the source of the voices heard by the authors. Was it God? Was it the Devil? Was it 'astrals'? Only the pure could be sure. Gandhi made it clear on numerous occasions that he regarded his inner voice as the voice of God, and that he practised his austerities partly to be sure of hearing that voice clearly and reliably. Truth, he told a group in Switzerland in 1931, was 'what the inner voice tells us'; and Truth was only revealed to those who had experienced the appropriate spiritual discipline.[80]

As Gandhi acquired a following in Europe comparisons to Jesus were inevitably made. He invariably deprecated them, but in terms which suggested that some day such comparisons would be more appropriate. Of Jesus and Buddha he said humbly in 1921, 'Who am I in comparison with these? Even so, I aspire to be their equal in love in this very life.'[81] In 1924 he did not consider himself 'worthy to be mentioned in the same breath' with them. But

> I am impatient to realize myself, to attain *moksha* in this very existence. My national service is part of my training for freeing my soul from the bondage of flesh. ... I am striving for the Kingdom of Heaven which is *moksha*. ... For me the road to salvation lies through incessant toil in the service of my country and therethrough of humanity. I want to identify myself with everything that lives.[82]

He reassured Indians disturbed by the talk of his Christian followers that 'the word Christ is a common name, an attribute not to be attached merely to one single historical person'.[83] In 1945 he endorsed in a preface J.C. Kumarappa's *Practice and Precepts of Jesus*, which argued that 'Jesus' whole life was a ... heroic attempt to assert the divinity of man and the absolute supremacy of the Spirit of Truth within him.' Gandhi observed that 'Prof. Kumarappa's interpretation ... reminded me of what I used to believe even as early as 1894–95. I can therefore speak from experience of the truth of the interpretation of the Gospels given'.[84] At the height of his powers, Gandhi would turn aside criticism with the observation that he 'danced to God's tune'. 'I have no desire to found a sect', he said in one of his characteristically ambiguous denials of divinity: 'I am really too ambitious to be satisfied with a sect for a following.' His aim was 'to follow and represent Truth as I know it'.[85] He was not preaching Esoteric Christianity but living it.

Pyarelal was clearly well informed about the extent of Esoteric Christianity's influence on Gandhi, and letters from Gandhi to close personal friends give the impression sometimes of referring to doctrinal matters uncommittable to writing. There is an account in Mahadev Desai's diary of a disagreement between himself and Gandhi about reincarnation, in which Mahadev did not believe.[86] Gandhi offers as evidence Anna Kingsford's belief that many Frenchmen, judging from the faces she saw on the streets of Paris, would be reborn as tigers. Mahadev demurs, but 'Bapu [Gandhi] kept gravely silent', and 'then said, "He who does not believe in it [reincarnation] cannot have any real faith in the regeneration of fallen souls. At least that man who wants to serve society ought to possess that faith."' This is Esoteric Christianity.

Just how, when and why Gandhi decided that his own liberation would be achieved through politics is unknown. Esoteric Christianity contains no political imperative. Though both his political and spiritual ambitions may have stirred at an early date, there is no indication that at first the former were conceived as the vehicle of the latter.

Yet, one further influence remains to be acknowledged – that of Tolstoy. Tolstoy's *The Kingdom of God is Within You* is a book about religion written in a state of political fury. It condemns politics but advocates a powerful political instrument. It takes up to a point a religious position similar to *The Perfect Way*. Gandhi recalled that when he read it in 1894 it 'overwhelmed' him.[87] It appears to have been Edward Maitland who sent it to him.[88]

*The Kingdom of God is Within You* remains an overwhelming book. With examples as vividly realized as anything in his fiction, Tolstoy lays out the argument that tyranny can be rendered impotent if individuals act according to their conscience and refuse, without offering violence, to submit to it. (With equal force, he shows that the authority of governments always depends on violence, that goodness and power are antithetical, and that 'The wicked will always dominate the good, and will always oppress them.' Few books more memorably collapse under the weight of their own contradictions.)

The political argument for non-violent resistance sustains its power not only because of the brilliance of the writing, but because it is so clear that Tolstoy loathes the Russian government and the injustice over which it presides, and though he advocates 'passive resistance' what he really means but does not acknowledge is rebellion. Every individual act of resistance to injustice described in the book possesses the significance of revolt. At the time he read *The Kingdom of God is Within You*, Gandhi had been reading books pressed on him by a Quaker friend in Pretoria. Some of these books presumably took a position against war and in favour of non-violent resistance to overweening authority. But Gandhi says that Tolstoy's book made these other books seem trivial.[89] The Quaker's aim has been relatively modest – to be left alone by the state. Tolstoy's book suggested non-violent resistance could produce political change. In 1910 Gandhi wrote that Tolstoy had taught that there is 'no government that can control' the man prepared to follow his conscience, 'without his sanction': 'Such a man is superior to all government.'[90] In 1928 he said that *The Kingdom of God is Within You* converted him from being a 'votary of violence' to 'faith' in non-violence.[91]

'Faith' to what end? Presumably that those aims he had supposed could only be achieved by violence could be achieved without it.

Like *The Perfect Way*, *The Kingdom of God is Within You* rejects the church's claim to authority, and requires men to overcome their animal nature if they are to make spiritual progress. (Tolstoy's struggles with celibacy are well known.) Both books connect goodness with suffering: refusal to submit to tyranny necessarily involves suffering.

Tolstoy contrasts 'the state conception of life' with 'the divine conception of life'. The divine conception of life requires that each individual assume responsibility for his own freedom. Not only this, but 'the freedom of all men will be brought about only through the freedom of individual persons'.[92] This is the political analogue of *The Perfect Way*'s argument that it was up to each individual to work out his or her own salvation.

Believing that the Christianity of the gospels was irreconcilable with state power, Tolstoy rejected the state and chose Christianity. This was the Christianity of the Sermon on the Mount, taken literally as a prescription for living, with perfection as the goal: 'Be ye therefore perfect, as your father which is in heaven is perfect.' Jesus' commands in the Sermon taken together constitute 'the commandment of love' – love being the essence of the divine – and man is required by God and his nature, which has the divine spark of love at its core, to strive to be a perfect embodiment of love. This all seems to echo *The Perfect Way*, and part of what overwhelmed Gandhi may have been seeing ideas he knew through his connection with the obscure Maitland appear in a work by so celebrated a personality.

Yet it is clear that Tolstoy believed that though progress towards perfection is the yardstick by which all endeavour will be judged, perfection itself cannot be attained. The Sermon encompasses, Tolstoy says, on the one hand, 'ideals' which we must strive to attain, and, on the other hand, 'precepts' which show 'the level below which we cannot fall in the attainment of this ideal'.[93] Tolstoy also denies that there is such a thing as love for the whole of humanity: 'Humanity is a fiction, and it is impossible to love it.'[94] He dismisses political parties, trade unions, conspiracies, and combinations of every kind as part of the 'state conception of life'. They cannot bring freedom but merely rivet on the chains. Gandhi said on several occasions that he could not agree with everything Tolstoy said.

He read more of Tolstoy's books while he was in South Africa – he mentions in the *Autobiography* that *The Gospel in Brief, What Then Must We*

*Do?*, 'and other works', helped him to realize 'the infinite possibilities of universal love'. Apparently, he read these books in Durban between 1894 and 1896. It is known that he read *A Confession*, Tolstoy's account of his religious conversion, and found it a 'soul-stirring' book. He also read and recommended *The Relation of the Sexes*, a compilation of Tolstoy's writings advocating celibacy.

A certain anxiety of influence seems to have arisen regarding the Tolstoyan element in *satyagraha*. In a letter written to Tolstoy in 1909, in hopes of interesting him in the South African struggle, Gandhi seemed at pains to convey the independence of his own conception. 'I and some of my friends', he wrote, 'were and still are firm believers in the doctrine of non-resistance to evil. I had the privilege of studying your writings also, which left a deep impression on my mind.'[95] He emphasized that *satyagraha* went far beyond anything Tolstoy had conceived, and was a force 'infinitely more active' than Tolstoyan passive resistance: through 'self-suffering' it drew out 'the limitless power of Truth'.[96] Tolstoy indeed never thought of any 'active force' which was not reducible to the cumulative effect of many individual acts of peaceful refusal to cooperate with authority.

In the end Gandhi decided that Tolstoy's 'life' was really what mattered. Tolstoy was great because he practised what he preached – non-violence, chastity, simplicity and 'bread labour' (the duty of physical work).[97]

He seems to have had no taste for Tolstoy's novels. Tolstoy too repudiated them. But Tolstoy never lost the hyper-lucid apprehension of the reality of human nature which illuminates his novels, and he never quite lost the ability to apply the same lucidity to himself. Having sinned and sinned vigorously he knew how far he was from God, and God remained for him essentially other. Whereas Gandhi, who was equally sin-obsessed, but hard put to think of any sins worth mentioning in his unexceptional personal life, set his course for perfection and union with the divine.

# THREE

# South Africa:
# *Satyagraha*

Summing up his time in Pretoria, Gandhi observed that 'Here it was that the religious spirit within me became a living force.'[1] His spiritual awakening was well timed. Not long after he got back to Durban, and was preparing to return to India and whatever prospects awaited him, he got his opportunity to go into politics. A bill before the Natal legislature proposed to deprive all Indians of the franchise, except those who had already registered to vote. Gandhi was hired by Dada Abdullah and others to help organize the Indian opposition.

Gandhi's account of this development in the *Autobiography* is well known.[2] At his farewell party he happened to see, tucked away in a corner of a newspaper which was lying around, news of the proposed legislation. He explained to his hosts that the new law would be ' "the first nail into our coffin" ', and struck ' "at the root of our self-respect" '. Confessing their ignorance of anything but trade, Abdullah and his friends asked Gandhi to ' "stay here a month longer, and we will fight as you direct us" '.

As Maureen Swan has shown, this account cannot have been true.[3] The Natal merchants had campaigned intermittently since 1891 against discriminatory legislation, including a previous attempt to take away the franchise. Gandhi's account glosses over this previous activity. Nor would they have been unaware that new legislation was in the offing. Debates on the question of the Indian franchise were reported in the press, and Gandhi himself had already spoken out, in a letter to *The Natal Advertiser* on 29 September 1893, against the growing agitation to deprive Indians of the vote.[4] When he looked back thirty years later he could not help seeing the circumstances of his entry into South African politics as part of God's plan for him. 'Thus God laid the foundations of my life in South Africa', he concluded his account of the occasion, 'and sowed the seed of the fight for national self-respect.'

Gandhi's legal training and command of English were assets to the campaign. His organizing ability was soon evident, and the month for which he had been retained was extended to a year. The petition he drafted in July was submitted with 9,000 signatures, a figure which alarmed the whites. In August the Natal Indian Congress was founded to represent the merchants' concerns on a permanent basis. This was the descendant of an earlier organization, the Durban Indian Committee which had came into existence in 1891, and the first president was the merchant Haji Adam, who had been active on the Committee. Gandhi was honorary secretary, a position he held until 1901, when he returned to India, he assumed for good.

The campaign focused on the political rights of the merchant class. The documents drafted by Gandhi put forward the merchants' view that they deserved to be treated better than those with whom the law would lump them – the indentured, or recently indentured, labourer and the African native. The July petition deplored a law which sought to put 'all Indians, indentured, and freed, and free ... in the same scale'.[5] In another document the race feeling which meant the Indian was treated like 'a raw Kaffir' was condemned.[6]

The glories of Indian civilization were cited in the merchants' favour. The whites countered with accusations that the Indians in Natal were dirty and untruthful – accusations which Gandhi conceded were, to 'a limited extent', true.[7] He accused the whites of being unchristian in treating Indians as if they would be 'polluted even by the touch of a fellow-being'. But the charge was duly flung back at him with reminders of the Indian practice of untouchability, a subject on which he was to remain publicly silent for the next sixteen years.[8]

He sought both to appeal to the British sense of fair play and to reassure the whites that if they let the Indians keep the vote (subject to the prevailing £50 property franchise) they need never fear the consequences. Relatively few Indians would qualify, and those who did would be 'too much taken up with their spiritual well-being' to claim a role in politics.[9] He made a point to which he would return in his dealings with the British in South Africa: that when the crown took over the Government of India from the East India Company in 1858, the queen's proclamation promised her Indian subjects admission to whatever positions they were qualified to fill.

The Natal authorities remained unmoved, and the Colonial Office, after squirming a bit because they were being asked to agree to legislation which clearly violated the rights of British subjects, eventually assented to a less offensively worded bill which achieved the same object. This was the normal course of legislation emanating from the African colonies. The government in London would not risk their open enmity, and, as Gandhi discovered once he began dealing directly with the imperial government in 1906, public sympathy with the Indians could conceal private complicity with the Europeans.

By 1901, when Gandhi made his first attempt to move back to India, the prospects for the Indian cause in South Africa were bleak.

Two more bills intending to drive Indian traders out of Natal received imperial assent in 1897. They were the Immigration Restriction Bill and the Dealers' Licenses Bill. Both were worded in such a way that the appearance of discrimination against Indians was avoided. The Immigration Bill set entry qualifications for immigrants to Natal – a written English test and assets of £25 – which effectively closed the door to most Indians. (The import of indentured labour was governed by separate regulations.) The Dealers' Licenses Bill gave the Natal government powers to deny trading licences on grounds of insanitation. Indians, as intended, were disproportionately affected. In the Transvaal, also, the Indians experienced reverses. In 1898 Gandhi was involved in a test case in the Transvaal High Court to determine whether the law requiring Indians to live in locations also meant that their businesses could only be in locations. The Indians lost the case. However, on this occasion they had the support of the British government, which, in the run-up to the Boer War, was looking for ways of defending the rights of British subjects against the tyranny of the Afrikaner government of the Transvaal.

Gandhi decided that if his compatriots were to obtain better treatment from the whites, they must remedy the defects of which they were justly accused. He began in earnest to berate them, and when *Indian Opinion* gave him a bully pulpit in 1903 he used it without mercy. In 1899 when Durban was threatened with plague he organized volunteers to get the Indian community to comply with the health regulations. It was a discouraging experience, but he felt his efforts were appreciated by the authorities, who saw 'that, though

I had made it my business to ventilate grievances and press for rights, I was no less keen and insistent upon self-purification'.[10]

It was quickly obvious that political campaigns could not proceed at the rate of collective self-purification, and the concept of *satyagraha* to some extent addressed this problem by making the campaign itself part of the self-purification process. *Satyagraha* was yet to come in the 1890s, but there were glimpses of the thinking that would eventually coalesce into the famous doctrine. In 1896, when Gandhi was in India to raise support for the Natal Indians and collect his family, he wrote that:

> Our method in South Africa is to conquer [the whites'] hatred by love ... We do not attempt to have individuals punished but as a rule, patiently suffer wrongs at their hands. Generally, our prayers are not to demand compensation for past injuries, but to render a repetition of those injuries impossible and to remove the causes.[11]

He soon got the opportunity to put principles into practice. An angry white mob attacked him as he went ashore at Durban, and, but for the bravery of the police superintendent's wife, who cleared a way for him, his injuries might have been serious. He would not press charges.

Support for the Congress dwindled as it failed to produce results. Gandhi's law practice flourished, however, with steady business from the Indian community, and he lived the life of a successful but sober professional man. His domestic establishment, at Beach Grove Villa overlooking Durban Bay, was simple but substantial. Dinner parties were given, strictly vegetarian.

To support his frequently repeated claim that Indians were loyal subjects of Her Majesty, Gandhi organized an Indian stretcher corps when the Boer War broke out in 1899, despite the awkward fact that 'my personal sympathies were all with the Boers'. It was a thousand strong and consisted mostly of labourers, with financial support from the merchants whose good name they were promoting.[12] It was not Gandhi's first venture into nursing. For some time he had been working as a volunteer in a mission hospital, and had found that nursing as a form of 'service' appealed to him.[13]

Congress activity fell into abeyance during the war, and by the time hostilities ceased in 1902 Gandhi was back in India, trying to break into Indian politics and having the usual trouble practising law under Indian skies. As a budding Indian politician he had only one selling point – his work in South Africa – and he discovered that it was not enough. The same Sir

Pherozeshah Mehta who had dismissed his problems with the Rajkot political agent dismissed his political aspirations with the verdict that South African Indians would have to solve their own problems. Gandhi used his allotted five minutes at the Calcutta Congress of 1901 to disagree with Mehta and to blame the South African situation on the Indian Congress's failure to intervene. The disappointment was bitter.

In November 1902 a telegram arrived from the Natal Indian Congress asking Gandhi to return. The war was over, and Joseph Chamberlain, the colonial secretary, was to visit South Africa and consider how much of the legislation concerning Indians in the former Boer republics should be retained. Would Gandhi present the Indian case? He was back in Durban by the end of December.

Chamberlain's visit came and went with nothing to show for it, though Gandhi organized and led a deputation. The Indians were in fact in an even worse position than before the war. The imperial government was anticipating the end of crown rule and the onset of responsible government, and thus felt its hand to be even weaker than usual. Lord Milner was now high commissioner for South Africa and in charge of the post-war reconstruction of the Transvaal. He intended to see it transformed into a modern industrialized state based on mining, its vast resources at the service of the empire, and to accomplish this he judged it necessary to keep all the elements of the Transvaal's white population – Afrikaners and English, rich and poor – politically quiescent. This combination of forces in London and Johannesburg spelled the end of Indian hopes, and Gandhi's political representations in the years remaining before his first *satyagraha* campaign met with no success.

Gandhi's base of activity meanwhile shifted to the Transvaal, and he settled down to a bachelor life in Johannesburg, having left his family in India. He seems to have resigned himself to making the most of his opportunities in South Africa, though hopes of an Indian career were not abandoned. He corresponded as often and as plausibly as he could with the Indian politicians Dadabhai Naoroji and G.K. Gokhale. But there was no knowing when India might be a possibility. He began in earnest to make himself the kind of man and the kind of politician he wanted to be. 'All the steps I took at this time of trial', he wrote in the *Autobiography*, 'were taken in the name of God and for His service.'[14]

He had been struggling for some time, at least since the birth of his last child in 1900 and perhaps since his reunion with Kasturbai in 1896, to become

chaste – partly out of a desire to avoid having more children, partly because
he had decided that sexual relations even with his wife compromised his
capacity for 'service'.[15] But he did not take his 'vow of *brahmacharya*' until
1906. Between the end of 1902 and the beginning of 1905 his physical if not
his mental chastity was assured by his wife's absence from South Africa.

Being without his family gave Gandhi latitude to experiment with his
way of living. He took his meals in a vegetarian restaurant in Johannesburg,
where, as in London fifteen years before, he found himself stimulated by new
friends and new ideas. One result was that the interest in 'nature cure' he
had in common with many vegetarians became a lifelong passion.

Nature cure arose in Germany in the nineteenth century and was part of
a reaction against the impersonality of scientific medicine and the increasing
power of the medical profession. It promised not only the cure of illness by
simple, 'natural' means, but the attainment of lifelong perfect health through
bringing oneself into harmony with natural forces, thus removing the necessity
for visits to the doctor. Its implicit product was the vigorous old man, his
powers undimmed by the passage of time. Nature cure's two most celebrated
exponents were Louis Kuhne and Adolf Just. Just made the life-enhancing
side of nature cure more explicit.

Gandhi already knew Kuhne's writings before he arrived in Johannesburg.
His most famous work, *The New Science of Healing*, had appeared in English
translation in 1893.[16] Kuhne saw disease as the result of foreign matter entering the body, usually in the form of an improper diet, and his system of
treatment was to encourage the elimination of this 'morbid matter' through
therapeutic baths: sun baths, steam baths and various water baths including
'sitz friction baths', which involved sitting in water up to hip level and rubbing
the genitals with a cold wet cloth. Kuhne believed that the body's nervous
system converged on the genitals, and their non-lustful stimulation therefore
produced general health, in addition to curing diseases from whooping cough
to epilepsy.

Gandhi had tried some of Kuhne's treatments (he is not specific) and had
felt better for them. Accordingly, when his son Manilal, then ten years old,
went down with typhoid while the family was living in Bombay in 1902, and
the doctor could only recommend eggs and chicken broth, both out of the
question, he felt just confident enough to try a version of Kuhne's hydro-
therapy. First Manilal was given hip baths, one hopes without friction. When
there was no result, he was wrapped up in a wet sheet and commended to

God with the thought that 'God would surely be pleased to see that I was giving the same treatment to my son as I would give myself'.[17] The fever broke, and Manilal began to mend.

Just's *Return to Nature!* was put into Gandhi's hands by a vegetarian acquaintance when the English translation appeared in 1903. Just developed Kuhne's idea that disease was the result of impure matter (in Just's opinion, primarily cooked food) entering the body, and argued that health was the result of getting rid of these impurities by switching to a raw, unprocessed, non-flesh diet. No idea would have seemed more reasonable to Gandhi.

Just believed that disease appeared in the world when men 'fell out of harmony with nature'[18] – wore clothes, started cooking, and so on – and that health ensued when men realigned themselves with nature and partook of its vital force. He emphasized that health could really only be acquired by individual effort – a man could not go wrong in matters of health if he listened to his 'inner voice'. The specific treatments and regimes he advocated were all ones which became part of Gandhi's repertoire as a naturopath: mudpacks (effective because they are made of earth, as man is), Kuhne-type friction baths (to stimulate the vital force), and massage. Massage Just interestingly associated with 'service', exactly prefiguring Gandhi's practice in later years of 'taking service' from favoured disciples in this form. The fact that massage was 'service' contributed to its efficaciousness; for, 'By the stroking and rubbing of the body vitality and health are always transferred from one person to another.'[19] To get the full benefit, one's masseur should be carefully selected, being – ideally – healthy, loving, good, innocent and anxious to serve. Vitality could also be communicated 'by the sleeping together of two persons. By this means, old men have often been rejuvenated by young men.'[20]

In the *Autobiography* Gandhi warned his readers who wished to purchase Just's book not to 'take everything in it to be gospel truth'.[21] But Just's ideas about vitality must have been in his mind when he lay in the sun after his bath in one of his ashrams, being massaged by some young admirer – and perhaps when at the end of his life he asked his great-niece Manu Gandhi to share his bed.

The self-help side of nature cure possessed a strong appeal. In nature cure the patient himself rather than the doctor had to decide, through observing and experimenting on his own body, 'what kind of remedies to employ and in what measures'.[22] As in the spiritual life, the individual assumed responsibility for his own salvation, with benefits both physical and mental. 'He who runs to the doctor', Gandhi wrote in the *Autobiography*, 'for every little ailment ... not only curtails his life, but, in becoming the slave of his body instead of remaining its master, loses self-control, and ceases to be a man.'[23] Curiously, he never showed any real awareness of the contradiction involved in his telling people – as he often did – what was good for their health. He invariably reminded them that they need not take his advice. But living in Gandhi's ashrams meant accepting his ministrations.

At the bottom of his enduring fascination with nature cure was the belief that, as he spelled it out in his *General Knowledge about Health* in 1913, 'The body is so closely bound to the soul that one whose body is pure will be pure in mind too.' And conversely, 'those whose minds are pure can never be ill and one who is ill can cure himself by cultivating purity of mind'. As he acknowledged, this was a principle developed in the West, though in the West it was sometimes misused.[24] Christian Scientists were condemned because they sought to use 'spiritual power' to cure ailments which were best left to simple physical remedies, or, preferably, endured.[25]

As a practitioner of nature cure Gandhi was always ready to take a chance in the belief that God would guide him. When Manilal recovered, he 'was sure that God had saved my honour'.[26] He once said to his grandnephew Kanu that when he took on a patient, 'God always helps me.'[27] Why would God do this? Because the very act of practising nature cure, as patient or physician, brought one 'nearer to God. ... Nature-cure treatment means going towards Nature, towards God'.[28]

When Gandhi set up his office in Johannesburg, among the pictures he hung on his walls were ones of Tolstoy, Jesus Christ and Annie Besant.[29] He had not lost interest in, nor lost touch with, the Theosophical Society.

Gandhi's long personal and political association with Lewis Ritch, a prominent member of the Johannesburg Lodge of the Theosophical Society, began in Durban, where Ritch sought him out.[30] Ritch became Secretary of the South Africa British Indian Committee, which Gandhi set up in London in 1906. Another theosophical friend going back to Durban days was Herbert Kitchin, whom Gandhi took in when he was evacuated from Johannesburg at the outbreak of the Boer War. Kitchin became one of the first settlers at Phoenix.[31] In 1903, when Gandhi arrived in Johannesburg, Ritch put him in touch with the Society. He also met theosophists at the vegetarian restaurant where he dined. Two whom he met at this time – Henry Polak and Herman

Kallenbach – were to become very intimate friends. However, though he was in close – for a while, daily – contact with theosophists, Gandhi did not join the Johannesburg Lodge. Instead he took part in 'a sort of Seekers' Club' whose members appear to have been theosophists. They 'had regular readings' and religious discussions. The readings included the *Gita*, and it was as a result of his discussions with this group that Gandhi began his serious study of the text which was to become his acknowledged guide through life.

Gandhi does not tell us who the Seekers were, or much about what they had to say to each other. But he suggests that he himself took an independent and critical line, arguing that what theosophy was really about was brotherhood, and pointing out to the other Seekers where their conduct fell short of the ideal. But the discussions also had a 'wholesome effect' on him. They 'led to introspection'. The fact that several Johannesburg theosophists joined him in the Phoenix venture suggests that in these little gatherings Gandhi may have begun his career as a teacher and spiritual guide.

The discussions among the seekers took place in the context of recent developments in the Theosophical Society, to which Gandhi does not refer but of which he and his friends must have known. Though theosophists were as preoccupied as ever with secret doctrines, Annie Besant was trying hard to stir their social conscience. In 1903 Besant was not yet president of the Society, but she was established in Benares as the reigning presence of the Indian Section, and the theosophy she preached developed the position taken by Blavatsky in *The Key to Theosophy*. Her sympathy with Indian nationalism was already well known. Not only was her picture on Gandhi's wall, but in a letter he wrote to her in 1905 he expressed his 'reverence' for her.[32]

Besant's distinctive contribution to theosophy was the 'Law of Sacrifice', which was set out most fully in *Esoteric Christianity* – a virtual recapitulation of *The Perfect Way* – which she published in 1902. The Law of Sacrifice was derived initially from Besant's reading of the *Gita* and only later discussed in connection with Christianity. Her text was the *Gita*, Chapters 3 and 4, in particular the verses in which the god Krishna explains to the mortal Arjuna, who shrinks from the coming battle in which some of his relations will be on the opposite side, why he must fight. Like Krishna himself, whose selfless activity brought the world into existence and keeps it going, Arjuna is obliged above all to act, and act without concern for himself – in the traditional language of *Gita* exegesis, act without thought for the fruits of action. Action performed in this 'sacrificial' spirit, says Krishna, is free from *karma*. From this Besant extrapolates the Law of Sacrifice – a form of 'spiritual alchemy'.[33] Through disinterested action, action 'cast upon the altar of duty' which 'turns the wheel of life but never binds the Soul', the soul becomes 'a fellow-worker with the divine in Nature'. The man who acts in harmony with the divine selflessness animating the universe becomes

> a force for evolution, … an energy for progress, and the whole race then benefits by the action which otherwise would only have brought to the sacrificer a personal fruit, which in turn would have bound his Soul, and limited his poten- tialities for good.

This was a very Fabian take on the *Gita*.

In *Esoteric Christianity* Besant went on to apply the Law of Sacrifice to the supreme sacrifice of Christ on the cross.

Anna Kingsford and Edward Maitland are nowhere mentioned in *Esoteric Christianity*, but, as in *The Perfect Way*, the New Testament is treated as myth with a kernel of historical reality, an allegory of the journey of the individual soul, through suffering love, to the status of 'Christ' or 'Initiate' – the terms are equated. The aspiring Christ (or Initiate) struggles to release himself from bondage to matter through a life of 'ceaseless service', until he is 'ready for the sacrifice on the cross', when 'the lower life is yielded up, its death is willingly embraced, the body of desire is abandoned'. This is the Atonement, which Besant spells without hyphens and defines as 'the identity of the Christ with His brother-men'. The Atonement exemplifies the Law of Sacrifice – which we now learn is also the 'Law of Love' – in 'concrete form'.[34] For in becoming one with humanity the Christ has become one with God and is filled with his power. He is then 'the Master triumphant, the link between God and man', and devotes the remainder of his earthly existence to helping 'every struggling soul'.[35] 'Such a one has become truly divine, a Saviour of men, and he takes up the world-work for which all this has been the preparation.'[36] The only way in which this differs from the teachings of the Esoteric Christian Union is that the suffering love of the aspirant Christ seems more robustly active in form. He vibrates experientially to the suffering of humankind, as in *The Perfect Way*, but also more explicitly lives a life of 'ceaseless service'. The rationale for achieving liberation through politics may perhaps be found here.

Though Kingsford and Maitland had acknowledged the spiritual authority of the *Gita*, in her teaching Besant linked the *Gita* with Christianity in a way which the Christocentric Kingsford and Maitland had not. She spelled out the equivalence of the perfect man, free from karma, of the *Gita* with the Christ triumphant of the esoterically interpreted gospels. She saw action as essential to perfection, and argued that, though every human being has the potential to become a Saviour, only those can do so who perform 'every act as a sacrifice, not for what it will bring to the doer but for what it will bring to others'.[37] She thus transformed the *Gita*'s injunction to act without regard for action's fruits into something few scholars would agree was already there in the text: the Christian ethic of selfless service whose motive is brotherly love.

We will put off until later consideration of what the *Gita* meant to Gandhi. But there is no doubt that his general approach to it was 'theosophical'. His treatment of it as an allegory of the struggle within the human heart between man's higher and lower natures was the standard starting point of theosophical interpretations, including Besant's.[38] And his elaboration of the idea of *yajna* (sacrifice) while discoursing on Chapters 3 and 4 in his *Discourses on the Gita* in 1926 was very Besant-like. There was no harm, he wrote, in 'enlarging' the meaning of the term, so long as the 'new meaning' was 'not inconsistent with the use of the term in the *Gita*'. The new meaning proposed was 'any action performed with a view to the public good'. If *yajna* thus conceived is faithfully performed, 'the sphere of our service will enlarge itself to embrace the whole world'.[39]

Gandhi and Besant fell out in 1916, but even in the days when he felt 'reverence' for her and had her picture on the wall he did not acknowledge in his writings or speeches any influence by her on his thinking. Yet a series of articles written for *Indian Opinion* in 1904 appears to reflect Besant's ideas. These articles, on 'Self-Sacrifice', were written at the time of Gandhi's first, unsuccessful, appeal to the Indian community to perform an act of disobedience to authority. They contained the germ of his theory of *satyagraha*.

In December 1903 the Transvaal government announced that Indians who wished to receive trading licences would have to show proof that they had been licensed traders before the war – a piece of official harassment which came at a time of increasing Indian anxiety about the future. The authorities were preparing to lay out locations to which Indians would be confined for both residence and trade – the long-delayed implementation of the court decision of 1895; and Milner was asking for 10,000 Indian contract labourers to work on railway construction – with automatic repatriation on completion of contract.

Gandhi urged the merchants to refuse to provide proof of earlier trading and, if prosecuted, to 'rise to the occasion, decline to pay any fines, and go to gaol'.[40] The merchants were disinclined to go to jail, and succeeded in getting the requirement waived by appealing to the government. But meanwhile Gandhi encouraged them by explaining the meaning and power of sacrifice.[41] Sacrifice, he said, was 'the law of life'. Life was 'sustained by sacrifice', and nothing could be achieved without it. With sacrifice, however, there was no virtuous object which could not be attained, for he who sacrificed his own self-interest to the common good could count on God's help: if we 'do our duty ... the will of God will then come to pass'.

> Christ died on the Cross of Calvary and left Christianity as a glorious heritage. Hampden suffered, but the ship-money went. Joan of Arc was burnt as a witch ...; the world knows the result of her self-sacrifice. The Americans bled for their independence.

Crudely expressed as it was, this was the belief which underlay the idea of *satyagraha* shortly to be born: that to the self-sacrificing sufferer came a power which was divine.

In 1905 Gandhi gave a series of lectures to the Johannesburg Lodge of the Theosophical Society.[42] They defined his point of departure from theosophical thinking as he encountered it in the majority of members of the Society. They also showed him rallying to the defence of his native religion, perhaps in response to what he felt to be misinterpretations of it by theosophical associates. 'There was a time', he said in 1921, 'when I was wavering between Hinduism and Christianity. When I recovered my balance of mind, I felt that to me salvation was possible only through the Hindu religion and my faith in Hinduism grew deeper and more enlightened.'[43] This may have been the time when the 'balance' was recovered – though there was to be no end to the attempt to reconcile the energizing intuitions of Esoteric Christianity with the tenets of Hinduism which they appeared to resemble. In these lectures Gandhi spoke of Hinduism's toleration and refinement, its absorption of the best of Buddhism, Islam and Christianity, and its emphasis on purity of conduct and 'self-abnegation'.

The final lecture made explicit his misgivings about theosophists. He criticized their dilettantism, their unreverential use of sacred texts for speculation, their disregard of the necessity of living a pure and truthful life, without which the meaning of the works for which they had such an appetite could not be understood. He deplored their preoccupation with 'the development of occult powers', and neglect of 'the central idea of Theosophy, the brotherhood of mankind and the moral growth of man'. He told them that 'Hindu sages' believed that 'to live life, no matter how hampered it might be, no matter with what limitations, was infinitely superior to having a mental grasp of things divine'. He said they should get out of 'Theosophical libraries' and find a purpose in 'real life'. Only in that way could 'a grasp of the whole of the divine teaching' be achieved. It was now evident to him, he said, 'that Theosophy was Hinduism in theory, and that Hinduism was Theosophy in practice'. It seems to have been not so much theosophy which was at fault but theosophists, who had betrayed its essence.

There was a confidence, a boldness and severity, in this address which must have been Gandhi's valediction to the Theosophical Society. He sounds like a man who has found his own purpose in life. He sounds like a man who will not have much further use for sects and societies. He also sounds like a man who has supporters. As he did.

When he delivered this lecture, on 25 March 1905, he had already taken the plunge and founded the Phoenix settlement, his first experiment in communal living; and two of the settlers – Herbert Kitchin and Henry Polak – were theosophists from the Johannesburg Lodge. Two others – Lewis Ritch and Herman Kallenbach – were to join the board of trustees. John Cordes, another Johannesburg theosophist, went to live at Phoenix in 1906. And Gabriel Isaacs, one of the South African theosophists who asked Annie Besant to become president of the Society in 1907, was a frequent visitor to Phoenix though he continued to live in Johannesburg. Gandhi later claimed to have pried Ritch loose from the Theosophical Society.[44]

The members of this group all became involved in the cause of Indian freedom. It may have been devotion to Gandhi as a friend and spiritual guide which propelled them into political activity. They all seem to have had a strong personal attachment to him: Kallenbach and Polak remained in a tutelary relationship to him for many years. They were among the first to experience what Gandhi occasionally referred to in his private correspondence as the 'glamour' of his personality.[45]

Gandhi's life had been moving towards greater 'simplicity' for some time before the founding of Phoenix, as he pondered the ideals of 'aparigraha (non-possession)' and 'samabhava (equability)' presented in the Gita. The question was how to put them into practice.[46]

How was one to treat alike insulting, insolent and corrupt officials, co-workers
of yesterday raising meaningless opposition, and men who had always been good
to one? How was one to divest oneself of all possessions? Were not wife and
children possessions? Was I to destroy all the cupboards of books I had? Was
I to give up all I had and follow Him? Straight came the answer: I could not
follow Him unless I gave up all I had.

The reference to opposition appears to mean the complaints by some Indians
that the community's support for the British war effort had done nothing to
improve its position.

The direct result of these meditations was that Gandhi took the first steps
towards putting his relations with his family on the same basis as his relations
with humanity at large. He wrote to his brother in Rajkot that there would
be no more remittances. Henceforth what he earned would be used for the
benefit of the community. He cancelled his life insurance, being 'convinced
that God, who created my wife and children as well as myself, would take
care of them'.[47] Kasturbai was still in India with the children and the point
would not have been lost on her that she was among the 'possessions' of
which her husband was divesting himself. The family's return to South Africa
was overdue and had been put off with the explanation that he wished to
spare them the disruptions arising from his public work.[48] Their presence
would indeed have complicated his life. Kasturbai had not liked his taking
in European friends and acquaintances and generally keeping open house in
Durban.[49] There had also been the question of the boys' education in South
Africa, which had not been resolved at the time of the family's return to India
in 1901. Unwilling to send them to local European schools (which would have
admitted them in acknowledgement of their father's standing as a barrister),
Gandhi had tried to find time to educate them himself, with unsatisfactory
results. The family's arrival in Johannesburg would have plunged him back
into the normal human mess which engulfs us all, and from which he was
trying to extricate himself in order to 'follow Him'.

Kasturbai and the three younger boys finally came back to South Africa
in early 1905, Harilal having married and remained in India. When Gandhi
gave up his house in Johannesburg to go off and serve as a stretcher bearer
in the Zulu Rebellion in 1906, they were moved to Phoenix. The 'rebellion'
was over in a matter of weeks and Gandhi returned to Johannesburg, but the
family stayed at Phoenix. He had just taken his vow of *brahmacharya*.

A more immediately pressing problem in late 1904 was that *Indian Opinion*
was overrunning its budget and a way had to be found to cut costs. On his way

to Durban for consultations with the printer, Gandhi happened to read *Unto This Last*, Ruskin's attack on modern political economy and its distorted ideas of wealth and value. Once more a book had a critical influence on Gandhi's mind. He spent the whole night reading it, and put it down 'determined to change my life in accordance with [its] ideals'.[50] He saw the solution to his immediate problem: a hand press operated by volunteers as part of a simple life of labour. The printer, the idealistic Albert West, agreed, and the decision to look for a suitable country property was made. (The hand press idea turned out to be impractical for producing a newspaper, and was abandoned. An engine was acquired, which then broke down. After that four Zulu women were employed to turn the handle.[51])

Phoenix was built on a 100-acre plot near Durban. The name 'Phoenix' had no significance, being the name of the property when Gandhi bought it. Each family received 2 acres of land on which they built themselves a house. A stipend of £3 a month was also paid – intended as the equivalent of Ruskin's 'living wage'. Though much time was spent together, the settlement was not strictly speaking organized along communal lines. Apart from their monthly stipend and an annual division of profits from *Indian Opinion*, the settlers were expected to be self-supporting and were given the option to purchase their plots. It was, theoretically, up to them how they lived, but ideally their lives would combine 'the ideas of Ruskin and Tolstoy' with 'strict business principles'. A nature-cure sanatorium and a boarding school for Indian children from all over South Africa were planned.

Though Ruskin was felt to be Phoenix's principal inspiration, the extent to which these arrangements could be termed Ruskinian is by no means clear; and it is difficult to account in terms of life at Phoenix for the sense of revelation experienced by Gandhi on reading his book. Gandhi summed up the 'teachings' of *Unto This Last* as:

1. That the good of the individual is contained in the good of all.
2. That a lawyer's work has the same value as the barber's, inasmuch as all have the same right of earning their livelihood from their work.
3. That a life of labour, i.e. the life of the tiller of the soil and the handicraftsman, is the life worth living.[52]

It has been pointed out that only the first of these ideas is clearly stated in *Unto This Last*. The second is not there at all, and the third is a stretch.[53]

The fervour of Gandhi's response can be accounted for by the meaning he attached to the first 'teaching', that the good of the individual is contained in the good of all. Ruskin argued that, in the world of work, disinterested action by everyone was in everyone's best interest. Unselfishness and restraint – as opposed to all-out pursuit of profit by the employer, and insistence on maximum wages by the employee – mean greater welfare (conceived as more happiness rather than more income) all round. Gandhi's approach to industrial relations was always 'Ruskinian' in its emphasis on mutual accommodation. But his paraphrase of *Unto This Last*, written for *Indian Opinion* in 1908, reveals that he saw accommodation as self-sacrifice in accordance with the 'divine law'.[54] The 'divine law' had been defined in an earlier article in *Indian Opinion* asking Indians to prepare themselves for going to jail. It was that 'one has to suffer pain before enjoying pleasure and that one's true self-interest consists in the good of all'.[55] This was the Law of Sacrifice. Gandhi found in Ruskin the basis for a political economy which accorded with his beliefs that all life was one and that the common welfare depended – in what was for him a religious sense – on individual sacrifice.

There were passages in *Unto This Last* hinting at the unseen power generated by sacrifice. In arguing that 'the affections only become a true motive power when they ignore every other motive and condition of political economy' Ruskin was not far off the message of the *Gita* as Gandhi understood it, though his inspiration was Matthew 10:39.

> Treat the servant kindly, with the idea of turning his gratitude to account, and you will get, as you deserve, no gratitude, nor any value for your kindness; but treat him kindly without any economical purpose, and all economical purposes will be answered; in this, as in all other matters, whosoever will save his life shall lose it, whoso loses it shall find it.[56]

In the chapter entitled 'The Roots of Honour' Ruskin argued that the various professions should be esteemed for the degree to which they practise self-sacrifice, even unto death.[57] Beginning with soldiers, whose trade 'is not slaying, but being slain' (a view to which Gandhi was to subscribe), he went on to show how lawyers, doctors, clergymen, and even businessmen might find occasion for inviting death or ruin. The doctor should be prepared to die 'rather than leave his post in plague'; the clergyman, 'rather than teach Falsehood'; the lawyer, 'rather than countenance Injustice'. As for the merchant or manufacturer, he must at all costs be true to his word; and rather than fail to keep a commitment, or permit deterioration in the quality of the goods he offers for sale, 'he is bound to meet fearlessly any form of distress, poverty, or labour'. Furthermore, as the captain of a ship is bound to be the last man to leave his ship in case of wreck, and to share his last crust with the sailors in case of famine, so the manufacturer, in any commercial crisis or distress, is bound to take the suffering of it with his men, and even to take more of it for himself than he allows his men to feel; as a father would in a famine, shipwreck, or battle, sacrifice himself for his son.

Gandhi had always exhorted Indian merchants to be honest in their dealings. Now here in the pages of Ruskin was the honest merchant as hero and martyr – a fact duly emphasized in Gandhi's 1908 rendering of the book. The merchant indeed deserved 'the highest honour', for the demands on him were so varied and so great.[58]

Ruskin's phrase 'The Roots of Honour' was rendered into Gujarati as 'the Roots of Truth [Sat]'. Gandhi had begun at this time to equate 'Truth' with God. To be prepared to sacrifice self for others was to align oneself with the divine.

Gandhi concluded his paraphrase of *Unto This Last* with some thoughts on *swaraj*. They were important as the first clear statement of his distinctive position. Already, he said, India was rushing to industrialize along the lines of Britain. But Ruskin had taught his countrymen that the true reward of labour was not the accumulation of money, but 'consists in having done one's duty'. 'Real swarajya', Gandhi wrote,

> consists in restraint. He alone is capable of this who leads a moral life, does not cheat anyone, does not forsake truth and does his duty to his parents, his wife, his children, his servant and his neighbour. Such a man enjoys swarajya wherever he may happen to live. A nation that has many such men always enjoys swarajya.

It was wrong, he went on,

> normally for one nation to rule over another. British rule in India is an evil but we need not believe that any very great advantage would accrue to the Indians if the British were to leave India. The reason why they rule over us is to be found in ourselves; that reason is our disunity, our immorality and our ignorance.
>
> If those three things were to disappear, not only would the British leave India without the rustling of a leaf, but it would be real swarajya that we would enjoy. ...
>
> If, therefore, every Indian makes it a point to follow truth always, India will achieve swarajya as a matter of course.
>
> This is the substance of Ruskin's book.[59]

Phoenix was kept going by subventions from Ratan Tata, the Indian industrialist, an arrangement in keeping with the views Gandhi held on the enlightened (self-sacrificing) use of wealth. His ashrams in India were also financed by industrialists – principally Ambalal Sarabhai of Ahmedabad, and the Marwari businessmen G.D. Birla and Jamnalal Bajaj. None of these institutions was ever self-supporting, and there was little effort to make them so. They were 'laboratories', as Gandhi put it, for experiments in spiritual development which would benefit the world, and training centres for 'public workers' – a term applied with astute indiscriminacy to the political agitators, promoters of handicrafts, and opponents of untouchability whose careers took shape under Gandhi's wing. Writing to Herman Kallenbach, a keen gardener, about the slaphappy horticulture practised at Phoenix, he confessed that he did 'not attach any permanent value to this work'.

> To me it is useful only insofar as it trains those who are engaged in it. The work itself is being continually done and undone. One man builds, another destroys and rebuilds according to his notions of rightness. Who is right? Who knows? But we do know when we act to our souls' profit and when we do not. And that is all that matters on this earth.[60]

This letter referred to planting banana trees, evidently without thought for fruits.

Phoenix, at the beginning, seems to have been one of the happier of Gandhi's settlements, owing probably to its improvisational character and pioneering spirit, and the fact that a significant number of its inhabitants were Europeans whose admiration for Gandhi, though in some cases extreme (particularly Kallenbach's), normally stopped short of the mahatma worship which blighted the Indian ashrams. Also, at Phoenix, sex was permitted between married couples, unlike at Tolstoy Farm – the second of Gandhi's South African settlements, founded in 1910 – where celibacy was required.

A few years after its foundation, when most of the European settlers had moved on, Phoenix began to take on a more regimented air.[61] At first there had been lively arguments about the qualities of different foods. Later, diets were prescribed by Gandhi, and dropped if he decided that a particular experiment was not a success. Western dress was banished. The hour of rising became earlier and earlier and a mania for time management began to assert itself. Bells announced the beginning and end of the activities into which each day was meticulously divided. Gandhi began sniffing out 'impurity' in his little flock. He would then 'atone' by fasting, in the belief that the lapses of others were due to imperfections in himself. These 'penitential' fasts marked the onset of the heroic stage in Gandhi's endeavour to identify himself with all that lived.

The spiritual life as lived at Phoenix under his supervision went largely unrecorded. But Millie Polak, who moved to Phoenix after her marriage to Henry in 1905, recalled conversations in which he maintained that all life was one and love meant 'identification' with others; that sacrifice was 'divine'; that the body was an impediment to spiritual progress, and that celibacy allowed one to concentrate on becoming 'perfect'; that God is good, and evil is the work of men who have yet to become aware of the God within; that brotherhood was the essence of Hinduism (and all religions properly understood); and that he was trying to follow Jesus' example. The practical application of non-violence in daily life was constantly discussed. There were Sunday evening services in Gandhi's house which opened with readings from the Gita and continued with readings from the New Testament and the singing of hymns – often, Gandhi's favourites, 'Lead, Kindly Light', and 'Take My Life and Let It Be'.[62]

In Phoenix School, children were offered instruction in their natal religion, Christians being taught 'the elements of the Christian religion ... on the basis of the teachings of Theosophy'.[63]

The elements of *satyagraha* were now ready to be knitted together. But there was one thing missing before an example of *satyagraha* could be delivered to the world. This was a final and binding commitment to *brahmacharya*. To Gandhi it was not coincidental that only a few weeks after he had taken his vows of *brahmacharya*, the opportunity to offer *satyagraha* presented itself. 'I can now see', he wrote in the *Autobiography*, 'that all the principal events of my life, culminating in the vow of *brahmacharya*, were secretly preparing me' for that day. He emphasized that his first *satyagraha* campaign 'had not been a preconceived plan. It came on spontaneously, without my having willed it.'[64]

The actual taking of the vow was important. The intention to be celibate had been there for some time; but taking a vow put the whole project on a higher level. It was done at Phoenix, after much discussion with 'co-workers' (though not with Kasturbai[65]), when Gandhi returned from stretcher service during the Zulu Rebellion, and was a solemn and public event. Vows from then on were central to Gandhi's rule of life for himself and those who joined him in his ashrams and campaigns. He saw them as keeping him in harmony with the nature of god's universe, which operated according to regular, predictable and inviolable laws. 'God', he said, 'is the very image of the vow.'[66] Taking a vow (like serving others) was acting as God did.

Gandhi said in the *Autobiography* that he did not know at the time he took the vow 'how indispensable [*brahmacharya*] was for self realization'. He saw, he said, in the long marches through Zululand, that a man 'aspiring to serve humanity with his whole soul' could not give himself up to the cares and pleasures of rearing a family. However, he summed up: 'In a word, I could not live both after the flesh and the spirit.'[67] This seems more in keeping with the views acknowledged through his promotion of the Esoteric Christian Union, and with the decision to make a public commitment before those who regarded him as a guide.

Long after the *Autobiography* was written, he acknowledged that it was in Zululand that his life's mission took shape. He returned from South Africa to India, he told Lord Linlithgow in 1942, 'with a mission which came to me in 1906, namely, to spread truth and non-violence among mankind in the place of violence and falsehood in all walks of life'.[68] The discovery of this mission, he said in 1937, came to him at the time when he took his vow of *brahmacharaya*. 'I took the vow of abstinenence', he wrote,

> when I was in the prime of youth and health, when I was young enough to enjoy married life in the accepted sense of the term. I saw in a flash that I was born, as we all are, for a sacred mission. I did not know this when I was married. But on coming to my senses I felt that I must see that the marriage subserved the mission for which I was born. Then indeed did I realize true dharma.[69]

The weeks in Zululand were a time of mental turmoil. According to the *Autobiography*, no sooner had he arrived at the front (with the temporary rank of sergeant major in the Natal Volunteer Defence Force) than he realized it was a terrible mistake. There was 'nothing there to justify the name of "rebellion".'[70] All that had happened was that there had been some resistance to the payment of hut tax, and the whites were teaching the Zulus a lesson. Too late, he understood he was part of 'a man-hunt'. Luckily, he and his corps were assigned to treat the Zulu wounded. They had been wounded, not in battle, but in floggings administered by the whites. (There were no European wounded to speak of.)

This account leaves out the fact that, though he may not have realized how trivial in reality was the reason for the 'war', he knew from its beginning in March – several weeks before he offered his services and three months before he got to the front – that the Africans could expect no quarter. He wrote uneasily in *Indian Opinion* on 7 April of the blowing away from cannon of twelve Zulus from a party which had killed two white policemen. The executions had been carried out after some bleats of protest from the imperial government were silenced by the intransigence of the Natal cabinet. Gandhi's conclusion was that 'whatever justice we may seek is to be had ultimately from the local government'. Indian interests therefore lay in supporting it.[71] Twelve days before he entrained for the front, Bambatha, the most troublesome of the Zulu chiefs, was killed and his head paraded through the countryside by the Natal Volunteer Force. Gandhi may not have known of the victory parade, though no effort was made to hide it.

Another fact missing from the *Autobiography* was that Gandhi's original desire had been to provide the Indians' services, not for nursing, but for fighting.[72] It was only the Natal government's resistance to arming Indians which led him to fall back on ambulance work. The Zulu trouble came at a time when he was following up his articles on 'self-sacrifice' with article after article in *Indian Opinion* on the heroes of the British race, whose bravery was held up for emulation. 'Those who have faith in God', he wrote in an article on Nelson, 'recognize that the British do not rule over India without His will. This too is a divine law that those who rule do so because of the good deeds they have done before.'[73] Gandhi was very receptive to the martial virtues, despite his admiration for Tolstoy. He had felt a coward when all his fellow lawyers had enlisted in the Boer War, and at that time too had offered to serve in any capacity.[74] He admired the bravery of the Boers and what he had seen of the British soldier's cheerfulness under arms. The Russo-Japanese war, which in 1905 catapulted Japan to the status of a world power, also stirred him. The virtues of the Japanese – bravery, honesty, order, obedience – were impressed on the readers of *Indian Opinion*.[75]

The circumstances, then, under which Gandhi decided to take his vow of *brahmacharya* included an element of needing, as it were, to get right with God. The *Autobiography* reveals that he endured agonies of conscience. Not long ago he had been telling the Johannesburg theosophists to get a life. Now his confident embrace of action had led him into appalling error.

He may have already begun to consult his 'inner voice'. He said later that he started to hear it 'about 1906'.[76] If he had gone to Zululand in the belief that God wanted him to go, then he could not have heard the voice of

God correctly. Did he decide that to avoid further mistakes, more strenuous purification was required?

Perhaps we can go a little further in attempting to reconstruct Gandhi's thought processes. It was to become a cardinal principle that, in recognition of his good intentions, God saved him from the worst consequences of his mistakes. He may have reasoned that the fact that he ended up caring for the victims of this cruel affray meant that God had 'saved him from error' (a favourite phrase); or it might have been that God had 'opened his eyes' (another favourite phrase) to the need to be truly pure.

The Transvaal Asiatic Law Amendment Bill of 22 August 1906 (which became known as the 'Black Act') proposed that all Asiatics, male and female, over the age of eight should take out registration certificates which they could be asked to produce at any time to prove their right of abode. The registration certificates replaced the permits which had formerly been issued to adult males. Fingerprinting, of all ten digits, was required. The old law had required only thumbprints. As drafted, the bill was a pointlessly intrusive piece of legislation guaranteed to produce outrage in any self-respecting Indian husband and father. And, as Gandhi pointed out, fingerprinting – a novelty at the time – was used for identifying criminals.

Nasty as it was, the proposed legislation was far from being what Gandhi declared it to be – an unprecedented attack on Indian rights and dignity, and the beginning of the end for Indians in the Transvaal. It appears to have originated in a bungled attempt by the imperial government to salvage what it could of the Indian position before the end of crown rule.[77] But Gandhi, fresh from the horrors of Zululand, was primed for battle.

The proposal to defy the registration ordinance was first floated in *Indian Opinion* on 8 September, in an article entitled 'Russia and India'.[78] The topic was the patriotic bravery of young Russian women who assassinated government officials, knowing they would be caught and executed. They had 'made themselves immortal', Gandhi wrote.

> Facing such risks, they serve their country selflessly. It will be no wonder if such a country succeeds in achieving freedom from tyranny. The only reason why it has not become free immediately is that such patriotism is misdirected, as we have pointed out before, and results in bloodshed. In consequence, these people cannot, according to divine law, obtain any immediate benefit.
>
> Do our people display patriotism of this order? We have regretfully to say "No". No one can be blamed, for we have not yet been trained for this. We

Lawyer and emergent political leader, South Africa, about 1906

are children in political matters. We do not understand the principle that the public good is also one's owns good. But the time has come for us to outgrow this state of mind. We need not ... resort to violence. ... We must, however, submit our bodies to pain, and the new Transvaal Ordinance offers an excellent opportunity.

That the 'excellent opportunity' was grasped was due to the ordinance's creation in the Indian community of a mood of defiance to which the spark of Gandhi's political and spiritual ambition could be applied. The inclusion of women in the ordinance was critical, accomplishing what Gandhi's regular accusations of cowardice in *Indian Opinion* had failed to do.[79] Suddenly, Indians were ready for action.

The mass meeting at the Empire Theatre in Johannesburg on 11 September, at which the pledge to defy the registration ordinance was taken, followed two and a half weeks of preparation, during which the idea of going to jail rather than submitting to the law acquired momentum.

First, on 23 or 24 August, at a meeting of prominent Indians called by the British Indian Association – the political organization formed to deal with Transvaal Indian issues in 1903 – Gandhi went over with those present the terms of the proposed legislation and said that in his view it was the most serious threat so far to Indian interests.[80] It was resolved to oppose it, and to find a venue for a public meeting. A strong letter of protest to the colonial secretary of the Transvaal, drafted by Gandhi and signed by Abdul Gani, president of the British Indian Association, followed on 25 August.[81] On 28 August a meeting was held in Pretoria at the house of Haji Habib, a prominent businessmen active in Transvaal Indian politics.[82] Gandhi was not present and indeed was criticized for the legal fees he was charging. But the meeting agreed to oppose the legislation and voted £25 for expenses. Going to jail was raised as a possibility, but apparently not in the context of a campaign of mass resistance in which jail sentences would be deliberately courted. At this point it remains unclear whether the presumption was that Gandhi would lead the proposed campaign. The likelihood is that it was not. Habib was no stranger to resistance: before the war he had persuaded 42 Indian traders to go to jail rather than seek bail after being arrested for trading without a licence. This was in the period immediately before the test case of 1898 gave the Transvaal authorities the legal right to confine Indian businesses to locations. Licences were often refused without any legal basis; some of the 43 who were arrested actually had valid licences. Habib had succeeded in enlisting the help of the British agent.[83]

Gandhi used the pages of *Indian Opinion* to stir up sentiment in the community. On 1 September an article appeared entitled (in bold print) 'Abominable!' It contained no reference to refusing to register but declared that the draft ordinance 'unsettles the Indian mind, as no other measure in South Africa has ever done' and 'threatens to invade the sanctity of home life'.[84] The same issue contained a brief article, entitled 'Colonial Indians, Note!', on the hardships being experienced by German troops campaigning in South-West Africa (the campaign against the Hereros which was to become a byword for colonial brutality). Indians were urged to emulate German fortitude in the pursuit of 'their communal duty'.[85] There is no reason to doubt that Gandhi's first reaction to the Transvaal Asiatic Law Amendment Bill was exactly as recalled in *Satyagraha in South Africa*: 'Better die than submit to such a law. But how were we to die? What should we dare and do so that there would be nothing before us except a choice of victory or death?'[86]

The next step was taken at a meeting with the colonial secretary, Patrick Duncan, on 1 September, at which Gandhi was present as a member of an Indian deputation, which included Habib and H.O. Ally, who had also been active in Transvaal politics since before the war and was president of the Hamidia Islamic Society. Gandhi's report to *Indian Opinion* said that Habib and Ally 'spoke in impassioned terms'.[87] There was no mention of any talk of jail, but in fact the topic came up. Immediately after the meeting Gandhi wrote to Chhaganlal Gandhi, the relative who was now at Phoenix editing the Gujarati edition of *Indian Opinion*, that 'I have informed Mr. Duncan, whom I met today, that, in the event of legislation going through, I would be the first one to go to gaol rather than be registered or pay the fine. I believe the people here, too, are determined, but I should naturally take the lead in a matter of this kind.'[88] There is no indication of who was the first person in the meeting to speak of jail, and a hint of concern for primacy in suffering.

Whether Gandhi was at this point leading or following, he was anxious that others maintain their resolve. No public commitment to jail-going had yet been made. On 4 September a development occurred which threatened to stifle the nascent *satyagraha* campaign. The Asiatic Law Amendment Bill was introduced into the Transvaal Legislative Council in a revised form which removed the requirement that women should register. In this form the bill passed its first two readings. The concession took much of the sting out of the legislation. This may have been why, in his 8 September article on 'Russia and India' in which he called for defiance of the law, Gandhi went public with the information that Duncan had been told on 1 September that 'Indians will not abide by' the proposed ordinance and would go to jail.[89]

On 9 September Gandhi addressed a meeting of Ally's Hamidia Islamic Society at which 800 people were present, and urged Indians to refuse to register. He himself would be 'the first to court imprisonment'.[90] All were asked to close their businesses on 11 September to attend the meeting at the Empire Theatre.

The meeting was the largest that had ever been organized by South African Indians. Three thousand people attended, many of them petty traders and street hawkers. Representatives of the petty traders (who were mostly Hindu) were included among the platform speakers, making the occasion an impressive display of unity. Gandhi credited Ally with being 'chiefly instrumental' in organizing it, and noted that for the past week 'leading Indians' had been in consultation every night at the Hamidia Islamic Society's hall.[91]

Though Gandhi framed the resolutions that were carried at the meeting, he was the last to speak, rising only after Habib and Ally had got the crowd to its feet in support of the jail-going resolution. It was Habib who proposed the swearing of a solemn oath to go to jail rather than submit. In his speech – of which there are no direct accounts – Gandhi claimed responsibility for urging people to go to jail, and reminded them of the sacred and binding nature of an oath.[92]

Gandhi had not yet emerged as the community's acknowledged leader, whatever his influence may have been behind the scenes: Ally and Habib were the ones to the fore. His task was now to ensure that the willingness expressed to accept imprisonment was not just an empty threat uttered in the heat of the moment, and that Indians' resolve was translated into a campaign conducted with dignity and order and in a sacrificial spirit.

The Asiatic Law Amendment Bill went through its final reading on 12 September and became law subject to the approval of the imperial government. The next move therefore was to send a delegation to London. Most of the cash promised in support of the campaign failed to materialize, so it was a delegation of two – Gandhi and Ally – which sailed on 3 October. Gandhi kept up the pressure meanwhile with articles in *Indian Opinion* and letters to the press. Indians were reminded that the British were moved only by bravery and self-sacrifice, and admonished that, if the community failed to honour its pledge, the whites would 'laugh at us ... spit upon us and call us cowards'.[93] In a practical vein, detailed instructions were left regarding the form that defiance of the law should take, if the act were to receive the royal assent. Gandhi undertook to defend in court anyone who was arrested. His argument would be that 'the real culprit' was not the defendant, but either himself or the British Indian Association, for it was they who had urged the people to disobey the law.[94]

In London, the delegation was received with suavity and the Indian case heard at the highest levels. All seemed to go well. But the Indians were crudely hoodwinked by the Colonial Office, which withheld assent to the

Act while secretly assuring the Transvaal government that, if they cared to wait until after responsible government arrived in January 1907, there would be no objection to the passage of similar legislation.[95] Gandhi returned from London to a hero's welcome – Ally had been ill and all the responsibility had fallen on him – and without any idea that he had been betrayed. In March 1907 the Transvaal government enacted legislation almost identical to that of 1906. Gandhi hoped the imperial government would object. It did not. The struggle which would occupy him for the next seven years then began.

Gandhi's opening salvo was to propose that Indians register voluntarily on the understanding that the law would then not be implemented. This would persuade the government, which had legitimate concerns about the illegal entry of Indians into the Transvaal, of the community's good faith, and, being voluntary, could not 'be regarded as humiliation'.[96] The Indian leadership, with evident bewilderment, accepted this reasoning. When the Transvaal government, surely to no one's surprise, rejected the proposal, Gandhi renewed his call for defiance and going to jail.

In the proposal for voluntary registration the influence of Gandhi's latest religious encounter – in London, with Ethical Culture – can be discerned. On his return to South Africa he wrote a series of articles summarizing William Salter's *Ethical Religion*, the bible of the movement.[97] The aim of Ethical Culture was to liberate the impulse to do right from sectarian religious consciousness. It emphasized that to be truly ethical action must be voluntary – that is, taken in deliberate obedience to the moral law we acknowledge in our heart, rather than in compliance with dogma however revered. This was Kant's moral imperative, which had inspired Ethical Culture's founder, Felix Adler: 'Act as if the maxim from which you act were to become through your will a universal law.' Ethical Culturists were at the forefront of social reform. The idea that moral action was distinguished by its voluntary (as well as its disinterested) nature may have suggested to Gandhi a broader range of permissible political tactics. Possibly it contributed to his later tactical use of 'compromise'.

The campaign began in earnest in July, when permit offices opened and Indians were notified to register in one month. It was then that Gandhi emerged as the leader of the South African Indian protest movement. He organized, he inspired, he found his voice. *Indian Opinion* became the movement's communication centre. With Indians refusing en masse to register – by 30 November, the final closing date, only 545 out of a possible 7,000 had done so – its calls to do or die were actually relevant. Gandhi's style became brisker, simpler.

In December came the crunch. The government began rounding up re-sisters and ordering them to leave the colony. Those who refused, including Gandhi, were sentenced to two months' imprisonment. By the end of January, about 2,000 people had gone to jail. This was magnificent, but could not be kept up. At the beginning of January the government started refusing trading licences to those who could not produce registration certificates – to many a more serious consequence of resistance than a spell in jail. As the movement approached its peak it began to collapse.

There now appeared on the scene the man who was destined to be Gandhi's historic antagonist in South Africa, Jan Christian Smuts. It was Gandhi's fate to have at crucial moments in his career opponents who were as morally aspiring and as instinctively political as himself. The high-souled Smuts – lawyer, soldier, farmer, politician, imperial statesman, holistic philosopher – was colonial secretary in the new Transvaal government of Louis Botha. Of Botha, Gandhi said that 'Though not an Englishman, he possesses the virtues of one.'[98] Smuts, too, he was prepared to treat as an honorary Englishman.

Gandhi's stay in prison was brief – only three weeks – and not too un-pleasant. He later claimed to have enjoyed it. Perceiving the weakening of Gandhi's position, Smuts did not wait long before sending an emissary to the jail, and a 'compromise' settlement was quickly reached. Gandhi committed the Indian community to voluntary registration, with full fingerprinting for all except a few prominent men, in the belief that Smuts had agreed that the Black Act would be repealed after registration was completed.

Gandhi felt he had little choice about reaching a face-saving agreement as quickly as possible. He was getting reports in jail that people were unwilling to undergo further imprisonment. Smuts told him that applications to register were coming in secretly.[99] Whether Smuts ever did commit himself to repeal of the Act, as Gandhi claimed, is not known. There was nothing in writing. But Smuts waited until May, when voluntary registration was almost completed, to make it clear that the Act would remain on the books. Gandhi, who privately expressed doubts about the government's intentions from the start,[100] spent the first few months after his release at the end of January declaring victory. It was a settlement, he said, honourable to all.[101] Both men had something to gain from an ambiguous situation. Smuts got Indian registration, and Gandhi got the chance to consolidate his leadership.

This was no easy task. When they were told by Gandhi that the settlement was an honourable one because it was not the provisions of the Act that were objectionable in themselves but their 'compulsory' nature, people naturally wondered why they had gone to jail. Only a few months before, they had been told the Act meant doom for South African Indians.

The dissatisfaction felt in the community was serious and almost cost Gandhi not only his claim to leadership but his life. On the way to the registration office to comply with the Act he was attacked by an outraged Pathan and beaten with an iron pipe. He felt, he said, not 'the slightest anger or hatred', and rejected prosecution.[102] A few weeks later, he had to be escorted to safety by the police after a speech justifying the compromise in Durban.[103] The resumption of mass resistance in August, after negotiations with Smuts which, though futile, kept Gandhi in the public eye as the Indian leader, was possible only because Smuts's perceived betrayal in declining to seek repeal of the Act eclipsed Gandhi's in agreeing to registration. After an initial loss of momentum, he was able to capitalize on resentment of the government.

In December 1907 Gandhi had asked readers of *Indian Opinion* to come up with Gujarati terms for 'Passive Resistance; Passive Resister; Cartoon; Civil Disobedience'.[104] Few suggestions were received, and Gandhi dismissed them all, except for the proposal by Maganlal Gandhi, his cousin once removed, who had followed him to South Africa in 1903 and was at Phoenix. Maganlal suggested *sadagraha*, meaning 'firmness in a good cause' (literally 'firmness [*agraha*] in good [*sad*]') for 'passive resistance'. The new word also meant 'firmness in truth', and this was the meaning Gandhi accepted and chose to bring out. He changed Maganlal's creation to the unambiguous *satyagraha*. The result was announced in January 1908, just before he went to jail.[105]

Not all the implications of the term occurred to Gandhi at once, though it obviously emerged into consciousness accompanied by an instant acceptance of its appropriateness. His amendment of *sadagraha* to *satyagraha* was expressly provisional. But he used the word constantly thereafter.

At exactly the same time, he began to use the word 'Truth' as a synonym for God. This conjunction is critical to understanding what Gandhi meant by *satyagraha*. 'Truth is God, or God is nothing but Truth', he wrote upon his release from jail at the end of January 1908. 'We come across this idea in every religion. It is a divine law that he who serves that Truth – that God – will never suffer defeat.' The divine law was the Law of Sacrifice – not mentioned, but there in the reminder which followed that success would come to him who fought, as enjoined by the *Gita*, 'with an equal mind', for God and duty's sake: he who fights thus will 'incur no sin'.[106]

The expression remains untranslatable, but it clearly contained what Gandhi believed about the power which flowed through the God-aligned man. The English equivalent which he proposed in 1909, 'soul-force',[107] indeed makes the role of divine energy explicit, for Gandhi believed that the individual soul only has power ('force') to the extent that it acts in harmony with the divine soul. *Satyagraha*, he explained in *Young India* in 1921, 'is literally holding on to Truth, and it means, therefore, Truth-force. Truth is soul or spirit. It is, therefore, known as soul-force.'[108] He emphasized from the start that *satyagraha* was a religious activity.

As he prepared to leave South Africa in 1914, Gandhi observed that the struggle had been prolonged because the development of soul-force in South African Indians had been imperfect. Had perfect soul-force existed, there would have been 'instantaneous relief'. But for this, 'prolonged training of the individual soul is an absolute necessity, so that a perfect Passive Resister has to be almost, if not entirely, a perfect man'.[109] He sometimes referred to Jesus as the perfect Passive Resister, or the perfect *satyagrahi*. Through the concept of *satyagraha*, Gandhi's spiritual and political aspirations were united.

Gandhi never really explained why God was Truth. It was an insight wholly taken for granted. Most likely it occurred as he pondered Maganlal's *sadagraha*, and was the overdetermined product of earlier beliefs and associations, as life-transforming insights generally are.

Gandhi was familiar already with references in the Hindu scriptures to 'Truth' as one of the attributes, even the principal attribute, of God. 'Truth is eternal Brahman', says the author of the *Mahabharata* – one of the quotations Gandhi assembled for an article written in 1905 to rebut a claim by Lord Curzon that ' "the highest ideal of truth is to a large extent a Western conception" '. 'Laws of nature are expressions of Truth, and Virtues are but forms of Truth, and all vices are forms of untruth', and 'Truth is That which Is, and Untruth is That which Is Not', were his summary observations.[110] There the matter rested for Gandhi (to judge from his writings) until he discovered Truth-force. But what appears to have taken hold in the meantime was the association of Truth (meaning what is real) with goodness, which

– in Bhikhu Parekh's words – 'lies at the heart of most Hindu thought'.[111] In Sanskrit, *sat* means the objective reality of things, their 'true' nature, and *satya* (derived from *sat*) means moral truth, integrity: the etymology of the two words is richly entwined.

'God is Truth' (or 'Truth is God', the form he later preferred) was Gandhi's most genuinely 'Hindu' conception. It was present in *The Perfect Way* and in some of Annie Besant's and Madame Blavatsky's writings, but not prominently; A.F. Hills had proclaimed that the sum of God's laws was 'absolute Truth', but had not identified Truth with God. Yet 'God is Truth' was really only Gandhi's way of expressing the belief common to them all that God was everywhere and God was good. Self-realization, as he would often say, meant realizing the Truth which lay within you: obviously, a moral imperative.

This is about as close as we can get to Gandhi's reasoning at the time about God, truth and *satyagraha*. The accusations of Indian untruthfulness with which he had constantly to contend – culminating in Curzon's insult – probably played some part in his thinking. To have Indians campaigning in the name of Truth was sweet revenge. Not that Gandhi would have had such a thought.

If God and the objective reality of the universe are somehow the same, then God in principle is knowable through rational inquiry. The sudden (though foreshadowed) discovery that God was Truth liberated Gandhi to pursue certain lines of thought, among them the idea that *satyagraha* was a 'science' whose 'laws' could be determined. From Hills and others[112] he had picked up the hopeful belief that, just as a scientist could discover the laws of nature through reasoned observation and experiment, so could the spiritual investigator discover, by the same means, the laws of God. Now he set to work.

The enterprise depended on three assumptions about the nature of reality: that matter and spirit are essentially one, differing only in degree of refinement; that all existence is one; and that a cosmic order therefore exists in which the 'divine law', applying equally to matter and spirit, embraces both the moral law and the laws of nature. The distinction between 'law' in the descriptive sense and 'law' in the prescriptive sense is ignored. For Gandhi, the idea that God was Truth tied all this together. In his view 'the Law and the Law-giver' were 'one'.[113] 'God', he said, 'would cease to be God if He swerved from His own laws even by a hair's breadth.'[114] And: 'Any departure conscious or unconscious from the laws of nature is a lie.'[115]

The advancement of the 'science of *satyagraha*' was one aspect of what Gandhi broadly termed his 'experiments with Truth'. The term covered a wide variety of activity and observation – with emphasis on self-analysis – which was intended to yield spiritual knowledge. The experiment could be as simple as observing the effect on his spiritual state of giving up salt. The question to which an answer was sought was always the same: Had what he had done brought him closer to, or taken him further away from, God?

He applied the same scrutiny to all experience that he applied to his deliberate 'experiments'. Unanticipated changes in his physical condition were observed for what they revealed about the state of his soul. Changes for the worse were attributed to some spiritual impurity whose exact nature was the object of careful inquiry.

Gandhi believed himself to be scrupulous in performing his experiments. But sometimes it became clear later that his conclusions had been mistaken. These turns of events necessitated refinements in the conception of 'Truth'. He proposed 'relative truth' to mean whatever appeared to be true at the time to a man of pure mind. Relative truth was not the same as partial truth but was what the 'inner voice' said, and it possessed equal status to absolute truth as a basis for action.[116] The moral validity of action inspired by relative truth rested on the exercise of spiritual discipline. 'In the same way that there are indispensable courses of scientific instruction to be undergone before anyone can carry out scientific experiments', Gandhi explained, 'a strict preliminary discipline is necessary before a person can be qualified to make experiments in the spiritual domain.'[117] A serious and humble spiritual aspirant would be spared calamitous error.

Obviously, Gandhi had no real grasp of scientific method. Nor did his devotion to experiment and to rational inquiry in the moral and spiritual realms really make him what he so often said he was: 'a humble seeker after Truth'. On the contrary, his experiments with Truth elevated his convictions (whatever they were at the time) to a level at which they were unassailable to criticism from anyone other than himself. Accepting the authority of 'relative truth', he attached no value to consistency.

Gandhi believed that 'Spirit is matter rarefied to the utmost limit' and, hence, 'whatever happens to the body must affect the whole of matter and the whole of spirit'.[118] Whatever he did, whatever happened to him, whatever other people did and whatever happened to them, was all connected, materially and spiritually, and causation operated in all directions. He was not overwhelmed by this connectedness, but hazarded conclusions about what was cause and what was effect regarding a great many events that engaged his attention. The moral lapses of associates were sometimes – depending on how close they were – seen as the direct result of his own imperfections. Or their moral improvement might be seen as the result of measures taken by him privately or publicly to become more pure. Similar processes were assumed to take place in the lives of other people.

The effects of these interactions could be experienced over long distances and long periods of time, in ways which might seem to be unconnected with what had originally been done, but were mysteriously in accordance with the divine law. Gandhi felt less certain of these connections than of the result of a simple experiment performed on himself. But by the time he started his first *satyagraha* campaign he was sure they existed. At this time his sense of God's involvement in human affairs, through the infinite ramifications of divine law operating on both the spiritual and the material level, became pronounced.

A cyclone in Hong Kong was reported in *Indian Opinion*, in October 1906 under the heading 'Divine Wrath in Hong Kong'.[119] In April 1907 'Divine Wrath' was the heading for a report by Gandhi on the unusual number of breakdowns in the Johannesburg tram system. Could these be, he asked, the result of 'God's wrath on the municipality which prohibits coloured persons from travelling by these trams?'[120] An article in December 1907 about the prevalence of plague in India was more specific.[121] 'After careful thought', he wrote, 'we have come to the conclusion that, if the plague, starvation, etc., have become more widespread in India, it is because of the sinfulness of the people.' The 'chief sin' was untruthfulness, but 'sensuality', and enmity between Hindus and Muslims, were also to blame. Untruthfulness in particular had 'a debilitating effect on our nerves': 'Our blood becomes poisoned with the impurities of sinfulness and succumbs to germs of any kind.' Plague and other diseases were the result.

To Gandhi, divine punishment for sin and divine reward for virtue were equally aspects of the divine law: the hand of God directed impartially the death from plague of the sensualist and the liar, and the triumph of the *satyagrahi*. Purification of body and soul was the remedy for sin, and the route to divine assistance. In public life, *satyagraha* was virtue's supreme expression.

In 1934 Gandhi shocked his admirers by announcing that a terrible earthquake in Bihar was God's punishment of India for the sin of untouchability.

Explaining his position at the time, he affirmed his belief in 'an indissoluble marriage between matter and spirit', from which he deduced that 'physical phenomena produce results both physical and spiritual', and that natural catastrophes, 'though they seem to have only physical origins, are, for me, somehow connected with man's morals'.[122] These beliefs were news to the majority of Gandhi's followers in 1934. But they had been part of his thinking for a long time. They were present at the birth of *satyagraha*, and they formed part of the context from which it emerged.

Though everyone had the potential to become a *satyagrahi* (even if not in this life), Gandhi made it clear that he meanwhile would define *satyagraha*, refine it, and authorize its practice. It was never presented as just an ethical political technique which anyone could use. It was more than a technique and required guidance.

The process of refining *satyagraha* occurred in response to events, and the agreement with Smuts in 1908 was the point at which 'compromise' became a cardinal virtue of *satyagrahi*s. A *satyagrahi*, Gandhi said, placed his trust in God and therefore trusted his opponent: resistance could always be resumed if necessary.[123] In 1908 Gandhi barely had the political and moral capital to survive the compromise with Smuts. But making a special virtue out of compromise was the key to surviving a number of later crises of confidence in his leadership. There was nothing cynical about this. Gandhi simply assumed that the delivery of *satyagraha*'s message to the world required his presence at the helm. He realized in 1908 that *satyagraha* could not be allowed to fail.[124] This was another reason why 'compromise' became an essential part of it. The practical advantage was that victory could be declared at a point short of total success if going for success seemed risky.

The conception of *satyagraha* lent itself to a definition of 'victory' which was not limited to the achievement of specific goals. The victory could be in the actual performance of *satyagraha*, which was a good in itself. In the uncertain days after his release from jail, Gandhi assured his followers that no matter what happened next the campaign had still been a 'perfect success'. Following truth, he said a few months later, 'is itself a victory'.[125]

While emphasizing that the Indians' 'victory' in the form of his agreement with Smuts was not a victory for any human being but for 'Truth', Gandhi at the same time began to claim a leader's discretionary powers. A leader, he said, should be chosen carefully but, once chosen, trusted to act in everyone's best interest. Under pressure from disgruntled supporters, he admitted that leaders could make mistakes. In that case, the true test of continued fitness for leadership was 'sincerity'.[126] He had been reading Carlyle in jail and may have been thinking of Carlyle's conception of sincerity as being 'in harmony with the Decrees of the Author of this World'.[127]

*Satyagraha* resumed on 23 August 1908 with a mass meeting at which Indians committed the odious registration certificates, symbols of the government's bad faith, to the flames. Arrests and deportations followed. In October Gandhi began his second stint in a South African jail, this time – in common with others – with hard labour.

Once again, support for resistance petered out after the first surge of enthusiasm. Working on the roads in convict uniform was more than had been bargained for. The government, fine-tuning its tactics, further discouraged resistance by fining many of the petty traders rather than sending them to jail. This could mean auctioning off their goods by court order to cover the fine. By February 1909, 97 per cent of the Transvaal Asians had taken out registration certificates.

Gandhi struggled on through two successive jail terms between October 1908 and May 1909, but by the time he came out of jail on 24 May the British Indian Association was bankrupt and many petty traders had been ruined. He appealed with little result to the wealthier men to 'lighten their pockets' in the cause.[128] Beyond a small group of loyal associates he could no longer count on the support of the merchants who had been his first constituency in South Africa.

H.O. Ally and Haji Habib now formed a 'conciliation committee' to negotiate with the government. The committee also met to decide on the composition of a deputation to be sent to England. Gandhi was not happy with either of these developments, which were a clear challenge to his leadership and an implicit vote of no confidence in his tactics. But he got himself on the deputation and sailed for England on 23 June without calling off *satyagraha*. Of the four who were selected, two members were arrested shortly before they were to leave for England, leaving only Gandhi and Haji Habib.

Gandhi had by now concluded that petitions and deputations were a waste of time, but could not afford to distance himself from the deputation and create an open split in the Indian community. He took the view that whatever success might come to it would be the result of the spiritual force generated by the *satyagrahi*s in the prisons of South Africa. 'Think of the deputation', he said, 'as a steam engine. Steam will be produced and the engine will move only if the coal needed for the purpose is supplied from there.'[129] Arriving in England and beginning what he soon suspected would be a futile round of visits, he wrote that the time and energy devoted to them, 'if spent merely in suffering', would 'ensure a very early solution'.[130]

Nevertheless, Gandhi's mood was one of impatience rather than despondency. The *satyagraha* movement was in disarray but he had emerged from prison in an exalted frame of mind, more convinced even than before that the *satyagrahi* was assured of 'divine help'. God, he believed, had seen him though the experience, and 'beyond any shadow of a doubt' he had 'grown in mental strength in consequence of having endured physical suffering'.[131]

His prison reading had been uplifting: the *Gita*, the *Upanishad*s, Carlyle, Ruskin, Emerson, Thoreau. Thoreau confirmed his faith in non-violent resistance; Emerson's essays he found 'worth studying', for they were 'Indian wisdom in a western garb'.[132]

But another author apparently encountered at around this time, the now forgotten Ralph Waldo Trine, seems to have made an equally powerful impression. Trine was not on the list of authors read in prison, but in a letter written on the eve of his departure for London Gandhi instructed Herman Kallenbach to include in his reading in the coming months, along with *The Light of Asia*, *The Song Celestial* and *The Voice of the Silence*, 'Trine's book'. 'Why not', he suggested, 'read aloud ... something from Trine or *Voice of the Silence* or some such work.'[133]

Trine was the best known of the authors associated with the American 'New Thought' movement, which took Emerson's lofty Transcendentalism and transformed it into a practical creed for successful living. His books were the earliest self-help books in the manner of Norman Vincent Peale, 'Werner Erhard', and other gurus who have advised people to stop worrying, get in touch with their inner selves and the cosmos, and embrace life.[134] Trine was a Christian concerned with morality. But his books held out the promise that virtue, correctly understood and practised, would be rewarded with power over men and events.

All Trine's books contained the same message: spiritual power – also termed 'thought power' and 'soul power' – could be acquired by making oneself one with God, who was immanent, through love and service of one's fellow men. The 1899 edition of his *What All the World's A-Seeking* included a postscript,

'Character-Building Thought Power', which was often reprinted separately. The Christ he followed was one familiar to Gandhi – the supreme spiritual exemplar who showed men the way to union with the divine essence.

Trine promised that the true seeker, fearless and forgetful of self-interest, will be so filled with the power of God working through him that he 'can sit in his cabin, in his tent, in his own home, or, as he goes here and there, he can continually send out influences of the most potent and powerful nature … that will reach to the uttermost parts of the world'.[135]

Gandhi's response to these inspirational notions was obviously enthusiastic. There may even have been some specific influence on his thinking. The term 'soul-force' made its first public appearance on 7 June 1909, shortly before he left for London. Casting out fear was an important part of Trine's advice to the spiritual aspirant – what Norman Vincent Peale was to epitomize as the power of positive thinking – and from this time exhortations to fearlessness become prominent in Gandhi's writing. 'Courage' often seems the cardinal virtue in the remaining years in South Africa.

Gandhi seems to have remained interested in Trine. He read his *My Philosophy and My Religion* (1921) in Yeravda jail in 1923, and in 1933, as he recovered from his 21-day fast for 'self-purification', he observed that the fast had sprung from 'a yearning of the soul to merge in the divine essence … How far I have succeeded, how far I am in tune with the Infinite, I do not know.'[136] *In Tune with the Infinite* was the title of Trine's best known book.

Gandhi took with him to London the manuscript of the first biography ever written of him, to be printed and distributed to his supporters. This was the Rev. Joseph Doke's *M.K. Gandhi: An Indian Patriot in South Africa*. Doke was a Baptist minister in Johannesburg who befriended Gandhi and became involved in the Indian movement. We can assume his book had Gandhi's approval.

Doke was the first of many sympathetic Christians to see Gandhi as more Christian than most who professed Christianity as their religion. Like some later admirers also he saw him as Christ-like, though this was only intimated through the choice of language. He described Gandhi walking to the Johannesburg jail with his face 'steadfastly set to go to Jerusalem', and lying 'helpless and bleeding' after the attack by Pathans, forgiving his assailants who knew not what they did: such scenes served 'to reveal the man'.[137] In the final chapter he described Gandhi's religious beliefs.[138] These were that Hinduism had once been 'a pure faith, free from idolatry', but had been 'corrupted by materialism', with the result that India had lost her place of spiritual leadership among the nations; that, periodically, God incarnated himself 'with the object of leading [men] back into the right path'; that Jesus had been one of these incarnations, and the Sermon on the Mount preached the same gospel of 'self-renunciation' as the *Gita* and *The Light of Asia*; that the goal of the spiritually minded man was 'the goal of Buddha, the goal, as [Gandhi] interprets it, of John the Evangelist – absolute absorption of redeemed Man in God'.[139] Doke's book was duly printed and handed out, but did nothing to prevent the failure of the deputation.

It was a bad time to go to London. The British public was preoccupied with Lloyd George's 'People's Budget', the Colonial Office with the imminent Union of the South African colonies. The man of the hour was Jan Smuts, who was in London for discussions with the British government. Smuts saw no need to make concessions to the Indians, whose movement was fizzling out. As in 1906 there were misunderstandings. But Gandhi's main problem was that he was the prisoner of a group of influential English well-wishers who were his intermediaries with the Colonial Office. He could make no move without them, and, assuming the Indian cause was safer in their hands, they effectively silenced him. Gandhi tried watering down his demands but still could make no headway.

Gandhi's position, weak as it was, was weakened further by an event which took place just before he reached London: the assassination by an Indian student, Madanlal Dhingra, of an official at the India Office, Sir William Curzon-Wylie. Gandhi's case was tainted by Dhingra's crime. At a time of increasing violence in India, British opinion was associating Indian nationalism with terrorism. There was some truth to this. The terrorists were dashing young men whose exploits brought them acclaim. Madanlal Dhingra made a fine end in August, proclaiming at the gallows that the 'only lesson required for India at present is to learn how to die, and the only way to teach it is by dying ourselves'.[140] This was what *satyagrahis* were supposed to do, but were not – the campaign in South Africa was fought with a remarkable absence of violence on both sides.

Gandhi left London in November with his demands unmet and *satyagraha* overshadowed by violent political crime. On the way home he produced the most honestly polemical of all his writings, *Hind Swaraj*. Despite its eccentric and embarrassing character, he never disowned it. (His admirers have disowned it for him.)

The book had two purposes: to discredit the terrorist case and prove the superiority of *satyagraha* for advancing the Indian cause; and to show that the way forward for India lay back in the past, through the revival of her ancient culture and rejection of 'Western civilization' as represented by industrialized Britain.

Dhingra had not acted alone but had been part of a radical group of London-based Indians which openly advocated political assassination. Their leader was Shyamji Krishnavarma, editor of the innocuously entitled *Indian Sociologist*. Gandhi met some of these people in London and opposed his belief in soul-force to their belief in physical force.[141] One of those whom he debated at a Dussehra dinner in an Indian restaurant was Vinayak Savarkar, the man suspected of being behind the Curzon-Wylie murder. He is thought to have exercised the guiding hand behind Gandhi's assassination in 1948.

The argument against the terrorists in *Hind Swaraj* was that the ends they sought were contaminated by the means they used.[142] The power released by *satyagraha*, on the other hand, Gandhi said, compromised neither the morality of the outcome nor the morality of the struggle itself. A force generated by personal suffering could not harm others – for 'only the person using it suffers'. Hence, mistakes are not irreversible, unlike those of the assassin. The argument marks the first appearance in Gandhi's writings of the idea that *satyagraha* can do no harm – a natural consequence of the view that *satyagraha* partakes of God's goodness.

Perhaps responding to a criticism heard in London, Gandhi defends *satyagraha*'s dependence on law-breaking, an act of social disruption to which the terrorist did not broadly commit himself. 'That we should obey laws good or bad', he claimed, 'is a new-fangled notion.' Formerly, people disregarded laws they disliked and 'suffered the penalties for their breach', a more manly approach. Ordinary laws, indeed, were 'not necessarily binding' on the man 'who has realized his manhood, who fears only God'. It was 'a superstitious and ungodly thing', he added, 'to believe that an act of a majority binds a minority'.

The manly man's manliness comes from his chastity. The unchaste are 'emasculated and cowardly', and 'not capable of any great effort'. Hence the necessity for the passive resister, even if married and desiring children, to avoid all sexual activity.

The assault on modern civilization in *Hind Swaraj* was not a new departure in Gandhi's thinking. But it was in *Hind Swaraj* that Gandhi's loathing of machinery, doctors, lawyers, formal education and all varieties of rapid transportation – the principal products of materialist civilization – became practically allied with his programme for Indian resistance to British rule.

It was the ancient civilization of India, he argued, which, above all others, was opposed in essence to regard for the material. Its revival was both the antidote to materialism and the key to the creation in Indians of the spirit both manly and devout which would mean the effective end of British domination. Only by rejecting the West and becoming true to themselves would Indians achieve *swaraj*. It was also the obligation of Indians to everyone else in the world to become free practitioners of the only culture which could provide the remedy for what ailed mankind. India, Gandhi said, had 'nothing to learn from anybody else'. Its simple technology and predominantly rural social organization were the results not of ignorance but of deliberate decisions by the wise Indians of long ago, who feared that the introduction of machinery would destroy people's moral fibre and turn them into 'slaves'. 'They, therefore, after due deliberation decided that we should only do what we could do with our hands and feet.'[143] To strive for Indian independence was thus a religious duty. The world's liberation from bondage to material existence depended on it.

The language of *Hind Swaraj* is uncompromisingly moralistic. Everything Gandhi disapproves of is a sin. Hospitals are 'institutions for propagating sin', because in curing disease, which is always the result of impurity, they allow people to escape sin's consequences and sin again. In a notorious passage, the British parliament is compared to a prostitute. The work of Indian lawyers is also compared to prostitution. MPs are prostitutes because they care more for advantage than principle (and ought therefore to be replaced by a few truly good men), Indian lawyers because they support the institutions of foreign rule. 'Prostitute' was the most abusive term the enraged and sin-obsessed Gandhi could think of. His denunciation of higher education contained the summation of his critique of Western civilization. He has studied, he says, 'Geography, Astronomy, Algebra, Geometry, etc.', but none of these has been any use for 'controlling my senses', which is 'the main thing'.[144]

An appendix to *Hind Swaraj* gives a list of authorities consulted – all western with the exception of Dadabhai Naoroji (*Poverty and Un-British Rule in India*) and R.C. Dutt (*Economic History of India*). Six works by

Tolstoy are cited, two by Ruskin, two by Thoreau. The list is completed by Mazzini's *Duties of Man*, Plato's *Defence and Death of Socrates*, Sir Henry Maine's *Village Communities in the East and West*, Robert Sherard's *The White Slaves of England* (a harrowing account of the lives of industrial workers), Godfrey Blount's *A New Crusade* (which advocated the revival of country crafts), Thomas Taylor's anti-railway polemic *The Fallacy of Speed*, a work by Max Nordau given as *Paradoxes of Civilization* (apparently a conflation by Gandhi of Nordau's *Paradoxes* and *Convential Lies of Our Civilization*), and Edward Carpenter's *Civilization: Its Cause and Cure*.

The last was one of only two works (the other was Dutt's *Economic History of India*) referred to in the text of *Hind Swaraj*, where it was respectfully presented as the work of a 'great English writer'.[145] Gandhi had written immediately to Henry Polak upon reading it in London, extolling its importance: its only drawback, he said, was that Carpenter was unable fully to understand the 'cure' for civilization because he had not 'seen the heart of India'.[146] (Carpenter in fact had been to India and noted the indifference to the fate of others inhering in the Indian pursuit of self-realization through non-attachment.[147])

Carpenter's conceit was that civilization was a disease, like measles, through which humanity had to pass in the course of its development. Unhealthiness, indeed, was civilization's distinguishing feature. Like other writers to whom Gandhi was attracted, Carpenter believed that health was the natural human state, and disease a falling away from that state due to the loss of man's harmony with nature. Health was 'unity' – the unity of body and soul as it had existed primordially – while disease was 'loss of unity'; for no distinction, Carpenter said, can truly be made between body and soul, the mortal individual being part of the divine and universal 'Man', who is also present in his consciousness. In the days when uncivilized men enjoyed perfect health, the 'divinity in each creature, being that which constitutes and causes it to cohere together, was conceived of as that creature's saviour, healer – ... the Man within the man, whom it was not only possible to know, but whom to know and be united with was the alone salvation'.[148] The fall of man into civilization and ill health came from paying too much attention to the demands of the body. Gluttony, for example, which is ruinous to health, replaced eating out of simple necessity. Then along came doctors, who made it possible for men to indulge their appetites without experiencing the natural and appropriate consequence of an early death.

Carpenter was a friend of Edward Maitland, with whom he co-authored a pamphlet on vivisection in 1893. A virile homosexual whose idea of unity of body and soul exalted both (Gandhi cannot have read carefully the concluding pages of *Civilization*), he was unlikely to have been a member of the Esoteric Christian Union. But to Gandhi his ideas would have made sense in terms of esoteric ideology. Gandhi's assertion that the self-realized man was above the law echoes the argument in *Civilization* that law and government came into being as men, responding to their appetites, ceased to be guided by their inner divinity and looked to authorities outside themselves. The problem with 'Modern civilization', Gandhi wrote to Herman Kallenbach in 1911, was that it 'either rejects the divinity or seeks to find it outside of ourselves'.[149]

A writer who was not on Gandhi's list of authorities for *Hind Swaraj*, but may have been more important than any of them in persuading him to write it was G.K. Chesterton, whose article in the *Illustrated London News* on 18 September, 'What is Indian Nationalism?', Gandhi thought worth summarizing for *Indian Opinion*.[150] The problem with Indian nationalists, Chesterton declared, was that they were not very Indian. They admired, of all people, Herbert Spencer, and subscribed to trivial ideas about progress and democracy, rather than looking for inspiration to their ancient civilization, which cared not a whit for those things and valued above all religion. Chesterton's careless paradoxes set Gandhi to wondering if 'we have been endeavouring to destroy what the Indian people have carefully nurtured through thousands of years'.

A curious footnote to Gandhi's visit to London was that, as he arrived, Annie Besant was just leaving, having emerged from India to take to the West a new message: the coming of the Christ (also referred to as the *avatar*, the *bodhisattva* and the World Teacher) was at hand.[151] While in London she gave eight public lectures, and seven private talks to theosophists, on this subject. Lewis Ritch, the Johannesburg theosophist who was secretary of the South Africa British Indian Indian Committee, was Gandhi's agent in London at the time. Did he know of Mrs Besant's good tidings? Did he convey them to Gandhi?

When she returned to India at the end of the year, Besant realized that the saviour had materialized already – in the form of a 13-year old boy, Jiddu Krishnamurti, the son of a poor Brahmin clerk employed at the Theosophical Society headquarters in Madras.

*Hind Swaraj* showed how occupied Gandhi's mind now was with thoughts of India. But it was to be five more years before the culmination of his South African campaign enabled him to return with some prospect of political success. Meanwhile, he prepared himself for the day when he could leave Africa and embrace his greater destiny.

There was still no major transformation in Gandhi's way of living. He continued to wear European dress and live mostly in Johannesburg. Tolstoy Farm, the second of his experimental communities, was founded in 1910 on land owned by Kallenbach near Johannesburg, initially to provide accommodation for the families of imprisoned resisters. Though celibacy was required, life was generally less austere than at Phoenix, perhaps in deference to Kallenbach, who liked to potter about there. Kallenbach did not share his friend's passion for self-denial in every area of life. At Phoenix, however, the daily routine became steadily more exacting, and also more 'Indian', in terms of what was taught to the inmates and how they lived. Phoenix was Gandhi's training ground for the coming Indian struggle – the place where he would prepare his chosen band for whatever horrors awaited them in the mother country. 'I always feel', he explained to a comrade as the movement in South Africa collapsed around him in 1910, 'that I shall be strong enough to welcome death in any form and at any time. I wish all may get this strength.'[152]

Life at Phoenix was minutely organized, even for the children.[153] There was no unauthorized play or roaming about. Right and wrong were rigorously defined. Food was consumed only at meals; plucking fruit from the trees, even wild fruit, was considered 'theft'. Everyone was conscripted into a heroic struggle for physical and spiritual renewal. The strictness of the regime took its toll on the inhabitants, few of whom had gone to Phoenix anticipating the earnestness of Gandhi's efforts to fortify and purify them. Many were relatives, or the relatives of colleagues. Gandhi took all evidence of 'lapses' as reflecting on himself. It particularly pained him that people deceived him about their transgressions. What must his spiritual state be, if sin and untruth flourished in his presence? This was a question he was to ask himself again as he surveyed the scenes of moral and emotional disorder prevailing in his various ashrams.

At Phoenix, Gandhi's unfulfilled sense of his own destiny drove him to be cruel. When boys and girls showed signs of awakening sexual interest in each other, he personally cropped the girls' hair. When he found out that his 12-year-old son Devdas and some other boys had bought snacks with money they had found, he fasted for a week. When Devdas illicitly ate lemons and failed to confess for fear of being slapped, he slapped his own face and wept inconsolably. In April 1914 disaster struck, from Gandhi's point of view, when a young woman and a young man were discovered to have 'fallen'. The discovery impelled him to fast for 14 days – at a time when Kasturbai was seriously ill, and negotiations with Smuts were at a critical stage. What drove him to this desperate act was probably the identity of the fallen pair. From his letters to Kallenbach it is clear that they were his son Manilal and a young teacher, Jeki, the daughter of Gandhi's close friend Dr Pranjivan Mehta and the wife of Manilal Doctor, who was in Fiji. Massive efforts at penance and self-purification were thus required. Jeki was sent home, and Manilal took a vow, in 'atonement', to postpone marriage for a length of time to be determined by his father.

Gandhi's relations with his children were a casualty of these years. Only Devdas, the youngest, who was treated less harshly and given some education, seems to have remained on relatively good terms with him. His letters to the two oldest boys during the final years in South Africa make melancholy reading. Try as they might to please him – and Harilal and Manilal did their stints in jail – they never could for long.

Gandhi's sexual preoccupations intensified at this period, in conjunction with his anxiety about the results of the political struggle.

In 1913 the words *tapas*, *tapasya* and *tapascharya* – Indian terms referring to the practice of austerities in pursuit of spiritual power – began to appear regularly in his writings. Jail-going was conceptualized as *tapascharya*. At the same time there flowed from his pen, in weekly instalments, the pamphlet entitled *General Knowledge about Health*, in which for the first time he wrote explicitly and at length, and in purely Indian terms emphasizing the conservation of the human male's 'generative fluid', of the exceptional physical and mental vitality enjoyed by the man who practised *brahmacharya* – he himself, he was not shy to say, being a good example.[154]

These were traditional Indian ideas, but Gandhi took them further than was done in India and laid down *brahmacharya* as the ideal state to be pursued by everyone, and not only (as was traditionally accepted) by the young man as he was preparing himself for life, or the old man who had moved beyond the duties and cares of family. He declined to discuss the 'religious issues' involved, but observed that if the human race came to an end through the universal observance of chastity it would be no matter for concern: 'He who has created the world will look after His affairs.' All those, he said, who practised *brahmacharya* would understand at some point what God's ultimate purpose was, for as they encountered other *brahmacharis* it would become 'as plain as daylight to them what will happen to the world if all did the same'.

These enigmatic observations were as far as Gandhi was prepared to go on this occasion in hinting at his hopes for the etherealization of the human race. He was more explicit in 1924 when he told a young admirer that the 'extreme logical result' of universal celibacy would be 'not extinction of the human species, but the transference of it to a higher plane'.[155] In 1922 he told Manilal, who wished to marry, that the cessation of procreation would 'only mean that all destruction will cease. *Moksha* is nothing but release from the cycle of births and deaths.'[156]

Gandhi took an unusual position in asserting the worthlessness of abstinence from sex without 'keeping the mind free from the very thought of it – one must not even dream about it'. To Gandhi, chastity meant imperviousness to desire. In India such purity of mind would only be expected from the most advanced aspirant to self-realization, not the ordinary striver.

There is a hint in Gandhi's private correspondence that his eventually notorious practice of sleeping in proximity to nubile young women, to get meritorious experience of restraint, began at Phoenix. 'We were most of us here on the verandah sleeping side by side', he wrote to Kallenbach in January 1913. 'Jeki was next to me.'[157]

Despite their problems, Phoenix and Tolstoy Farm established Gandhi as a spiritual and moral leader. They gave him a coterie of followers who accepted his right to inflict on them the consequences of his personal spiritual aspirations. What these aspirations were was becoming a bit more explicit. In July 1913 he wrote to Jamnadas Gandhi – brother of Chhaganlal and Maganlal – with some thoughts on the *avatar* – to Hindus, a god who has assumed human form. 'Krishna, Rama and others', he wrote,

were divine incarnations, but we, too, can be like them when immense *punya* [merit] has accrued to us. The *atmans* about to attain *moksha* are so many divine incarnations. We need not believe in their perfection while yet alive.... *Avatar* is, and always will remain, a necessity. It is only when people are in utter despair and immorality is widespread that a belief in *avatar* comes to prevail. A small number following normal morality in the midst of a wicked majority looks for support. In a situation of this kind, a man of great moral strength who has no fear of the wicked but of whom the wicked stand in fear, is looked upon as an *avatar* after his death, or even during his life-time. It is not probable, in most cases, that such a person regards himself as an *avatar* right from the beginning.[158]

Gandhi's return empty-handed from London in 1909 meant that his active following was reduced to those who felt a personal commitment to him. In the next two years he barely escaped oblivion. His career was kept alive by Smuts, who chose to treat him as the Indian representative.

As his hold on the merchant community loosened, his position as spokesman for Indian interests was challenged from another quarter. Colonial-born Indians, the partly assimilated children mostly of indentured labourers, were organizing themselves, and making demands not heard before. They wanted education, they wanted freedom as South Africans to move round the newly created Union, and they wanted better treatment for the indentured and the formerly indentured – in particular, repeal of the £3 annual tax which drove many back into servitude. They were not much interested in the cause of India: South Africa was their home.

Gandhi had protested against the £3 tax but the issue had never been seriously taken up, his political strategy for most of his South African career having been to show that the Indian merchant deserved better treatment than the Indian labourer. But, after a barely face-saving 'provisional agreement' with Smuts on Union immigration policy in May 1911, and further complications with Smuts, Gandhi was ready to stake his future on an attempt to broaden the movement. The £3 tax was moved up the agenda, though not without misgivings. Gandhi was conscious that repeal of the tax already had a more credible advocate in P.S. Aiyar, the moving spirit of the Colonial Born Indian Association. He also professed to distrust the existing agitation against the tax as not 'unselfish', meaning it was not coming from those directly affected but from those who sought to exploit it as a political issue.[159] If he were to move beyond sanctioning sympathetic articles on the subject in *Indian Opinion*, he would have to include himself in that category. There was no denying, however, that resistance to an iniquitous tax provided the perfect opportunity for *satyagraha*, whereas the complex negotiations on immigration, in which he had become bogged down, did not.

The visit to South Africa from October to December 1912 of the prominent Indian 'moderate' politician G.K. Gokhale was the event which revived Gandhi's fortunes, and enabled him to emerge as the leader of a truly representative South African Indian movement.

Gandhi had met Gokhale in India and, being courteously received, had been pressing him for years to come on a 'fact-finding' visit. When he finally came, his timing, from Gandhi's point of view, could hardly have been better. As a leading constitutionalist politician he had access to the highest level of the South African government, at which he presented the Indian case. He toured the country addressing huge crowds of Indians, with Gandhi, his host, always at his side, the visible representative of the South African Indian community. At the Mount Edgecombe sugar estate, one of the biggest employers of indentured labour in South Africa, Gokhale promised to work for repeal of the £3 tax. He left South Africa believing that, in response to his representations, the government had agreed to move towards repeal; he also believed that the government was prepared to make concessions on the immigration issue. Neither of these beliefs turned out to be correct.

The relationship between Gandhi and Gokhale was a curious one. Gandhi despised Gokhale's Servants of India Society as out of touch with the real India,[160] but would permit no criticism of Gokhale himself and treated him with fantastic deference during his visit. In 1915, after his return to India, he tried to join the Servants of India Society, but after Gokhale's death in that year, the Society declined to admit him. Gokhale's feelings about Gandhi were obviously mixed. He knew political talent when he saw it, and was open to Gandhi's political originality: the Servants of India Society, in its more conventional way, required righteousness and self-sacrifice from its members. But he resisted Gandhi's efforts to use him as an entry into Indian political life. He took a dim view of *Hind Swaraj*,[161] and when Gandhi finally arrived in India in 1915 he sent him off on a year's study tour. He was amused by Gandhi's reverent ministrations on his South African tour.

His contribution to Gandhi's political career in 1912 was decisive. By the time Gokhale left South Africa, Gandhi was a credible public figure to an immensely larger number of people than he had been before, and a settlement of the long struggle seemed in sight. Planning to follow Gokhale to India as soon as everything was wrapped up, he closed Tolstoy Farm and took the inhabitants to Phoenix to begin practising the necessary austerities.

But the government denied having given Gokhale any assurance that the tax would be repealed. And it soon became apparent also that the current round of negotiations with Smuts on immigration would not be reaching a satisfactory conclusion. In April 1913 the Union government published an immigration bill which Gandhi was bound to oppose.

When negotiations with the government finally broke down in September, he announced the resumption of *satyagraha*. The issues were the immigration bill, the status in law of non-Christian marriages (women married according to rites which recognized polygamy had been refused admission to South Africa) and the £3 tax.

The merchants did not respond to the call. Instead, at a public meeting in Durban on 12 October, at which Gandhi was present, they expressed strong criticism of his leadership as autocratic and unproductive. The meeting became so rowdy that the police were called. Gandhi undertook to return in a week and seek consensus. But by then he had called the indentured labourers of South Africa out on strike against the £3 tax. On 16 October the strike began in the coalmines of Natal.[162]

The strike was Gandhi's last stand in South Africa, and an enormous gamble. To admit defeat and leave the field when, only a few months before, the settlement had seemed in reach which would allow him to depart for India was not an option. It was now or never.

Once the strike had begun, it spread rapidly and spontaneously, affecting mines, railways and sugar estates. Little groups of *satyagrahi*s – often women – courted arrest under the immigration laws by crossing provincial borders. But the strictly *satyagraha* element in the campaign was overshadowed by the far greater upheaval which seemed to have been waiting to happen. Many who took part in the struggle had only the dimmest idea, if that, of what Gandhi's campaigns had been about. There was violence on both sides, particularly on the sugar estates, which eventually led the Government of India to make a public request for a commission of inquiry – the first step towards a settlement.

Gandhi's strategy was to get the striking workers out of their compounds and on to the roads, where illegal border crossings would in due course provoke mass arrests. The jails would then be swamped, and the campaign's organizers relieved of the burden of feeding the large number of destitute people for whom they had suddenly become responsible. Despite financial help coming from India, the provision of strike rations was a serious problem.

At the height of the strike Gandhi led over 2,000 strikers across the Transvaal border. More followed. Smuts held back from ordering the mass arrests he knew would hand the moral victory to Gandhi. But when the disruptions caused by the strike became severe, he had no alternative. The world soon learned of the expedients to which his government resorted in order to cope with the mass of people in custody, including incarceration in mine shafts.

It was important to Gandhi that there should be martyrs in the ranks of the *satyagrahis*. No one, he had written in 1910, 'can be accepted as a true satyagrahi till he has met death, being faithful to his pledge right up to the end.'[163] In 1909 he had organized a ceremonial funeral for a *satyagrahi* who had died of pneumonia after being let out of jail, and done what he could to invest the death with the aura of martyrdom. Another Indian who was released on health grounds had survived. Gandhi publicly hoped that he would soon be back in jail, perhaps to die there. 'Death in prison', he said, 'will uphold our honour and will serve the cause of India.'[164]

In 1913 there were deaths resulting from police action among the striking workers. But these deaths lacked the element of conscious renunciation of concern for the body which marked the death of a *satyagrahi*. Some were contaminated by violent provocation. Only one example of 'absolutely pure sacrifice', the kind which 'bore fruit' in enlisting God's aid, occurred in 1913: the death of a young Tamil woman named Valliamma, who became ill in prison and died shortly after release.[165] Gandhi began a campaign to erect a building in her memory.

It is painfully clear that Kasturbai, who served three months in jail with hard labour from September to December 1913, and fell seriously ill thereafter, was regarded as a prime candidate for martyrdom in the 1913–14 campaign. In the first *satyagraha* campaign, when she was close to death during a gynaecological illness, Gandhi had declined to pay his fine and leave jail to be with her. 'If you die', he wrote to her, 'even that death of yours will be a sacrifice to the cause of satyagraha.'[166] Now the prospect of a spiritually productive demise for Kasturbai arose again. In February, Gandhi wrote to Kallenbach of his disappointment that there had been no Gujarati martyr. 'If anybody should have died', he wrote, 'it was Mrs. Gandhi' (whose health at that moment happened to have taken a turn for the better).[167] Writing a few days later with news of a relapse, he expressed his acceptance of God's will should she be taken away. Meanwhile, he forebade medicines, prescribed fasting, and made arrangements for her funeral. But she continued to 'linger' and then began to improve. When she rallied sufficiently to complain of the behaviour of Jeki, of whom she clearly thought her husband was too fond, and he 'gently but rebukingly remarked' that her illness was largely due to her sinful thoughts, she unburdened herself. 'I had made her leave all the good food, in order to kill her', Gandhi reported to Kallenbach; 'I was tired of her, I wished her to die, I was a hooded snake.' He reflected that his love had 'not been sufficiently intense and selfless to make her change her nature'. She was 'the most venomous woman' he had ever met.[168] A week or so later he discovered the affair between Jeki and Manilal and decided to fast for 15 days. But realizing that a 15-day fast 'would mean Ba's [Kasturbai's] death', he hesitated. Finally, he decided to fast for 14 days![169]

Gandhi's letters to Kallenbach reveal how trying he still found his wife, who had remained illiterate, who thought his way of life absurd, and who much resented his treatment of their children. For her to die in jail or soon enough thereafter to be awarded 'the martyr's crown' would have solved a good many problems. Not only that, it would have put the finishing touch to a glorious campaign, perhaps helped to assure its success, and launched him unencumbered into the life he hoped to live in India. That he desired his wife's death seems obvious. But it was a desire of which he managed to remain unaware.

Like many people with inadmissible desires, Gandhi found himself referring to them in jest ('Only joking!'). When Kasturbai was ill in 1911 and cried because he was too busy to stay with her, he felt, he told Maganlal, 'somewhat awkward', but recovered himself and 'said to her with a smile, "Nothing to worry about if you die. There is plenty of wood. We shall cremate you on this Farm itself."' At this, he reported, 'she also laughed'.[170] In 1913, he made her promise to offer *satyagraha* against the ruling regarding non-Christian marriages. According to the account by Gandhi's admirer Ravjibhai Patel, who was present, Kasturbai protested that she might die in prison. With 'a hearty laugh', Gandhi replied: 'Of course, I do wish that. If you die in jail, I'll worship you as *Jagdamba*' (the goddess of valour).[171]

In December 1913 Gandhi and Smuts began negotiations, Gandhi being released from jail for the purpose. The strike had collapsed in many areas, and he was in no position to make a credible threat of renewed resistance. But Smuts's position had also been weakened by criticism of the government's manner of dealing with the strike, and he was under pressure to make concessions. The eventual result was once again a compromise. No other outcome was really possible, but, as before, Gandhi's willingness to back down at the negotiating table came as a shock to those who had been exhorted to do or die. There were unruly meetings of the Indian community, at which he was called to account. There were even threats of murder, which he took seriously enough to make a will. His 'compromises', which to him possessed spiritual merit, were arrived at on his own initiative; from the perspective of his supporters, they were unauthorized negotiating positions.

The agreement reached in June 1914 passed into law in July as the Indian Relief Act. Gandhi could now join Gokhale, who was in London and about to return home, and go on to India in the company of the great man.[172] He left for England on the first leg of his journey on 18 July. Thirty years later he attributed Smuts's 'conversion' to 'the working of truth and non-violence expressing themselves through me'.[173] Upon his departure, Smuts noted that 'The saint has left our shores, I sincerely hope for ever.'[174]

The gains to South African Indians from the Indian Relief Act were repeal of the £3 tax and the recognition of the right of one wife of a polygamous marriage to join her husband in South Africa. All other matters were left to be settled by administrative action within the framework of the Smuts–Gandhi correspondence at some future date. The immigration issue was not resolved. But, as Gandhi explained to his fellow Indians as he prepared to depart, a force had arisen in the world – the force of Truth – which, if it spread and became perfected, would transform it.[175] Despotism and militarism would pass away; social ideals would undergo a revolution. The training given to the children at Phoenix and Tolstoy Farm meant that the rising generation would understand 'what the soul is, what truth is, what love is, what powers are latent in the soul'. As for himself, he was departing for India in hopes of there understanding better his 'imperfection as a Passive Resister', and then trying 'to perfect myself, for I believe that it is in India that the nearest approach to perfection is most possible'.

# FOUR

# Return to India

As Gandhi's ship sailed up the English Channel news came that war had broken out in Europe. Gokhale was stranded in France where he had gone for medical treatment, and there was no knowing when he would return. After a welcome reception by London Indians, Gandhi was left with nothing to do.

A week after arriving, he contacted the India Office with an offer from himself and 52 other Indians to place their services 'unconditionally, during the crisis, at the disposal of the Authorities'.[1] Maganlal and others reminded him of statements made in South Africa that, for a *satyagrahi*, no form of war work was appropriate. But he explained that, first, 'unconditionally' was not meant to include fighting, as 'Everyone knows' that, having fallen ill after his arrival in London, he himself was 'not fit for active service'; and, second, that to sit back and do nothing while eating food whose importation was protected by the Royal Navy was cowardice – and 'So long as I have not developed absolute fearlessness, I cannot be a perfect satyagrahi.' He could either, he said, take to the hills and live by foraging, thus foregoing naval protection, or he could justify the food he ate by doing something useful: the former was not an option for which he was 'ready'. As a public figure, he added, he could not act alone, but must involve others in non-violent self-sacrifice.[2] In the *Autobiography* he mentioned that hopes of improving the Indian position had also been in his mind.[3]

The offer of help was accepted and an ambulance corps formed. Training went well until the authorities appointed several corporals from among a

With Kasturbai shortly after returning to India in 1915

group of British university students assigned to the unit for non-combatant
duties. Gandhi protested as the corp's unofficial head and representative that
the Indians should be allowed to choose their own leaders. Receiving no
satisfaction, he announced that the corps was 'obliged to abstain from further
drilling and week-end camping' until the appointments were recalled.[4] Much
official correspondence followed. But support for Gandhi faded among the
volunteers after a reminder that they were under military discipline, and as
they became aware that Indian troops were going into action and required
their services. Gandhi was given assurances that he would remain in charge
of recruiting and be consulted 'informally' on non-military matters. He was

also 'informally' prevented from joining the corps at the hospital to which they were assigned.[5]

Meanwhile, Gokhale had left for India. Gandhi, ill with pleurisy, hung on in London for another month and then followed on 19 December. His poor health obliged him to give up temporarily the 'fruitarian diet' begun before leaving South Africa.

In India Gandhi received a hero's welcome, but, in an already crowded field, he had to establish a position. Gokhale, upon whose good offices he was depending, enjoined on him a year's silence on political matters. Other Indian politicians made no move to befriend him. They were wary of him, or hostile. The outstanding figure at the time was the brilliant Maharashtrian, Bal Gangadhar Tilak. Without openly endorsing political murder, Tilak was prepared to do whatever it took to remove the British and restore India to its lost (Hindu) glory. Like Gandhi he was an admirer of the *Gita* and took from it a message of action.[6] In 1915 he stood poised to take over Congress from Gokhale and the 'Moderates'. In this struggle Gandhi had as yet no part to play.

Gandhi began his study tour of India in Gujarat. In Rajkot he told his audience that the love they professed for him would one day be 'put to the test'.[7] In Gondal, the epithet 'mahatma' was bestowed upon him, perhaps for the first time.[8] He visited Shantiniketan, Rabindranath Tagore's community in Bengal, where a group of Phoenix inmates had been staying; he made an attempt to simplify its manner of living. He found in India, he reported to Kallenbach, 'much to criticize, much to disappoint', but still felt the 'basis of life' was 'spiritual', which meant one could therefore 'build straightaway'.[9]

In March Gandhi made up his mind to found a community of his own at Ahmedabad. There were to be 40 settlers to begin with, and the principal activity in addition to agriculture was to be handweaving. As at Phoenix, the inmates were to be trained 'for long service to the Motherland'.[10] This was the beginning of what became the Sabarmati ashram.

Ahmedabad, the business centre of Gujarat, at first seems a surprising choice for a settlement whose ultimate aims were not of this world. It was a city at the forefront of Indian's industrialization, about as far removed in spirit from the ideals of *Hind Swaraj* as it was possible to get. But the money Gandhi needed was available from the owners of the local cotton mills, and it was the centre of such nationalist political activity as there was in his native province. In 1915 Gandhi had to go to the mountain and not wait for it to come to him. Gokhale's death in February and Gandhi's subsequent failure to gain admittance to the Servants of India Society were setbacks. He needed a base, and followers. He was very conscious that all his achievements could come to nothing if at this juncture he failed to inspire others.[11]

His hopes to inspire were dealt a blow from an unexpected quarter at the end of March. After a failed attempt to mend relations with his father, Harilal circulated an 'open letter' which, in addition to his personal complaints, contained the frankest criticisms of Gandhi's conduct and character ever to see the light of day in India.[12] Phoenix was described as a place ruled by fear, its daily round governed by Gandhi's petty obsessions.

> Not to take salt, not to take *ghee* …, not to take milk has no bearing on character. You say this is necessary in pursuit of self-control. But my view is that even before one cultivates self-control, there are other even more desirable qualities that need to be stressed – such as being unselfish, that is, charitable, being endowed with courage, simplicity, etc. If one does not have these qualities, giving up salt etc. will not help one to acquire self-control. For the spirit of renunciation will be lacking.

Gandhi's treatment of Kasturbai was a major item in the arraignment.

> I saw her insulted and humiliated. … 'Mrs. Gandhi takes too much sugar, which has led to increased expenses'; 'Mrs. Gandhi has no right to assign work to the employees of the press' and so on and so forth. I have not the words to describe the misery Mother went through.

Harilal apologized later to his father for writing this letter, but seems not to have issued a public withdrawal.[13]

A week after Harilal's broadside Gandhi was in Hardwar, on the Ganges, for the Kumbh Mela – the religious festival held there every 12 years which attracts to this day many thousands of devotees, including every conceivable variety of holy man. Here was popular Hinduism in concentrated form and Gandhi reeled from the impact. There was the dirt, there was the five-legged cow. There was everywhere the unmistakable presence of religion as a way of making a living rather than as a sacred way of life. Gandhi did not attempt to record his reaction until long afterwards in the *Autobiography*.[14]

He found himself at Hardwar, apparently for the first time, the object of religious veneration. He was pursued all day by people desiring his *darshan* (the blessed sight of a holy person) and was both touched and annoyed by the experience – touched by the appreciation of what he had done in South Africa, and annoyed by the 'blind love' and ceaseless proximity of his admirers. But veneration it was, however tainted, and it appears to have prompted some heart-searchings about how worthy he was. Hardwar was full of *sadhu*s (holy ascetics) and he had noted their enjoyment of 'the good things of life' – a reference presumably to the food offered them by devotees. He thought 'of the unnecessary trouble' he had caused his hosts on recent visits to Calcutta and Rangoon, where his dietary requirements had been lavishly taken care of. In a letter to Kallenbach he had described rather ungratefully a meal provided by Dr Pranjivan Mehta in Rangoon[15] – for the first meal of the day, taken at 10 a.m. after rising between 4 and 5: '4 bananas, 2 tiny tomatoes, 1 tiny unripe mango chopped, 2 spoonfuls of grated fresh coconut, 4 walnuts, perhaps 2 ounces of date, ground-nut meal mixed, 1 naarangi, 2 slices of wretched melon, 2 lemons and a drink of coconut water'. He remorsefully decided that he would never in future 'take more than five articles [of food] in twenty-four hours and never ... eat after dark'. Otherwise his hosts would be engaged in serving him, when it ought to be the other way round.[16]

The decision took the form of a vow and it was a set of vows – six principal ones and three additional ones – which constituted the rule of life at the new ashram.[17] These were: truthfulness, non-violence, celibacy, control of the palate, non-stealing, non-possession, *swadeshi*, fearlessness, and refusal to practise untouchability.

The vow of non-violence included an obligation to love one's enemy and win him over by 'love'. Celibacy included the eradication of lust from one's heart, and was stated to be the essential precondition for successfully observing the vows of truthfulness and nonviolence. Control of the palate was necessary for the practice of celibacy, and meant abandoning 'such articles of food as may tend to stimulate animal passions' and, in general, eating only to sustain the body. Non-stealing, as at Phoenix, meant not just avoiding what was normally understood by 'theft' but also not eating or possessing anything which was not really needed. 'Non-possession' was the same idea more stringently expressed: for instance, 'if one can do without chairs, one should do so'. The term *swadeshi* was employed in an unusual sense. It meant originally, when the *swadeshi* movement began in the nineteenth century, not using goods of foreign manufacture. But Gandhi included in it not using mill-made cloth and (less explicitly) any other machine-made articles. The observer of *swadeshi* would 'never use articles which conceivably involve violation of truth [in the special Gandhian sense] in their manufacture or on the part of their manufacturers' and would only wear handwoven clothing in a simple Indian style: handspinning had not yet come into the picture. The vow of fearlessness included defending oneself or others from violent attack only by 'truth-force' or 'soul-force'.

The vow against untouchability was added when an untouchable family joined the ashram in September, at the suggestion of Amritlal Thakkar, a member of the insufficiently radical Servants of India Society, who had devoted himself for some years to the uplift of untouchables in Bombay. Bravely, Gandhi took them in, immediately putting his ashram at risk. Kasturbai and others were appalled, donations from the rich and pious stopped coming in, and Gandhi considered going to live in the untouchable quarter of Ahmedabad.

But rescue came from a Jain millowner, Ambalal Sarabhai, in the form of a gift of 13,000 rupees. Kasturbai came round, though only after Gandhi had undertaken 'partial starvation. I lived without nuts for a few days.'[18] In the end, though some people left the ashram, most settled down to make their accommodations. The experiment appears to have been a modest success – in the Indian context perhaps a big success – though Gandhi found the untouchable daughter trying and was not happy when her father asked him to adopt her (which he did).[19] The Dudabhai family remained the ashram's only untouchables. But untouchables were admitted to the Sevagram ashram as servants in the 1930s, as part of the uplift programme.[20]

Gandhi had not previously come out in favour of the abolition of untouchability, though he had deplored the treatment of untouchables in *Indian Opinion*.[21] He recalled in the *Autobiography* having quarrelled with Kasturbai when she refused to empty the chamber pot of an Indian Christian clerk, born of untouchable parents, who was staying at the house in Durban.[22] When he got back to India he found advanced Indian opinion in favour of abolition and was confronted with the need to define a public position. Thakkar undoubtedly forced his hand on the issue, but after that he made it his own.

When he began to speak out, he condemned untouchability not just as a social evil but as 'irreligion'. He was sure that it could not have been part of Hinduism in its earliest form, for Hinduism, he believed, meant above all 'recognition of the unity of all life'.[23] 'None can be born untouchable', he wrote, 'as all are sparks of one and the same Fire.'[24] Untouchability was an excrescence on Hinduism which would have to be removed before India could exert its proper spiritual influence on the world. His campaigns against it were campaigns for the purification of Hinduism from this 'blot'.

Gandhi believed in the caste system, purged of untouchability. He accepted and approved of the division of Indian society into four hereditary *varnas* or caste groupings: the Brahmins, who are born Brahmins because of the excellence of their past lives and perform the priestly functions; the Kshatriyas, whose *dharma* is to rule and fight; the Vaisyas (Gandhi's own caste), farmers and merchants; and the Sudras, who till the soil and perform menial tasks. The future to which he aspired for the untouchables was to be absorbed into the Sudra caste. His plan for reforming the caste system was to abolish the thousands of subcastes within the four main divisions and encourage mutual respect.

These views were similar to those of Dayanand Saraswati (1824–1883), the founder of the Arya Samaj and Vivekananda (1863–1902), the Bengali sage, both of whom had sought to preserve and revive Hinduism by reforming it. Gandhi thought (as Vivekananda had) that the caste system was what prevented India from becoming an individualistic, competitive, materialistic free-for-all like the West. He believed that caste, like rejection of machinery, was a great 'spiritual discovery' of the ancient Hindus. They had perceived that men whose occupation was settled at birth would be able to keep their minds off bettering themselves materially and concentrate on their spiritual progress.[25] The idea of a Brahmin class (though not Brahminism in practice) appealed to him because Brahmins constituted a group which had 'been set apart from generation to generation for the exclusive pursuit of divine knowledge and consigned to voluntary poverty'.[26] In 1913 he observed that the caste system was 'a perfectly natural institution' which in India had been 'invested with religious meaning' as an 'agency for ensuring self-control'. Caste defined 'the limits within which one may enjoy life'; being content with the restrictions it imposed on conviviality required 'discipline of the flesh'.[27]

Gandhi could not have survived politically in India had he launched an all-out assault on caste. Fortunately, caste in the 'purified' form advocated by him and other reformers fitted in well enough with the belief that the purpose of life was to transcend all earthly desires. Anna Kingsford had seen in caste an acknowledgment of spiritual hierarchy: castes were karmic 'ladders whereby to ascend from the lower to the higher'.[28] Annie Besant had also been attracted to caste, as a spiritual and social discipline, though by 1913, the year in which she founded her anti-caste organization Brothers of

Service, her concern for social justice had overcome her romantic attachment to the ancient ways of India.

Gandhi's support for the caste system, which softened a bit towards the end of his life, was firmly rooted not just in his beliefs but in his nature. He possessed to a high degree the horror of personal defilement which seems to be a fundamental part of the experience of caste consciousness.

The ashram vow against untouchability did not envisage 'inter-dining'. 'This vow', the ashram constitution said, 'does not extend to association for purpose of eating.'[29] Gandhi's antipathy to inter-dining, which remained with him for life, was not limited to dining with untouchables. He would not share food with anyone, even his wife and children, though it is not known when this practice began: it may have been towards the end of his time in South Africa. 'Eating', he said, 'is as dirty a business as evacuating, the only difference is evacuation is a matter of relief.'[30] 'Just as we attend to evacuation, etc., in private', he wrote in 1916, 'we should likewise eat and perform other actions common to all animals always in private.'[31] It seems an understatement of the feelings involved to say eating alone and without enjoyment ('control of the palate') was part of a religious effort to transcend his material nature.

Gandhi also had what appears to have been a natural liking for affably conducted hierarchy. On his fifth and last visit to England in 1931, when he went as India's representative and was received as a distinguished guest at Eton, Oxford, and the houses of the political and social elite, he noted with pleasure how true equality could coexist with rank and station. Had not Lady Astor 'brought out all her servants to shake hands with me'? Had not Lloyd George 'encouraged all his servants, as he would his own children, to hand me their autograph books for signature'? In England, he observed, there was 'a living family tie between its noblemen and their domestic servants'.[32] This was the model he proposed for relations between India's purified castes.

It was ironic that Gandhi had to take on conventional Hindu opinion over untouchability at a time when he was steadily Hinduizing his public persona, his manner of life, and his beliefs.

The critical moments in his emergence as a Hindu personality were the invention of *satyagraha* in 1906 and his blessing of it with a Hindu name, the writing of *Hind Swaraj* in 1909, and his return to India in 1915, which focused his mind on finding what he 'needed', as he would put it, in his natal branch of that great tree which is the world's religions. (The metaphor, which Gandhi adopted, is Madame Blavatsky's.)

In an important speech to a meeting of Christian missionaries at Madras on 14 February 1916 Gandhi outlined his relationship as he now conceived it to the Hindu religion.[33] His subject was *swadeshi* and his point was that making do with what was home grown was as necessary in religion as in the use of manufactures.

> Swadeshi is that spirit in us which restricts us to the use and service of our im-
> mediate surroundings to the exclusion of the more remote. Thus, as for religion,
> in order to satisfy the requirements of the definition, I must restrict myself to
> my ancestral religion. That is the use of my immediate religious surroundings.
> If I find it defective, I should serve it by purging it of its defects. ... Hinduism
> has become a conservative religion and therefore a mighty force because of
> the Swadeshi spirit underlying it. It is the most tolerant because it is non-
> proselytising, and it is as capable of expansion today as it has been found to be in
> the past.

Acknowledging Christian influence, he went on to propose that Christians concentrate on keeping alive the best in their own religion and abandon the work of conversion.

> Quoting again from experience, a new birth, a change of heart, is perfectly pos-
> sible in every one of the great faiths. I know I am now treading upon thin ice.
> But I do not apologise ... for saying that the frightful outrage that is just going
> on in Europe, perhaps, shows that the message of Jesus of Nazareth, the Son of
> Peace, has been little understood in Europe, and that light upon it may have to
> be thrown from the East.

It was to the Hinduization of the concept of non-violence that Gandhi first turned his attention.

That 'soul-force', being immaterial, was non-violent was axiomatic. But the nature of non-violence had not yet been explicitly worked out. The foundation on which Gandhi now chose to build was the Hindu concept of *ahimsa* – harmlessness. The idea of *ahimsa* had developed in India in the context of an essentially passive concern with non-killing as a personal virtue: the Jain monk with his gauze mask to avoid breathing in microorganisms was the emblem of that virtue. Gandhi transformed a moribund notion into something consistent with a non-violent approach to active living.

He says in the *Autobiography* that it was during his South African cam-
paigns that the all-embracing significance of non-violence had begun to be clear to him. Through the experience of political struggle he learned that

he must attack the system without attacking the people representing it – for we are 'all tarred with the same brush' and all 'children of one and the same Creator', with the same potentially 'infinite' divine powers. To attack one's opponents personally was like 'attacking oneself' and the divine spark within, thus harming 'the whole world'. Non-violence, he realized, had to be 'the basis of the search for truth'.[34]

Gandhi's development of the idea of *ahimsa* took him a long way from this early insight. The 'law' of *ahimsa* – the 'law of regenerate man'[35] – absorbed the Law of Sacrifice, explained its magic power, reconciled action with non-attachment, and guaranteed the moral standing of every act performed with non-violent intent. This was all possible for Gandhi because he defined *ahimsa* as before everything a state of mind.

Just as *brahmacharya* meant abstention not just from sex but from lust, *ahimsa* meant abstention not just from physical violence but from even the thought of doing harm. Anger was its true antithesis. 'For one who follows the doctrine of ahimsa', Gandhi said in a speech delivered to a Christian audience in Madras on 16 February 1916, 'there is no room for an enemy; he denies the existence of an enemy.' Even to resent someone's action, whether friend or 'so-called' foe, implied a falling away from *ahimsa*. *Ahimsa*, indeed, was universal love, and its practice the goal of the religious life.[36]

In the same speech he referred to the 'efficacy' of *ahimsa*. A man who believed in this efficacy, as he approached the state of mind from which all intent to do harm had been banished, would find 'the whole world at his feet':

> not that he wants the whole world at his feet, but it must be so. If you express your love – ahimsa – in such a manner that it impresses itself indelibly on your enemy, he must return that love.

*Ahimsa* meant being ready for instant self-immolation in the service of others. If it fell to one to be someone's protector, and that person were attacked, the only course would be to deliver *'ourselves* into the hands of the man who would commit the sacrilege', standing our ground and receiving his blows. Then, 'I give you my promise', Gandhi said, 'the whole of the violence will be expended on you, and your charge will be left unscathed'.

This speech attracted attention, including a critical article by the Congress leader Lala Lajpat Rai.[37] Lajpat Rai came from a Jain family and had observed the doctrine of *ahimsa* at work among his relations: the grandfather who meticulously practised non-killing but cheated at business; the great-uncle, a religious leader, ascetic and model of Jain piety, whose life Lajpat Rai had concluded was, 'according to the best standards of ethics, ... barren and unnatural'. The perverted practice of *ahimsa*, he suggested, was a reason why 'There is no country on the face of the globe which is so downtrodden, so bereft of manly virtues', as India. The idea that taking upon oneself the blows intended for another would infallibly protect that person he could not take seriously.

Gandhi backed down scarcely at all in response to these criticisms, merely conceding that there might on rare occasions be situations in which for some reason *ahimsa* failed to work.[38] Without referring to the Law of Sacrifice he explained how 'deliberate self-suffering' for others' sake – *ahimsa* in its 'active' form – pitted the soul of the non-violent resister against the mere body of the attacker, with the overwhelmingly probable result that the soul in the latter would be 'awakened'. He cited a passage in the Hindu scriptures saying that the true practitioner of *ahimsa* 'so affects his surroundings that even the snakes and other venomous reptiles do him no harm'. He dismissed the idea that the 'active *Ahimsa*' he was proposing could have any connection with cowardice. It was 'the most soldierly of a soldier's virtues', for it 'necessarily' involved 'truth and fearlessness': he was the true soldier who knew 'how to die and stand his ground in the midst of a hail of bullets'. The example of General Gordon, who had gone into battle armed only with a cane, was put forward – though he would have done better to discard the cane. *Ahimsa* was given a special place among the virtues – not displacing the others but rendering 'their practice imperatively necessary before it can be practised even in its rudiments'. What this seems to be saying is that it is *ahimsa* which converts goodness into power. It is the supremely enabling virtue.

In 1921 Gandhi declared *ahimsa* to be 'spiritual *brahmacharya*'. Abstention from violent thought or action created a 'form of energy, an invisible one' analogous to that created by retention of the 'vital fluid': only that could 'truly be called non-violence' which was 'combined with strength and energy'.[39]

Gandhi's many later references to 'failures of my ahimsa', and the fasts he undertook to compensate for these 'failures', make sense once we know that he saw *ahimsa* as an efficacious state of mind. When he spoke of failure, he meant that his mental non-violence had not been pure enough to produce a desired result, or prevent an undesirable result. Fasting was then necessary to purify the mind through renunciation of the body – attachment to the body being, in Gandhi's view, the root of all violence: 'a votary of ahimsa always prays for ultimate deliverance from the bondage of flesh'.[40]

*Ahimsa* was always connected in Gandhi's mind with purity of intention. If he meant no harm, no harm could be done. Later, in his interpretations of the *Gita*, he wove this absolving aspect of non-violence (the purest selflessness, the loving intent) into his conception of desireless action. Judging his own intentions to be harmless, he made his mind easy in the face of unanticipated consequences. It pained him to hear it said, in 1914, that the effect of *Hind Swaraj* had been to stir up hatred of the British. How could this be, when he bore the British no ill will? All living souls were, to him, as drops of water in the same ocean.[41]

When apparent contradictions arose in the practice of *ahimsa*, it was to purity of intention that he appealed. In 1928 he made a humane decision to euthanize a sick calf in the ashram, arguing that the act was not violent because the 'final test' of the violence or non-violence of an action was 'after all the intent underlying' it.[42] The same argument was applied to situations in which he could imagine himself killing another human being. It would be 'the purest form of *ahimsa*', he wrote, to kill his daughter were she threatened with rape, and after that surrender himself 'to the fury of the incensed ruffian'.[43] There was some adverse comment on this lurid little fantasy, but he was unmoved by it.

Gandhi acknowledged to his missionary friend Mary Chesley in 1934 that his conception of *ahimsa* was an importation into the Hindu religion from Christianity, notwithstanding its Hindu name.

> I think Christianity's particular contribution is that of active love. No other religion says so firmly that God is love, and the New Testament is full of the word. Christians, however, as a whole have denied this principle with their wars. The ahimsa of Hinduism is a more passive thing than the active Christian love.[44]

By developing his conception of active, self-sacrificing love within the framework of the Hindu religion Gandhi sought to accomplish two things. He would breathe new life into Hinduism, and he would show Christians that it was the Hindu belief in the oneness of all life that was the logical foundation of the active practice of non-violence – which was 'love'. This was the light 'from the East' which would be shed on the message of Jesus.

How was this light to be shed? In what way was the power of *ahimsa* to be displayed? It would be through India winning her independence by non-violent means. Speaking to the Arya Samaj in March 1916, Gandhi said that he would 'like to use the British race for transmitting this mighty message of ahimsa to the whole world'. That would only happen, he said, when 'we have conquered our so-called conquerors'.[45]

As he rose to prominence in Indian politics, he left behind any doubts that he was the predestined deliverer of this message. There must, he said in 1921, 'be some significance in the fact of my being born in India instead of in Europe'.[46] It was his sense of his destiny being linked to his Indian-ness, and having to be worked out through it, that led him further down the road to a 'Hindu' identity.

The consequences were tragic and he did not foresee them. He thought he could represent in his life and teaching a catholic and enlightened Hinduism; but the communal realities of India gradually sharpened the outline of the Hinduism he professed in practice. Even in 1916, in his address to the Arya Samaj, he described himself as a *sanatani* (orthodox) Hindu – on the grounds that Hinduism was hospitable to every variety of belief![47] But he must have known well enough the connotations that the term *sanatani* had for an audience of Hindu revivalists. It was self-deception to expect the personal meaning he attached to the term (which he continued to use) to be given much weight. The same was true of his advocacy of Hindi, which began in 1916, and of cow-protection, into which before long he was inexorably drawn.

Gandhi emerged from his year of silence on politics with a provocative speech at the opening of Benares Hindu University on 6 February 1916, which ended with the platform party leaving the stage in protest, apparently at Annie Besant's instigation. Other distinguished departees included the maharajah of Dharbanga (the reigning aristocrat of Benares) and a variety of other notables, princely and otherwise.

The facts of this curious affair have remained obscure. Gandhi spoke without notes, and no reliable contemporary accounts survive. But it appears from his own recollections that any number of the things he said could have precipitated the dignitaries' departure: his disparagement of the institution for not teaching in Hindi; his remarks on the filth of Benares; his proposal that the assembled princes donate the jewellery they were wearing to the nationalist cause; his ambiguous observations on the patriotic, but ultimately misguided, bravery of the terrorists; his odd (but typical) suggestion that if British officials in India were overbearing, it was the fault of Indians, who surrounded them with an 'atmosphere of sycophancy and falsity'; and, finally, his call to the audience to 'take' self-government from the British rather than wait for ever to receive it – at which point the honoured guests departed amid pandemonium.[48]

Gandhi may have been aiming to appeal to the students over the heads of their elders. He may have had some thoughts of showing Annie Besant she had backed the wrong horse in Krishnamurti. Perhaps he knew of the furore a few years back at Central Hindu College (as Benares Hindu University was then known) over Besant's demands that the staff and students venerate the semi-literate boy. Besant never trusted Gandhi after the 'Benares incident'. Later on this did not matter. But in 1916 she was a power in the Congress, having entered the political arena at the bidding of the Rishi Agastya, one of the Himalayan Masters, and shaken up Indian politics with inflammatory articles in *New India* and (in 1916) the founding of the Home Rule League. Her star rose higher in 1917 when she was interned by the government for three months, and emerged to become Congress president. The deep exception she took to Gandhi's oratory at Benares completed his isolation from the Indian political establishment of the day.

This isolation, as it turned out, was no bad thing. Gandhi was forced to stop beating his head against the wall of Congress and go directly to the people to find a political base. This done, he was able to claim the position at the top level of Indian politics which had been denied him in 1915–16.

*Satyagraha* was the obvious way forward. But for what, and where? He contemplated offering *satyagraha* over the operation of the government customs barrier at Virangam in Gujarat, about which there were many complaints; but representations to the authorities proved sufficient to get the barrier removed.[49] When the great opportunity shortly came to demonstrate *satyagraha* at work in India, he almost missed it.

At the Lucknow Congress in December 1916 he was approached by a peasant farmer from Champaran in Bihar, Raj Kumar Shukla. Shukla asked him to go to Champaran and involve himself in the peasants' struggle against the European owners of the local indigo plantations, who over the years had acquired a wide range of dictatorial powers. The Champaran peasants not only had to put part of the land they leased under indigo cultivation, and sell the crop at a price fixed by the planters, but were also subjected to forced labour, to various arbitrary demands and levies known as *abwab*, and to large increases in rent as world demand for indigo decreased after the invention of synthetic dyes and the acreage under production declined.

Shukla was not, as one might think from the *Autobiography*,[50] just an ignorant fellow who mysteriously turned up in Gandhi's life begging him for help for the downtrodden. He had been involved for years in organizing resistance to the planters, had served three weeks in jail in 1914, had submitted petitions to various officials including the viceroy, and was a member of the Bihar delegation to the Lucknow Congress, at which he spoke. Champaran (like much of India) had not yet got an active Congress organization, but it was not innocent of political activity. Shukla was part of a relatively well off group of small farmers. He held about five hectares of land, owned two houses, and lent money (presumably at the high rates of interest usual in rural India). He had worked as a clerk and a manager of land for an absentee owner. He was one among a number of similarly placed people who wished to be rid of the exactions of planter *raj* in order to take advantage of the rapidly growing market for food grains. None of this appears in the *Autobiography*, which presents him as a 'simple agriculturist' who was 'perfectly innocent of everything'.

Gandhi at first declined to help Shukla and it was not until April that he agreed to his repeated requests and went to Champaran. A week later he offered *satyagraha* for the first time on Indian soil, when he disobeyed an order to leave the district. He did not go to jail. The government of Bihar had nothing much invested in the preservation of the dying indigo industry and a great deal invested in the preservation of its own prestige, which would suffer if Gandhi were allowed to become a martyr. The local officials were ordered to drop proceedings and cooperate in the investigations he said he had come to make.

These investigations were of an ambiguous nature, for they were clearly preliminary to demands for reform. In pursuing them Gandhi came in contact with large numbers of local people who treated him as a saviour. Many came to see him in order to receive his *darshan*: certain hours of the day had to be set aside for him to be exhibited. Some compared him to Rama, the hero of the *Ramayana* who had rid Bihar of demons, and rumours flew about that rebellion in his name bestowed invulnerability.

There was a long history of violent protest against the system of indigo cultivation in Champaran, and a few weeks after Gandhi's arrival fires were set at two of the indigo factories. He declined to accept that they could be connected with his activities.[51] Alarmed, the Bihar government requested his removal from the district, but the request was refused by the Government of India.

Gandhi's investigations and persistent pressure resulted in the Champaran Agrarian Act of 1917, which abolished forced cultivation of indigo and reduced the rent increases, though they were not required to be returned to the original level. These were significant victories and were accepted by Gandhi as the conclusion of his campaign. But they did not meet the millenarian expectations which had arisen. Some of the peasants refused to pay even the reduced rents and after Gandhi left the district relations between planters and peasants remained antagonistic. The struggle in which he intervened was not a simple one, and the principal beneficiaries were the relatively affluent peasants represented by Raj Kumar Shukla.

Gandhi succeeded in Champaran because of the novelty of his methods and because the Government of India was prepared to let him succeed, up to a point. He never knew how much the local administration's hands had been tied by higher authority.

He was the only person to offer *satyagraha*, and the longer he stayed in Champaran the more doubtful he became that the local peasants had the stuff of *satyagraha* in them. But there were moments which seemed to indicate the hand of God at work. 'None of us could have imagined', he wrote to Maganlal when jail seemed imminent, 'that I should be sent to jail in Bihar, a province hallowed by the footsteps of Ramachandra, Bharata, Janaka and Sitaji' – the heroes of the *Ramayana*.[52]

Gandhi did not involve Congress in his activities in Bihar, and imposed silence on the subject of national politics on the little group of politically conscious lawyers and schoolteachers who collaborated with him locally. He raised money for the campaign from wealthy Biharis, often Marwari businessmen, whose India-wide trading connections, ambition to supplant British merchant interests, and involvement in pious Hindu concerns such as cow-protection and promotion of Hindi, with which Gandhi was beginning to identify himself, formed the basis of a natural alliance. Reporters were discouraged from coming to Champaran. Gandhi distributed information to the outside world when he wished to do so, and through channels which he chose.

The Champaran *satyagraha* gave a tremendous boost to his career. The Indian press was ecstatic. In November he was included in a deputation of leading politicians who met the viceroy and Edwin Montagu, the first secretary of state for India ever to visit it. In December he received an ovation at the Calcutta Congress. As Judith Brown shows in *Gandhi's Rise to Power*, he also acquired a power base in Bihar which gave him votes in Congress when he needed them later.

Champaran saw the birth of Gandhi's 'constructive programme'. Volunteers were recruited for social and educational work among the peasants. But in the remote and difficult conditions of Champaran their efforts did not long survive his departure.

Gandhi lost no time in seizing other opportunities for *satyagraha*. He considered a *satyagraha* campaign aimed at releasing Anne Besant from internment – 'an insult to our manhood'.[53] But she was released anyway, the Government of India deciding that she was less of a menace at liberty than in detention, where she became more popular with every passing day.[54] From the government's point of view, this was the right move. Though Congress could not help but offer Besant the presidency on her release, her inaugural speech, in which she claimed as of long-merited right the leadership of India, and the high-handed fashion in which she followed it up, resulted in her speedy eclipse from eminence in Indian politics. 'India the Crucified among Nations', she announced to delegates of the Calcutta Congress, 'now stands on this her Resurrection morning, the Initiated, the Glorious, the Ever Young, and India shall soon be seen, proud and self reliant, strong and free, the radiant Splendour of Asia, as the Light and Blessing of the World'.[55] By the end of Besant's year of office, only Tilak remained as a significant impediment to Gandhi's advance to pre-eminence in Congress.

Gandhi consolidated his position through two more *satyagraha* campaigns, conducted simultaneously in 1918 in the Kheda district of Gujarat and in Ahmedabad. During this period he also campaigned for the release of the Muslim politicians Mohamed and Shaukat Ali, whose fiery pan-Islamist speeches and articles had landed them in jail in 1915 – the beginning of the process of reaching out to the Indian Muslim community which culminated in Gandhi's Khilafat campaign of 1920.

The Kheda *satyagraha* was an agitation for relief from payment of land revenue after partial failure of the crops.[56] The opportunity to undertake it arose out of Gandhi's activities during the previous year in Gujarat, where he established a political footing through his presidency of the formerly somnolent Gujarat Sabha. Whether the Kheda farmers approached the Gujarat Sabha, or the Gujarat Sabha approached them, was later disputed. Gandhi claimed it was the former; the government was convinced it was the latter. In any case, the opportunity was appreciated. 'It is our supreme duty', Gandhi wrote to a volunteer in January at the outset of the campaign, 'to take every occasion to show in action the wonderful power of satyagraha.'[57]

Like Champaran, Kheda had not yet been penetrated by the Congress, but there the similarity ended. Kheda was an area dominated by energetic peasant proprietors of the *patidar* caste, who were not at all new to political organization at the national level – Annie Besant's Home Rule League and the Arya Samaj were strongly represented; and 1918 was not the first occasion on which they refused to pay land revenue. The *patidar*s were the principal recruits to Gandhi's *satyagraha* campaign.

The government decided that its interests on this occasion lay in standing firm against what it believed to be outside agitation, and moved to confiscate land and property belonging to resisters. Most of the *satyagrahi*s then paid the revenue – which as men of comparative substance they were able to do. The government strengthened its position by showing some leniency towards those who could not pay – a move which also gave Gandhi the opportunity to arrange a compromise settlement of the collapsing campaign, declare victory, and depart. But he acknowledged later that the Kheda campaign had been a hastily concluded failure.

Nevertheless, Kheda also made its contribution to Gandhi's rise to power. In Ahmedabad, where he was involved in February and March in his campaign on behalf of striking millhands, his activities in Kheda made a useful impression, strengthening his position with both workers and employers. In Kheda itself he appears to have become the object of widespread personal devotion, even though people let him down when faced with unanticipated penalties. His chief organizer was the Ahmedabad lawyer Vallabhbhai Patel, himself a *patidar*, who entered Gandhi's life at this time. Patel did not hesitate to advertise his leader's sanctity. He told the villagers of Ras that their land had been made holy by Gandhi's presence.[58] The constructive programme was developed effectively and did not fizzle out when Gandhi left. It remained an important presence in the region for many years, and provided a permanent organizational infrastructure. Gandhi bestowed upon the programme's staff the title 'public workers', which removed any taint of politics from what they did.

Once again, Gandhi did not involve Congress in the campaign. When a team from the Servants of India Society (including Amritlal Thakkar) arrived in Kheda in January to investigate independently, he was not pleased, and was even less pleased by their report, which suggested that the degree of hardship suffered by the farmers was exaggerated. 'Where was the necessity for publishing the report at all?' he wrote to the Society in February. 'When I entered upon the scene, you might well have left the judging of the moment of publication to me.'[59] Nor was Congress appealed to for funds. This time, money was raised mostly from Gujarati businessmen in Bombay.

In the Kheda campaign, all the *satyagrahi*s were required to bind themselves in a solemn pledge, which emphasized the duty of the better-off not to undermine the resistance of the poor by paying revenue under pressure, even if they could afford it – which suggests that Gandhi was concerned at the outset about the fortitude of his principal recruits. In Champaram there had been no pledge, as he was the only one to offer *satyagraha*. One feature the two campaigns had in common was that they did not remain non-violent. There was no major outbreak in Kheda but there was violent resistance to government officials. Compliance with the withholding of revenue was enforced by boycotts and withdrawal of services from the guilty parties – a definite grey area in the practice of non-violent protest which was to attract attention later on.

The Kheda settlement was reached in June, three months after the conclusion of the Ahmedabad *satyagraha*. Like the Kheda *satyagraha*, the Ahmedabad *satyagraha* ended in a hasty and graceless compromise – a fact obscured by the drama of Gandhi's first public fast, which brought the campaign to an end.

The issue was what amounted to a reduction in wages for workers in the Ahmedabad textile mills, when employers announced the withdrawal of the 'plague bonus' which had been paid to keep workers at their posts, instead of dispersing to their villages, during an outbreak of plague which began late in 1917. The plague bonus had meanwhile offset a rise in the cost of living, and its termination was a hardship.

Gandhi had become involved in the Ahmedabad labour situation before the withdrawal of the plague bonus. In December 1917 he wrote to Ambalal Sarabhai, his benefactor of 1915, whose rebellious sister Anasuya had gone to help him in Champaran, asking for a wage increase for the millhands.[60] On 2 February 1918 he met Sarabhai in Bombay, shortly after the announcement was made that the plague bonus would end. According to the account in Mahadev Desai's *A Righteous Struggle*,[61] Sarabhai asked Gandhi to intervene to prevent a strike over the bonus issue. Gandhi then went to Ahmedabad and advised the workers to go to arbitration. Arbitration failed, sporadic strikes broke out, and the employers responded on 22 February with a lockout. Gandhi could hardly withdraw. He advised the workers, who had been asking for a 50 per cent increase, to settle for one of 35 per cent, and when this also was rejected, and the employers offered to take back anyone willing to accept 20 per cent, gave his support to those who refused to return to work.

The workers had already, at Gandhi's request, taken a pledge not to resume work without a 35 per cent increase. He now threw himself into making the strike a success. His goal was Ruskinian concord between employers and employed, all working for the good of all – a state of affairs he now identified with traditional Indian ways. You would never, he observed in one of a series of leaflets published during the strike, 'find in ancient India that a situation in which the workers starved was regarded as the employers' opportunity.'[62] He summoned Sarabhai to Sabarmati, and went to his house, to show how concord might be approached. To Sarabhai, he wrote a letter sadly comparing him to Ravana, the demon king of the *Ramayana*.[63] This was less morally dismissive than it might appear, for Ravana's strength came from his practice of austerities, making him implicitly, like Milton's Satan, a casualty of spiritual pride.

The strike proper began on 12 March, after the lifting of the lockout. Support for it quickly declined under pressure of need: Gandhi would allow no dole to be paid, though funds were available, and expected the strikers to keep themselves through casual labour. In spite of picketing, which he did permit, workers were drifting back to work when he announced on 15 March that he would fast until either a settlement was reached or all the workers stayed out. Gandhi made three statements explaining the reasons for his fast – a speech to the millhands on 15 March, a leaflet published on 16 March, and a talk to the ashram inmates on 17 March.[64]

In the speech of 15 March he explained the importance of honouring a pledge and said he wished to give the workers an example of that by not eating until his objective had been attained. He said also that he had been stung by 'your bitter criticism of me' – a reference to an occurrence of the previous day, when Chhaganlal Gandhi had gone to urge workers to attend the daily strike meeting and had been told: 'What is it to Anasuyabehn and Gandhi? They come and go in their car; they eat sumptuous food, but we are suffering death agonies; attending meetings does not prevent starvation.'[65] (That at least is the gist of what they said.) Gandhi felt that fasting would prove his sincerity, to the workers, and to himself. 'I must', he said, 'see that my conscience is clean. I wanted to show you I was not playing with you.' In his leaflet of the following day he said nothing of the workers' criticism of him; nor did he mention it in his talk at the ashram. In the leaflet he explained again a pledge's importance, and his desire to show by fasting how much he himself valued one. He was not, he said, trying to influence the employers, which would be 'misusing his position and would lose his good name'. In the talk at the ashram, given as workers were responding to his call to stay out, he outlined the 'great idea', the 'beautiful idea', behind the fast. It was to demonstrate the power of suffering voluntarily undertaken for a spiritual purpose. In making this demonstration, he would show 'what India's soul is'. He had gleaned, he said, from 'the ancient culture of India ... a truth which, even if it is mastered by the few persons here at the moment, would give these few a mastery over the world'.

A curious feature of the ashram talk was the interest Gandhi showed in the effect of his 'demonstration' on his two chief political rivals – Tilak and the more moderate Madan Mohan Malaviya. Tilak, he acknowledged, had known suffering – he had returned in 1914 from six years' internment in Burma – but had learned from the experience only 'courage of the European variety', that is, courage not informed by an appreciation of suffering's spiritual value. Malaviya, though of holy character, had not 'properly understood the soul of India in all its grandeur'. He, Gandhi, had now been given the 'opportunity' to provide him with 'a direct demonstration'.

In this talk, given during the fast, Gandhi also admitted that he was 'aware that it carries a taint'. He knew it was probable the mill owners would cave in because they feared he would die. This knowledge filled him with shame. But it had been important to show the mill hands what a pledge meant, and so he had taken 'no thought of my shame'. He was spared having to decide whether the taint of coercion warranted calling off the fast by Sarabhai's capitulation that same day.

Gandhi then made a counterproposal to Sarabhai, who represented all the mill owners. On the first day of the settlement the wage increase should be 35 per cent; on the second day 20 per cent (the amount earlier conceded by the mill owners); and on the third day, and thereafter, whatever was decided by an arbitrator. After a further proposal was accepted that the interim increase should be 27.5 per cent (splitting the difference), the arbitrator got to work, and, six months later, awarded an increase of 35 per cent.

Gandhi's announcement of the settlement to the workers was reproachful.[66] He said the letter of the pledge had been fulfilled and not its spirit, but: 'Spirit does not mean much to us and so we must rest content with the letter'. In future, he told the men, they must take no oath 'without consulting your seniors'. 'He who has no experience, and has attempted nothing big, has no right to take an oath. After twenty years' experience, I have come to the conclusion that I am qualified to take a pledge. I see that you are not yet so qualified.' But in later statements he pronounced the settlement to be a victory for both parties. There was no climbing down, he said, in accepting 35 per cent for just one day, for: '"We will not resume work without securing a 35 per cent increase [the terms of the pledge]" may mean one of two things; one, that we will not accept anything less than a 35 per cent increase at any time and, two, that we will resume work with a 35 per cent increase, it being enough even if we get it just for a day.'[67] Gandhi's conscience did not allow him to settle for plain capitulation by the mill owners. As he explained to the millhands: 'It is extremely humiliating to me that they offer you 35 per cent for my sake.'[68]

The Ahmedabad strike gave Gandhi an urban, industrial base. In 1920 he founded the Ahmedabad Textile Labour Association, the union which afterwards set the tone of industrial relations in the city. Its approach was mild, but Gandhi's standing with the workers guaranteed a constructive response from the mill owners, who feared him.

In 1918 Gandhi became the most powerful politician in Gujarat, and a figure of national significance who owed nothing to any established party or institution. But he was not satisfied. He was afraid his victories were hollow, his triumphs premature. Events were racing ahead of their capacity to be exploited in the service of mankind. By the time the Ahmedabad strike was over he had accepted that whatever had determined the outcomes of the campaigns in Champaran and Ahmedabad, and would determine the nature of the settlement in Kheda, it was not soul-force alone. 'I fear that the people whether in Champaran or in Kaira [Kheda] would not fearlessly walk to the gallows, or stand a shower of bullets', he wrote to his friend the Indophile Anglican missionary Charles Freer Andrews in July.[69] What was to be done? The answer was found in military service.

In August 1917, during the Champaran campaign, Gandhi had written to Esther Faering, another missionary to whom he had become close, that he had been mistaken in thinking that India could take on the world through soul-force.[70] *Ahimsa* meant being willing to die rather than harm another being. But what if this willingness were absent? What if there was 'want of will altogether'? In that case, there was nothing he could do but advise a man 'to exert his will and fight'.

> There is no love where there is no will. In India there is not only no love but hatred due to emasculation. There is the strongest desire to fight and kill side by side with utter helplessness. This desire must be satisfied by restoring the capacity for fighting. Then comes the choice.
>
> Yes, the very act of forgiving and loving shows superiority in the doer. But that way of putting the proposition begs the question, who can love? A mouse as mouse cannot love a cat. A mouse cannot be commonly said to refrain from hurting a cat. You do not love him whom you fear. Immediately you cease to fear, you are ready for your choice – to strike or to refrain. To refrain is proof of awakening of the soul in man; to strike is proof of body-force. The ability to strike must be present when the power of the soul is demonstrated.

Not until India had acquired 'the ability to fight and suffer', he said, could she 'speak to the world with any degree of effect'.

At the time he wrote this letter, not only was Gandhi concerned about what he perceived (not entirely correctly) to be the abject state of the peasantry of Champaran and (whatever he might say in public) their paradoxical proclivity for political violence, he was finding their pathetic demands on himself almost more than he could bear. Day after day, people arrived on his doorstep expecting him to solve their problems. He was unsure, he wrote to Faering, whether his love for humanity was greater than the annoyance he felt at their helplessness.[71]

Gandhi wanted two kinds of followers: a relatively small group of helpers (whom he referred to as 'co-workers') who like himself were committed to getting people on the road to true self-rule; and a necessarily larger group which was capable of the moral awakening he and his co-workers were trying to bring about. The latter comprised the potential foot soldiers of *satyagraha*. They would offer themselves up for sacrifice, not in obedience to a mere human leader, but in obedience to the inner moral promptings that leader had inspired. They would act, that is to say, in response to God's command.

In Champaran the possibility entered Gandhi's mind that the majority of people in his beloved India were a long way off qualifying even for membership in the second group. The experiences of Kheda and Ahmedabad, where resistance melted away under pressure, confirmed the fears which had arisen in Champaran. His long letter to Charlie Andrews in early July, an important letter in which he showed a degree of realism about the unexceptional quality of human nature in India which he was never to show again, revealed his state of mind.[72]

Gandhi began by dismissing Andrews's contention that ' "Indians as a race did repudiate it, bloodlust, with full consciousness in days gone by and deliberately took their choice to stand on the side of humanity." ' True, Gandhi replied, the doctrine of *ahimsa* existed in India. But what of the bloodthirstiness of the great epics, the *Mahabharata* and the *Ramayana*? What of the extinction of Buddhism in India, its original home? The code of Manu, the ancient compilation of Indian legal practice and social behaviour, 'prescribes no such renunciation that you impute to the race'. The Jains 'have a superstitious horror of blood(shed), but they have as little regard for the life of the enemy as an European'. And 'take the Mahomedan period. The Hindus were not less eager than the Mahomedans to fight. They were simply disorganized, physically weakened and torn by internal dissensions.'

Gandhi would not allow to stand even Andrews's point that non-violence ' "has become an unconscious instinct, which can be awakened any time" '. In Kheda and Champaran, people had only gone along with his non-violent methods 'because they were too weak to undertake methods of violence'. Not until they 'have received the training to defend themselves' would they 'regain the fearless spirit'.

He went straight into the theological basis of his thinking. If only one Indian were to realize within himself the meaning of the morning prayer which millions heedlessly intoned, he would be 'enough to repel the mightiest army that can approach the shores of India':

I am changeless Brahma, not a collection of the five elements – earth, etc. – I am that Brahma whom I recall every morning as the spirit residing in the innermost sanctuary of my heart, by whose grace the whole speech is adorned, and whom the Vedas have described as '*Neti, neti*' [not that, not that].

Now he could state his difficulty. How could Indians realize the soul's power, which if they only knew it they acknowledged every day, in the current atmosphere of (as he saw it) servility and fear?

It is clear that before I can give a child an idea of *moksha*, I must let it grow into full manhood. I must allow it to a certain extent to be even attached to the body, and then when it has understood the body and so the world around it, may I easily demonstrate the transitory nature of the body and the world, and make it *feel* that the body is given not for the indulgence of self but for its liberation.

Even so must I wait for instilling into any mind the doctrine of ahimsa, i.e.,
perfect love, when it has grown to maturity by having its full play through a
vigorous body.

This is a good statement, in its elliptical way, of the Esoteric Christian
doctrine of renunciation: spiritual progress comes only through conscious
repudiation of the desires associated with the material state.

Gandhi was explicit in a letter to Maganlal.[73]

Violence is a function of the body. *Brahmacharya* consists in refraining from
sexual indulgence, but we do not bring up our children to be impotent. They
will have observed *brahmacharya* only if, though possessed of the highest virility, they can master the physical urge. In the same way, our offspring must be
strong in physique. If they cannot completely renounce the urge to violence,
we may permit them to commit violence, to use their strength to fight and thus
make them non-violent.

There was, therefore, 'non-violence in violence' – this was the insight that had
come to him. (It can be noted here in passing that Gandhi was often to use
sexual terms – 'emasculated', 'effeminate' and so on – to describe the craven
condition of the Indian male, implying a mental equation between sexual
potency and moral strength not entirely explained by his religious convictions.
But speculation about Gandhi's sexual psychology is pointless.)

To Esther Faering, Gandhi wrote revealing a further aspect of his thinking:
'Ahimsa can be practised only towards those that are inferior to you in every
way. It follows therefore that to become a full ahimsaist you have to attain
absolute perfection.' However, for most Indians, all that was necessary was
to acquire the courage 'to face the world without flinching'.[74]

In April 1918, after some hesitation, Gandhi attended the war conference
convened by the viceroy in Delhi, the government having taken him up on
his lamentation that, being engaged in agitation in Kheda and elsewhere,
he had not pulled his weight in the war.[75] The conference's purpose was to
get support from prominent men for the government's plan to raise 500,000
more Indian troops.

Almost a million and a half Indians served in the Great War, of whom over
half were combatants; 36,000 died and 11 were awarded the Victoria Cross.
The Indian Army fought in all the theatres of battle from France to East
Africa; and it was Indian regiments which were annihilated in the botched
Mesopotamia campaign of 1915–16 – one of the most shameful failures of
British generalship in the entire war. No one could have argued in 1918 that

India – a subject nation! – was not doing its bit. And no one would have been surprised if India's foremost exponent of non-violence had found some way not to associate himself with the government's appeal for more live bodies.

On the eve of the conference the Bolsheviks disclosed the existence of the secret treaties Britain had made with its allies agreeing to divide up the Middle East after the war. Charlie Andrews begged Gandhi not to go. But he accepted the viceroy's assurance that he himself knew of no such treaties, and hastened to Delhi, where he gave his unconditional assent to the government's resolution on recruiting.

Gandhi's action enraged the Home Rule League, whose members were then helping him in Kheda. League representatives at the conference demanded early responsible government in India in return for supporting recruiting, and Gandhi fought this proposal in committee. His own position, as he explained to the viceroy in writing immediately after the conference, was that he assumed India's ungrudging sacrifice would be rewarded by the grant of responsible government without delay.[76] It was anathema to Gandhi to demand a quid pro quo; for action to bear fruit it had to be disinterested.

The viceroy (Lord Chelmsford) must have smiled when he read this letter, as also the one with which Gandhi followed up, in which he made efforts to link an offer to go about recruiting – which he would do regardless – to demands for the release of the Ali brothers, and a request for government cooperation in reaching a settlement in Kheda.[77] That the viceroy did not take Gandhi seriously as a moral force, whatever weight he may have given to his political standing, appears from his private secretary's response to Gandhi's earlier note saying that 'In fear and trembling' he had decided to attend the conference after all. 'The viceroy does not believe in your "fear and trembling"', wrote Mr Maffey. 'Nor do I!'[78] There must have been general hilarity over the note Gandhi wrote to Maffey two days later concluding: 'I always feel that I am committing a sin when I write to you.'[79]

Where his relations with the Government of India were concerned, Gandhi had painted himself into a corner. The position he took in London in September 1914, that accepting the benefits supplied by the state carried an obligation to assist it in time of war, was one he had taken with him to India, and though he involved himself in nothing of a practical nature before 1918, he had made a political point of refraining from embarrassing the British government during wartime. When the Government of India thought he might be useful, he found it hard to avoid being used. Nevertheless, it was recruitment for armed combat, not auxiliary services, to which he gave his assent.

Gandhi generally discerned in the turn of events 'opportunities' provided by God. In the case of his unforeseen attendance at the war conference, he descried an opportunity to do something about the cowardly and helpless nature of the Indian common man, as it had been revealed to him over the campaigns of the last twelve months.[80] It was an opportunity he dared not forgo. How could he introduce *satyagraha* on the all-India stage without more confidence in his troops? The question was a political as well as a religious one.

When the Kheda campaign wound up in June, Gandhi went back into the villages to recruit for the army. His support for the government at the war conference involved no obligation to do this. But it was important to him that Indian troops be raised through voluntary enlistment, reflecting a genuine desire to help India and Britain, not conscription – which he feared might take place if recruits did not appear. There would be no moral virtue (or political advantage, as he explained in his recruiting speeches) in serving under compulsion.

His aim was to raise a Gujarat contingent, which he would lead to France. It would include members of the ashram, and one of his sons, Ramdas, who was without settled occupation, was selected to represent the family. Gandhi himself would neither kill nor harm. But beyond that, he was unsure whether he preferred his recruits to fight so hard they would contribute decisively to a British victory, or 'lay down their guns and challenge the Germans to shoot them', thereby melting German hearts and bringing about victory by effectively disarming them.[81] In his own heart, he believed mass *tapascharya* on the battlefield would have instant results for India: 'if we were to sacrifice ourselves silently in our thousands, swaraj would be ours today'.[82]

He hoped to raise 12,000 men from Kheda district alone – as he pointed out, 1.7 per cent of the population, which was lower than the natural death rate. If we were not prepared, he told the villagers, 'to make even this sacrifice for the Empire, for the sake of swaraj, no wonder that we should be regarded unworthy of it'.[83] The idea of 'partnership' with Britain in a reformed empire was a regular theme. As there could be 'no friendship between the brave [the British] and the effeminate [the Indians]', Indians who wished to become free of the reproach of cowardice were advised to learn the use of arms.[84] Another theme, one which ventured some way beyond the original mission statement, was the necessity of creating a national army for the defence of independent India – here was the opportunity. There were even suggestions that such an army might be used against the British, should they 'play foul with us'.[85] The fiery young organizer Indulal Yajnik, who was in Gandhi's recruiting party, later said that his own aim had been to get as many Indians into the army as possible, with the idea of training them for operations against the Raj.[86]

Gandhi was prepared in 1918 – not for the last time – to contemplate the death of a large number of Indians for the sake of the spiritual regeneration and political emancipation of the nation. He was not in practice inclined to put a high value on life itself. It was better to die a fine death, and then move on to a superior spiritual start in the next incarnation, than to continue living with an unawakened soul. 'No one', he believed, 'dies before his time.'[87] As he traipsed from village to villiage in Kheda with little result, he found to his disgust 'that not one man has yet objected because he would not kill. They object because they fear to die. This unnatural fear of death is ruining the nation.' He was thinking, he added, of the Hindus: 'Total disregard of death in a Mahomedan lad is a wonderful possession.'[88]

He could be harsh in his judgement of the worth of other people's lives. During the Champaran campaign he published an article on orphanages in which he doubted that the case for taking in foundlings was 'ethically sound'. He suspected the practice led to 'increase in indulgence'. It could furthermore 'in no way be proved that keeping alive every creature that is born … is a part of humanitarianism. … Unclean flour is infested with numberless lives. To preserve such flour is no humanitarianism. It lies rather in covering up the flour with earth or destroying it, though either way the vermin in the flour perish.'[89] Behind these remarks lay a set of ideas about the influence of biological heredity, karma accumulated in previous lives, and the parents' moral state at the moment of conception, on the spiritual condition of a newborn child. They need not detain us. The point is Gandhi's certainty that these infants, whose spiritual prospects seemed so dim to him, were best left to die.

The probability of his succeeding in his recruiting mission was very low. Except for a few tribals, Gujarat had never supplied recruits to the Indian Army. Bihar, where he made a brief and unsuccessful pitch in May, had once been a principal recruiting ground for the East India Company's army, but

recruiting had ceased after these units mutinied in 1857; the end of recruiting
had contributed to Bihar's subsequent impoverishment. India contained few
less promising areas for finding military recruits.

Even so, Gandhi's failure was spectacular, his personal humiliation extreme.
At the end of a month he had less than a hundred volunteers. Eventually he
scraped up a few dozen more. In the same villages where he had not long
before gone to organize *satyagraha*, he was refused transport and even food,
and insults heaped upon him. He had misjudged the extent of his influence
– or, as he put it, the degree of his *tapascharya* – on which he had relied to
pull it all off.[90] A few weeks into his wanderings, the British government announced a historic programme of reform (the 'Montagu–Chelmsford reforms')
which would vastly increase Indian participation in government – reducing
immediately the appeal of Gandhi's argument that only through sacrifice on
the field of battle would further political progress be made. To add to his
troubles, Harilal had got into business difficulties, and only avoided prosecution for financial irregularities because the injured party was reluctant to
embarrass his father.[91] In August Gandhi fell ill with dysentery.

All these setbacks and problems were taken personally. What had he done
that they were inflicted upon him? Falling ill was a particularly cruel blow,
for it could only denote a fall from spiritual grace. He referred to his illness
as 'my humiliation',[92] and tried to accept it as necessary suffering.

The dysentery itself cleared up quite quickly. But it was followed by a
long period of prostration, which was eventually diagnosed as a nervous
breakdown, though not before Gandhi had laid himself on his deathbed and
bade farewell to all the ashramites. He spent the last two months of 1918 in
great mental distress. Rajendra Prasad remembered him repeatedly weeping
and saying 'I do not know what God's will is.'[93] He wrote to Harilal, of
all people, that he was often 'filled with shame by the unworthiness of my
mind'.[94] He turned over and over in his head the problem of how exactly,
in reality not theory, his brave and gentle Indians were to be produced. He
began to doubt whether he would attain *moksha* in this life, a prospect he
had approached with confidence not long before.[95]

The political situation in India after the announcement of the Montagu–
Chelmsford reforms in July also disturbed his peace of mind. Tilak and
the Extremist party in Congress denounced the reforms as inadequate; the
Moderates wanted to try to make them work. A Special Congress was called
for late August in Bombay to resolve these differences which threatened

to produce a schism. Gandhi was on the whole receptive to the reforms, but loathed the idea of going down to Bombay to fight his corner in the contentious atmosphere of the Special Congress. 'There are things which are done, ought to be done, only behind the scene', he wrote in a letter which he requested the recipient not to publish. He expected to find himself isolated at the Congress and for this reason as much as his illness would not go. But: 'My absence itself will strike the people. Everyone will begin to ask questions; if necessary, I will state my views then.'[96]

Gandhi's condition did not improve until January 1919, when he suddenly began to make serious efforts to get better. He allowed a doctor to give him injections of arsenic, strychnine and iron, and accepted the same doctor's recommendation that he start to drink milk. This decision was accompanied by much public introspection, for he had taken a vow, in protest against the cruel practices involved in extracting the last drops of milk from Indian cows, never to drink milk. It was Kasturbai who suggested he could accept the doctor's advice if he restricted himself to goat's milk, which was not known to be obtained by these methods. Two weeks later, he had an operation for piles, which, except for some residual weakness, essentially completed his recovery.

What spurred Gandhi along was the prospect of a national *satyagraha* campaign against the government's new security measures, under consideration since the previous July – the Rowlatt Bills, which extended into peacetime the emergency powers to deal with sedition held by the government under the Defence of India Act during the war. These bills were not formally proposed until the beginning of February, but the December Congress session at Delhi (which Gandhi also did not attend) had condemned the report of the Rowlatt Committee which outlined the proposed legislation. 'My intense eagerness to take up the satyagraha fight had created in me a strong desire to live', he recalled in the *Autobiography*, 'and so I contented myself with adhering to the letter of my vow only, and sacrificed the spirit. ... The memory of this action even now rankles in my breast.... But I cannot yet free myself from that subtlest of temptations, the desire to serve'.[97] Explaining himself at the time to Maganlal, he wrote: 'We cannot cease wholly from activity and, therefore, everything we do must tend to *paramartha* [the highest good]'.[98]

In fact, he had not ceased wholly from activity even in the latter part of 1918 and had been contemplating a major campaign on behalf of the Ali brothers.[99] But the prospect of a fight against the Rowlatt Bills meant the

Ali brothers had to take a back seat. By early February Gandhi was fully committed to the Rowlatt agitation and was anticipating 'the greatest battle of my life'.[100]

By the time he rose from his sickbed to lead the Rowlatt *satyagraha* the principal features of Gandhi's political style in India were apparent. He exploited specific issues, first locally then nationally, which were suited to his style of agitation. He relied on and developed his relations with local collaborators. He was prepared to compromise to stay afloat as a leader. He preferred to remain aloof from Congress and hold himself ready to appear as a saviour when the moment required the qualities and experience he alone possessed. Instinctively political, he was never just a politician. He followed his personal convictions in recruiting, striking out in a direction he felt compelled to go. The price he paid for this particular misjudgement was less than what he gained by his removal from the bearpit of Congress politics at the time.

In his relations with British officials Gandhi displayed the combination of sanctimoniousness and obvious calculation which was to keep them on their toes for thirty years.

On a more personal level, he began to establish a claim, which few Indians later dared question, for the state of his soul to be considered a matter of public interest. His concerns about his 'tainted' fast in Ahmedabad, and about his decision to drink the milk of the goat, were aired before his followers. Similar concerns would eventually be aired before the whole of India.

When Gandhi threw himself back into politics in 1919 he put aside the question which had tormented him such a brief time ago: how could he initiate *satyagraha* with such poor material as had been his to command? He lowered his standards, though he did not admit it. He then had to find some other justification for simply going on campaigning. He was to find it in the *Gita*. When Edwin Montagu said to him in November 1917: ' "I am surprised to find you taking part in the political life of the country!" ', he replied, without 'a moment's thought': ' "I am in it because without it I cannot do my religious and social work" '.[101] It was work nothing could now make him give up.

# FIVE

# The Battle Joined

The Rowlatt *satyagraha*, as it turned out, was just the range-finding shot in Gandhi's opening cannonade against the Raj. As a bid for all-India leadership, it had mixed results. India's politicians, for the most part, shrank from the violence amidst which the campaign ended. But such had been the tumult in Gandhi's name that they had to acknowledge that he now occupied a unique position. The *satyagraha* ended in July with a compromise: civil disobedience would be 'postponed' while the government reflected further on the Rowlatt legislation (which was not in the event withdrawn). But by then Gandhi was moving on to other agitations: the campaign started by Indian Muslims to maintain the authority of the Turkish sultan as caliph of Islam (the 'Khilafat' movement); and the campaign against the 'Punjab wrongs' – the brutal punishments dealt out during the disturbances occasioned by Gandhi's brief arrest in April.

Gandhi's opportunity to organize *satyagraha* came when the Rowlatt Act became law in March 1919, in the teeth of Indian opposition, and conventional politicians found their resources of protest exhausted. Breaking the new law, for those prepared to contemplate it, was the logical next step. But what form was law-breaking to take? Most of the Act's provisions were concerned with abridgement of the rights of people suspected of terrorism. Gandhi decided that civil disobedience would take the form of distributing proscribed literature 'which one sincerely believes to be harmless'.[1] This, however, would hardly involve action on a mass scale. Proscribed works only began to be passed out on 7 April. Gandhi chose as his instrument of mass action *hartal* – voluntary closing of shops and other businesses – to be accompanied by prayer and fasting, for self-purification. All this was organized without benefit of Congress, primarily through the Home Rule League which, with misgivings, was transferring its allegiance to Gandhi from Annie Besant whose star had now set. The level of participation seems to have exceeded all expectations (except probably Gandhi's).

*Hartal* was observed in Delhi on 30 March. The occasion did not remain peaceful. A crowd went to the railway station to close down the sweet-sellers' stalls, and when they refused to leave the police opened fire, killing ten people. On 6 April there was *hartal* in a number of other cities. On 8 April the government authorized Gandhi's restriction to the Bombay Presidency, and the following day removed him from the train on which he was travelling to Delhi and returned him to Bombay, where he was released. The uproar then began. Rioting in Bombay subsided when mounted police and cavalry charged the crowds. In Ahmedabad, where it was rumoured that Anasuya Sarabhai had been arrested, the disturbances were more severe. Public buildings were burned, Europeans were beaten up, and a British soldier was taken from a house where he had sought refuge from a mob and killed. A train was derailed near Nadiad, and an unpopular Indian official was burned alive in Virangam. In Amritsar in the Punjab rioters rampaged through the streets and four Europeans were killed. The corpses of a bank manager and the bank's accountant were burnt on pyres constructed from their office furniture.

On 14 April Gandhi wrote to the viceroy's private secretary acknowledging that he had 'over-calculated the measure of permeation of satyagraha amongst the people'. He asked that the restriction order on him be withdrawn in order to avoid inflaming the people further, and to permit him to use his calming influence outside the Bombay Presidency: 'Rightly or wrongly, I seem to command, at the present moment, in an excessive degree the respect and affection of the people all over India. The non-withdrawal of the orders would be resented by them.' He proposed that the Ali brothers be released to go to London as advisers on the peace settlement in the Middle East, and in conclusion reminded the viceroy that the events of recent days demonstrated the desirability of withdrawing the Rowlatt Act.[2] This letter must have brought another grim smile to Lord Chelmsford's lips. But civil disobedience was not called off until 18 April, after more violence, when Gandhi announced a 'temporary suspension' while the principles of *satyagraha* were instilled into the people.[3] Less than two months later, he called for civil disobedience to be resumed: 'A movement like satyagraha, designed as it is to work a moral revolution in society so far as the method of attaining reforms are concerned, cannot be stopped for the vague fear of unscrupulous or ignorant persons misusing it.'[4] This time, violence would be avoided by *satyagraha* being offered in the first instance only by himself. If after his arrest the country remained calm, the government would then, he was sure, withdraw the Rowlatt legislation. But if the government were stubborn, there would be further acts of *satyagraha* by a small number of volunteers selected in advance. These would be people of law-abiding character who understood the solemn and exceptional nature of an act of civil disobedience. They would proceed 'only if it is found that no violence has been offered after my incarceration by the satyagrahis so called or others acting in co-operation with them'.[5] He himself would offer *satyagraha* by disregarding the order restricting him to the Bombay Presidency – a conspicuous act of solitary defiance ominously recalling the circumstances of his arrest in April.

This *satyagraha* did not materialize. Instead, Gandhi sought a compromise settlement with the government. His statements at the time do not suggest that it was the prospect of violence which deterred him. On 21 July he announced that civil disobedience was being suspended because the government and others had warned him that resuming it meant further outbreaks were inevitable. The announcement gave no indication that the decision was taken for any reason other than deference to their concerns – and indeed the government had given him permission to state that the suspension was at its request.[6] He may have concluded that a tactical withdrawal was necessary from a campaign which was beginning to crumble, or over which he was losing control; or the government may have convinced him it was going to stand firm.[7] He damped down the Rowlatt agitation and concentrated on organizing the Khilafat (caliphate) campaign. On 23 November, at the Khilafat Conference held in Delhi, at which he was the only Hindu present, he proposed complete withdrawal of cooperation from the government if the Khilafatists' demands were not met.

None of this conveys the state of exaltation in which Gandhi spent the early months of 1919.[8] Twenty-eight years later he recalled how he 'shook with rage' when the Rowlatt Act was passed.[9] He rose from his bed with the intention of bringing about a much bigger eruption than eventually occurred, with disobedience of a wide range of laws other than the Rowlatt Act – possibly all the laws of British India – and non-payment of taxes. His inner voice had spoken.[10] Political India was not ready for this, and almost every politician of note urged Gandhi to be cautious. After years of wartime privation and political repression, the country was a tinderbox, and only Gandhi believed that the kind of campaign he initially had in mind, or even the one he settled for, could be peacefully carried off. He dropped his most alarming proposals but later said that the *hartal* had been conceived as 'a prelude to a series of direct actions', whose execution had been interrupted by 'Satan whispering fear into the ears of a Government conscious of its own wrong' and causing it to arrest him.[11] In February, after 50 men and women signed a *satyagraha* pledge at the ashram – an event he described as 'probably the most momentous in the history of India'[12] – he anticipated 'a mighty conflagration', which, if it came, could 'but purify the atmosphere and bring in real swaraj'.[13] At the beginning of April, he was 'happy beyond measure' over the confrontation at the Delhi railway station on 30 March, and rejoiced that the blood spilt 'was innocent': 'It is possible that the satyagrahis in Delhi made mistakes. But on the whole, they have covered themselves with glory. There can be no redemption without sacrifice. And it fills me with a glow to find that full measure was given even on the first day and that too at the very seat of the powers of Satan.'[14] 'This is not a bad beginning', he told the crowds assembled at Bombay on 6 April – the more brutal the government's response, 'the better'.[15] Blood righteously shed was the order of the day. In 1918 the battlefields of France had held the key to *swaraj*. Now it was the streets of India.

Gandhi's reaction to the violence that followed his arrest was to decry it but also to claim that *satyagraha* could in no way be connected with it. *Satyagraha* could not by definition be violent but was always a counterforce to violence and served to check it. It was the government that provoked violence by actions which inflamed the grievances of the (imperfectly evolved) people.[16] These were to become standard arguments. Accused in the run-up to *satyagraha* of fomenting 'bolshevism' – that is, bloody revolution – Gandhi responded that *satyagraha* was the antidote to Bolshevism, because Bolshevism arose from 'insensate worship of matter' and *satyagraha* represented the rule of the spirit. To reject *satyagraha* was to 'disobey the law of the final supremacy of the spirit over matter, of truth and love over brute force'.[17] *Satyagraha* by its nature could not be held accountable for an act of violence.

His role as commander-in-chief in the war of spirit against matter on the planet earth led Gandhi to take a surprising position on the most notable event connected with the Rowlatt campaign – the massacre on 13 April of 379 people, members of a crowd assembled illegally in the Jallianwala Bagh at Amritsar, by troops under the command of General Dyer. Gandhi did not join in the outcry against Dyer, but remained silent for a long time, claiming insufficient knowledge.[18] It is true that the government kept the news about the Punjab, which was under martial law from 14 April, out of the Indian papers. But information trickled out nonetheless and on 21 April Gandhi complained to the viceroy – citing an Associated Press report – about the public floggings ordered by Dyer.[19] He did not begin to refer publicly to the massacre until November, and refrained from criticism of the government until the Congress report on the Punjab disturbances – whose production he supervised – was published in March 1920.

There was perhaps policy in this restraint. The publication of the Congress report and, two months later, the government's own report (the Hunter report), provided the perfect launching pad for non-cooperation. But policy was not the whole story. The deaths at Amritsar did not meet Gandhi's criteria of martyrdom. The panic-stricken crowd, trapped in a public space with only one proper exit, scrambled in all directions when Dyer, without any warning, ordered his Gurkhas and Baluchis to fire. (Ten minutes later, after 1650 rounds accounting for approximately 1500 casualties had been discharged, Dyer marched his troops out of the square leaving the dead and wounded where they lay.) In a speech in October 1920, Gandhi announced that 'The men and women who died in Jallianwala Bagh were not martyrs or heroes. Had they been heroes, when General Dyer came on the scene in all his pride, they would have fought with swords or sticks or would have stood up before him and faced death.'[20] Gandhi was disappointed in the people of Amritsar. They had scrambled to save their bodies and forgotten about their souls. His reaction to news of the notorious 'crawling order' – Dyer's decree that all Indians passing through the street where an Englishwoman had been attacked should do so crawling on their bellies – was also singular. 'In Amritsar', he wrote in the *Autobiography*, 'innocent men and women were made to crawl like worms on their bellies. Before this outrage the Jallianwala Bagh tragedy paled into insignificance in my eyes, though it was this massacre principally that attracted the attention of the people of India and the world.'[21]

By May Gandhi was seeking to broaden his assault on British rule beyond opposition to the Rowlatt Act. At a conference of *satyagrahi*s on 30 May he proposed demanding a government inquiry into the administration of martial law in the Punjab, and following up with *satyagraha* if the demand were refused.[22] He tried without great success to drum up a protest over the deportation of B.G. Horniman, the radical English editor of the *Bombay Chronicle*. He involved himself in the growing Muslim agitation over the Khilafat, pressing the Muslim leaders to resort to *satyagraha* and promising them 'Hindu' support.[23] He also took up in earnest the issue of *swadeshi*, advocating not the boycott of foreign cloth (which being revengeful was immoral), but its destruction (which was purifying).[24] This was the origin of the bonfires of foreign cloth which accompanied non-cooperation. It was at this time also that hand-spinning was introduced into the ashram, which had been experimenting with hand-weaving, so that completely handmade cloth (*khadi*) might be produced to replace the foreign cloth consigned to the flames.

Clearly the idea was to keep stirring the pot. In 1919 Gandhi had been back in India for almost five years. He had come through his breakdown and regarded his six months of physical and mental suffering as an account settled. The time for *swaraj* – true *swaraj* – was now. But Gandhi did nothing which was not according to religion, and he had discovered in the *Gita* the reason why *satyagraha* need not be confined to the attainment of a particular object but could – in fact should – take the form of a ceaseless process unconstrained by immediate or concrete results. Gandhi had been thinking for a good while of *satyagraha* as a process first and an instrument second. But in 1919 he moved towards dissolving any remaining distinction implied in it between ends and means.

On 4 May he called for *hartal* on 10 May in Bombay to express grief over Horniman's deportation, the close of business to be accompanied, in the case of Hindus, by the reading of the *Gita*. On 8 May he published Satyagraha Leaflet No. 18, entitled 'True Meaning of "Bhagavad Gita's" Teachings'.[25] This 600-word pamphlet was the Indian public's first glimpse of Gandhi's personal understanding of the *Gita*.

The *Gita*, he said, was a great religious allegory in which the warfare between two families (the Pandavas and the Kauravas, protagonists of the *Mahabharata*, of which the *Gita* is a part) represented 'the war going on in our bodies' between the forces of Good and the forces of Evil – a war in which, as Krishna makes clear (allegorically) in explaining to Arjuna why he cannot forsake the warrior's duty to fight, there can 'be no remissness in carrying on the battle against the forces of Evil'. The same idea, Gandhi noted, was found in all religions, as in Christianity's 'war between God and Satan'. 'To confuse the description of this universally acknowledged spiritual war', he said, 'with a momentary world strife [that depicted in the *Mahabharata*] is to call holy unholy.'

On 19 May he wrote to the educational reformer Sakarlal Dave, explaining that it was this allegorical reading of the *Gita*, which he had 'accepted for so many years', that affirmed for him the correctness of 'the principle of satyagraha'.[26] 'As far back as 1889', he said, 'when I had my first contact with the *Gita*, it gave me a hint of satyagraha, and, as I read it more and more, the hint developed into a full revelation of satyagraha' – though, had the *Gita* preached a contrary message, he would have said that the *Gita* was wrong and the principle of *satyagraha* right, for the principle of *satyagraha* was one he had derived from 'experience'. It was the *Gita's* teaching that 'one should go on working without attachment to the fruits of work', he said, from which the principle of *satyagraha* could be deduced. The time was now 'ripe' for the true meaning of the *Gita* to be placed before the people.

There were three principal sets of assumptions involved in the interpretation of the *Gita* which Gandhi was now presenting to India.

The first was that there is a universal obligation to take part in the spiritual war going on in the world between the forces of evil and the forces of good, so that good might eventually triumph. To Gandhi this meant the struggle going on in every awakened individual between the yearning towards spirit and the attachment to matter – 'the war going on in our bodies', which can only be fought by individuals yet possesses cosmic significance, and is the 'war between God and Satan'.

Second, this war has to be fought 'without attachment to the fruits of action', which to Gandhi signified several things: fighting without 'desire and anger' and being 'the same to friend and foe'; acting without concern for self, in a spirit of love and sacrifice; and – something which in practice assumed great importance – not worrying too much about the consequences of a well-intentioned act, but rather leaving God, in his goodness and wisdom, to take care of them. A God-fearing man, Gandhi said in December 1920, on the eve of the Nagpur Congress at which he would secure decisive support for non-cooperation and control over its execution, 'must have faith in a good deed producing only a good result: that in my opinion is the *Gita* doctrine

of work without attachment'. 'I say with Cardinal Newman', he also said,
' "I do not ask to see the distant scene; one step enough for me." '[27] This
capacious conception of the moral validity given to an action by the actor's
non-attachment to fruits was vital to the preservation of Gandhi's good conscience in the world of political action he had chosen to enter. When things
went wrong he discerned some trace of attachment left within himself after
all, and tried to purge it before acting again.

The third component of the interpretation of the *Gita* that he offered was
implicit in the language he employed – the language of moral struggle. It was
that the struggle itself possessed moral value: there must 'be no remissness
in carrying on the battle against the forces of Evil'. Inaction meant moral
lapse. Conversely, 'a good deed' must produce 'a good result'. The end was
contained in the means, the victory contained in the struggle.

The existence of such a 'war' as Gandhi envisaged is not acknowledged
in the *Gita*. Nor is the notion of moral struggle as a process having value
in itself. Nor is the slightest autonomy conceded to good intentions. The
*Gita* concerns itself with the liberation of the individual soul from ignorant
attachment, and at its heart is an ambiguity about the nature of action far
more radical than any Gandhi was prepared to entertain. In the course of
the argument, all motives for action, except two, are found wanting, being
compromised by desire. These two are the performance of duty and the
love of God.

Duty is that which is enjoined by membership of a caste. To try to perform
another's duty, it is emphatically stated, is wrong. Given the *Gita's* general
position that all action motivated by desire for results is antithetical to the
process of liberation, there is logic in the limitation of action to the strict
observance of caste *dharma*. To do what is expected of one, in one's station,
offers a way of fulfilling the obligation to act (which is universal, the alternative
being the end of existence) while avoiding the danger of craving results. It is
in performance of his duty as a member of the Kshatriya caste that Arjuna
is urged on to the battlefield by Krishna: it is extremely doubtful that the
author had in mind any general injunction to 'fight'. Krishna then says that
to act out of conscious devotion to God's will makes dutiful action even more
meritorious. Knowing God's will is less of a problem than it might appear
because caste *dharma* defines it.

The poem opens with Arjuna agonizing, in his ignorance, over the right
thing to do. Is he really required to kill all his relatives arrayed on the

opposing side? But Krishna tells him to get on with the job God has given him. They will have to die sometime; he is merely the agent of their deaths; and what could be better than that they die performing their duty? The *Gita*'s sublime unconcern with the struggles of the individual conscience is striking. Yet Gandhi seems to have missed this. The language of moral endeavour in which he wrote of a text so bracingly indifferent to it indicated the fundamental problem with his approach. To work without attachment to the fruits of work, if that work is conceived as strengthening the forces of Good, seems a logical impossibility. For how can such work be reconciled with a supposedly superior state of desirelessness, which must exclude (as is made clear in the *Gita*) even a desire for good?

In the life of a campaigning politician, such a contradiction was bound to assume a practical form. When it did, Gandhi glossed over it. 'There is no harm in desire', he wrote to a Bengali follower in 1931, 'provided it is accompanied by detachment. For example we may desire an increase in the sale of khadi but no harm will come from so desiring if there is no dejection in case the sales do not increase.'[28] Gandhi's doctrine of *ahimsa* was in part an attempt to find a basis of moral action consistent with the renunciation of desire. Hence assertions such as this one: 'When doing anything, one must ask oneself this question: "Is my action inspired by egoistic attachment?" If there is no such attachment, then there is no violence.'[29]

Gandhi's difficulties arose from two sources: the paradoxical nature of the *Gita*'s simultaneous advocacy of action and disparagement of its intrinsic significance, and the fundamental difference in outlook between the author of the *Gita* and the author of his other inspiration, *The Perfect Way*.

He took both works to be about 'renunciation'. But he failed to distinguish clearly between renunciation of two different kinds, which might be but are not necessarily connected. The *Gita* is about renunciation of desire. *The Perfect Way* is about *both* the renunciation of desire and the renunciation of self in the service of others. It represents, in fact, an attempt to integrate the two. Renunciation of desire appears in *The Perfect Way* as transcendence of all attachment to the material; renunciation of self reflects the authors' essentially Christian ethic. *The Perfect Way* endorses moral effort, as an essential element of the spiritual life. The ethos of struggle – against flesh, against evil in such concrete forms as vivisection – permeates its pages. And for all its doctrinal unorthodoxy, its account of the soon-to-be perfected Christ's final renunciation of the body for others' sake remains unmistakably the great agonal drama of the New Testament – the renunciation which all but exhausts the resources of the soul.

Gandhi's mental outlook was unquestionably closer to that of *The Perfect Way* than of the *Gita*. But he took from the *Gita* what he needed, in a manner which involved for him no conscious distortion or manipulation of the text but rather extracted from it its true meaning in accordance with the universal religion. In 1919, what he needed was a rationale, in terms meaningful to Indians, for a campaign that in his mind had no foreseeable end and took forms no one could predict, but currently was the struggle against the British.

If *satyagraha* was the practical expression of the working of the forces of Good against the forces of Evil, there was no reason why its use should only be intermittent. In a war which was continuous, and comprehended in itself all manner of experience involving pitting the good against the bad, there could be 'no remissness' in carrying the struggle forward – and no succumbing to discouragement when events appeared to go awry. For the *Gita* taught that 'one should go on working without attachment to the fruits of work'. There was thus no need to wait for opportunities to offer *satyagraha* but rather an obligation to find them where God had strewn them in one's path. A person who 'has become a satyagrahi', Gandhi observed in a letter to the 'Satyagrahis of Surat', written the day after his letter to Dave, 'will always find opportunities for offering satyagraha. How can those who are full of doubts and fears be reckoned as satyagrahis? To be a satyagrahi is like walking on the blade of a sword.'[30]

With the disturbances of April 1919, a new element entered Indian politics: the people. At this point in Gandhi's career, it would be wrong to say that he had 'mobilized' them. They had begun to mobilize themselves, around his person. It was anger at his being laid hands on by the British that got them out into the streets. The Indian political establishment could not help but take notice. At the Amritsar Congress of December 1919 Gandhi was an honoured guest.

During 1920 Gandhi's position in Congress became progressively stronger. To his emerging popular appeal as a hero–saint was added the support, even devotion, of the many small-time political workers and organizers who were becoming involved in his personal campaigns. These 'followers', as Gandhi called them, were often people who had little or no contact with Congress politics. For some, active participation in Gandhi's campaigns superseded a more passive association with the Congress.

The arrival of Gandhi's supporters in large numbers at the Special Congress at Calcutta in September, and at the annual Congress session at Nagpur in December, played a significant part in swinging Congress round to the endorsement of *satyagraha* as the chosen method of agitation against the Raj. Though in appearance Congress was a talking shop for the elite, in practice its organization was very open – almost anyone could be enrolled as a voting delegate to one of its public sessions – and once Gandhi's 'followers' reached a critical mass, it required mainly their transportation to a Congress session for their influence to be felt. When the Congress met at Nagpur, Gandhi was poised to take it over, and did. The death of Tilak on 1 August cleared the way. But it was his capture, organization and inflation of the Khilafat movement, and his emergence as the principal spokesman for redress of the 'Punjab wrongs', which ultimately ensured his triumph.

The Khilafat movement arose among Indian Muslims after the defeat of Turkey, the only remaining independent Muslim power, in the First World War.[31] Confined at first to a small group of politicians, foremost among them the Ali brothers, with pan-Islamist sympathies, the movement gained ground as it became clear that the victorious Allies were planning to break up the Ottoman Empire. The Allies did not – could not, as Christians – deprive the sultan of his title as caliph. The issue raised by the Khilafatists was whether the sultan could fulfil the duties of the caliphate, in particular the duty to protect the holy places of Arabia, if his temporal authority extended no further than Turkey itself. This was a roundabout way of arguing that the Ottoman Empire should remain intact.

It was principally in India, where the sensibilities of Muslims were heightened by their minority status and memories of past glory under the Mughals, that the Khilafat movement took hold. For the most part the Muslim political classes elsewhere were content to leave the Ottoman Empire to its fate and were not much concerned about the moribund institution of the caliphate, Ottoman claims to which had in any case long been disputed. The Arab Revolt of 1916 against Turkish overlordship, led by the guardian of the holy places himself, the Sherif of Mecca, had contributed to the defeat of Turkey in the war. In Turkey, support for the sultanate and its appurtenances was crumbling even before the war. When Ataturk came to power in 1922 he deposed the sultan, and in 1924 declared the caliphate defunct. After a brief attempt by the Sherif of Mecca to assume the title himself, the institution fell into abeyance with the Sherif's defeat by Ibn Saud in the struggle for control of Arabia. The Khilafatists embraced a cause which was already lost. They would have had little impact on Indian politics had it not been for two developments: the decision by the movement's leadership in 1918 to reach out for support to the Muslim clergy, a group hitherto ignored by politicians; and the patronage of Gandhi.

The leaders of Indian Muslim opinion had not previously shown much trace of pan-Islamist sentiment. Men like Sir Syed Ahmed Khan had concentrated on improving the Muslim position in British India, a task to which they had taken a basically secular, modernizing, and loyalist approach. The Khilafatists were a new breed. Romantics driven at first more by cultural nostalgia than religious zeal, they often appeared confused about their ultimate aims but were clear on one point: the British were the enemy of Muslims and must go. Their enlistment of the clergy in the cause of endangered Islam changed the whole complexion of Indian Muslim politics, making them not only more confrontational but inevitably more communalist. The mullahs brought into the movement large numbers of people who saw the issues in the crudest religious terms. Some of them were the kind of people who might at other times have been found provoking their Hindu neighbours by killing cows, or raising the cry of 'Allah-o-Akbar!' when their neighbours provoked them. Nirad Chaudhuri noted the unsavoury appearance and threatening demeanour of the Khilafat volunteers at the Calcutta Congress of September 1920.[32]

There was nothing non-violent about the Khilafat movement. The leadership welcomed the Afghan invasion of India in May 1920 and issued calls to join the invaders in driving the British out. Abdul Bari, the religious preceptor of the Ali family and a prominent Khilafatist, proclaimed *jihad* and reportedly urged soaking Christians in kerosene and setting them alight.[33]

Gandhi was well acquainted with the inflammatory rhetoric and excitable character of his Khilafatist associates. When violence broke out in Delhi in April 1920 at the instigation of militant Khilafatists, he was, in the words of a sympathetic biographer, 'disturbed, but not surprised'.[34] He urged non-violence and moderation on the Alis and their friends, while also (in a style now beginning to be familiar) warning the Government of India of the dire consequences of provoking Muslims. In taking up the Khilafat cause he not only allied himself with the most blatantly communalist elements of Indian Muslim opinion, but compromised the non-cooperation movement's non-violent character before it began.

Gandhi declared himself a Khilafatist in the face of the outright opposition or unease of almost every established Congress politician and the criticism of some of his closest friends and associates. Henry Polak and Charlie Andrews argued with him in vain that Ottoman imperialism was no different from any other. He turned their concerns aside with the assertion that his viewpoint was 'religious'.[35] Vallabhbhai Patel and Indulal Yajnik, his two closest political lieutenants at the time, were baffled by their leader's sudden fascination with Ottoman affairs and desire to prop up the Ottoman empire.[36] He carried his identification with the Khilafat movement to the point of taking against the Armenians, expressing reluctance to believe reports of the Armenian massacres and referring disparagingly to Armenian-financed propaganda.[37] The Khilafat episode has remained one of the most perplexing of Gandhi's career.

It was not just a case of my enemy's enemy being my friend. Gandhi did indeed have a viewpoint which was 'religious', and he explained it clearly in a letter to Maganlal, in which he sought to respond to Maganlal's accusation that he was going around seeking opportunities for public activity, rather than waiting for them to come to him.[38]

> You may be sure I don't go seeking work. Which activity, do you think, did I go out of my way to take upon myself? If I had not joined the Khilafat movement, I think, I would have lost everything. In joining it I have followed what I especially regard as my dharma. I am trying through this movement to show the real nature of non-violence. I am uniting Hindus and Muslims. I am coming to know one and all and if non-co-operation goes well, a great power based on brute force will have to submit to a simple-looking thing. The Khilafat movement is a great churning of the sea of India. Why should we be concerned with what it will produce? All that we should consider is whether the movement itself is a pure and worthy cause. I cannot leave any field in which I have cultivated some strength. My *moksha* lies through them.

The 'great churning of the sea of India' was a reference, as is made clear in the less elegant translation of the Gujarati original found in the English edition of Mahadev's diary,[39] to a story well known in India – that of the occasion on which the gods could only recover *amrita*, the life-giving nectar which sustained them and therefore the universe, by enlisting the help of demons in churning the milk ocean, of which *amrita* was the cream. The cream duly rose to the surface – but also a deadly poison, which Lord Shiva swallowed and kept in his throat for the good of all. What Gandhi thus appears to be saying is that if, in the furtherance of his greater mission, he took up a cause which in itself was a worthy one, the moral standing of his associates, and the possibility that the joint endeavour might produce something evil (violence? – but perhaps in the Khilafat case also communal ill-feeling), were considerations which could, for the moment, be set aside. He was duty-bound, for the sake of his salvation, which implicitly involved the salvation of India, not to abandon any endeavour which was contributing to his spiritual progress. (How the Khilafat movement's purity and worthiness were determined was never elucidated. Gandhi sometimes suggested that the sincere fervour of the Khilafatists' belief was enough reason to support them.)

In an article in *Young India* written a few days after his letter to Maganlal, he gave a further reason for his support of the Khilafat cause – 'to transform ill will into affection for the British and their constitution which in spite of its imperfections has weathered many a storm'.[40] Once said, this was no doubt believed.

He acknowledged publicly a month later that the Khilafatists were not non-violent, and had signed up to non-violent non-cooperation only as an 'expedient' forced on them by their physical weakness vis-à-vis the British.[41] But he was sure that 'the use of a pure weapon even from a mistaken motive' was bound to do good.

Driven on by the urge to show the world the power of *satyagraha*, Gandhi made his preparations for a non-cooperation campaign if the Khilafatists' demands were not met. In March the Central Khilafat Committee accepted his plan for withdrawal of cooperation from the government in a series of stages, beginning with relinquishing of British titles and honours, moving on to mass resignation from government service, and culminating in refusal to pay taxes. At Gandhi's suggestion, 19 March was observed as Khilafat Day with a countrywide *hartal* in which Hindus were invited to join. To organize this event, Khilafat committees were formed throughout India. On 18 May Gandhi issued a statement to the press that non-cooperation was the only possible response to the publication a few days before of the Treaty of Sèvres, which liquidated the Ottoman Empire. On 22 June he wrote to the viceroy that he had advised his Muslim friends and their Hindu supporters 'to withdraw their support from Your Excellency's Government' if the peace terms were not revised.[42] These preparations were given urgency by the imminence, in November, of elections to the new legislative councils created by the Montagu–Chelmsford reforms of 1919. The councils offered Indians their first opportunity to take part in government on the basis of popular election. They were a powerful inducement to cooperate with the

British and the slow process of 'reform'. After some equivocal statements, Gandhi denounced participation in the elections as a distraction from the truly important political work of the country, which was non-cooperation.[43]

Hindu support for the Khilafat movement was crucial to Gandhi's plans for non-cooperation. But it was by no means clear that he could provide it. Nor was it clear that most Muslims wanted Hindus involved in a matter concerning their religion. The Khilafat leadership, however, saw the importance of support from the majority community, and looked to Gandhi to deliver it. Hindu–Muslim unity, presented as a step towards the unity of India, became an important element in Gandhi's programme, though he was careful to make it known that 'unity' – as with caste reform – need not embrace inter-dining or intermarriage. He himself, he noted, 'for years', had 'taken nothing but fruit in Mohammedan or Christian households'.[44] Nor did unity involve being any less devoted to one's own religion: to each community its route to God. In 1926 he refused permission to his son Manilal to marry a Muslim girl: it was 'contrary to dharma' and 'like putting two swords in one sheath'.[45]

Unity lay in cooperating to achieve a common goal, with 'mutual help, mutual tolerance and the feeling of mutual sharing of suffering by all'.[46] It was his duty, Gandhi claimed, to share his Muslim brethren's pain. If he failed to stand by them, he told the viceroy, 'in their hour of trial', he would be 'an unworthy son of India'.[47] He strove to promote this idea through *Young India* and the presidency of the All-India Home Rule League, which he assumed in April 1920.

Unity through shared suffering was a very Gandhian inspiration. And what suffering could be purer than suffering for the sake of someone not of one's ilk, whose beliefs and customs were assumed to be inferior to one's own – as Hindus would suffer if they embraced non-cooperation for a Muslim cause? On 16 June an article on 'The Law of Suffering' appeared in *Young India*, hammering home, for his ever-expanding audience, Gandhi's key ideas.[48] 'No country', he wrote, 'has ever risen without being purified through the fire of suffering.' In addition: 'The purer the suffering, the greater is the progress. Hence did the sacrifice of Jesus suffice to free a sorrowing world.' The sages of old had mortified the flesh to set the spirit free, and if Indians of the present day wished to see 'the Kingdom of God established on earth instead of that of Satan which has enveloped Europe', then terrible sufferings would have to be borne. Mistakes were possible. There might be 'avoidable suffering'. But this was preferable to 'national emasculation'. Even Jesus, in 'his onward march', did not 'count the cost of suffering entailed upon his neighbours, whether it was undergone by them voluntarily or otherwise'.

For the benefit of his Gujarati-speaking readers, the same ideas were cast into 'Hindu' form in an article which appeared in *Navajivan* on 20 June.[49] Suffering was *yajna* (sacrifice), without which 'this earth cannot exist even for a moment'; and without very great sacrifice India would never 'advance'. What were people frightened of, Gandhi asked? Of starving? Of dying? They should welcome such suffering as a test of their 'devotion to dharma'. 'I am convinced', he said, 'that the severer the repression the sooner will the problem [of the Khilafat] be solved.' Only one thing bothered him – the possibility that people might 'make a mistake, put themselves in the wrong and invite punishment', or 'yield to anger and assault or kill an official', in which case 'the pure law of self-sacrifice will be tarnished and to that extent the desired end will be delayed'.

To Charlie Andrews, also on 20 June, writing of the Treaty of Sèvres, he revealed a more personal ambition: 'If only I could infect India with my belief in the weapon of unadulterated suffering, i.e., self-suffering, I would bring down this insolence from its pedestal in a moment and reduce to nothingness the whole of the powder magazine of Europe.'[50]

But Hindu politicians did not come forward to embrace non-cooperation for the sake of the Khilafat. They were keeping an eye on the forthcoming elections, and they were wary, after the Rowlatt debacle, of another 'non-violent' campaign which could go out of control. In any case, as the enlightened Motilal Nehru pointed out, 'Pan-Islamism or Pan-Hinduism does not enter into the programme of the Indian Nationalist'.[51] But while the politicians held back, the Khilafat cause, under Gandhi's guidance, assumed ever greater prominence. Soon they would have to decide what to do about it. If it was a tiger they chose to ride, Gandhi, the prophet (however deluded) of non-violence, offered the best hope of keeping it under control.

Gandhi meanwhile had been active in the cause which was in the event to bring about a Hindu–Muslim alliance and a truly national non-cooperation campaign.

His silence on the Jallianwala Bagh massacre had been matched for some time by an almost equal restraint regarding the government's actions under martial law in the Punjab, which other politicians had rushed to condemn. As with the Jallianwala Bagh, Gandhi gave insufficient evidence as the reason for his reluctance to comment. When he did begin to speak out in June 1919 it was to condemn unjust convictions by the martial law tribunals, whose judgments were a matter of public record. To the embarrassment of his Congress colleagues, he stayed away from the allegations of government brutality which began to circulate shortly after the imposition of martial law.

It was the violence perpetrated by his supporters in the Punjab that held him back. The government's violence he regarded as inevitable, and even, when visited on the innocent, desirable: it was the suffering of the innocent – especially the consciously, militantly innocent – which was the point of *satyagraha* and gave it its power. But in the Punjab it had been on the whole the guilty who suffered. Their suffering was merited and warranted no complaint: their cause was not pure.[52]

This view was to be implicitly abandoned as Gandhi waited in vain for Congress to rally to the Khilafat cause. He could not remain forever aloof from the Punjab agitation, and by the end of May had decided to push for a government inquiry. Failing an inquiry, he would resort to *satyagraha*.[53] When the government obliged with the appointment of the Hunter Commission he professed his satisfaction and fell silent. He did not join the Congress subcommittee dealing with the investigation until October, when relations between the subcommittee and the government had begun to deteriorate amidst disagreements over Congress's conditions for cooperation. There is evidence that the subcommittee's final decision to break off relations with the government in November was reached after a threat of resignation from Gandhi.[54] His earlier restraint on the Punjab had belied his generally militant frame of mind, and now he needed a new string to his non-violent bow.

The Congress decided to produce its own report on the Punjab. The investigative committee met from November 1919 to March 1920 when it published its findings, and during this period Gandhi through industry, concentration and competence became the committee's dominant member. The report when it came out was essentially his, and it was masterly, omitting nothing which might plausibly discredit the government, but avoiding all irresponsible speculation and rhetorical excess. Gandhi displayed his grasp of method and his flair for the judicious understatement. Nevertheless, his condemnation of Dyer and the random brutality of some British officials, on the basis of the now carefully collated evidence, was severe.

Before completing his own report, Gandhi gave evidence before the Hunter Commission.[55] He was asked to explain his practice of *satyagraha*, and as always under direct questioning his asseverations sounded less plausible, his logic less certain. He could not offer a resolution of the contradiction involved in organizing a disciplined political campaign according to a theory which accepted the autonomy of the individual conscience. He had no adequate response to the question why *satyagrahis* were bound by the pledge they had taken to defy those laws deemed unjust by the Satyagraha Committee directing the Rowlatt campaign. He declined to see his seeking arrest as connoting anything but a desire for 'self-suffering'. He claimed that the practice of non-violence eliminated any possibility of mischief arising from individuals following the dictates of their conscience. He discounted the idea that it was naive of him to expect large numbers of people under the stress of political disturbance to observe his own standards of non-violence; it was only necessary, he said, for them to 'understand' those standards. He responded to a pointed question about the legitimacy of *satyagraha* against a democratically elected and democratically replaceable government with a categorical statement of the dissident minority's right to disobey the law. He did not reveal to the committee his belief in his superior ability to hear the voice of God. In spite of close questioning from the distinguished advocate Sir Chimanlal Setalvad about his evident working belief that even in a *satyagraha* campaign some must lead and some must follow, he scarcely permitted himself to be drawn. Setalvad never followed up on Gandhi's observation that: 'In satyagraha the success of the movement depends upon the existence of one full satyagrahi.'[56]

The Congress report was published before the Hunter report, to avoid it seeming like a riposte. The Hunter report in fact was not published until two months later, a longer interval than had been anticipated. But the timing of its eventual release at the end of May turned out to be just right. It followed two weeks after the publication of the Treaty of Sèvres, which fulfilled the worst fears of the Khilafatists. The moment for national unity had come. Gandhi denounced the report as 'page after page of thinly disguised official whitewash',[57] even though it was in fact scarcely less critical of the Punjab government's actions than he had been himself. The time had come, he said, to have done with talk and embrace action. At the end of June he announced that the Treaty of Sèvres and the Hunter report were twin blows to Indian self-respect to which there could only be one response: mass withdrawal of cooperation from a government demonstrably indifferent to national opinion.[58]

With the publication of the Hunter report, and the expressions of public support for Dyer which followed it in Britain, feeling in Congress over the Punjab came to the boil. Gandhi was the author of the official Congress report, however measured, and his voice raised now to advocate the most extreme Indian opposition to government since 1857 could not be ignored. The All-India Congress Committee called a Special Congress for September in Calcutta to consider his call to arms. Meanwhile, he moved to pre-empt their decision by inaugurating non-cooperation independently on 1 August – the day on which the old warhorse Tilak conveniently died.

There is no need to go into all the details of Gandhi's triumphs at Calcutta and Nagpur. At Calcutta, after a narrow victory in the Subjects Committee, he carried his motion proposing non-cooperation in general session, promising 'swaraj in one year' if his programme were followed. At Nagpur he had to concede some points about the way non-cooperation would be put into effect. But these were concessions of a type which did not matter very much to a man whose motto was 'One step enough for me'.

He took the opportunity at Nagpur to push through an overhaul of the organization of Congress, making it both more amenable to central direction and more capable of mobilization at every level of Indian society. The vast All-India Congress Committee was superseded by a Working Committee of fifteen, and Congress organization was extended to the level of the district subdivision.

The governor of Bengal, Lord Ronaldshay, who had read *Hind Swaraj*, taxed Gandhi with attempting a radical transformation of society under the guise of a political campaign. He replied that the two were not incompatible, but 'parliamentary swaraj', being what the people wanted and were presently capable of attaining, was the immediate aim.[59] Some aspects of non-cooperation – withdrawal of students from schools and colleges, boycott of law courts by lawyers and litigants – strongly resembled the programme advocated in *Hind Swaraj*, and as he travelled the country drumming up support Gandhi spoke to the people in language in which it was hard to tell where political objectives stopped and millenarian dreams began. If the non-cooperation programme were adopted fully, he said again and again, *swaraj* would be achieved not in one year but in one day.

In the excitement of the hour he spoke frequently of the 'Satanic' nature of British rule and the enlistment of Indians for God's purpose in the struggle against it. When he was accused of fomenting hate, he replied that his aim was conversion, not destruction, of his opponent. He made explicit public statements – no doubt a little mystifying to people not familiar with their context in his thinking – explaining the religious nature of the struggle, in particular the article entitled 'The Inwardness of Non-Co-Operation' which appeared in *Young India* on 8 September 1920.[60] The movement, Gandhi said, was 'a struggle between religion and irreligion, powers of light and powers of darkness'. Europe today, imbued with 'the spirit of Satan' – that is, 'mammon' – represented the latter. It was 'only nominally Christian', being really wrapped up in the worship of material things. The world war and still more the peace settlement imposed by the Allies, who had stopped at nothing to assuage their gross appetite for the fruits of material power, had revealed decisively its 'Satanic' nature. That was what India was 'really fighting through non-violent non-cooperation'. His identification of thralldom to matter with the operations of Satan – 'Mammon and Satan', Gandhi was to say, 'are synonyms'[61] – was Esoterically Christian. (He never developed a conception of evil which matched the complexity and scale of human malevolence.)

In this terrible struggle the British had a divinely appointed role to play. Despite their attachment to matter, God had made them the rulers of the Indians – who with all their faults were naturally inclined to accept the supremacy of spirit over matter – because, above all other nationalities, they were capable of appreciating the power of the soul. No other people, Gandhi said in May 1920, 'excepting Indians, recognize soul-force as quickly as the British do. This is the basis on which I have conducted my many campaigns.'[62] His study of their history and its heroes – passed on in the form of thumbnail sketches to the readers of *Indian Opinion* and *Young India* – had persuaded him that they were so constituted that true sacrifice would move them – but only after true sacrifice had been offered would they be moved.

It almost beggars belief that Gandhi could have had any faith left in the British after his dealings with them in 1906 and 1909. But it was British toughness he admired, and the way they respected toughness in others. On the personal level, he adored the British indifference to comfort, and acceptance of privation and even mortal danger if needs must. 'I like the Englishmen', he wrote, 'for their grit.'[63] He even liked the Englishman's frank enjoyment of luxury when it came his way, because he could as easily do without it. Observing the English passengers on the SS *Armadale Castle*, which was taking him to England in 1906, he wrote, in an assessment few self-consciously English people would have disputed:

> When he [the Englishman] chooses to enjoy wealth and power, he excels in doing it and he makes the best of poverty, too. He alone knows how to give orders; and he knows how to take them. In his behaviour he is great with the great and small with the small. He knows how to earn money and he alone knows how to spend it. He knows how to converse and move in company. He lives in the knowledge that his happiness depends on the happiness of others. The [English]man I observed during the [Boer] war seems to be an altogether different person now. Then he did all his work himself, trekked over long distances and felt happy with dry bread. Here on board ship he does not do any work. He presses a button and an attendant stands before him. He must have nice dishes of all kinds to eat. Every day he puts on a new dress. All this becomes him, but he does not lose his balance. Like the sea, he can contain all within himself. Though, generally speaking, he has little sense of religion, yet living in society, he is disciplined and observes sabbath. Why indeed should such a people not rule?[64]

He spoke from the heart when he marvelled at the Englishman's equanimity in the face of the ebb and flow of fortune. 'I sometimes feel', he wrote in 1918, 'that many of these Englishmen who go through the terrible strain of war without collapsing must be *yogis*. They would be fit for *moksha* if their *yoga* was employed for a better cause.'[65] The *yogi*, says the *Gita*, is the man of steady mind, neither losing himself in joy at his good fortune, nor hating bad fortune when it befalls him.[66] It was to these intimations in the British character of transcendence of attachment to mere flesh that Gandhi responded.

Gandhi admired from his earliest youth the English ideal of the gentleman. In his maturity he saw it as no less than the social expression of the capacity for renunciation. When Tilak, casting a disdainful eye over the columns of *Young India*, declared that politics was a game for worldly people not *sadhu*s, Gandhi retorted that the essence of all our activity in the world, in a life informed by religion, was 'nothing but a desperate attempt to become sadhu, i.e., to become a gentleman in every sense of the term'.[67] A gentleman subordinated immediate advantage to the higher goal of consistently right action; Gandhi was proud of the gentlemanly fashion in which he conducted his campaigns.

The British with whom he had dealings in India, however, mostly thought of him as shifty. His political twists and turns baffled them. His 'gentlemanliness' seemed too much paraded, too much according to measure, to be quite the real thing. Had he known this, Gandhi would have been mortified. He took British displays of contempt for the ungentlemanly ways of his fellow Indians much to heart. Lord Willingdon's dismissal of Indian politicians, in a speech in 1916, as dissimulating yes-men rankled for a long time.

He felt enormous admiration for the way a handful of Englishmen had come to India and carved out an empire, and enormous shame at the way Indians had let them. The British ruled over weaker nations, he said, because the sufferings they themselves had undergone in the course of their history for the sake of personal liberty had fitted them to do so. This was how the 'divine law' of suffering operated 'in political matters'.[68]

God's design for the world was that Indians' suffering for the sake of liberation from British rule would stiffen up their ancient notions of *ahimsa* and world renunciation and bring them to fruition. British repentance for the evil they had done would spiritualize their capacity for sacrifice and suffering, and in abandoning their exploitation of India they would perform an act of renunciation which would contribute to the spiritual progress of mankind: Gandhi was insistent that Britain should leave India not in disgust or expediently but in a spirit of self-chastisement. Indians and British would then together transmit a message to the world, 'a message not of physical might, but a message of love'.[69] The immediate practical result would be 'a partnership between two races the one having been known for its manliness, bravery, courage and its unrivalled powers of organization, and the other an ancient race possessing a culture perhaps second to none'[70] – a partnership which would take the form of founding a multiracial commonwealth of nations to replace the old British Empire, which had been based on the exploitation by the strong of the weak.

The idea of such a 'partnership' between Britain and India was one Gandhi never abandoned. Independence accompanied by severance of relations with Britain was always to him a counsel of despair. It would mean that Indians had failed to grasp that their liberation from British rule constituted their first and principal step in the conversion of the world to non-violence. If the British truly repented (as a result of India's accession of moral strength), it would be 'vindictive and petulant' to insist on independence. Not only that, it would be 'religiously unlawful', being a denial of the divine awakening in the British people.[71]

Indian politicians never grasped either the religious nature of Gandhi's position on independence or its reach and ambition. His views on the subject were openly stated but evidently discounted as part of the clouds of mahatma–speak emanating from *Young India*. His views, however, were not stated in their entirety. During non-cooperation a French adventurer called Paul Richard turned up at Sabarmati. After long conversations with Richard, an ardent religious tourist of the East, Gandhi embraced him as a soulmate. He was stung when Richard later told a newspaper reporter that Gandhi's aim was not so much the independence of India as the inauguration of an era of non-violence in the world, and that he was prepared – the real betrayal of confidence – to sacrifice the first to the second.[72] The interview created a mini-sensation and dogged Gandhi for some time. He had less to say on the subject for a few years, but was compelled by Jawaharlal Nehru's introduction of the resolution demanding full independence at the Madras Congress of 1927 to reveal that 'My ambition is much higher than independence. ... If India converts, as it can convert, Englishmen, it can become the predominant partner in a world commonwealth of which England can have the privilege of becoming a partner if she chooses.'[73] Oddly enough, the commonwealth idea was being promoted in Britain at the time by those (the 'Round Table' group under Lionel Curtis) who also saw it as a transition to moral influence from brute force – but with Britain in the lead. The anticipated British Commonwealth of Nations, Curtis said, would be 'simply the sermon on the mount translated into political terms'.[74]

Some of the fancies entertained by Edward Maitland about the spiritual benefit to the world of British rule in India may have influenced Gandhi.[75] Without the lost Gandhi–Maitland correspondence – which surely must have touched on a topic of such mutual interest – we cannot know. Gandhi's ideas were similar to those held by Annie Besant, who also saw Anglo-Indian concord as the basis of a new world commonwealth, in which India might have an equal place with Britain by virtue of its being the custodian, through Hinduism, of the great truth that all human life is one. To be worthy of such a position, India would first have to purify itself.[76]

Besant, however, disapproved of Gandhi's provocation of head-on conflict with the British so that India could progress through suffering. That was not how the Law of Sacrifice was supposed to work. How could 'non-cooperation' bring about the brotherhood which was her lifelong desire? How could Gandhi delude himself that his campaigns would remain non-violent? He was hubristically mistaking a distant vision for the present reality. Besant's conclusion was that Gandhi had attracted the attention of the evil ones known to theosophists as the Lords of the Dark Face, who were using him to retard the progress of evolution. Throughout the 1920s pamphlets poured from her presses arguing that it was not through Gandhi that the world commonwealth would be brought into existence.[77]

Gandhi chose non-cooperation as a tactic likely to yield results because British rule depended on Indian collaboration – by 1900 only about 4000 of India's 500,000 civil servants were British. The withdrawal of that collaboration, it was reasoned, would mean the collapse of British rule. 'If every Hindu and every Muslim resigns from the service of the Government, what will be the result?' Gandhi asked in March 1920. 'The British will either have to leave India or respect our wishes.'[78] He put it less baldly in 1921. 'My reading of history', he said, 'is that [the British] do not yield to justice pure and simple. It is too abstract for their 'common sense'. But they are far-seeing enough to respond to justice, when it is allied with force. Whether it is brute force or soul-force, they do not mind.'[79]

The question was, could mass non-cooperation be brought off? As the hour of confrontation approached, Gandhi took thought for India's preparedness. Active celibacy was the key. By this he meant perfect self-control in the presence of the opposite sex. As he put it in a speech in October 1920: 'If you are men who would never cast lustful glances at chaste and devoted women like Sita [consort of Rama], then alone will you be able to mobilize sufficient strength to destroy this Empire.'[80]

Shortly before that Gandhi had decided to have coeducation at all levels in the ashram school at Sabarmati, with the intention of providing opportunities to learn self-control.[81] (Boys and girls, however, would avoid physical contact in the classroom and play separately after class.) Explaining the decision to the ashramites, who were all vowed to celibacy, he reminded them of chastity's physical benefits, which would be needed in the coming struggle. Surveying the little band of disciples before him, he wondered aloud what 'service' he could take from their 'lean and lanky' bodies. How could a person 'whose body is as thin as a stick', he asked, 'cultivate the virtue of forgiveness'? First he would have to achieve the superior physical condition resulting from 'preservation of the vital fluid'. He proposed himself and Lord Kitchener as examples.

There was a eugenic side to the question – which he also linked to the national struggle. He blamed the ashramites' parents' heedless expenditure of semen, which declined in quality with use, for their runtish physiques. He subscribed to the traditional belief that when a *brahmachari* stooped to procreate, the offspring would be of superior quality,[82] and wished for the sake of the next generation to put a stop to frequent ejaculations. In October he issued a call for celibacy to be adopted until further notice by all Indians.[83] The cessation of sexual relations, he said, was 'a temporary necessity in the present stage of national evolution'. When India was a free country, reproduction could resume. Meanwhile, the exercise of 'perfect self-restraint' would produce the 'physical, material, moral and spiritual' strength required for battle. The English, he reminded Indians, were often celibate. Though he did not say so, it can be assumed he would have felt no perturbation had the cessation of sexual activity proved permanent.

His perspective was undeniably male: only men could conserve (or squander) their vital fluid. Yet he expected women to benefit physically and spiritually from the renunciation of desire. He wanted their participation in the national struggle, and was at ease with such manly women as Sarojini Naidu, who was Congress president in 1925.

In 1920 Gandhi was 51 and was anxious not only to be chaste but for everyone to know that in his case sexual inactivity and sexual inadequacy were not to be confused. 'There is hardly any meaning', he said when he called on the nation to be celibate, '... in preaching continence to an enfeebled person.'[84] But after at least fourteen years of abstinence, he might well have wondered about his current capacity for sexual performance. It was a nice dilemma: how could he be sure he was truly, actively chaste, if the practice of chastity was a habit? One solution was to put his chastity to the test.

As he moved closer to national leadership, evidence of potency held in check was urgently required, and he allowed himself to enter into intimate relationships with two attractive women. One was Esther Faering, a young Danish missionary who spent some time at Sabarmati. The other was Saraladevi Chaudrani, a great-niece of Rabindranath Tagore, who accompanied him on his travels around India promoting *swadeshi* and *swaraj*.

Gandhi poured out his heart to Esther Faering in a series of letters, which were published in book form after his death.[85] The tone was indulgent, flirtatious and deeply disloyal to his wife, who was making life difficult for her husband's young friend at the ashram. He wrote of the 'evil' in Kasturbai's nature: 'If you or I love, we act according to our nature. If she does not respond, she acts according to hers.'[86] For a while he was sending Faering daily 'love-letters'. He pined for her when she was away from the ashram. 'Another evening', he wrote, 'has come to fill me with thoughts of you.'[87] 'I shall certainly miss you', he wrote on another occasion, 'at the time of retiring.'[88] When Faering decided to marry an Indian doctor Gandhi immediately fell ill. For a while he lost the use of his legs: 'I cannot understand the cause.'[89]

Sexual attraction was obviously present in Gandhi's relationship with Faering, but it cannot be said to what degree he was conscious of it. He seems to have been more involved than he knew. Mahadev evidently expressed misgivings to him about the nature of his attentions.[90]

The relationship with Saraladevi – a stylish, cultivated, independent-minded, politically committed woman of 37 – involved an awareness of sexuality and conscious efforts at sublimation. Gandhi later said that he had come close to having sexual relations with her.[91]

Long before Gandhi came on the scene, Saraladevi had been a pioneer in the revival of hand-spinning and hand-weaving, and in 1920 she delighted Gandhi by appearing on platforms with him wearing *khadi* saris, designed by herself, in rich and sombre colours which looked the height of chic. Gandhi was used to seeing *khadi* in the form of the limp white garments worn by the ashramites, but he was far from oblivious to its aesthetic potential. Saraladevi was a revelation to him in many ways of a new type of Indian womanhood: brilliant, bold and resolute, yet no less of a woman for it. She was married and the mother of children and ran a comfortable house in Lahore, at which he was a guest. She was musical and composed patriotic songs. She had edited a nationalist journal, *Bharati*, and had been close to Vivekananda. She was handsome. 'Our relationship', Gandhi wrote to his old friend Kallenbach, 'is indefinable. I call her my spiritual wife. A friend has called it an intellectual wedding. I want you to see her.'[92]

When he was away from Saraladevi he dreamt of her. Once he dreamt of her return, and woke up filled with joy. In this dream she told him her husband had tricked her into going home.[93] Her husband was right, Gandhi told her, to call her 'the greatest *shakti* of India': 'You may have cast that spell over him. You are performing the trick over me now.'[94]

The term *shakti* has a number of interconnected meanings. It can mean the female embodiment of the life force, female power, the mother goddess, the energy without which God is incapable of creation, and, in tantric forms of Indian mysticism, the spiritual consort of a spiritual master, in a relationship where both are conscious of but liberated from their sexuality. Gandhi sent

Saraladevi verses from the *Ashtavakra Gita* arguing the enlightened man's freedom from conventional morality: being without attachment, his pleasures can only be innocent. 'You will note', he said, 'that the verses ... are somewhat dangerous. It is strong food for a delicate stomach.'[95]

Gandhi was dragged back from the edge of the antinomian pit by family members and associates who warned him of the scandal that was becoming attached to the relationship. At the end of August, he broke it off. 'It is my claim', he explained to Saraladevi, 'that I have selected as my companions my superiors in character, superiors, that is to say, in their possibility. My progress can only be little. Theirs is still illimitable. They are jealous of their ideal which is my character. ... They want to run no risks and they are right.'[96]

He did not seem wholly displeased with his companions' concern for his virtue: Saraladevi had become demanding. They did not part friends. Later, he told her that he had not been sufficiently confident of his mental purity to continue the relationship. They should now think of themselves not as spiritual husband and wife, but as brother and sister.[97] She was not the last woman with whom he would besot himself.

Saraladevi taxed Gandhi with initiating a campaign based on hate. On the contrary, he replied: '*I am gathering together all the forces of hate and directing them in a proper channel.*' In the process, hatred would inevitably rise to the surface as dirt did during the refinement of sugar.[98] He was clearly allowing for and rationalizing the possibility of violence. Just before his formal inauguration of non-cooperation on 1 August 1920 he announced in *Young India* that the campaign would not be halted the moment violence broke out. Great movements, he said, could not 'be stopped altogether because a government or a people or both go wrong. We learn to profit through our mistakes and failures. No general worth the name gives up a battle because he has suffered reverses, or, which is the same thing, made mistakes.'[99] 'I would risk violence', he said a week later, 'a thousand times [rather] than risk the emasculation of a whole race.'[100]

He appeared unconscious of the effect his own rhetoric had on the crowds who flocked to see him as he travelled the country. Qualify as he might the meaning of the term 'Satanic' as applied to the British government, the message actually received cannot have been subtle. Increasingly, he identified the conflict between India and the British with the immortal struggle familiar to all Indians from the *Ramayana* between the god-hero Rama and the demon Ravana, and described the outcome to be desired as the replacement of *Ravanarajya* (British rule) by *Ramarajya* (God's rule). Such language was not associated in India with non-violence – it was much closer in fact to the traditional language of rural revolt.

Gandhi felt obliged to explain more than once that he himself was not claiming to be Rama. It was the non-cooperation movement as a whole which was Rama, and if Indians purified themselves sufficiently God would work through them to destroy evil. So Gandhi scattered the seeds of chiliastic anticipation throughout India in 1920 and 1921.

His hopes and expectations for himself were in an equally high key. The desire to achieve *moksha* in this life reasserted itself, and his timetable was the same as that for *swaraj* – one year, which was to say by the end of 1921, a year after Congress's commitment to non-cooperation at Nagpur. He had said from time to time that he was seeking *moksha* through his efforts to win *swaraj* for India; now he sometimes spoke as if his attainment of *moksha* was the event that would bring about India's freedom. He saw this happening through the extraordinary powers which were known to accompany the enlightened state. If he could 'always practise truth, non-violence and *brahmacharya* in action, speech and thought', he said to an audience of *sadhu*s of the Swaminarayana sect in January, he would possess 'all the supernatural powers' they talked of, and 'the world would be at my feet'.[101]

As the year wore on with little prospect of either *swaraj* or *moksha* arriving within the time frame set for himself, he wrestled ever more forlornly with the everlasting difficulty presented by the karmically binding nature of action. 'I cannot attain freedom', he said, 'by a mechanical refusal to act, but only by intelligent action in a detached manner. This struggle resolves itself into an incessant crucifixion of the flesh so that the spirit may become entirely free.'[102] But even in November he had not given up hope that, 'If we have, before 31st of December, even one person who will follow truth to [a] perfect degree, swaraj is a certainty, for everyone will have to obey his word as law.'[103]

Formally, non-cooperation was not a success. Despite some locally intense activity, in the end few people responded to Gandhi's calls in the early months of the campaign for return of British titles, boycott of elections, boycott of law courts and boycott of educational institutions. The response to the call for boycott of schools and colleges was at first promising, but most students soon returned to their studies, in spite of the excitement created by Gandhi's appearance on campuses demanding – even at Benares Hindu University, the brainchild of Annie Besant and the life work of Madan Mohan Malaviya – the students' abandonment of sinful Western-style educational practices. 'National' schools and colleges sprang up under Gandhi's auspices but it was immediately clear they could not provide an alternative education that would satisfy either the students' parents or the students themselves. Similarly, the traditional *panchayat* courts Gandhi tried to revive never got properly organized and quickly disappeared.

By the end of March 1921, with such non-cooperation as had occurred subsiding, Gandhi had to find some other way to keep the campaign going. Without abandoning the existing programme, which remained morally obligatory for all who sought true *swaraj*, he changed the emphasis to the boycott of foreign cloth, the production of *khadi*, and exhorting everyone to spin. There was aggressive picketing of shops selling foreign cloth, and social ostracism of people who bought the cloth – neither of which Gandhi unequivocally condemned, though he said after the riots in Bombay on 17 November 1921 that he regretted this.[104] There were huge public bonfires of clothes made of imported cloth. At one such bonfire in Bombay, at which Gandhi was present, 200,000 people watched a great pyramid of clothing go up in flames. In response to criticism of these spectacles as wasteful and implicitly violent, Gandhi defended them as no different from destroying one's liquor store once abstinence had been embraced. No one, he added, who felt hatred of the British in his heart, should burn foreign cloth. He was 'not fit to do so'.[105]

As in 1919, the country was disturbed to a far greater degree than could be explained by compliance with the formal requirements of Gandhi's programme. The Indian masses were barely touched by non-cooperation per se. They were not enrolled in schools and colleges. They neither practised law nor normally went to law. Ninety-seven per cent of adult Indians still had no vote to withhold. Even the foreign cloth boycott, which was enforced with enough success to alarm the British, had little impact on Indian life outside the cities and towns. Yet there is no doubt that Gandhi evoked a national response.

Wherever Gandhi went on his travels around India there were huge crowds eager just for a glimpse of him. The trains on which he travelled sometimes had to stop at every station, where hundreds or even thousands waited to receive his *darshan* – the blessing of his presence. At times he could not sleep for the crowds which lined the tracks shouting 'Mahatma Gandhi ki jai!' – 'Victory to Mahatma Gandhi!' Songs were sung about him, prayers were offered to him, his picture appeared in shrines, talk of miracles worked by the mere mention of his name gained currency in areas where the existence of the Indian National Congress was still a distant rumour.

Thousands of workers on the tea gardens in Assam walked off the plantation and began the long journey home to Bihar or the United Provinces, saying they were obeying Mahatma Gandhi's orders. Hundreds of Santal tribesmen attacked a police post, wearing Gandhi caps (the little folding *khadi* headpiece later associated with Nehru) which they thought made them immune to bullets. There were jailbreaks in a number of places by inmates who thought the end of the British Raj was at hand. In the hill districts there was widespread disobedience of the forest regulations, in the belief that Gandhi was about to restore the people's ancient freedoms; in Kumaon division alone 250,000 acres of forest were destroyed.

Gandhi's response to the people's adulation was complex, but he did not dismiss it. He deprecated the crude ideas which circulated about his magic powers; but he did not rule out the possibility that one day he might acquire powers most people would think of as magical. He denied that he was divine; but he implicitly aspired to a state which partook of divinity. 'Your sentiments are pure', he wrote in 1933 to a woman who said he was like God to her, and asked to be granted happiness, 'but I do not at all possess the power you attribute to me. I too am a sinful being like others but am eager to see God face to face and striving to that end.'[106] His point was always that he was not there yet, that he remained imperfect. Asked why he tolerated people touching his feet in reverence, he replied that the practice was 'not in itself wrong or sinful'. Though wearisome to him, he accepted it because it was the way the 'simple-hearted, loving peasants' expressed their feelings.[107] If he felt no craving in his heart for such expressions of adoration, no harm was done by putting up with them. If he did come to crave them, his spiritual progress would be at an end.[108]

Believing that nothing happened which was contrary to God's will, Gandhi knew the outpourings of devotion he was receiving must have some significance. He took them as a kind of validation – an idea which took clearer shape in the 1920s but had already occurred to him. Visiting Lahore in 1919 in connection with the Punjab inquiry, he was followed by crowds wherever he went. A stream of *darshan* seekers passed through the room in which he was working. He was sure he was unworthy, but:

> It is perfectly clear to me that this is the miracle wrought by even a small measure of devotion to truth and service. I cannot claim that I always conduct myself, in thought, word and deed, according to the truth as I know it. Nor can I say that I always follow the principle of service as I understand it. My only claim is that I am making a prodigious effort to live up to these two principles. And the incomparable love that I have received has made it clear to me that they in whom truth and the spirit of service are manifested in their fulness will assuredly sway the hearts of men and so accomplish their chosen task.[109]

He did not, then, reject the adoration that was showered upon him, though he thought it was excessive (in view of his imperfection) and undisciplined in form. He found the physical proximity of his devotees trying. Indeed there were times when he was in danger of being crushed to death by people trying to touch the dust of his feet. He would prefer it, he said, if they stood quietly at a distance and greeted him with folded hands, and gave up shouting 'Mahatma Gandhi ki jai!' Most of all, he said, he would like to see their veneration of his person transformed into action for the cause. 'The only worship that I ask for', he explained after a man sent him ten rupees in gratitude for recovery from an illness, 'if I have at all earned it, is that the people should promptly act upon any suggestion of mine which they approve of and secure swaraj. That is the only real worship worth offering; worship in any other manner may be misplaced and we should refrain from offering it.' He kept the ten rupees, 'since it was for a charitable purpose'.[110]

The ideal Gandhi was reaching towards was the true touching of the heart from which would arise an understanding of the necessity for action. But he saw that if *swaraj* was to be achieved with the speed he desired, the process would have to be helped along. Touring Madras in August 1920, after declaring non-cooperation, he expressed disappointment with the tour's practical results. Some people had left their jobs and so on, but 'the result has not come up to one's expectations, considering the people's love [for me]'.[111] He saw that only if these demonstrations of extreme devotion – of 'love run mad' as he put it after a harrowing train journey to Cawnpore – were 'regulated and harnessed for national good' would they 'procure swaraj for India'.[112]

He chided leaders who distrusted the people. 'My faith in the people', he said, 'is boundless. Theirs is an amazingly responsive nature.' He would use the non-cooperation movement 'to evolve democracy' through 'a process of national purification, training and sacrifice'.[113] He saw both the spiritual and the political opportunity. In learning to show their love for their leaders in an orderly and practical fashion, the people would take their first steps on the road to deliverance. There was 'no deliverance and no hope without sacrifice, discipline and self-control. More sacrifice without discipline will be unavailing.'[114]

He ceaselessly reminded his audiences of their obligation to 'purify' their way of living. A temperance movement sprang up, apparently spontaneously. Gandhi and the Congress gave it their blessing and organized the picketing of liquor stores. The decline in alcohol sales resulted in a significant loss of excise revenue to the government.

Gandhi saw, as other politicians did not, the potential usefulness to the cause of vast, organized displays of popular feeling. At first as a practical matter, he organized a volunteer corps trained in methods of crowd control. Spectators were requested to remain 'motionless and silent', except for the utterance – at intervals, in unison, and on a given signal – of 'national cries'. The cry of 'Mahatma Gandhi ki jai!' should be replaced with cries of 'Vandemataram!', 'Bharat Mata ki jai!', 'Allah-o-Akbar!' ( to be sung out jointly by Hindus and Muslims) and 'Hindi-Mussulman ki jai!'[115] It was to be a long time before Gandhi achieved this level of control over the Indian crowd. Only at the end of his life, when he began to hold vast open-air 'prayer meetings' at which speeches followed performances of religious music and congregational chanting of the Hindu invocation known as *Ramdhun*, did he hit on the formula which ensured the silent attention of an enthusiastic multitude. But he saw the potential of music as a form of crowd control in 1920. 'Music means rhythm, order. Its effect is electrical. It immediately soothes.' He recommended that boy scouts and service organizations 'make compulsory a proper singing in company of national songs' and that the best musicians perform at Congress gatherings and teach 'mass music'.[116]

Gandhi's political associates regularly exploited his deification by the masses. In Champaran in 1917 local leaders had encouraged the peasants' millenarian beliefs about him. In Kheda, Patel had not been above invoking the sacred. Shahid Amin has shown how Gandhi's workers in Gujarat in 1921–22 exploited the peasants' willingness to see him as a saviour.[117] In 1928 a Gandhian agitator in Bardoli presented him to a local tribal group as a new god in their traditional pantheon, come from Africa to save them.[118] Not all of this was cynically done: some of Gandhi's closest associates, people of education and experience, came to think of him as divine, or at least not quite human. Sushila Nayar, his doctor, disciple and biographer, told Ved Mehta long after his death that: 'He was a god. I have always been drawn to the supernatural.' By then she was a devotee of Satya Sai Baba, another god incarnate.[119] Mahadev Desai, upon seeing the room in which Gandhi was born, experienced its *darshan* and reflected on how God 'had sent Bapuji down to the earth specially to remove the intense darkness that prevails now'.[120]

In Bihar in 1921 Gandhi acknowledged that people were talking of him as an *avatar*. But he told his audience that *avatar*s – God's 'special messengers on earth, upon whom the effulgence or the glory of God specially shines' – only appeared after people had purified themselves 'by hard, strenuous work on right lines'.[121] An *avatar* was recognized as such through the acclamation of the just. The moral progress of society and the full revelation of the *avatar* thus went hand in hand.

Unrest (to employ the classic British term) in 1921 spread beyond grievances directly connected with foreign rule. The expectations created by the arrival on the national political scene of a holy man calling for the establishment of *Ramarajya* could not be contained within the bounds of a programme for the removal of British rule. For many Indians, *Ramarajya* would only arrive when they were freed from exploitation by other Indians. In the United Provinces and Bihar, and in Malabar, there were serious disturbances when the non-cooperation campaign set a match to existing local conflicts.

In the United Provinces and Bihar the non-cooperation campaign became entangled with the Kisan Sabha (Cultivators' Association) movement, which had grown up to demand agrarian reform.[122] The atmosphere of 1920 and 1921 emboldened the Kisan Sabhas and the movement spread in an unorganized way to much larger numbers of peasants. At Rae Bareli early in January 1921 thousands of armed men – armed, that is to say, not with firearms, which were prohibited, but with spears, axes, stones and bricks – raged through the district robbing moneylenders, merchants, and any others identified with their misery, and attacked the police. In Fyzabad district bands 500-strong roamed from one estate to another destroying property and intimidating landlords. Local officials reported that Congress organizers had been in the area promising people that if they gave money to Gandhi's Tilak Swaraj Fund, Gandhi would shortly bring *swaraj*, and tenants would then be free from eviction and the landless would be given land.[123] In March there was a pitched battle between rioters and police in which the Rae Bareli police station was set afire and rioters sustained heavy casualties from police firing. Among the leaders who sprang up were 'babas', or holy men, who sometimes claimed to be acting for Gandhi, sometimes were actually confused with Gandhi by the local population. There was even a bona fide local agent of Gandhi who became involved in the movement, was styled 'mahatma', and went on a hunger strike at the local police station after his arrest.

One of the demands of the Kisan Sabhas was the restoration of the traditional village courts, the *panchayats*. Gandhi also was calling for *panchayats* to be set up, as part of the constructive side of non-cooperation which aimed at taking Indian society back to its pre-colonial state. It was understandable that peasant radicals and revolutionaries thought Gandhi might be their man. But Gandhi quickly dissociated himself from the Kisan Sabhas, as did Jawaharlal Nehru and other Congressmen who had at first shown sympathy with them. The problem was not just the movement's violence but its obviously uncontrollable nature, and the gaping hole it opened up in the facade of Indian unity against foreign rule. Gandhi found its stridency offensive. He had a deep horror of Indians demanding their due from other Indians. Like his campaigns against the British, the campaigns he undertook against social injustice in India were meant to get the wrongdoer to make a voluntary, heartfelt concession. It was violence to do otherwise than respect a man's capacity for sincere reform.

The Kisan Sabha outbursts showed how easily a Gandhian campaign could become enmeshed with a local protest movement of a radically different type. The reason was Gandhi's resemblance to the saviours who periodically arose in rural India to lead the downtrodden to the promised land. Even his demands for 'purification', in the form of giving up alcohol, *bhang* and tobacco, would not have been novel. Oppressed groups in India had often tried to raise their status by giving up such habits and adopting the more rigorous lifestyle of the upper castes. In one remarkable development in south Gujarat in 1922, local Gandhians managed to gain such influence over a spirit possession movement which had arisen in a tribal group that the divine spirit's original commands – to desist from drinking toddy and eating meat, and practise higher standards of both personal and public hygiene – were supplemented by commands to boycott foreign cloth and wear *khadi*. On one occasion Vallabhbhai Patel and Kasturbai Gandhi (Gandhi himself was by then in jail) arrived to address an assembly of 20,000 tribals and convey Gandhi's desires to them directly. When they tried to speak the spirit mediums went into a state of mass possession, wagging their heads and crying 'garam, garam, garam!' (hot, hot, hot!) – the appropriate response to a potent manifestation of the divine spirit's presence among them.[124]

An even more serious disturbance than those in the United Provinces and Bihar was the rebellion of the Moplah community in Malabar in the summer of 1921.

The Moplahs were poor Muslim cultivators, descended originally from Arab traders of the ninth century, with a tradition stretching back almost a hundred years of violent uprisings against their Hindu landlords. These land-lords had formerly been rent collectors, and had been given what amounted to proprietary rights of the most arbitrary character by the British administra-tion, which saw them as a bulwark of its authority. The Moplah uprisings – of which there were 31 in the years between 1836 and 1898 – were of a distinctive character. Thirty or so men would gather together, undertake a period of ritual cleansing and devotional exercises, divorce their wives, put on the white robes of martyrdom, and go forth to deal with their oppressors. Afterwards they would confront the police and die fighting.

The outbreak of 1921 was more serious. Around 600 Hindus and – according to wildly diverging official and unofficial estimates – between 2,000 and 10,000 Moplahs died. Over 2,000 Hindus were forcibly converted to Islam. It took six months to put down the rebellion, and afterwards nearly 200 Moplahs were hanged. There has been controversy over the causes of the outbreak.[125] Presumably both social discontents and religious feelings were involved – among the Moplahs they could not be disentangled. But in the early months of 1921 Congress became active in Malabar organizing support for non-cooperation, and the religious leader of the Moplahs, who was president of the Malabar Khilafat Committee, publicly pledged his support. A tenants' conference then called for non-cooperation against the landlords. At that point the local administration decided to show the iron hand. Meetings were banned, leaders arrested, and a subsequent demonstration met by soldiers with fixed bayonets. The full-scale rising which followed was initially against the British but soon took on an anti-Hindu character. There seems no doubt that Congress propaganda, and, as the summer wore on, rumours that British rule was collapsing in the face of non-cooperation, contributed to the violence.

Gandhi's reaction was ambiguous.[126] He did not consider calling off non-cooperation. He condemned the violence but praised the bravery of the Moplahs. He acknowledged that non-cooperators in Malabar were not 'in full control' of the non-cooperation movement, but declined to accept any responsibility for the outbreak. It was not non-cooperation, he said, but the government that was to blame – a charge which was lent weight by the administration's heavyhandedness and refusal to allow Gandhi and others into the area to try to calm the people down. The government, Gandhi pointed out, 'could have avoided the trouble by settling the Khilafat question'. He admitted that the Moplahs had not absorbed the message of non-violence: 'A change of heart has not been brought about in them to such an extent that they will never resort to violence.' Their violence, he said, 'impedes our progress'.

The failure of the Hindus to die resisting forced conversion distressed Gandhi more than the Moplahs' resort to violence. 'What was the more detestable', he asked, 'the ignorant fanaticism of the Moplah brother, or the cowardliness of the Hindu brother who helplessly muttered the Islamic formula or allowed his tuft of hair to be cut or his vest to be changed?' Bad as 'the Moplah madness' was, 'the fact of others having submitted to the madness' was 'worse'. 'Let me not be misunderstood', Gandhi said; 'I want both the Hindu and Mussulmans to cultivate the cool courage to die without killing.' But it was better 'to cultivate the art of killing and being killed' than to be a coward. The man who failed to stand up to violence was in his heart violent. He fled because he had 'not the courage to be killed in the act of killing'. Once again, the Hindus had let Gandhi down.

One of Gandhi's hopes for the communal alliance created in the Khilafat campaign had been that it would infuse the whole national movement with manly vigour. Despite the trouble they gave him, Gandhi relished his public appearances with the Ali brothers, who reliably proclaimed their willingness to die for their religion. But the Moplah rebellion put an end to his hopes for Hindu–Muslim unity. The fear and distrust aroused in the Hindus by the *furor religiosus* of the Moplahs gave a shot in the arm to the Arya Samaj's *shuddhi* movement for the reconversion of Indian Muslims, which in turn encouraged Muslim separatism. Once Gandhi's campaign against the British penetrated to the level where Muslim peasants saw oppression personified every day in the shape of Hindu landlords backed by the British courts – or, as happened to be the case with the Hindu Kisan Sabhas of the United Provinces, Muslim and Sikh landlords backed by the British courts – the fragility of the alliance was revealed.

Gandhi himself contributed to the heightening of communal consciousness by an over-clever campaign beginning at the end of 1920 to link noncooperation with cow protection. The aim was to stiffen the Hindus for the struggle against the British by reminding them of the British love of beef – 'Whereas Muslims slaughter cows only occasionally for beef, the English cannot do without it for a single day'[127] – while continuing to suggest to Muslims, as he had been doing since involving himself with them over the Khilafat, that ceasing to kill cows would be a way to show their appreciation of Hindu support. Gandhi's rhetoric took flight. So long as a single cow was being killed in India, he declared to a Hindu audience in January 1921, 'my very flesh and muscles and blood turn into water. I am going through the necessary training for protecting the cow, doing *tapascharya* and acquiring spiritual potency to do a great many things, and I shall die with the holy message of cow-protection on my lips.'[128] At a conference of untouchables in April he announced that 'Two of the strongest desires that keep me in flesh and bone are the emancipation of the untouchables and the protection of the cow. When these two desires are fulfilled there is swaraj, and therein lies my own *moksha*.'[129]

It was only in Malabar and the United Provinces and Bihar that violence related to the non-cooperation movement occurred on a large scale. But there were violent incidents directly connected with the campaign throughout the country. One of the ugliest was at Melagaon in April, when a police subinspector and four constables were killed by non-cooperators enraged by the arrest and imprisonment of some Khilafat workers. Gandhi's reaction was mild. He condemned the murders as an 'unworthy act' which had 'definitely harmed our struggle' and would 'delay the coming of swaraj', and prescribed 'atonement' in the form of confession and acceptance of punishment where applicable, an end to inflammatory speeches and irresponsible agitation, and a sincere effort at self-purification – giving up 'harmful addictions', discarding foreign cloth, and spinning.[130] There was no suggestion that the campaign had been so tarnished it would have to be abandoned. Until February of the following year, when he called off civil disobedience following the murder of policemen at Chauri Chaura, Gandhi consistently interpreted incidents involving violence, intimidation or abuse by non-cooperators as 'setbacks' – events whose effect was not to invalidate the campaign but to diminish the accumulated force of non-violence. 'We would have all power in our hands today', he said in August, 'if we had, in thought, action and speech, remained peaceful, respectful and humble towards all our opponents.' A non-violent campaign was the political analogue of an individual's quest for spiritual perfection. It involved error and did not stop because errors were made but continued after corrective measures (dispassionate analysis, 'atonement') were taken. Non-violence was 'like the vital fluid', a 'form of energy', which had to be built up to the level at which it had a decisive influence on events.[131]

Gandhi consistently overestimated the extent to which non-violence, even of an 'expedient' nature, was accepted by the people. He would return from his tours convinced that his rapturous reception meant that his message in its entirety was getting across, and India was now ready for a non-violent assault on British rule. He began to think that it was the masses who understood him best. Their lives were 'more righteous than ours', and they knew that *swaraj* meant 'the establishment of the Kingdom of Righteousness on earth'.[132] When violence occurred he hesitated to say at what level it became, in practice, incompatible with his general aims and principles. He concentrated on keeping up the momentum of the campaign in the hope that on balance the forces of non-violence would prevail.

The Government of India bided its time in responding to non-cooperation. It feared a national uprising if Gandhi or other prominent leaders were arrested, and through most of 1921 its reaction was restrained. But it made no political concessions.

By September the campaign was in danger of losing its focus altogether and degenerating into a general state of disorder which the government might legitimately act to contain. At this point, it was the Ali brothers who fanned the campaign back into life. At a Khilafat conference in the second week of July a resolution was passed, with Mohamed Ali in the chair, demanding that Muslims not serve in the armed forces. Gandhi had all along seen refusal to serve as one of the final stages of non-cooperation. But the indifferent success of non-cooperation in its early stages had not augured well for such an open challenge to government authority. It was not until the Alis were arrested on 14 September that Gandhi took the plunge and announced that it was a sin for any Indian, Muslim or Hindu, to serve in the Indian Army.[133] On 4 October he and 46 other leaders issued a manifesto proclaiming that it was 'the duty of every Indian soldier and civilian to sever his connection with the Government and find some other means of livelihood'.[134] In his speeches Gandhi invited the government to arrest him for sedition. But it did not. On 4

November he announced his intention to initiate civil disobedience, including non-payment of taxes, in a selected district of Gujarat. Plans were made for *hartal*s, bonfires of foreign cloth, and complete boycott of all celebrations during the visit of the Prince of Wales to India, which was to begin on 17 November.

This was a period of despondency for Gandhi. There was still no sign of any concession from the British government. There was no response to the call to leave the army. The foreign cloth boycott had begun to lose momentum. But he saw no other way to go but forward. The risks involved in starting civil disobedience – actual breaking of the law – in the current state of the country, with non-cooperation fizzled out but violence in the air, were too obvious to ignore. He decided to limit it to an area he felt he could prepare and control. He pushed through the Congress Working Committee, against opposition, the requirement that all civil resisters would have sincerely to embrace non-violence and Hindu–Muslim unity, forswear untouchability, spin, and wear *khadi*. To avoid action had no merit; the consequences of action seemed increasingly uncertain.

Gandhi began publicly to question whether, if *swaraj* had not come by 31 December, he would survive. He was 'likely to be pained so deeply that this body may perish'. Should he live, he would 'retire to a solitary place'. His 'remaining alive, therefore, or continuing to live in society' depended on 'the success of swadeshi'.[135] In response to pleas that he not commit suicide, an article appeared in *Young India* on 17 November bemoaning his 'imperfec-tions' – were he perfect, he said, he could fulfil all his aspirations for India 'by the force of unchallengeable Truth in me' – and explaining that his plan was to 'kneel down before my Maker and ask him to take away this useless body and make me a fitter instrument of service'.

Perhaps sensing that a request to be taken away from this life if he failed to liberate India by New Year's Eve suggested attachment to the fruits of action, he added that he had 'but shadowed forth my intense longing to lose myself in the Eternal and become merely a lump of clay in the Potter's divine hands so that my service may become more certain because uninterrupted by the baser self in me'.[136] Whatever this meant to the readers of *Young India*, it meant to Gandhi a supremely efficacious act of renunciation.

On the day this article appeared, the Prince of Wales arrived in Bombay. A crowd consisting mostly of Europeans, Eurasians and Parsis cheered him off the boat and along the road to Government House. Gandhi meanwhile was in another part of Bombay addressing a much bigger crowd, exhorting them to remain non-violent but at the same time reminding them that they would never get *swaraj* until they were prepared to die for it.[137] Hostility to the visit was widespread, and several thousand millworkers left work and rioted, attacking Parsis, Eurasians and Europeans, stripping people wearing foreign cloth, and burning wine shops (which were usually owned by Parsis). 'We have had a foretaste of swaraj. I have been put to shame', Gandhi wrote that night to two of the organizers who were preparing Bardoli district in Gujarat for civil disobedience. If the riot 'turns more violent' – six policeman, he noted, had been killed – the start of civil disobedience, which was set for 23 November, would have to be postponed.[138]

The rioting continued for five days, with attack and counter-attack by the different communities. Parsis went round beating up people wearing *khadi*. Europeans took potshots at Indian passers-by. Gandhi went immediately to some of the affected areas and remonstrated with the crowds, but then did not venture out again for the duration of the riots. Shaken, he agonized that the 'power' of his *ahimsa* had deserted him. His humiliation was keen that volunteers were at his behest out in the streets trying to bring peace to the city, while he remained indoors. Yet what, he asked himself, was he to do? 'If I allowed myself to be torn to pieces by justly incensed Parsis or Christians, I would only give rise to greater bloodshed. Whilst as a soldier I must avoid no unavoidable risk, I must not recklessly run the risk of being killed.' He decided to fast. 'If I may not give myself to be killed through human agency, I must give myself to God to be taken away by refusing to eat till He heard my prayer.'[139] The fast began on 17 November and ended on 21 November as the city returned to normal. No more was heard of perishing through sheer despair. Years later his recollection was vivid of how he had sat in his room in Bombay with people 'shouting why I was not coming out', of how he had felt extreme reluctance to go into the disturbed areas, how he had arrived at the scene of rioting with fear and trembling and pounding heart, how urgently he had wanted to go home. Had there been 'real love in my heart', he said, and 'a feeling of oneness', he would have overcome fear.[140]

Civil disobedience was postponed after the Bombay riots until such time as Gandhi could be sure the country was ready for it. 'If you want to win swaraj this year, despite Bombay's error', he told the civil resisters awaiting his call in Bardoli, 'you will have to bring about a far higher degree of self-purification than you have done so far.'[141] This was on 24 November, leaving not much time for purification to be accomplished. But it was not being ruled out.

The Government of India then came to Gandhi's rescue. The viceroy, Lord Reading, under increasing pressure to be firm, invoked the Criminal Law Amendment Act and the Seditious Meetings Act, and the long anticipated crackdown began. A whole range of activities tolerated up to that point became illegal – including wearing 'Gandhi caps' – and the British began to fill the jails. Leaders were not spared. Motilal and Jawaharlal Nehru, Lala Lajpat Rai and C.R. Das were arrested early in December. Das's wife, sister and niece were arrested for selling *khadi* – an event which caused Gandhi particular joy.

Eyewitness accounts of Gandhi at this time testify to the complete transformation in his mood as reports of the arrests came in.[142] 'His whole frame', remembered the ashramite Krishnadas, 'seemed to be tingling with joy.' The 'setback' represented by the Bombay riots, he told the members of the ashram, was now overcome: 'Our victory is certain, there is no more cause for fear. By God's providence the Government have set their foot in the trap, and they are bound either to bend or to break.' 'He serves best who suffers most', he announced in *Young India*.[143]

Scenting victory, he now with his usual sincerity shifted ground. The issue, he said, was no longer the Khilafat or the Punjab wrongs, but government repression – the 'unsexing process'.[144] He rejected a proposal for a round-table conference floated by the viceroy and a group of Moderate politicians, observing that such a conference would only be useful when the government had 'tried the non-co-operators to its satisfaction and measured their strength in quantity and quality'.[145] He was in no mood to talk when the real campaign – as it appeared – had just begun.

On 11 December Gandhi announced in *Navajivan* that purification was now sufficiently advanced in Bardoli that 'within a very short time' the people would be 'completely fit for offering civil disobedience'.[146] *Swaraj* by the end of December was acknowledged to be an unrealistic target; the campaign would have to continue into the following year. Civil disobedience would begin in Bardoli on 12 February.

By the end of December thousands had been arrested and volunteers continued to come forward to court imprisonment for violating the sedition laws. Harilal Gandhi was among those arrested. But Gandhi was now feeling that imprisonment was not enough: only death could meet the case. He no longer, he said on 31 January, had any desire to go to jail and wished to be 'killed by a bullet, or die by hanging'. There was only one 'remedy' for the government's policy of repression – 'another Jallianwala Bagh', if necessary 'many repetitions of the Jallianwala Bagh'.[147]

On 4 February he published an ultimatum to the viceroy, threatening 'national revolt' beginning in Bardoli unless the government accepted his demands. These were, that all non-cooperators now in jail should be released, that there should be no more prosecutions for non-violent infractions of the sedition laws, and that all fines and forfeitures imposed on publishers of newspapers should be returned.[148] On 7 February, after the ultimatum was rejected, he announced that in view of the 'official lawlessness and barbarism' everywhere to be seen, no alternative remained but to inaugurate civil disobedience – 'with all its undoubted dangers'.[149] Political India was poised for the final showdown.

Then on 12 February, at Gandhi's request, the Congress Working Committee announced the immediate and indefinite suspension of all activities designed to court arrest and imprisonment, and their replacement by nationwide spinning, weaving and other 'constructive' projects. The brakes had been slammed on.

Gandhi's decision to suspend the campaign came after learning of the violent incident that had taken place on 4 February at the railway junction of Chauri Chaura, near Gorakhpur in the United Provinces. An unarmed crowd, several thousand strong, had marched to the police station to protest against police intimidation of Congress and Khilafat volunteers who were picketing liquor shops. There was a fracas, the police opened fire, and the crowd torched the police station. Some of the constables who tried to escape were pushed back inside, and in all 21 policemen and two protesters died. These were the facts that later emerged. The brief Associated Press news item which appeared in the *Bombay Chronicle* on 7 February referred to the burning of the police station, the death of 17 policemen, and the stripping and burning of bodies.[150]

The decision to shut down the campaign was not taken right away. On 8 February Gandhi wrote to the Working Committee saying that he was considering suspending mass civil disobedience either 'for the time being' or for 'a definite and sufficiently long period to enable the country to do organizing constructive work and to establish an indisputably non-violent atmosphere', and would like to hear their views.[151] As he had taken pains to make clear in his rejoinder the previous day to the government's rejection of his ultimatum, the term 'mass civil disobedience' referred to the programme which would shortly begin at Bardoli, and not the current jail-going in defiance of the sedition laws, which was 'defensive civil disobedience otherwise described as passive resistance', involving only 'technical' breaches of the law.[152] At this point he was thinking of once again postponing the Bardoli campaign, not of stopping all activities intended to invite arrest.

As 'sole executive authority' of the Congress – a position given him at the Ahmedabad Congress in December – Gandhi was not obliged to consult the Working Committee. He had not done so after the Bombay riots. After Chauri Chaura he not only convened the Committee but invited members to bring interested colleagues to the deliberations at Bardoli on 11 February – a move which suggests that his mind was still open to arguments for going ahead. 'I want', he said in his letter, 'to have the guidance of all the friends I can.'[153] Satan, he later confessed, had tempted him to continue as planned. Would it not be 'cowardly' to back down now?[154] But on 9 February he told Madan Mohan Malaviya, and other Moderate leaders who were urging postponement, that he would advise the Working Committee to postpone mass civil disobedience to the end of the year.[155] And by 11 February his position was firm. At his insistence the Committee voted not only for the postponement of the Bardoli campaign but for the cessation, also for an indefinite period pending 'further instructions', of all deliberate law-breaking including defiance of the sedition laws.[156]

How severely was Gandhi tempted? Perhaps severely enough that he went ahead and announced the start of the campaign even though he already (by 7 February) had news of the outbreak.

Romain Rolland, whose biography of Gandhi was published in 1923, recorded in his diary on 27 January 1924 that Paul Richard, who was visiting him, had told him that Gandhi knew about Chauri Chaura 'before writing his letter to the Viceroy and declaring his war of non-co-operation', but then decided to suspend the campaign after 'a letter from his son, shocked by the sight of the massacred people' and 'the intervention of a disciple'.[157] Gandhi's son Devdas did go to Chauri Chaura shortly after the event, and Charlie Andrews wrote to Gandhi on 8 February urging him to halt the campaign.[158]

At the time of the deaths at Chauri Chaura, Devdas was living at Allahabad, about a hundred and fifty miles away, running the local campaign and putting out a manuscript edition of the proscribed *Independent* newspaper. He went to Chauri Chaura when the news came in and began wiring reports from there to the Allahabad *Leader*, one of which makes it clear that he was on the scene by 6 February.[159] It seems unlikely that he failed to communicate at any point before 7 February directly with his father.

The assumption has been that Gandhi learned of Chauri Chaura from the 7 February (datelined Allahabad, 6 February) article in the *Bombay Chronicle*, which reached him in Bardoli on 8 February. But some accounts – including his own – suggest that he learned of events directly. 'My agony had begun', he later said, 'the moment telegrams about Gorakhpur were received.'[160]

Charlie Andrews weighed in with a letter on 7 February, having heard the news and learned that Devdas had 'gone at once' to Gorakhpur. He expressed horror but shrank from giving advice. Then after meeting Malaviya, witnessing his agitation, and passing a sleepless night, he sent a telegram and a further letter on 8 February urging postponement. He recalled the earlier postponement of mass civil disobedience after the Bombay riots, noting sadly 'the suddenness with which Bombay seemed forgotten even by you'. Chauri Chaura, in his view, was 'an event of even greater magnitude'.

Devdas did not stop at describing the carnage but recorded the view of local notables, including the president of the local Congress committee, who went to Chauri Chaura on 5 February, that the murders were the result of ' "carrying on a propaganda among the inflammable masses with the avowed object of destroying respect for law and authority by persons posing as apostles of non-violence" ' and showed ' "the grave danger with which the country is confronted" '. Devdas was also reported to have said that 'after what he had seen he must now ask his father to forget the Punjab wrongs'. On 11 February he wired a detailed account of the 'crime of Chauri Chaura' from Gorakhpur.

Paul Richard's version of events (though, as recorded by Rolland, incorrect in details – the announcement of 7 February which was indeed Gandhi's declaration of war took the form not of a letter to the viceroy but of a statement dictated for release to the press, and Devdas's letter was more likely to have been a telegram) cannot then be dismissed.

Gandhi himself acknowledged the importance of Devdas's interventions in a letter on 19 February to Jawaharlal Nehru, who was aghast that the campaign had been called off. The letter revealed that his feelings on hearing from his son had been mixed.[161] 'Let us not', he wrote, 'be obsessed by Devdas's youthful indiscretions. It is quite possible that the poor boy has been swept off his feet and that he has lost his balance, but the brutal murder of the constables by an infuriated crowd which was in sympathy with non-cooperation cannot be denied.' The news from Chauri Chaura, he went on, was the 'last straw'.

> I was much disturbed by the Madras doings [riots during the Prince of Wales' visit on 13 January], but I drowned the warning voice. I received letters both from Hindus and Mohammedans from Calcutta, Allahabad and the Punjab, all these before the Gorakhpur incident, telling me that the wrong was not all on the Government side, that our people were becoming aggressive, defiant and threatening, that they were getting out of hand and were not non-violent in demeanour.

He referred to other incidents which had taken place in recent weeks, including the forcible takeover of town halls at Shahajanpur and Jajjar. 'I have bitter complaints about Jajjar', he said. But at the time he had praised the local Congress Committee's occupation of the town hall as 'audacious and inspiring', though admittedly 'fraught with the greatest danger'.[162]

Chauri Chaura, then, was no bolt from the blue. The campaign was not, as many accounts have it, suddenly 'marred' by violence. Nor was Gandhi ignorant of the violence that was taking place. Nor was the campaign stopped 'on the spur of the moment' when he heard the news – as Romain Rolland put it in what was to become the orthodox version in 1923.[163] The decision to call off the campaign was a painful one, and but for the intervention of others might not have been made.

Once the decision had been taken, and the brakes successfully applied, it was clear to Gandhi that it was the right one. Not only would *swaraj* not be 'real swaraj' if it came through violence, as he had said in his exploratory letter to the Working Committee on 8 February, but the fact was that the campaign had been rapidly slipping out of his control.

The Khilafatists had openly demanded the abandonment of non-violence at the Ahmedabad Congress in December. In Bengal as well as the United Provinces, peasants were refusing to pay rent – the published decision of the Working Committee suspending the campaign explicitly condemned this. In Rajputana there was agitation for non-payment of taxes to the governments of Indian states. Of all the many thousands of new volunteers enrolled, only a few wore *khadi* or otherwise observed Gandhi's stipulated code of behaviour. As long as he saw the spirit of non-violence spreading, he said, he would be 'ready to run many risks'; but he could not allow his movement to be exploited by other people.[164] Suspending the campaign gave him the opportunity to reassert control.

But first there had to be a fast, and this took place from 12 to 16 February. The intention at first was to go without food for 14 days, but in acknowledgement of others' concern, Gandhi 'let it be five days'.[165] Later he said that five days had not been enough. The fast had a deliberate air, as though his conscience had already been relieved by calling off the campaign, but he had some further points he wished to make. He felt 'stronger', he wrote on the eve of the fast, for having confessed error: confession was 'like a broom that sweeps away dirt and leaves the surface cleaner than before'. Fasting would continue his purification and make him 'a fitter instrument able to register the slightest variation in the moral atmosphere'. The fast was also intended as a punishment of those who had committed violence in his name, and as a 'warning'. He believed, he said, that the country wanted him to live. If so, 'it should not deceive me .... so long as it accepts my services, it will have to accept non-violence and truth'. If he had to undertake another fast, who could say for how long it would be?[166] The fast was Gandhi's first step towards regaining control.

Even before it was over, he was looking forward to a resumption of civil disobedience in some form. Buoyed up, it appears, by his success in bringing the campaign to an instant halt, he announced that in spite of some 'aberrations', India had 'become solidly non-violent'.[167] Mass civil disobedience would remain out of the question 'at least to the end of the year' – but individual civil disobedience would only have to stop 'for some time'.[168]

Individual civil disobedience, in Gandhi's lexicon, meant defiance of designated laws by individuals acting alone or in small groups – a group of people might, for example, hold a prohibited meeting. So long as such acts were not centrally coordinated, and involved no incitement to mass lawbreaking, they remained 'individual' even if undertaken by many people overall. On 24 February, in a resolution Gandhi moved before the All-India Congress Committee, the provinces were given permission to resume individual civil disobedience at a time of their choice – ideally, as Gandhi said, under conditions of 'perfect non-violence', which would 'really add to the strength of the movement'.[169]

His confidence waxed and waned. There was strong condemnation of his decision to call off the campaign at the AICC meeting, and incredulity expressed at the suggestion that the country should now devote itself to a programme of purificatory and constructive work. Congress, after many hesitations, had got the bit between its teeth, and had seen that Gandhi's tactics could bring the finishing post in sight. It resented being reined in, and had little real interest, apart from its being the price of Gandhi's leadership, in his 'constructive programme'. Gandhi become anxious about how durable his hold over the political classes might be. It disturbed him that many had voted for his AICC resolution whose non-violence was 'skin-deep'. But he had neither withdrawn the resolution nor offered to resign. He had said already that he felt no inclination to remove himself from politics as a result of Chauri Chaura. He said the country could reject him if it wanted, but made no move to go. He was like a man, he said, finding his way by trial and error through a trackless forest, who 'must continually make mistakes and retrace'.[170] There had been no contradiction, he told Mathuradas Trikumji on 6 March, in his moving the AICC resolution: 'Had I been rigid .... it would have been violence on my part.'[171]

Yet he so much identified the movement's progress with his own that he could scarcely conceive of political events whose significance did not relate to himself. Upon reflection, he now welcomed the events of Chauri Chaura as a personal communication from God, saving him and India from error. 'God has been abundantly kind to me', he wrote in *Young India* on 16 February; 'He has warned me for the third time that there is not as yet in India that truthful and non-violent atmosphere which and which alone can justify mass disobedience'.[172] The first warning was during the Rowlatt *satyagraha*. 'I retraced my steps, called it a Himalayan miscalculation', and 'humbled myself before God and man'. The second warning was Bombay. 'The humiliation was greater than in 1919. But it did me good. I am sure that the nation gained by the stopping.' God warned him in Madras, but he ignored that. Then came Chauri Chaura, when 'God spoke clearly'. His decision after that had been 'religiously sound', and the country would gain 'by my humiliation and confession of error'.

Talk such as this may have been in Lord Reading's mind when he described Gandhi during these weeks as displaying 'unmistakable symptoms of megalomania'.[173] In an interview on 15 February a journalist had questioned the rationality of Gandhi's faith in non-violence. He was silenced with the rejoinder that nothing was being attempted 'that Jesus, Buddha or Mahomed failed to achieve'.[174]

By March Gandhi was marking time. There were daily rumours of his impending arrest and indeed the government had decided to make its move. He was arrested on 10 March and removed to Sabarmati jail to await trial. He seemed almost to be looking forward to imprisonment: the difficulties and uncertainties of his position were becoming ever more apparent.

It was only in a negative sense that Gandhi had satisfied himself that when he spoke, men would obey. If things went wrong, he could 'retrace', and he could fast. But the force within him was not yet reliably experienced positively by those he wished to guide. His conclusion was that it would remain so until their lives were sufficiently purified for it to be otherwise. This could only come about through the constructive programme. Enforce the constructive programme today, he said in a letter of 7 March, 'and the whole country is ready for mass civil disobedience tomorrow. Fail in the effort, and you are not ready even for individual civil disobedience.'[175]

But the slow process of purification could hardly keep pace with events. Political considerations influenced Gandhi's decisions to a degree he was unable to admit.

In May 1920, as he prepared for non-cooperation, he had written that 'the politician in me has never dominated a single decision of mine, and if I seem to take part in politics, it is only because politics encircle us today like the coil of a snake from which one cannot get out, no matter how much one tries.' Since 1894, his aim had been 'to wrestle with the snake' in the name of religion – that religion which 'is the permanent element in human nature which counts no cost too great in order to find full expression and which leaves the soul utterly restless until it has found itself, known its Maker and appreciated the true correspondence between the Maker and itself'.[176]

The authors of *The Perfect Way* had seen the story of Apollo's struggle with the python as an allegory of the struggle between matter and spirit, light and darkness; and had taken the god's triumph over the encircling beast to represent the soul's triumph, 'wherever it has succeeded in obtaining full manifestation', over materialism – the 'Serpent of Matter'.[177] Gandhi wished to be like that divine Apollo who spread light where there was darkness, and confounded the forces of matter with the power of the soul. But he was not always mindful that as a mere mortal he was yet to separate himself from the dark forces with which he strove, that he was still engaged in his spiritual journey, and was perhaps far from reaching its anticipated end. He found himself calling up tumults which he might sometimes control but could rarely direct.

# SIX

# In the Wings

Exhorting everyone to spin, spin, spin, Gandhi disappeared from the Indian political scene to begin a six-year sentence for promoting disaffection towards the government. Two years later he was released after falling ill with appendicitis, but it was not until 1928 that he was able to make a comeback. These six years were a period when Gandhi and his programmes were 'at a discount', as he put it, in Indian politics. But they were the years when his international reputation took shape.

Once Gandhi was in jail Indian politicians awoke as if from a dream and got on with their daily business. The Montagu–Chelmsford reforms gave them plenty to do, particularly at the provincial level, where the foundations of the political system of independent India were being laid. Gandhi had owed his position in the crowded marketplace of Indian politics to a highly differentiated product. With his imprisonment, that product went off the market. As they absorbed the shock of the collapse of non-cooperation, many Congressmen decided that was just as well.

Gandhi went to jail believing he had purified himself 'thoroughly' of all his recent errors. He had called off civil disobedience, fasted, heard without complaint the criticisms aired at the AICC meeting, and written appropriate articles in *Young India*. When the process of purification had reached 'the highest point', he had 'offered' himself for arrest.[1] His trial, at Ahmedabad before a courteous judge who acknowledged his sanctity, was a personal

triumph. Pleading guilty, he offered no extenuation, and in a dignified statement announced his intention to repeat the offence.

After a bumpy few weeks before he got his living arrangements and dietary
requirements sorted out with the prison authorities – the mention of the
word 'fast' was followed by provision of a spinning wheel, a diet of fruit and
goat's milk, and the free run of the jail compound – he settled down to a
life of reading, mostly on religious topics, and spinning, to which he devoted
four hours a day. When he came out of prison two years later, his views on
the way forward for India were exactly the same as when he went in: mass
purification through spinning, Hindu–Muslim unity and the eradication of
untouchability, followed by civil resistance when purification was deemed to
be sufficiently advanced.


It had become Gandhi's habit to pay no attention to criticism, 'except when
thereby I acknowledge a mistake or enforce still further the principles criti-
cised'.[2] Operating on the self-correcting principle, he set his course according
to his inner voice. From time to time he conceded that something had been
said which prompted him to examine his own position, to make sure it was
'free of error'. But during non-cooperation, a voice had been raised in public
rebuke which could not be ignored – that of Tagore.

Had Gandhi not lived, Tagore would be remembered as the quintessential
Indian of the first part of the twentieth century. His poetry, written originally
in Bengali, was read throughout the English-speaking world, despite losing
almost everything in translation. His life as a public man – as an educationist,
as a patron and resuscitator of the Indian arts, as a principled supporter of
the national cause, and as the most famous representative of a distinguished
Bengali family – gave his pronouncements on things Indian authority with a
large and devoted audience in India and abroad. He received the Nobel Prize
for literature in 1913, and a knighthood in 1915. It was to Tagore that C.F.
Andrews first attached himself when he decided to make his life in India,
and many of Andrews's reservations about Gandhi are decidedly Tagorean.
Tagore was no armchair patriot. He involved himself in *swadeshi* and rural
reconstruction, and in 1919 renounced his knighthood in protest against the
Jallianwala Bagh massacre. He believed like Gandhi that the heart of Indian
life was in the village, but saw its survival in intelligent adaptation and reform.
He denounced the caste system.

His relations with Gandhi were uneasy. Gandhi was always respectful in his public statements about rival personalities on the Indian scene, and Tagore was no exception. But from the start he claimed the right to moral instruction. On his visit to Shantiniketan in 1915, at a time when Tagore happened to be absent, he persuaded the boys they ought to be doing their own cooking, and dismissed the kitchen staff.

Gandhi's hatred of the flesh was alien to Tagore. Tagore wanted to reconcile the flesh and the spirit, and universalize the simple beauty of his own surroundings and the spirit of cooperation and obligation he believed could flourish in them. His personal beauty and refinement of mind and taste were so extreme that he was often mocked by those who laid claim to greater seriousness. But he never lacked courage in his public life, and did as much, in a practical way, for the poor of India as Gandhi did.

He recognized in Gandhi a personality who could inspire Indians to stand up to the arrogance of the British – of which the Tagore family, despite its celebrity, had experienced its share. But he disliked the self-righteousness, narrowmindedness and irrationality which seemed to go with nationalism, and Gandhi possessed all these traits. In two of his novels – *Gora* (1907) and *The Home and the World* (1919) – he had tried to show that even love of his beloved India could assume perverted forms in minds dominated by it.

His first criticisms of Gandhi concerned the moral extremism of his statements on non-cooperation with the British. Tagore did not in fact express these criticisms very well. Like others he found it hard to get a grip on what Gandhi was saying, did not know how literally to take him, and experienced the disadvantage in argument of knowing that for many people he was criticizing someone who was already beyond criticism. He seemed to hit the mark with the observation that Gandhi's wholesale rejection of Western civilization was at odds with the Indian conception of the oneness of life.[3] Taking it for granted that oneness was the condition entered into by the spirit after all attachment to the flesh was dead, Gandhi retorted that all religions 'teach that two opposite forces act upon us', and rejection of evil was as necessary as acceptance of good.[4] Tagore's apprehensions about Gandhi's moral assurance and its mesmerizing effect on weaker personalities prompted his subsequent broadside 'The Call of Truth', in October 1921, to which Gandhi made a celebrated reply.[5]

Tagore described how he had returned home from a long journey abroad during the early months of non-cooperation to find not an exhilarating atmosphere of freedom, but an oppressive atmosphere of conformity. Everyone seemed to speak with the same voice, 'to work at the same mill'. Hardly anyone dared to criticize Gandhi's campaign of cloth-burning, express doubts that mass spinning was the solution to India's problems, or question the rationality of expecting *swaraj* to arrive on a particular day. He saw that many had doubts but 'felt some admonishing hand clutching them within' if they opened their mouth to express them. What was the point, he asked, of exchanging subservience to a foreign ruler for subservience to an Indian one? Wonderful as Gandhi was – and Tagore felt obliged to say repeatedly how wonderful Gandhi was – he was not infallible, and to treat him as such was to fall prey to 'the illusion-haunted magic-ridden slave mentality that is at the root of all the poverty and insult under which our country groans'. The burning of cloth to make oneself pure, the idea that spinning could bring *swaraj* – these were nothing but instances of the Indian weakness for a 'magical formula' that could bring about the heart's desire, and: 'We have enough of magic in the country – magical revelation, magical healing, and all kinds of divine intervention in mundane affairs'.

These criticisms could not have been more to the point. But Gandhi evaded them and concentrated on demolishing Tagore's credentials for making them. He could see no evidence of a 'slave-mentality'. Had he not 'again and again appealed to reason'? If 'happily the country has come to believe in the spinning-wheel as the giver of plenty, it has done so after laborious thinking'. For himself: 'When all about me are dying for want of food, the only occupation permissible to me is to feed the hungry.' It was made plain without actually being said that Tagore could hardly claim to be concerned about the poor if he baulked at spinning. 'I have found it impossible to soothe suffering patients with a song from Kabir', Gandhi said, referring to Tagore's setting to music of Kabir's poems: 'The hungry millions ask for one poem – invigorating food.' There could be no effective response to this and Tagore fell silent, but he resumed the argument after Gandhi's release from prison in 1924.

Another who criticized Gandhi, more directly than Tagore, was Sir Sankaran Nair, whose book *Gandhi and Anarchy* was published shortly after Gandhi went to prison. Nair was a high court judge and member of the viceroy's executive council – a position he resigned in protest over Jallianwala Bagh. His criticisms were detailed and unabashed. He questioned Gandhi's motives for taking up the Khilafat cause, accused him of pandering to the

Hindu elite by his support of the caste system, deplored the 'emotionalism' of his fasts and other penances and the contempt for legal process implicit in his exaltation of soul-force, and argued that his real objective was to establish in India the primitive society described in *Hind Swaraj*. Gandhi, being in prison, did not reply. His admirers have always considered the book an outrage. Sushila Nayar, in her continuation of her brother Pyarelal's biography of Gandhi, dismissed Nair as a government tool. Geoffrey Ashe, most judicious of Gandhi's biographers, referred to *Gandhi and Anarchy* as 'a carefully prepared diatribe', a 'savage' outpouring inflicted on a helpless victim in a jail cell. These reactions to an able polemic of the type politicians must expect to endure suggest how right Tagore was to fear the deadening effect on thought of Gandhi's personality.[6]

Gandhi was never shy, in his self-deprecating way, of drawing attention to his superior ability to know, speak and act upon the truth. Though still far from attaining the vision of absolute truth, he wrote a few weeks after composing his rebuttal of Tagore, being at least on the way towards it he was like 'the castor-oil plant which, as they say, is king on a tree-less heath'.[7] He claimed greater purity and hence greater insight. At times he claimed more. 'My book is true', he wrote in response to a South African friend who questioned the accuracy of his *Autobiography*, 'because it is a faithful reproduction of my recollections.'[8] He did not mind being accused of inconsistency, so long he was 'true to myself from moment to moment'.[9] The self to which he was true was the higher self – the projection of God into matter – with which his pure life brought him into alignment.


Assent was also a problem. Expressions of support from fellow Indians inevitably aroused mixed feelings. They might be expedient, or not backed up by correct behaviour. So Gandhi was usually pleased to receive the approbation of foreigners, which could be taken to be disinterested.

He had collected European admirers in South Africa, but as demands were made on their discipleship, they tended to drop away. Henry Polak remained active in the Indian cause, but was critical of Gandhi and disliked the atmosphere of a court which surrounded him in India.[10]

The prototype of Gandhi's later admirers, who were attracted to him after he became a public personality, was Joseph Doke. Doke and his many successors felt it as a reproach to the un-Christian state of the supposedly

Christian West that a man of such radiantly self-abnegating character should be a Hindu. The Western cult of Gandhi arose in the context of a desire, acquiring urgency after the war, for the resuscitation of Christianity's moral power. The marvel of it all, Doke said in a sermon in Johannesburg in 1908, was 'that a little handful of Indians and Chinese should have so imbibed the teachings of Christ in regard to the inherent nobility of man that they should become teachers of a mercenary age, while Christians stand by and smile or are silent as they suffer'.[11]

Charlie Andrews was another who went to Gandhi in South Africa, arriving in 1914 from India as an emissary from Gokhale. Meeting Gandhi on the Durban dock, he fell on his knees and touched his feet. Thereafter he was as firmly attached to Gandhi as he was to Tagore, and served him selflessly until his death in 1940. Tagore he adored as supremely Indian, Gandhi he adored in a different fashion, with religious awe and a conviction of his universal significance for mankind.

Gandhi seems not to have minded Andrews's many disagreements with him. They were framed in the context of discipleship and treated as requests for enlightenment. Andrews seems to have rationalized his misgivings about Gandhi by thinking of him as a 'volcanic force', transmitting the great message of 'the hidden power of a living freedom from within' – a force which must inevitably destroy before it could rebuild. The embodiments of such force, he reflected, were always 'men of strange uncouth ways which shock our normal habits'.[12]

Andrews was without pride, worldly or spiritual. But he had a need for personal validation through the service of others, which could make him trying to the special objects of his love – a word he used with as much abandon as Gandhi. Tagore banished him from time to time; and after the first flowering of friendship in South Africa Gandhi saw little of him and relied on correspondence. He was a man in constant motion, ever about the world's business. Gandhi once observed treacherously that 'his comings and goings signify nothing'.[13] But he was useful to the cause as an intermediary and a publicist. He had a wide acquaintance among the influential, and the relatives of the influential, and had the knack of plausibly inserting himself into the presence of the powerful. His books on Gandhi, which began to appear in 1929 and reached a wide audience, were mostly compilations of Gandhi's writings, with the addition of narrative and background material.[14] They emphasized Gandhi's attraction to Christianity and particularly his reverence for the Sermon on the Mount. Their rather impersonal format gave them an apostolic air.

Gandhi's appearance in Andrews's life precipitated a personal religious crisis, which is of interest in showing on what type of Western soil the seeds of Gandhism tended to fall.

Andrews's encounter with Gandhi at the height of the South African campaign was the decisive influence on his abandonment of Anglican orders and cessation of missionary work in India. But the crisis which brought about these events had been a long time in brewing. Born into unorthodoxy in the form of the eccentric Catholic Apostolic Church (known after its founder as the 'Irvingite' church), in which his father was a minister, Andrews had rebelled against unorthodoxy, sailed into the safe haven of Anglicanism at Cambridge, and then found the foundations of conventional belief crumbling as his teaching position at St Stephen's College in Delhi brought him into contact first with Indian culture, and then with the 'fulfilment theology' being propounded by missionary theologians who took as their text Christ's words: 'I come not to destroy but to fulfil.'

Life as an Irvingite primed Andrews for his encounter with Gandhi, the cardinal points of Irvingite doctrine being, in Andrews's words, 'the direct divine leading of the believers by the voice of the Holy Spirit',[15] and the imminent Second Coming of Christ. Church services featured speaking in tongues and prophecy, and there was emphasis on keeping the inner light bright through purity of heart. The prospect of Christ's return became terrifying to the boy Andrews when he took up 'impure' (presumably homosexual or masturbatory) practices at school and it dawned on him that he had consigned himself to the flames of hell. Unbelief being also a terrible prospect, there was no escape except into the Church of England. There he sought to become a better person through work at a university mission in a South London slum, throwing himself into the task of reclamation with a zeal which brought about the first of many breakdowns. This was the combustible youngish man (33) who arrived in Delhi in 1904.

'Fulfilment' or 'sympathy' theology was the Protestant equivalent of the accommodations to India made long ago by the Jesuits as they established their stupendous mission at Goa. A kind of proto-Christianity was discerned by the proponents of 'fulfilment' in the Buddhist and Hindu ideals of poverty and renunciation, which it was the task of Christian missions to bring to fruition through the Indian acceptance of Christ. The Christianized Hinduism of the Brahmo Samaj and Vivekananda was also thought to point in the direction of fulfilment. As Andrews made friends with Indians and came to know something of India, he gravitated towards the 'fulfilment' party. But his sympathy with Indian nationalism, and friendship with Tagore, who was plainly a bigger man than any of his missionary associates, meant he was not satisfied with it.

The South African visit both completed his estrangement from official Christianity and pointed the way to something else. South African racism stunned him. At St. Stephen's College, Indians and Englishmen taught and worshipped together. In Durban, when he preached at the cathedral, Gandhi had to stay outside because the church was for whites only. Yet Gandhi and his *satyagrahi*s, 'the humblest and lowliest and lost', seemed closer to Christ's spirit than the Christian congregation that excluded them.[16]

Within a few months Andrews had rejected what he saw as the European version of Christianity and constructed an 'Indian' one to which he transferred his allegiance. Unbelief, as always, was out of the question. Christianity, he now saw, was not a Semitic religion but the direct descendant of Buddhism and Hinduism: all were part of 'one stream' and what connected them was *ahimsa* – a concept alien to the exclusive, domineering spirit of Judaism and historical Christianity now manifesting itself in European imperialism. He thought it possible that Jesus had been influenced by Buddhist sages, and St John instructed by Indian philosophers. He decided that Christ's divinity was not unique, that God was there in all men, to be revealed by suffering, and that it was currently India's privilege among nations to suffer the most.

How much if any of this came from Gandhi during the intense initial experience of mutual attraction in South Africa, Andrews was never to say. But he did say of the letters he wrote to Tagore at the time, revealing his spiritual turmoil, that he had discussed the contents of them at length with Gandhi. They were written with a view to publication, but Gandhi advised waiting for at least three years. Tagore also advised against publication. They eventually appeared, somewhat revised, in the *Modern Review* in 1922. The war, which seemed the last nail in the coffin of European Christianity, confirmed for Andrews the correctness of the path he had just taken.

Jesus remained supreme for Andrews. But he believed that God was 'visible in great human souls', 'formless, yet He takes form in man';[17] and page after page of his apologia, *What I Owe to Christ*, reveals his belief that Gandhi was a being of that order. He persuaded himself that the scene in India at the time he arrived in Delhi recalled 'that of the Roman Empire nineteen hundred years ago' – the same deceptive calm, the same vast creative force bubbling up below.[18] He knew as soon as he met Gandhi that 'there had come into the world, not only a new religious personality of the highest order, moving the hearts of men and women to incredible sacrifice, but also a new religious truth, which yet was not new, … that long-suffering and redeeming love is alone invincible'.[19] Christ, he said, 'comes again to His own right in our day. He comes to set us free.'[20]

Others besides Andrews were to see Gandhi as suggesting the possibility of a new, 'Indian', form of Christianity – notably the American missionary E. Stanley Jones and the Indian Christian S.K. George.[21] The influence of Gandhi was also felt in two missionary groups – the 'Kristagraha Movement' and the Christa Seva Sangh – which appeared in India in the 1920s.

The Unitarian minister John Haynes Holmes, of the Community Church in New York, wrote the introduction to the American edition of Andrews's *Mahatma Gandhi: His Own Story*. He became Gandhi's chief publicist in North America. Holmes was a pacifist who denounced American participation in the war. After the war he looked around for a man who might lead the world away from destruction and found Gandhi, whom he introduced to his congregation in 1921 in a sermon entitled 'Who is the greatest man in the world?'[22] He proclaimed Gandhi the suffering Christ of the twentieth century. 'Clothed upon with the frailest garment of fleshly incarnation ever known', he wrote in his introduction to Andrews' book, 'the Mahatma walks among us as pure spirit'. He was offering to mankind ' "the way of life" ': would they refuse it, 'as they refused it once before?'[23]

In fact Holmes the Unitarian minister regarded neither Christ nor Gandhi as divine. They were 'saviours of the race', like the Buddha and a few other outstanding religious personalities, through whom God was active in history. Men could learn, if they wished, from Gandhi's message and example that non-violence was as great a force as violence. Gandhi had come to save the world from the horror of war.

Holmes was impressed by Gandhi's command of events. During non-cooperation 300 million Indians had felt the power of his will, which made him 'the most potent personal force the world has known'. Like other saviours of the race, he could tap into the 'quickening powers, unfathomable springs of being', which lie quiescent in the human soul.[24] There is something of New Thought in this. But Holmes was ever conscious of the distance separating himself from Gandhi and his kind. Not self-transformation but world-transformation through making known Gandhi and his ideas was his aim.

It was the French man of letters Romain Rolland who first brought Gandhi worldwide attention. The French edition of his book *Mahatma Gandhi: The Man Who Became One with the Universal Being* sold 100,000 copies within a year of publication, and was soon translated into English, German, Russian, Spanish, Portuguese, Polish and Japanese. Like Holmes, Rolland was a pacifist, and his pacifism was in the heroic vein. He was a man of manifestos. 'The way to peace', he wrote in *Mahatma Gandhi*, 'is not through weakness. We do not fight violence so much as weakness. Nothing is worth while unless it is strong, neither good nor evil. Absolute evil is better than emasculated goodness. Moaning pacifism is the death-knell of peace; it is cowardice and lack of faith. Let those who do not believe, who fear, withdraw! The way to peace leads through self-sacrifice.'[25]

These views preceded Rolland's acquaintance with Gandhi. Their spirit permeated all his writings before the war. They can be found in the essays he published during the war.[26] His biography of Beethoven (his inspiration before Gandhi) exalted a man made great by suffering – the only route to greatness, in Rolland's view.[27] Though not a Christian, like Gandhi he esteemed 'faith' and thought it carried the obligation to right action. He was outraged by the churches' acquiescence in the war.

Rolland was by nature reclusive and austere. He had a romantic soul but a puritan work ethic. He believed the service of art required the renunciation of pleasure. His passions were for peace, social justice and the truly noble in life and art. After 1914 his aim was to rescue some idea of the moral significance of the human personality from the immense wreckage of the war. Gandhi, a kindred spirit but with a force he himself lacked, seemed to offer that possibility. His renunciation of power when it was within his reach in 1922 greatly moved Rolland. He saw the calling off of civil disobedience as one of the supreme moments in history, a milestone in 'humanity's spiritual progress', and a manifestation of the force which had been present in Jesus and the Buddha; and if Gandhi himself ultimately failed, the force would manifest itself again, until there appeared, 'in a mortal half-god, the perfect incarnation of the principle of life which will lead a new humanity on to a new path.'[28]

Rolland had the religious temperament and once described to Freud his continuous awareness of all being and the force at work in it – an 'oceanic feeling' which he believed connected him to all men and to the divine core of existence within them, and was the foundation of human progress in every area of endeavour. (Freud, however, wrote back explaining that the oceanic feeling was a regression to the undifferentiated egoism of the infantile state.[29]) Inevitably, Rolland was drawn to Indian ideas of the immanence of the divine. He was already in contact with Indian thinkers – Tagore and the art historian Ananda Coomaraswamy – before he became aware of Gandhi, and in 1929 published biographies of Ramakrishna and Vivekananda.[30] He thought that the idea that God was present in all men offered Europeans a superior rationale for the pursuit of their own values – liberty, equality, fraternity – and that exposure to Indian thought could therefore be a regenerative influence on Europe. He was treading where Annie Besant had trod. Like her he accepted the corollary to the fraternal implications of God's immanence – the existence of beings of superior enlightenment and power. This was the reason for giving his book on Gandhi the subtitle *The Man Who Became One with the Universal Being*. But in writing the book he did not address these ideas directly. His purpose was to convey to as large an audience as possible the power of non-violence through its most brilliant exponent.

A fervent appreciation of the power of Gandhi's personality ran through all the admiring accounts of him. He had that mastery over life which seemed to have eluded a generation of Europeans caught up in the most destructive and – so it seemed to many – senseless war the world had known. After the war, as the dictators arose in Europe, and the left appeared morally compromised by Bolshevism, Gandhi began to represent to some people a countervailing force. His appeal was to political men who had lost faith in the ordinary process of politics, and were drawn to a personality in which power seemed to inhere and find expression without moral compromise or visible ambition. Rolland begged him to come and save Europe.[31]

There were people who saw Hitler in this light – the 1920s were a boom time for saviours. And it was certainly no coincidence that the European cult of Gandhi arose at the same time as the cult of T.E. Lawrence, another life-denying and power-hungry ascetic who was credited with exceptional powers, and thought by some to be capable of dealing singlehandedly with Hitler and Mussolini.[32]

An Indian admirer, K.M. Munshi, well summed up the *Übermensch* aspect of Gandhi's appeal. In all his multifarious activities, Munshi wrote, the one thing that forcefully strikes even a casual observer is that Gandhi is the master.... He has willed his body to perform its appointed task. He has created his own surroundings, and shaped the lives of those around him. He has forged the formidable organizations which struggle to liberate India.... The words of the *Gita*, 'Yoga is perfection in action' have come true in him.[33]

Gandhi read Rolland's book in prison and found 'a real vision of truth' in it, a 'real sage-like vision'.[34] A relationship developed in which Rolland became, in Gandhi's words, 'my self-chosen advertiser' in Europe.[35] The relationship did not survive, on Rolland's part, a disillusioning meeting in 1931. Faith and hope crumbled upon the arrival of the saviour in the flesh.

Gandhi was equally welcoming to Holmes, and indeed to all his foreign admirers. Paul Richard, who had written apocalyptically of the rise amid the ashes of the old materialist civilization consumed in the war of a new Christ, not 'of the white race', enjoyed high favour for a while.[36] Holmes was accepted by Gandhi as his promoter in North America, and his advice sought on American matters. Plans for an American visit in 1931 were put aside when Holmes warned that his message would be trivialized by the American press.[37]

After the publication of Rolland's book comparisons of Gandhi to Christ became common. He responded invariably that he was but a striver after perfection. But he allowed himself some calculated ambiguities. Taken to task by an Indian Christian in 1924 for tolerating talk of himself as ' "the modern Jesus" ', he replied that he did 'not like these comparisons': 'They serve no useful purpose and cause unnecessary hurt to the feelings of the devotees of the masters with whose life mine is compared.'[38]

Doctrine as well as prudence restrained him from saying that if all went well he would be a Christ. It was his esoteric opinion that Jesus never preached belief in himself as a condition of salvation, but rather offered his life as an example whose power was magnified inexpressibly by the ultimate renunciation of the cross. An Indian Christian, P.V. George, wrote a book correcting this view with numerous quotations from the gospels.[39] But Gandhi continued self-consciously to tread the exemplificatory path.

The title 'mahatma' was now regularly appended to his name. His feelings about it were painfully mixed. He detested its vulgar use but could hardly consider it inapt. If he were not a 'great soul', why would he be aspiring to *moksha* in this life? Asked in 1924 why he allowed himself to be referred to as 'Mahatma' Gandhi on the list of executives published by his organization, the All-India Spinners' Association, he replied that had he 'offered satyagraha against it, the word might not have appeared. But I did not consider the offence to be serious enough to call for the use of that terrible weapon. Unless some catastrophe takes place the offensive word will always be associated with my name, and the patient critics must tolerate it even as I do.'[40] In time he came to speak matter-of-factly of his mahatmahood.[41]

The problem of popular acclaim was in fact on the way to being solved. It struck Gandhi that the 'affection of the masses' was reciprocated in the love he bore for them. The resulting 'bond' was an intimation of his potential oneness with all mankind, and hence with God himself. 'I see in the fellowship with them', he said, 'the God I adore. I derive from that fellowship all my consolation, all my hope and all the sustaining power I possess.'[42]

As for the extraordinary 'expectations' his foreign admirers were entertaining of him, it was clear they were 'a tribute not to me, a curious mixture of Jekyll and Hyde, but to the incarnation, however imperfect but comparatively great in me, of the two priceless qualities of truth and non-violence'. Though 'dazed', he would 'not shirk the responsibility of giving what aid I can to fellow-seekers after truth from the West'.[43]

Gandhi was released from jail in February 1924 after an emergency appendectomy. He knew God's hand must be at work in this development, but exactly how was a matter for anxious introspection. Obviously, God wanted him out of jail.[44] But to be stricken with such an illness? What could it say about his spiritual state? And what of his submission, in the hour of crisis, to the ministrations of Western medicine, so thoroughly execrated in *Hind Swaraj*? Would it have been better to accept that his time had come?

He could not but acknowledge that he was not yet 'absolutely free of egoism'.[45] But, the appendix being a 'superfluous' body part with no known function, its inflammation failed to qualify as 'a serious illness'. Hence, whatever transgressions had brought it on could not be too serious either. He had caught himself enjoying his goat's milk. Perhaps this was what had provoked divine chastisement: 'Failure in conquering the palate is the "offence against God".'[46]

Meanwhile the appendectomy passed into the folklore. The story circulated that the mahatma had refused anaesthetics, felt no pain, and 'chatted cheerfully with his devotees' as the surgeon did his work.[47]

After being released from prison, spring 1924

Indian politics had moved on while Gandhi was doing time. The 'No-changers' in Congress, who held out for Gandhian non-cooperation, had failed to prevent the 'Pro-changers' (also known as the Swarajists) from taking advantage of the electoral opportunities created by the Montagu-Chelmsford reforms. Under the leadership of Motilal Nehru and C.R. Das the Swarajists were moving Congress on to the constitutional path, even as they purported to be entering the legislatures only to obstruct them. The alliance between Congress and the Muslim League had collapsed amid a general deterioration of communal relations. The hollowness of the cause which had bound them together under Gandhi's direction was revealed when the Turkish Assembly voted to abolish the caliphate in April. The spinning wheel had made no headway.

Gandhi briefly quailed before all this but then met his difficulties head on. His meditations of the last two years had made him 'a firmer believer than ever in the efficacy of the Bardoli programme and, therefore, in the unity between the races [sic], the charkha [spinning wheel], the removal of untouchability and the application of non-violence in thought, word and deed'.[48] He rejected a compromise with the Swarajists and in June presented to the AICC at Ahmedabad his terms of leadership.

He prescribed for Congress a thorough detoxification programme. Only those who observed the five elements of non-cooperation – boycott of mill cloth, law courts, schools, titles and legislatures – were to be elected to Congress office. On pain of dismissal, all Congress office-holders were to spin for at least half an hour daily, and send in to the secretary of the All-India Khadi Board each month – arriving no later than the 15th – at least 2,000 yards of evenly spun yarn. The AICC was asked as well to condemn a recent political assassination as violating the Congress creed. In Gandhi's view it was 'discipline' which Congress required, and without discipline there was no point in his resuming his post as its 'general'.[49] Congress was free to reject his proposals. In that case he would leave.

The audacious move failed. After a Swarajist walkout, Gandhi was left with a majority of votes but clearly not an invitation to resume his general-ship. The motion to condemn assassination carried by less than ten votes. He wept. He threatened to go but was persuaded to stay. The Swarajists remained in Congress. Gandhi was not testing the waters at Ahmedabad but anticipating a victory.[50] Defeat prostrated him. He considered trying to take the No-changers with him out of Congress, but finally decided 'to drink the bitter cup' of remaining in an organization he did not control.

The cause of his miscalculation was the belief that 'the country expects me to lead it'.[51] He had gone into jail in what he knew to be good spiritual condition, he had undergone a purificatory incarceration passed in spinning, reflection and prayer, and he had emerged – evidently by divine dispensation – to global acclaim. Once his feelings about the appendectomy were sorted out, he looked forward to taking up the leadership of Congress where he had left off.

In the two months between his release and the confrontation at Ahmedabad his mood was increasingly buoyant. On the eve of what proved to be defeat he declared that, should the vote go against him, he would 'walk out cheer-fully, with no complaint, no bitterness'.[52] In the event he stood before the Committee, laid bare his heart, 'and let them see the blood oozing out of it'.[53] Until the moment the votes were announced, he said, he had been 'enjoying the whole thing' – meaning the antics of the Swarajists – 'as a huge joke'.[54]

After Ahmedabad Gandhi set about salvaging what he could from the wreckage. He made the spinning resolution a test of loyalty by insisting that all who voted for it carry it out. He interested himself in the *satyagraha* taking place on local initiative at Vykom in Travancore, where volunteers were trying to get a road past a temple opened to untouchables. Before Ahmedabad he had damped down attempts to make it a national issue. He saw the unwisdom of having forced a vote, and set out to recapture Congress by acclamation when it met in open session at Belgaum at the end of the year. Whatever happened there, he told Motilal Nehru, 'must be by agreement'.[55] To this end he devised one of his most extraordinary and – to his supporters – most baffling 'compromises'.

It came to him suddenly at the end of August. He would accept the suspension, for one year, of all boycotts except the boycott of mill cloth, and would cease all opposition to entering the legislatures. The official activities of the Congress, however, would be confined to propagating *khadi* and working for Hindu–Muslim unity and the removal of untouchability. All members of Congress would have to spin for half an hour a day and send in 2,000 yards of yarn.

To Gandhi, this amounted to 'surrender up to the very margin of principle'.[56] It was an act of renunciation from which he expected great results – purification of the atmosphere and true unity. His Congress colleagues were about to experience the operation of the Law of Love. There was no major public statement to that effect but he talked vaguely of *satyagraha*: through 'sacrifice', through 'love', he would prevail. Readers of *Navajivan* were reminded that a believer in non-violence 'never fights for power', and propagates his creed 'not on the strength of a majority', but through spiritual force, accepting only power which comes 'unsought', through the working of public opinion. He had no doubt, he said, that opinion among the Congress rank and file would be with those 'who are prepared to sacrifice themselves to the uttermost for the sake of their service'.[57] Only if victory at Belgaum came 'without any special effort' would he remain in Congress.[58] It proved difficult to convince his supporters – who still held a majority in Congress – that by giving up power they would ultimately receive it. But if he could not convince by argument, he told Rajagopalachari, his lieutenant in the south, neither could he 'suppress the clear voice within'. And of what use would he be if he 'once stifled that monitor'?[59]

He meanwhile sought an explanation for the state of the country and concluded that it was all his fault. He had misjudged Indians' readiness for peaceful non-cooperation. The non-cooperation actually practised had been 'that of the weak', not of the truly loving and strong, and it was this that was responsible for the discord now existing between Hindus and Muslims, and between the two factions of Congress. After the collapse of the campaign, Indians, their passions aroused, had begun to 'non-cooperate' against each other. 'Once we take a weapon out of its sheath', he said, 'it does not turn back but leads to our own destruction.' It was up to him to get India back on track by resort to the 'potent weapon' of 'pure love'.[60] There was some truth in this, but the point of view was Gandhi-centric, both as to the problem and the remedy.

An opportunity shortly arose both to do penance for error and to provide a public demonstration of the potent weapon of pure love. On 9 September an especially ugly outbreak of communal violence occurred in Kohat, in the North-West Frontier Province. Thirty-six people were killed and the entire Hindu population had to be evacuated. A week later, Gandhi announced a 21-day fast as a 'penance' and as a 'prayer'.[61]

The 'penance' was for his misjudgement regarding non-cooperation. The prayer was for reconcilement of the two communities. The fast has been known since as the 21-day fast for Hindu–Muslim unity. But Gandhi was emphatic that his concerns were much broader than that.[62] The objects of his previous fasts, he said, had been 'limited': the object of this one was 'unlimited'. Such a fast, he said, had been a possibility in his mind since first conceiving non-cooperation, knowing full well the risk he ran. It was a fast for self-purification – 'a pure matter of religion' – and its 'meaning' was like that of the fasts after Bombay and Chauri Chaura. It was, though he did not quite say so, the fast he knew he should have undertaken after Chauri Chaura, perhaps after Bombay.

But what prompted him to undertake it now? – after an event for which, as Mahadev pointed out, no one held him responsible. Could he not, inquired Shaukat Ali, visit the affected areas instead? He had failed in his non-violence, Gandhi replied. He was to blame for everything because, had he been 'practising non-violence to perfection', all would have been well. It was thus pointless for him to visit Kohat or anywhere else. 'I have lost the power', he lamented, 'wherewith to appeal to people. Defeated and helpless, I must submit my petition in His Court. Only He will listen, no one else.'[63] The fast is perhaps best described as a fast for Hindu–Muslim unity, for unity in Congress and for national unity under Gandhi's revitalized leadership.

The fast ended on 8 October. Foss Westcott, the Metropolitan of Calcutta, sang 'Lead, Kindly Light'; Charlie Andrews sang 'When I Survey the Wondrous Cross'. Vinoba Bhave, a disciple since 1916, recited verses from the Koran. Mohamed Ali bought a cow from a butcher and presented it to Gandhi for transfer to a *pinjrapole* (retirement home for cows). A 'Unity Conference' had meanwhile convened in Delhi, and representatives of the communities had with some difficulty passed a series of hopeful resolutions. But there was no improvement in the communal situation and within a week riots had broken out in Allahabad and Jubbulpur.

Gandhi emerged from his fast with hope that his *tapas*, as he put it in a note sent immediately to *Navajivan*, would keep him afloat in the 'stormy ocean' into which he was about to plunge.[64]

The political situation remained unaffected by the fast. The Swarajists and Gandhi were no closer to an agreement than before. But at the end of October the issue was resolved by an unexpected development. The government cracked down on the Swaraj party in Bengal, claiming it was involved in a recent revival of terrorism, and the urgent need for a show of solidarity in Congress produced the elusive agreement. Gandhi was summoned to Bengal by C.R. Das to work it out. The agreement announced on 6 November stipulated that the Swaraj party would henceforth carry on its activities in the name of Congress, that all boycotts except the cloth boycott would be dropped, and that Congress would adopt Gandhi's 'spinning franchise'. No one was happy but Gandhi sought consolation in the spiritual merit accruing from further concession.

Accepting the presidency of Congress which was pressed upon him, Gandhi was conscious of the depleted powers he would be taking to Belgaum. Despite his stupendous fast, it was all too clear that he did not possess 'that power by which my words once uttered would have an immediate and permanent effect': 'I have to be near the persons all the time.'[65]

The agreement with the Swarajists was ratified at Belgaum and Gandhi transferred his activities to the constructive programme and the cloth boycott. If a complete boycott were achieved by the end of the year, he told his follow-ers, he would unveil to them a new plan of civil disobedience.[66] In June the sudden death of C.R. Das presented him with the opportunity for another attempt at 'unity'.

Das had been a power in Bengal and on the national scene since 1917. His political inspiration was Aurobindo Ghose in his brief revolutionary career before his departure in 1910 for Pondicherry and eventual seclusion. Aurobindo

had taken the *swadeshi* idea – boycott of all foreign manufactures and promotion of indigenous products – which had swept Bengal after Curzon's attempt
at partition in 1905, and developed it into a programme of non-cooperation
with the foreign oppressor involving four boycotts: of foreign and particularly
British goods, of government schools, of law courts, and of the government
bureaucracy (meaning that Indians would neither work in it nor accept its
services). Published in 1907, Aurobindo's programme anticipated Gandhi's.[67]
But it was not non-violent and it was not an attempt to resurrect the pre-
industrial past. The development of Indian industry was a principal aim; the
revival of handicrafts was merely welcomed.

Das, then, represented an alternative tradition of political protest with a
secure base in Bengal – a province long accustomed to being at the leading
edge of India's response to British rule. He and Gandhi had always mistrusted
each other. Temperamentally, they were opposites – Das the emotional 'real-
ist', Gandhi the calculating idealist. Their alliance in 1921, when Das threw
his support behind Gandhi's non-cooperation campaign, renounced his law
practice, gave away his property, and put on *khadi*, was the result of his
calculation that it would be political suicide to do otherwise. His belief in mass
spinning as the solution to India's problems was nil. The effect of his death
for Gandhi was to remove an increasingly powerful rival from the scene.

Nevertheless, upon his death, Gandhi, who happened to be in Calcutta
and had just been with Das in Darjeeling for a few days, went into action
to organize his obsequies and appropriate his memory for the constructive
programme. Collections began under his supervision for a memorial fund,
along the lines of the earlier and equally egregious Tilak Swaraj Fund, to be
devoted to 'the universal propagation of the spinning-wheel and khaddar'.[68]

In accordance with Das's wishes, said to have been expressed privately
to him in Darjeeling, Gandhi proposed a merger between the Swarajist and
Gandhian wings of Congress. But the Swarajists, their position fortuitously
strengthened by a blimpish attack on them by Lord Birkenhead in the House
of Lords, responded with a demand that Congress drop the spinning franchise. Gandhi was at last forced to concede defeat. In September he founded
the All-India Spinners' Association, which was to be part of Congress yet
independent of it. Its members were to spin 1,000 yards a month.

Gandhi now betook himself to Sabarmati. He continued to attend public
sessions of Congress but confined his involvement in policy to whatever

influence could be exerted through his protégé, Jawaharlal Nehru. He promoted spinning and his other causes, touring the country to great acclaim and extending his organizational base through the AISA.

The attempted comeback of 1924 had been doomed by his insistence on the spinning franchise, for which there was very little wholehearted support. The American Samuel Stokes, who had left wealth and privilege in Philadelphia to do social work in India, had joined Congress, had gone to jail during non-cooperation, and was a committed spinner, denounced it publicly as an un-Gandhian attempt to legislate virtue and as an assault on the democratic nature of Congress. Gandhi replied that Stokes's 'excessive regard for the liberty of the individual has disabled him from distinguishing between voluntary compliance and compulsion'.[69]

As usual it was Gandhi who was having difficulty distinguishing between the two. He wanted voluntary compliance but there was an undeniably authoritarian aspect to his advocacy of organized spinning. He compared it to the 'discipline' of military conscription in more patriotic but less spiritually enlightened countries. The *charkha*, being 'the embodiment of willing obedience', was the essential prerequisite for a successful resumption of civil disobedience.[70] He had a point. Had he ever truly managed to impose a spinning franchise on Congress, he would have had the disciplined non-violent army of his dreams. (The spinning requirements he did manage to impose were immediately bogged down in a host of special regulations, including ones permitting vicarious spinning – sending in yarn spun by somebody else.)

Though keenly aware of the organizational value of compulsory spinning, it was not for this that Gandhi risked his political career. Spinning had acquired a religious significance for him. He had quoted to Tagore in 1921 the verses from the *Gita* (Chapter 3, 8–16) which recommend work free of attachment to results as the route to liberation. Afterwards he explained in *Young India* that, in seeking to apply the doctrine to India, he could 'only think of spinning as the fittest and most acceptable sacrificial body labour'. Through spinning, those who had no need to clothe themselves, or eke out a living, could identify themselves with the poor, 'and through them with all mankind'.[71]

Spinning has been from ancient times a symbol of the very process of living. In Greece the three Fates presided over human destiny: one spun the thread of life, one measured it, and one cut it. The Germans had the Norns, similarly employed. The *Gita* refers to turning the wheel of life through sacrifice, an image that predates it. Annie Besant had emphasized the *Gita*'s imagery of the wheel in expounding the 'Law of Sacrifice'.[72] Perhaps some such thoughts were in Gandhi's mind when he adopted so potently symbolic an avocation.

Gandhi's interest in handmade cloth went back to his student days in London, where hand-woven and hand-spun garments were in vogue among fashionable advocates of the simple life. (The Indian aesthete Ananda Coomaraswamy may also have been an influence.[73]) Wearing handmade garments was rejection of mass production made visible. When Gandhi returned to India he interested himself in hand-weaving and hand-spinning as possible solutions to the problem of rural poverty. Hand-weaving was by no means dead in India in 1915, but it was the occupation of low castes using mill-produced yarn. Spinning was a skill which had fallen into disuse. In 1919 it occurred to Gandhi that spinning was an activity in which Sabarmati (where hand-weaving had already been taken up) might specialize. 'We should drop or curtail', he told Maganlal, 'one by one, those of our activities which we think others are likely to take up; and pay more attention to those in which others have less faith or none, but which are all the same essential. Spinning is one such activity.'[74] Before long spinning was everywhere associated with his name. On his tours of India during non-cooperation he promoted it as an economic activity which could be pursued during the relatively idle seasons of the agricultural year, and at spare moments during the day. These tours opened his eyes to the wretchedness of the Indian poor – 'To read of semi-starved millions', he wrote to Henry Polak, 'was so different from seeing them'[75] – and convinced him of the spinning wheel's unique importance. Spinning did not displace but supplemented other activities, and anyone could learn to do it. By 1921 it was 'the secret of swaraj'. It was also 'the least penance we must do for the sin of our forefathers in having succumbed to Satanic influences of the foreign manufacturer'.[76]

But it was Gandhi's experience in prison, when he spun for four hours a day, which convinced him beyond possibility of argument that spinning possessed such spiritual value that all Indians must do it. 'The spinning is growing on me', he wrote after three weeks in Yeravda jail; 'I seem daily to be coming nearer to the poorest of the poor and to that extent to God.' What was more, he was discovering that 'Not an impure thought enters my mind during the four hours.'[77] Spinning, as he was often later to put it, 'stilled the mind'. He was to recommend it particularly to the young: 'They will find that shortly after they sit down to spin, their passions begin to subside.'[78]

The full doctrine of spinning took time to mature but the essential point was that 'when millions take to it as a sacrament, it will turn our faces godward'.[79] Gandhi looked upon the spinning wheel 'as the means of supreme *yajna* in this age. He who plies it will have lived worthily, will have won the battle of life.'[80] He enunciated a 'Law of Swadeshi', a 'self-enacting' spiritual law, which, when observed by Indians in the form of sacrificial spinning, would ultimately through the extension of the sacrificial spirit to all areas of life bring about 'the final emancipation of the human soul from its earthly bondage'. The body being a hindrance to the soul 'in its outward journey', standing in the way of its 'realizing its oneness with other lives', the 'votary of swadeshi ... in his striving to identify himself with the entire creation seeks to be emancipated from the bondage of the physical body'.[81]

'There are many who assert and some who believe', wrote Tagore in his essay on 'The Cult of the Charkha' in 1925, 'that *swaraj* can be attained by the *charkha*; but I have yet to meet a person who has a clear idea of the process.'[82] Tagore was deploring the Indian propensity for symbolic action. But he had failed to take Gandhi's measure. Spinning was no mere symbol to him but a supreme example of that desireless action which was the route to liberation.[83] Sufficiently collectivized and coordinated, spinning would generate the spiritual force which would propel Indians – and ultimately all humanity – towards union with God. Swaraj would be arrived at on the way. For the Law of Swadeshi was no other than that Law of Sacrifice through which the enlightened efforts of mankind were assured of divine assistance.

During the 1920s Sabarmati attracted many foreign visitors. Some came for a short visit and were enchanted. Those who stayed longer – including Gandhi's comrade of many years, his 'Mirabehn', Madeleine Slade – often arrived at a less positive view.[84]

Like Phoenix, Sabarmati was ruled by the clock, and ashramites trooped at the sound of the bell to the activities of the day. For most these involved varieties of ritualized toil such as spinning, peeling vegetables and cleaning latrines: paid labourers were employed to do much of the heavy work. The ashramites' lives revolved worshipfully around Gandhi, for whose attention competition was keen. Quarrels were frequent – about the performance of duties, about possessions, about the organization of the kitchen (a particular and perennial source of discord). Sex being a constant preoccupation, lapses were common.

A significant part of Gandhi's correspondence between 1925 and 1933, when Sabarmati was disbanded, dealt with problems at the ashram, in which he took an intense and detailed personal interest, particularly when they involved sexual misconduct. Like many puritans he liked to hear people confess. In 1925 Mahadev and others had to step in to prevent him requiring the public reading of confessions by some boys found guilty of unclean behaviour.[85]

There were other problems to deal with, including petty theft, which proved impossible to eradicate, and the persistence of untouchability. As late as 1933, when Gandhi's untouchable ward Lakshmi was married at the ashram (to a foundling of unknown antecedents) he had to make sure the untouchables were not seated apart from the other guests.[86] Matters came to a head in 1929 when it was revealed that Chhaganlal Gandhi, the manager of the ashram, had for years been embezzling ashram funds. Gandhi was the last to know.

The eventual disbandment of the ashram in July 1933 was announced to the world as an act of solidarity with those who were experiencing repression at the hands of the government. But Gandhi was later to speak of the 'failure' of Sabarmati.[87] He started a new ashram, at Segaon near Wardha in central India, in 1934, but it fared no better. By 1940 he was considering closing it down, but had no heart for starting up yet again. Quit India, internment, and the horrors of partition spared him a decision.

The failure of the ashrams represented personal failure of the most discouraging kind. It being axiomatic with Gandhi that the influence for good acquired through self-purification was visible in the first instance in one's immediate surroundings, the shortcomings of the ashramites could only reflect his own. He decided that the ashramites must be judged not according to their lapses but according to the effort they were making – logical if the journey and the arrival were somehow the same – and he justified to himself in this way whatever faith he continued to muster in the ashrams as spiritual experiments. He made a point of not being too choosy about the people who settled at Sabarmati. Their commitment to self-improvement, he emphasized, was what was important. The result was that standards declined. Both Ramdas and Manilal, who had endured the rigours of Phoenix, noted the laxness at Sabarmati.[88]

But if the ashrams failed in their spiritual purpose, they succeeded in their practical one of providing soldiers for Gandhi's peaceful army. 'Public

workers' were despatched from them to man the constructive programme as
it took shape around India. And at any given time a body of men and women
could be mobilized for civil disobedience. The supreme sacrifice was never
far from Gandhi's mind. Pyarelal long remembered the evening at Sabarmati
when Gandhi observed that

> he looked forward to the day when he would call out the inmates of the Ashram
> ... to immolate themselves at the altar of non-violence. Unmoved, he would
> watch them fall one after another before a shower of bullets, without a trace of
> fear or hatred but only love in their hearts. And then, when the last one of them
> had fallen, he would himself follow.[89]

Family troubles were if anything an even more brutal reminder than the
failings of the ashramites of the uncertain extent of his spiritual power.
Ramdas and Manilal – in 1925 respectively 27 and 33 – rebelled against the
imposition of celibacy. When Manilal, who was still living in South Africa
but anxious to return to India, wanted to marry a Muslim woman, Gandhi
told him that such a marriage, besides being 'contrary to dharma', would
have an adverse effect on the Hindu–Muslim problem. It would thus prevent
his return to India and perhaps require removing him from the editorship of
*Indian Opinion*. All the same, it was up to him.[90] In 1927 Gandhi married off
both Ramdas and Manilal to women of his choice. Kasturbai too continued to
present problems. She was unkind to Gandhi's female favourites at Sabarmati,
resisted his dietary stringencies, and in 1929 was discovered to have kept back
a small amount of money for herself from money given to her for the ashram,
earning a public rebuke. In 1927 Devdas, hitherto the model son, fell in love
with a daughter of Rajagopalachari, and wished to marry. Rajagopalachari was
a Brahmin and neither he nor Gandhi would sanction an inter-caste marriage.
(The couple persisted and were married six years later.)

But the main problem as usual was Harilal. In June 1925 his shady business
dealings in Calcutta were brought to Gandhi's attention. Perhaps because
Gandhi happened to be in Calcutta at the time, promoting the *charkha* and
mending fences with the Swarajists, and thus felt compelled to distance himself
from his erring son, he chose to denounce him publicly and at length in an
article in *Young India*.[91] He was odious. 'Men may be good', he wrote, 'not
necessarily their children.' The statement was more an articulation of doctrine
than the simple piece of sanctimoniousness it appeared to be. As he explained
a few weeks later to Ramdas, he believed that the differing characters of his

sons reflected the degree of spiritual development he had attained at the times they were conceived: 'There can be a mistake in my calculations', he said, 'but so far my predictions have proved correct. ... I am experiencing my four states in you four brothers.'[92] He had long assumed that the unalloyed carnality of his conception meant that Harilal's spiritual prospects in this life were dim. He could therefore without embarrassment or self-consciousness explain to readers of *Young India* that it was his 'desire to non-co-operate with all that is evil' which necessitated the repudiation of his firstborn.

Harilal kept on giving trouble, leading a rackety life, drinking too much and drifting around. In 1936 he converted briefly to Islam. He was the only one of the four sons to take serious issue with his father's ideas. At the time of Manilal's request to marry the Muslim girl, he sent a letter to *Navajivan* in favour of inter-faith marriages, but Gandhi refused to print it or make a public reply.[93] In 1927 he was writing to the papers accusing his father of propagating Buddhism.[94] But there were moments when reconciliation seemed possible, and in spite of his efforts at non-attachment Gandhi was always overjoyed at the prospect. His hopes came to nought, as they were bound to do. 'I have always believed', he wrote to the most spirited of his sons, 'that I was a bad man when Ba carried you in her body, but after your birth I have been doing greater and greater penance for my former life. How can I, therefore, give up all hope?'[95]

In 1928 a further blow fell with the death of the man who 'was dearer to me than my own sons, who never once deceived me or failed me', Maganlal. 'He whom I had singled out as heir to my all is no more', Gandhi announced to the world, grief-stricken, in *Young India*.[96] Maganlal had been his spiritual disciple, his confidant and the effective manager of the ashram – a 'born mechanic', who had mastered and made technical improvements to the processes of spinning and weaving, built up the dairy herd, and designed the buildings whose simple elegance is his memorial today. He could not be replaced and Gandhi could only hope that 'He who has subjected me to the ordeal' had some purpose in mind and would get him through it.[97] For a time, he moved into Maganlal's room at the ashram, 'to commune with his spirit'.[98]

In 1926 Gandhi imposed on himself a 'year of silence' on public matters. The main product of this year was his *Discourses on the 'Gita'*. These were talks given to ashram inmates, on which notes were taken by Mahadev Desai. They were not published until 1955.

In 1927 Gandhi began writing his formal commentary on the *Gita*, *Anasaktiyoga*. This was first published in Gujarati in 1930 and then in English in 1931. In 1946 the English version of *Anasaktiyoga* was reissued together with a commentary written by Mahadev in 1933–34, in a single volume entitled *The Gita According to Gandhi*, to which Gandhi contributed a foreword. Together with *Letters on the 'Gita'*, a simplified commentary written in 1932 for ashramites who had difficulty with the earlier work, these materials give us Gandhi's mature thoughts on the *Gita*.[99]

The text is treated always as a prescription for self-realization. The large part of it, which deals with the necessity of worship (*bhakti*), is either passed over without comment, or dismissed with the argument that 'to be a real devotee is to realize oneself'.[100] This alone would make Gandhi's interpretation highly idiosyncratic to most Indians, for whom the *Gita* is pre-eminently, as the title says, the 'Song of the Lord'.

One of several distinctive features of the interpretation offered in the *Discourses* was the argument that Krishna, the *avatar*, who in the poem reveals his divinity and instructs Arjuna to 'love and worship' him, was not a god come to earth but a man who in the process of his own self-realization has become like God. This was the idea Gandhi had sketched out to Jamnadas in 1913 and hinted at in Bihar in 1921.[101] In the privacy of the ashram he now developed the idea in terms which left no doubt that the word *avatar* might one day be applied to himself.

In the *Discourses* Gandhi referred often, and as something to be taken for granted, to his progress towards a perfection which might in the end prove unattainable, but to which he was far closer than his audience. Taken together with the belief expressed from time to time that public adulation was somehow a validation of his divine calling, these remarks provide the context for his observations on the *avatar*.

God, he says, never incarnates himself as an *atman*, and is 'never born as a human being. He is ever the same.' But when human beings 'see special excellence in some individual', they think of him as an *avatar*. 'When evil spreads in the world', he goes on, 'some persons, inspired by God, feel in their hearts that it is not enough for them to be a little good, that they must do *tapascharya* and be exceptionally good, so good that people would look upon them as perfect manifestation of the Divine in man. That is how Shri Krishna came to be worshipped as the fullest avatar.' Through their *tapascharya* these persons 'generate goodness in the world' and wield its power. 'This can happen even in the present age. Anyone who has completely shed hatred and ill will, who has succeeded in making his life a perfect embodiment of truth, can command everything in life. He does not have to ask that anything be done. He has only to wish and the wish will be fulfilled.' (Here the state of *avatar*-hood seems equated with that of *moksha* while still alive.) He himself, Gandhi observes, had been 'passionately eager to do such penance' that Hindus and Muslims would cease to feel enmity for each other – presumably a reference to the 21-day fast – but God for his own good reasons had seen fit to humble his pride. Things would have to get much worse, he concluded, before He stepped in.[102]

In *Anasaktiyoga*, which was written for publication, Gandhi more cautiously interpreted the doctrine of the *avatar* enunciated in Chapter 4 of the *Gita* as an allegorical assurance that in the eternal conflict between right and wrong, right – 'which is Truth' – will always prevail; for God's nature is good and 'Wrong has no independent existence'.[103] Mahadev elaborated a little in his commentary. The belief that God periodically comes to earth to save mankind, he says, is a product of the imagination:

> But the same belief rationalized becomes a belief not in God embodied as man, but either in God working out the cosmic purpose through the universal law or in man ascending to the estate of God by wholly divesting himself of all his earthliness and completely spiritualizing himself, or sacrificing himself in God.[104]

Self-realization and self-purification were treated as equivalent by Gandhi in his observations on the *Gita*. Some of his most colourful animadversions on the filthiness of the flesh are to be found in the *Discourses*. How can anyone, he asks, feel attracted to the body, 'which excretes dirt through countless pores, such dirt as we cannot bear touching'?[105] It was being imprisoned 'in the cage of the body', 'like a criminal', which was the chief impediment to achieving the final object of life, union with the divine.[106] The process of birth itself is pronounced 'repulsive'.[107] Yet it is through the body that self-purification and thus self-realization will be achieved.[108] 'Enjoyment of sense-pleasure', Gandhi instructed his flock, 'leads to death. *Brahmacharya* leads to immortality.'[109]

Patiently Gandhi squeezed out the familiar messages of non-violence and selfless service from the recalcitrant text. Fulfilling his self-imposed obligation to propagate the universal religion through his native scriptures was not easy. The *Discourses* seem to peter out a little dispiritedly; it may have been with

relief that he turned to his other exegetical task of 1926 – the series of talks
on the New Testament given to students at the Gujarat Vidyapith.

Responding to accusations of crypto-Christianity when word of these
talks got out, Gandhi declared himself 'a staunch *sanatani* Hindu'. But he
observed that if Hinduism, Christianity and Islam were understood correctly,
they would all be perceived to be the same.[110] In these talks – of which the
only surviving record appears to be some notes found in Mahadev's papers[111]
– Gandhi's ideas find relatively unforced expression. He sketches out a portrait
of the esoteric Jesus – the 'spiritual aspirant' of human, not divine birth, who
may have been inspired by 'Eastern philosophers'. This Jesus subdues the
flesh (the 40 days' fast, the temptations in the wilderness) before beginning
his ministry, which means that during these final years his very presence
'purifies the atmosphere' around him. Though 'a soul far more advanced',
he permits himself, for form's sake, and so as not to 'disturb the even tenor
of the mass understanding', to undergo initiation at the hands of John the
Baptist. (Gandhi here compares Jesus' reluctance to get too far ahead of
'mass understanding' to his own advocacy of spinning. He knows, he says,
that there are many things other than spinning that could be done, but 'if
I did not spin, there would arise doubt and confusion in the people's mind.
That is why I must ply the wheel.') Jesus' message to the people is '*Repent*'
– purify yourself – and in the Sermon on the Mount he delivers his gospel
of self-purification through world-renunciation and non-violence. As Jesus
makes clear in its final words, the 'laws' laid down in the Sermon 'are meant
for leading a man to perfection': 'Be ye therefore perfect, even as your Father
which is in heaven is perfect.' 'This verse', Gandhi says, 'means that you must
be completely lost in God. If you wish to become God (to use the language
of the Vedanta), you must observe *ahimsa*.' 'Love your enemy' is the Sermon's
supreme command. 'What else should a man do', Gandhi inquires, 'if the
principle of *advaita* (non-duality in life, matter and everything) is true?' For
if a man desires 'to see others as himself', he 'must forget the separateness
of one physical frame from another'. This is presumably what Jesus learned
from the 'Eastern philosophers'.

His year of silence over, Gandhi ventured forth to test the political waters.
They were chilly. The Congress–Muslim alliance had by now disintegrated,
and the Muslim League was calling for a federal form of government with
largely autonomous provinces to be created along communal lines – a pre-

cursor of the demand for Pakistan. At the same time, the Hindu revivalist movement under Madan Mohan Malaviya, a founder of the Hindu Mahasabha, had acquired a firm footing in Congress, and by 1926, the year of elections to provincial and central legislatures, was sufficiently organized at the grassroots to challenge the claim of Motilal Nehru's Swaraj party to be Congress's political voice. After an unsuccessful attempt to outmanoeuvre the Malaviya party in the run-up to the elections, Motilal, the old secularist, acknowledged its indispensability at the polls and was reborn as a good Hindu. Congress propaganda became more overtly Hindu in its appeal; and by 1930, except for a few 'nationalist Muslims' who adorned its committees, Congress had become an essentially Hindu body.[112] Meanwhile, the number of violent incidents involving communal antagonism continued to increase through the 1920s, the responsibility lying chiefly with the Hindus who persuaded themselves their religion was in danger from the Muslim minority.

By 1926 Gandhi had resigned himself to communal violence and was vaguely hoping it would be purgative – fighting for your beliefs was at any rate 'better than utter helplessness and unmanliness'.[113] He resisted attempts to enlist his mediation. Indeed he failed to take the firm stand against Hindu militancy his beliefs appeared to require, with what mixture of conviction and calculation is impossible to say. Unlike Buddhism and Christianity, Islam could not really be fitted into what he chose to regard as the universal religion of mankind. He viewed Muslim iconoclasm with some irritation. 'I have found not the slightest difficulty in Hindu circles about evoking reverence for the Koran and the Prophet', he said. 'But I have found difficulty in Mussulman circles about evoking the same reverence for the Vedas or the incarnations.' He hoped this 'illiberalism and intolerance' would be 'a passing phase', and Muslims would come to appreciate Hinduism's 'inclusive' nature.[114]

The critical moment came on 23 December 1926, with the assassination by a young Muslim of Swami Shraddhanand, the leading figure in the movement to reconvert Indian Muslims to Hinduism (and incidentally a dear friend of Charlie Andrews, for whom he epitomized the virile Hinduism of yore[115]). Gandhi heard the news as he was on his way to the Congress session at Gauhati – his first foray into national politics after the end of his silent year – and it was he who moved the resolution in open session deploring the as-sassination and memorializing the victim, whose 'pure and unsullied life' he held up for emulation. The Swami's reconversion (*shuddhi*) campaign – which Gandhi had opposed – was passed over with the observation that it involved no ill will.[116] With some equivocation, he endorsed the Hindu Mahasabha's Shraddhanand Memorial Fund and appealed for donations.

The rise of the Malaviya party in Congress affected Gandhi closer to home. Its victorious candidate for the Benares and Gorakhpur division in the central legislature was the Marwari magnate G.D. Birla, his principal financial backer and indispensable supporter of the Sabarmati ashram. Birla's victory was a triple betrayal: he had succumbed to the lure of legislative office, done so under the communalist flag, and not even bothered to inform Gandhi of his candidacy. 'There must be some mistake', had been Gandhi's reaction on learning of it from Motilal Nehru.[117] But there was no mistake, and no choice but to digest it. Defeat would have been better, Gandhi told him, but what was done was done. Meanwhile he would be paying him a visit in Calcutta.[118]

These accommodations to the spirit of the times did Gandhi little good. At Gauhati, to which he had gone professing his usual reluctance, there was no movement in his direction. The legislatures were the object of everyone's attention, and though he spoke on a number of topics, it was rather forlornly. 'I do not need your patronage', he told the Subjects Committee as it deliberated a motion requiring delegates to wear *khadi*.[119] 'Please eliminate me from your mind', he advised the framers of the Independence Resolution (which was rejected).[120] After Gauhati he set off on a long tour to promote the *charkha*.

The tour did not go well. He tried to stay off the subject of *shuddhi* and was accused of being a Muslim agent. He was asked what was the point of *khadi*. In Maharashtra he was presented with an open letter claiming that the local notables only put on *khadi* for his visit. He was also asked what he had done with the Tilak Swaraj Fund. On 5 February he was visited by an Indian Communist member of the British parliament, Shapurji Saklatvala, who told him that spinning was a waste of time and he should organize the workers. Saklatvala followed up with an open letter to the *Hindustan Times* on 17 March to 'Dear Comrade Gandhi', denouncing him for betraying the nationalist movement in 1922 and accusing him of encouraging the mahatma cult. Saklatvala himself had observed Gandhi allowing people to touch his feet: how could he tolerate this? Gandhi's long reply lacked force. The touching of feet was dismissed in a humorous aside.[121] The following week an interviewer from the *Bombay Chronicle* told Gandhi his response to Saklatvala was disappointingly vague.[122] On 19 March he visited Swami Shraddhanand's Gurukul Kangri, the epicentre of militant Hinduism. Here he tried awkwardly to blend praise of the institution's services to religion with criticism of its intolerance: some of the students had sent him abusive letters.[123] During all this time he was trying to deal at long distance with the problems of the ashram. He pushed on, his days crammed with engagements, and on 26 March he collapsed with what appears to have been an attack of high blood pressure.

Gandhi was 57 and hypertension is not unknown among men of that age under great physical and mental stress. But once again he felt confronted with the spiritual humiliation of serious illness and his thoughts turned to the imperfections of his *brahmacharya*. 'If it were not for human passion', he wrote to the women of Sabarmati, there would be no disease: a true *brahmachari* at the moment of death would drop 'gently down like a ripe fruit'.[124]

It was not merely impure thoughts which stood between him and the attainment of perfect *brahmacharya*. In 1924 he had announced to the consternation of his admirers that he was still having nocturnal discharges.[125] This was not the last of such confessions, which were made in the name of truth and edification but were not devoid of a hint of advertisement. Until Gandhi's thoughts acquired wings, he had to be credibly presumed to be still struggling with the demons of desire. To his dying day (at age 78) he thought of himself as a man whose capacity for sexual intercourse was unimpaired.

An outbreak of self-abuse among the ashram boys was the occasion for opening a correspondence with an authority on yoga, S.D. Satavalekar, whose book on *brahmacharya* Gandhi read while confined to bed after his collapse.[126] It was soon obvious that his interest was primarily on behalf of himself. (He also contacted another yoga practitioner, one Nanabhai, asking for advice.) The correspondence was extremely respectful on Gandhi's side, and he arranged for Satavalekar's publications to be distributed at the ashram.

But the *pandit*'s advice was eventually found wanting, being too much concerned with the retention of semen and too little with the conquest of desire, and the correspondence lapsed in June. It appears to have clarified for Gandhi the extent to which his conception of *brahmacharya* differed from the traditional one. He never abandoned his belief in the physical and psychological value of retaining semen. But, as he pointed out, the existence of 'a certain process in Western medicine [vasectomy, presumably] by which a man can retain the vital fluid but is not freed from passion' suggested the limitations of the hydraulic approach. He experienced some benefit from the use of yogic breathing exercises, but concluded that – like the cold baths he recommended – they were but 'a stage on the way' which it might be 'necessary for an aspirant to pass through'.

The correspondence with Satavalekar apparently emboldened him to make a public demonstration of the nature of true *brahmacharya*, and the degree of indifference he could now claim to the sexual charm of women. The practice of putting his hands on girls' shoulders when walking began at this time. There were soon complaints, and he gave it up. The practice was resumed – and dropped again, several times, in response to objections – and then continued for the remainder of his life, though it was some time before he appeared in public with his 'walking sticks'. He claimed inspiration from his experience in Europe and South Africa, where he had known men and women practise celibacy without observing the customary Indian restrictions on casual physical contact. But he also emphasized that such freedom as he permitted himself was not for everyone. (In Europe, in fact, the practice would have seemed just as provocative as it did in India.)

Recovery from his collapse was swift and he experienced the usual exhilaration at escape from the jaws of death. The change in his mood was marked. Resigned to his end in April, he was full of energy by June. There was a temporary acceptance of the possibility that he was not the awaited one,[127] which seemed to contribute to his recuperation. The pursuit of perfection was enthusiastically resumed. Dietary matters claimed his close attention: milk, he decided, would have to go; it was costing him all his strength 'to keep the brute in me under disciplined subjection and control'.[128] He threw himself into completing the *Autobiography*, and began to explore the possibility of installing Jawaharlal Nehru as president of Congress. He even began to consider the possibility of *satyagraha*, for which there was no lack of 'occasions'.[129] An attempt at a comeback was in the air.

What he took in the end from the experience of physical collapse and recovery was a renewed sense that his life on earth had meaning to the extent that he kept himself accountable to God alone. He formulated a new doctrine rationalizing his determination to truckle no further: the 'discovery' that 'really speaking, there is no distinction whatsoever between individual growth and corporate growth, that corporate growth is therefore entirely dependent on individual growth.' The advancement of one meant the advancement of all.[130]

This was a refinement of the position that all life was one which struck Gandhi with great force and had an immediate effect. He spoke out forthrightly on the communal question.[131] It was beyond him at present, he said, to contribute to a solution, and the 'humiliation' he felt was 'too deep for words', but there was no attempt to disguise the disgust he felt with the sectarian follies of Hindus and Muslims alike. It was not true religion, he said, which led them to do each other harm. He recovered his eloquence and a number of correspondents felt the force of his plain speaking.[132] Life was too short, seems to have been his feeling, to permit himself any weakening of his purpose, any concession to the forces of disorder which assailed him on every side. Through his progress, all would progress: his weakness would mean the weakening of all.

He was presented almost immediately with a situation to which prevarication was the only practical response: the uproar created in India by the publication of the American journalist Katherine Mayo's *Mother India* in the summer of 1927. *Mother India* was an accomplished piece of muckraking, by an author entirely in sympathy with those who shouldered the white man's burden. It dealt principally with Indian sexual mores and the problem of child marriage, but lambasted in passing the practice of untouchability, the ignorance of traditional Indian medical practitioners, and the general absence of sanitation. Many Indians assumed it was written at the direct instigation of the British government – a possibility to which Gandhi discreetly alluded in the critical review he eventually published in *Young India*.[133]

The book was well documented and quotations from Gandhi's writings were used to support the author's case. This was Gandhi's problem and presumably the reason why it was nearly three months before he made a public response.

At the time Gandhi wrote his critique he was touring south India and was everywhere attacking two of the practices denounced in *Mother India*: child marriage and the maintenance of the sacred prostitutes known as *devadasis*. Child marriage he had campaigned against for many years, assigning it a large part of the blame for both the moral and the physical feebleness of the Indian race. The line he eventually took on the book was to condemn Mayo's motives for writing it. There was little which was untrue, he said, in the sense of departing from the facts – but the book as a whole was 'untruthful' because the author had set out to present India to the world in the worst light. His article was entitled 'Drain Inspector's Report'. Later his comments became less equivocal – 'libellous' was a term employed – and he lent his prestige to attempts to discredit the book.

# SEVEN

# Salt

It took another 18 months for Gandhi to return to power. His opportunity came with the British government's blunder in sending out an all-British commission – the Simon commission – to report on the future of responsible government in India. The failure to include even a single Indian in the commission's composition produced such outrage that Indian politicians patched up their differences and united in refusing to cooperate with it. In this atmosphere of wounded national pride and sudden doubts about the significance of the Montagu–Chelmsford reforms, Gandhi and civil disobedience became relevant again. At the Calcutta Congress of December 1928 he stated his terms. They were as before: *khadi*, support for the social causes in which he took an interest, and complete control.

After recovering from his breakdown, he was active behind the scenes. Deciding that his old friend the nationalist Muslim Ansari was a better bet for the time being as Congress president than the 'high-souled' Jawaharlal, he managed to secure his election in the name of giving Congress more credibility with the Muslims. Ansari displayed an unanticipated independence of mind and had to be reminded that his job was to express hopes for Hindu–Muslim unity and not to 'meddle in anything else'.[1] Even with Ansari in charge, the long discussed but never previously adopted 'Independence Resolution' was passed at the Madras Congress of December 1927, at the instigation of Jawaharlal Nehru and the Bengali radical Subhas Bose. Gandhi was able to get the resolution watered down. Afterwards he told the mutinous Jawaharlal that if necessary he was prepared for an open break.[2]

When the Simon Commission arrived in India in early February 1928 it was greeted by a countrywide *hartal*, and demonstrations wherever it went. Gandhi stood aloof: his time was not yet. Huge demonstrations were all very well, he told a missionary friend, but 'There is no reality behind them'. He could only lead a movement whose organizers had a 'living faith' in *khadi*.[3]

While staying out of the limelight himself, he began to move forward on two fronts. The cloth boycott programme was resurrected and offered to the country in the pages of *Young India*; and he moved to reopen *satyagraha* in Bardoli, with Vallabhbhai Patel as the man publicly in charge. His intention was to put civil disobedience back on the national agenda.

God handed Gandhi an opportunity in the form of the falling due of the periodic revenue assessment for Bardoli in 1926. In view of the increased prosperity of the district since the last assessment in 1896, the land tax was raised in 1927 by 22 per cent.

Patel was approached by the peasant proprietors of Bardoli with a request to support a proposed campaign to withhold the additional amount of tax. Gandhi then stepped in with a proposal that no tax at all should be paid until the government rescinded the increase.[4] The stage was thus set for a significant confrontation with the government at a time when the hostile reception given to the Simon Commission had increased its vulnerability, and *satyagraha* commenced on 12 February 1928. Gandhi urged the *satyagrahis* on in articles in *Young India* and *Navajivan*, but it was not until July, as the struggle was approaching its climax, that he made public the fact of his involvement in the *satyagraha* 'from its very beginning'.[5]

He was determined this time to have power thrust upon him. He would respond only to a 'call' in the form of beseechings by Congress politicians which were felt to coincide with the promptings of the inner voice. In the early part of 1928 his inner voice was telling him that national purification was insufficiently advanced – a practical as well as a religious concern, because he would have to count on the country's steadfastness in any campaign of which he was given charge.

Even in Bardoli, as Gandhi reminded the *satyagrahis* on the eve of battle, the vows 'about khadi, untouchability and so on' had not been observed to the proper extent; they would have to dispel his doubts by their 'determined conduct'.[6] In assigning leadership of the campaign to someone else he hedged his political bets on the results and reserved judgement on the moral fitness of the troops. As the campaign progressed, he emphasized its inherently 'purifying' nature, and its successful outcome, in August, laid his concerns to rest. In 1937 he expressed 'shame' that Bardoli had still 'not fulfilled the condition of the charkha', nor achieved prohibition, nor eradicated untouchability; he would not presently, he said, consider launching a campaign 'on the strength of Bardoli'.[7] In 1928, as the movement for national resistance ripened, he overcame his hesitations.

Gandhi's detachment from the day-to-day operation of the campaign gave Patel a free hand to manage it in his own fashion. The weapon of caste sanctions was effectively employed to ensure that no one broke ranks and paid his taxes: 'Why should the peasant not make his own social arrangement to fight against injustice?' Vallabhbhai inquired.[8] Not only individuals but whole villages were boycotted if they failed to join the campaign. Yet the sacred nature of the struggle was assumed. In a preview of Gandhi's later prayer meetings, most gatherings included a communal rendering of the *Ramdhun*. Ritual prostrations were accepted by Vallabhbhai.

Social pressure and religious cajolery were applied to untouchable groups – who of course did not pay land tax – to support their superiors by refusing to assist the government: their gods, they were advised, had sent Gandhi to save them.[9] Patel refused to countenance any tampering with the system of bonded labour. Gandhian social workers in the district had already accepted that their hands were tied by the opposition of the farmers who constituted the political cadre: their hope was to inspire feelings of 'kindness and fairness' in them.[10]

Under Vallabhbhai's generalship – after Bardoli he was known as 'Sardar' ('chief') Patel – the farmers stood firm against both official intimidation and attempts to divide the movement by piecemeal concessions. As on previous occasions, Gandhi declared victory on the basis of a compromise. His judgement was sound. In the political circumstances in which the government currently found itself, its agreement to an inquiry led rapidly to concession of almost all the campaign's demands, and even the cancellation of fines already collected.

Bardoli was a huge personal triumph for Gandhi, re-establishing his reputation as a fighter after his reversal of 1922. During the months of resistance the struggle took on a national significance, and demonstrated to an Indian public already aroused by the despatch of the Simon commission the power of civil disobedience. To some disgruntled resisters who wanted to fight on, Gandhi posed the question: 'And why are you impatient? The bigger battle is still before us – the battle for freedom of which the campaign was planned in 1921 and which has yet to be fought.'[11]

Before battle could be joined – of necessity, through a Congress in which political Hinduism was now a powerful force – Gandhi's credentials as a good Hindu had to be in order.

He had remained active in the protection of the cow. He had come implicitly to the defence of his fellow Hindus in his condemnation of *Mother India* – for it was their customs which Mayo, who had not been reticent about preferring the hardy, clean-living men of the North, had chiefly censured. Now an occasion presented itself, as with the passing of Swami Shraddhanand, to speak well of the communalist dead. On 17 November 1928 the powerful Punjabi politician Lala Lajpat Rai, who with Malaviya had organized the Hindu communalist threat to the Congress vote in 1926, died of a heart attack, 18 days after being injured in a police *lathi* charge while leading a demonstration against the Simon commission. Gandhi immediately pronounced the death of the more or less martyred Rai – with whom his relations had always been difficult[12] – a national calamity, and moved swiftly to take a leading part in the obsequies and raise money for the usual memorial fund. Appearances notwithstanding, he observed, the deceased Arya Samajist and Hindu Mahasabhite had been a true 'friend of Mussulmans and sincerely desirous of promoting Hindu–Muslim unity'.[13]

On 30 November he made a more explicit move in the direction of Hindu solidarity, effectively ending his relationship with Shaukat Ali, who had been outspoken about the increasingly Hindu coloration of Congress politics and Hindu responsibility for communal violence. In a letter intended for publication, Gandhi informed him that, with respect to communal misdeeds, 'the Mussulman is at least equally guilty with the Hindu, if not on the whole more so', and that it was now up to him and his brother to seek a rapprochement with their old comrade if they so wished.[14] A week later Gandhi made his decisive move into the Hindu camp. An article appeared in *Young India* giving his imprimatur to the Nehru report, recommending that it be approved in its entirety by Congress at the Calcutta session due to take place in three weeks' time.[15]

The Nehru report on the future constitution of India, whose chief author was Motilal Nehru, now the president-elect of Congress, was an attempt to formulate an all-India response to the Simon Commission. It recommended dominion status as India's goal. In addition it addressed the constitutional issues of particular interest to the Muslims: the degree of control to be exercised from the centre, the organization of the provinces, and the questions of separate electorates and reserved seats. In 1927 Congress had agreed to the reservation of seats in the Muslim majority provinces of Bengal and Punjab in proportion to the Muslim population, and to the reservation for Muslims of a third of the seats in the central legislature. But the Nehru report recommended reservation of seats for Muslims only in the Muslim minority provinces. There was to be a strong central legislature with no reserved seats, and joint electorates. These recommendations were opposed by the Muslim League, which, though it did not altogether reject joint electorates, demanded that the agreement of 1927 be upheld, with a weaker central government and residual powers vested in the provinces. When Jinnah presented these demands (his '14 points') at the All-Parties Convention called to consider the report in November they were all overwhelmingly rejected by the predominantly Hindu assembly, and he was told by the prominent Mahasabhite Congressman M.R. Jayakar that he was without standing as a representative of the Muslim community. For Jinnah, it was the parting of the ways.

Gandhi had told Motilal in March that though he disliked reservation of seats Congress should abide by its commitment to them.[16] But by October he thought that acceptance by Congress of the Nehru report was essential to the 'unity' of the country in its struggle with the British. Uncertainty about his attendance at Calcutta was ended when he decided to 'obey' the urgings of Motilal who wanted his help in getting the report through Congress.[17]

It was, then, in the context of the anticipated struggle against the common enemy that Gandhi turned his back on the Muslims. They were after all mostly outside Congress, which remained the only practical instrument for disciplined, non-violent, mass action against the Raj. The energizing effect of his insight of the previous year that to his own self he must be true had not diminished – but neither had his ability to reconcile political objectives with spiritual concerns. He served truth as he saw it by accepting a personal duty to act with the utmost selflessness towards Muslim aspirations. At Calcutta that duty was of necessity subordinated to his duty to the nation. In the future it would take some interesting forms.

His contribution to the debate on the report at Calcutta focused on the issue which was creating division within the Congress ranks: whether dominion status or full independence should be the stated aim. He produced a formula which for the time being was accepted by both parties, that dominion status should be agreed on as the immediate goal, to be replaced by complete independence should the British reject the Nehru report. The issues of communal representation would have to be settled, he said, another day.[18]

His views on the Hindu–Muslim problem had already changed in a fundamental way. He had been thinking for some time in the terms which later dictated his preference for the bloody resolution of communal differences within a unitary state over the partition of India into two separate countries On 29 April 1928 he told C. Vijayaraghavachariar, who later joined the committee working on the Nehru report, that 'My solution to the problem is so different from what is generally expected. I am more than ever convinced that the communal problem should be solved outside of legislation and if, in order to reach that state, there has to be civil war, so be it. Who will listen to a proposal so mad at this?'[19] (And who could doubt what the outcome of a civil war between Hindus and Muslims would be?) It followed that, though Hindu–Muslim unity remained a prerequisite of *swaraj*, failure to attain it need not delay formal independence. True *swaraj* would have to come later, perhaps only after the two communities, in an essentially purificatory process sometimes compared by Gandhi to the rising of dirt to the surface, had fought each other to a standstill.[20] Then people would understand at last that Islam and Hinduism were mere variants of the way Indians made their way to God.

Gandhi said in November he was not going to Calcutta with the intention of resuming leadership. He would only lead India 'when the nation comes to me to be led, when there is a national call', and he was certain of his 'power over the masses'.[21] But he had registered the quickening pace of confrontation, had contributed to it with the Bardoli campaign, and could smell gunpowder in the air. Bardoli, he said, was only a local struggle, but all such struggles in habituating people to 'corporate suffering' brought India nearer *swaraj*.[22] Lajpat Rai's injuries were welcomed with an immediate wire: 'Hearty congratulations'; and he confessed that his reaction on hearing the news had been: ' "Well done! Now we shall not be long getting swaraj." ' It was 'the most economical thing', he said, given the inherent difficulty of executing a mass campaign of perfect non-violence, 'that leaders get assaulted or shot'. The assault on Rai he saw as 'the first trial of strength, the strength of non-violence against violence', and 'part of the game we have to play, to turn the irritation by the wanton assault into dynamic energy and husband it and utilize it for future purposes'.[23]

It was the God-given power of *ahimsa* of which Gandhi spoke, the power of which he had said not long before: 'That which gives *moksha*, that which is the supreme dharma, in whose presence ferocious beasts shed their violence, an enemy sheds his hatred, a hard heart is softened, this ahimsa is a supernatural power and it is only attained by a few after great effort and penance.'[24] Through non-violent resistance to violence, some of this power could be attained by the many.

The final obstacle to Gandhi's appearance at Calcutta was resolved only in early December when, after a protracted correspondence with the Bengali organizers, all non-*khadi* products were excluded from the contemplated *swadeshi* exhibition and the displays were arranged to his liking. Still professing reluctance but having satisfied himself that human voices at least were calling him, he descended on Calcutta with a large entourage, for which special accommodation had to be provided, and in a masterly performance brought Congress to its knees.

His first proposal at Calcutta was that the British be given two years to accept the Nehru report. Failure to accept it by 31 December 1930 would activate a broad Congress-directed campaign of civil disobedience, including refusal to pay taxes. Under pressure from the Young Turks of Congress he reduced the time limit to one year. 'Unity' was the theme of all his speeches and the reason given for the revision of the timetable. This amended motion was carried. He then laid down his terms for leadership.

The 'yoke' he would impose on them, he said, would be 'much tighter and much heavier than it was in 1920', for one year was 'nothing' to create the discipline required.[25] In fact, the yoke as described in Gandhi's list of terms presented at Calcutta appeared noticeably lighter.[26] Prohibition of intoxicating liquors was item number one. The requirements for promoting *khadi* and removing untouchability were vague enough to disturb no one, as was the obligation on Congressmen to 'devote the bulk of their time to the constructive work settled from time to time by the Congress Committee'. Promotion of Hindu–Muslim unity was not mentioned. These were terms to which most could vaguely assent and which few would vigorously oppose. The alternative to acceptance, Gandhi said, was his retirement to Sabarmati. They were accepted amid scenes of patriotic enthusiasm.

All attempts to press on him the presidency of Congress were resisted, and he saw to it that Jawaharlal was installed instead. There was no point using up his political capital in struggling with its problems on a daily basis.

After Calcutta, there was not much to do in the political arena but wait. It was up to the British to make the next move. Gandhi devoted himself to propaganda and promoting the foreign cloth boycott. He kept himself before the people in a series of spectacular tours, remaining in splendid health despite the hectic pace.

1929 was the year when scandal struck Sabarmati. Chhaganlal's and Kasturbai's lapses came to light, and word got out of the seduction of a widow by another ashramite. Gandhi moved swiftly to contain the damage. An article appeared by him in the *Bombay Chronicle* on 8 April condemning the guilty parties and attributing their sins to his own shortcomings, which he would try to 'discover and remove'.[27] His public shaming of his wife raised some eyebrows. G.D. Birla wrote to castigate him. 'I doubt if anyone else', Gandhi replied, 'has experienced to the extent that I have the sweet joy of publicly confessing one's guilt. I am surprised you were not to able to appreciate this.'[28]

In May Gandhi resumed the experiment of living on uncooked food, hoping to achieve the passionless state: 'I do not differentiate', he said, 'as between health, non-violence and the ultimate aim of life.'[29] Twenty-two ashramites joined him, at first with encouraging results, but constipation set in and most of them had to withdraw. Gandhi went down with dysentery, and the experiment was abandoned in August.

On 31 October the wait was ended when the viceroy, Lord Irwin, announced that 'the natural issue of India's constitutional progress is the attainment of Dominion status'.

The 'Irwin declaration' was a carefully thought out attempt to forestall civil disobedience and rally 'moderate' support. It could be argued to be no more than a clarification of the statement in fact contained in the viceroy's official instructions three years before, that India would one day have a place among His Majesty's dominions. No timetable for implementation was suggested. But an assurance of good faith was given by a simultaneous announcement that a conference would be held at which Indians and British together would discuss India's constitutional advance. Irwin's private belief was that the attainment of dominion status by India was a goal not realistically in sight, and that even if granted it could be made to mean little. He attached much significance to a comment made to him by Gandhi in February that if Indians were free to order their destiny, they would prefer, through lack of self-confidence, to leave much in British hands.[30]

In spite of his earlier impatience for combat, Gandhi was at first inclined to welcome the declaration. Dominion status was what he wanted, and after ten months of supposed preparation Congress had yet to reach the point where it could be judged ready for battle. There was little visible activity in the areas of constructive work adumbrated, however vaguely, at Calcutta, and the foreign cloth boycott merely sputtered along. Political divisions had emerged about how to deal with the alienation of the Muslims which since Calcutta had become impossible to ignore. Gandhi's instinct was to take what was offered and work with it.

But he had reckoned without Jawaharlal and the other independence-wal-lahs, who were unwilling to settle for dominion status to be bestowed at a suspiciously indeterminate date. Debates in the British parliament made it obvious that there was no commitment on the part of the (Labour) government to grant dominion status to India any time soon. He was forced to harden his position. In December his inner voice began to tell him with increasing clarity that the situation was one which would only be resolved by *satyagraha*.[31] India was weak, the British Labour Party, no matter how willing, was also weak; the way forward therefore would lie not through the conference table, but through creating conditions that would ensure in advance that any conference would produce the appropriate result. On 23 December 1929 he informed Irwin that he would only take part in the proposed Round Table conference if he were assured in advance that the British Cabinet would back the demand he would make for immediate dominion status. Negotiations between Congress and the British government then broke down.

At the Lahore Congress a week later Gandhi proposed that India's goal should now be complete independence (*purna swaraj*), and asked Congress to authorize immediate boycott of the legislatures, followed by civil disobedience at a time and a fashion to be determined by the All-India Congress Committee. His resolution was passed by a large majority, but only after much hand-to-hand fighting in committee and obstruction in open session from both ends of the Congress political spectrum, and the defeat of many disabling amendments. The deciding factor was the desire to retain Gandhi's leadership. If there were to be a confrontation, who else could lead it? In the end his personal triumph at Calcutta was repeated at Lahore. But there was a string implicitly attached.

In his speech of welcome, the chairman of the Reception Committee, Saifuddin Kitchlew, said that, if civil disobedience were to be Congress's choice, there should be no repeat of Gandhi's suspension of it in 1922.

On the eve of what was to be his greatest campaign, Gandhi was at a loss what to do. Like a great conjuror, he had produced the appearance of unity of purpose in Congress, but Congress, it was apparent, could not be relied on as his instrument in the forthcoming struggle. He had not even tried to enlist its support at Lahore for boycott of schools, courts, or local municipalities, knowing he would not get it. When the Working Committee, now under his personal control, tried to implement the council boycott decision there was resistance, and many Congressmen refused to give up their places in the legislatures even when their resignation from Congress was demanded. He concluded that civil disobedience would have to take some form other than the mass campaign under Congress direction anticipated since Calcutta.

It was to the ashram that Gandhi now turned. For all its faults, it was an institution over which he had some real control. Civil disobedience would be offered, he told Jawaharlal on 10 January, either by himself alone, or 'jointly with a few companions'. He was not sure where Congress would come in.[32]

The voice was yet to speak regarding the precise form that disobedience would take. But one thing was clear. The hour of destiny had struck: 'The great trial of strength in this country is at hand.'[33] If non-violence were not now to carry the day, it would be 'thoroughly and rightly discredited'.[34] 'I have made up my mind', he told Charlie Andrews, 'to run the boldest risks. ... Lahore revealed it all to me.'[35] Did God really mean him to live his life in vain? He had 'no interest in living', he said, if there was no work for him 'in the direction for which He appears to me to have called me. If all this be hallucination I must perish in the flames of my own lighting.'[36] 'I admit', he said, as civil disobedience was about to begin, 'that this may be my last chance, and if I do not seize it, it may never come again.'[37]

Violence, as before at times propitious to Gandhi's leadership, was in the air in India in 1929. In December 1928 the assistant police superintendent of Lahore had been shot dead. In April bombs were thrown in the central assembly. In December a bomb was thrown at the viceroy's train, and Gandhi's motion at Lahore deploring the attack was passed by only 904 votes to 823. At Lahore there were unruly demonstrations by radical groups in Congress. In Bengal and the Punjab support for revolutionary terrorism was gaining

ground. Meanwhile the government had promulgated a Public Safety ordinance, and was prosecuting 31 leading agitators, mostly trade unionists,
in the Meerut Conspiracy Case. It was folly to imagine that any campaign
would remain non-violent. Yet it was unthinkable that there should be no
campaign at all, or even one that would begin and end with action taken by
Gandhi and a few others.

The plan Gandhi devised was this. In the first instance, civil disobedience would be offered only by himself and companions chosen for their
absolute commitment to non-violence, acting independently of Congress.
After their arrest and imprisonment, direction of the campaign would pass
to others. Then, and only then, would the mass movement begin. At that
point, 'everyone' would be expected to take up 'civil disobedience or civil
resistance'.[38] This formula, which Gandhi described as 'not so much a political
as a religious effort' on his part,[39] was accepted by the Working Committee
on 15 February. His *ahimsa*, and the force of his *ahimsa*, would not now be
compromised by acting in the name of an organization in which there was
little principled support for it.

His hope was naturally that the mass campaign, when it came, would
remain non-violent. But were it not to, then a new kind of battle would
begin. This would be the 'struggle ... of non-violence against violence, no
matter from what quarter the latter comes'. It would continue 'till a single
representative is left alive'.[40] The nature of this struggle had been spelled
out in a speech to the students of the Gujarat Vidyapith a month before.[41]
He reserved for them, he said, a higher destiny than just going to jail in
disobedience to British laws. They were to be 'pure sacrifices' in this second
struggle he saw coming. If there were violent outbursts after his arrest,
they would have to 'immolate [themselves] in the flames', not hiding while
violence was raging around them, but rushing 'into the conflagration with
a view to extinguishing it'. This was the 'higher and severer ordeal' he had
in mind for them.

What had been 'revealed' to Gandhi at Lahore and had convinced him
beyond doubt of the necessity for civil disobedience was a better understanding of the active nature and continuous applicability of non-violence.
After 'deep and prayerful thinking' it had come to him that only 'non-violent
*action*' could prevail against both the violence (in its 'extended meaning' of
'Greed, pilfering, untruth, crooked diplomacy') of the British and the violence
which was taking hold of the minds of Indians impatient for freedom. It

followed that to hold back from action at this juncture would be 'stupid if not cowardly'.[42]

Thus Gandhi rationalized his intention to continue the campaign come what may. And by postponing the mass campaign until he was no longer in charge, he relieved himself to the extent humanly possible of responsibility for it. It would be up to his *satyagrahis* to go in and quench the flames, securing perhaps the final triumph of non-violence in the process. Who was to be in charge was left open – it might be Congress, or it might be some 'successor' who would emerge in the press of circumstances.[43]

The crux of the scheme was anticipation of an early arrest. He made clear his expectation that he would be arrested very quickly. In the event this was not to be, and he was not spared the sight of violence. The Government of India, fearful of the consequences, refrained from arresting him for a month after he committed his ritual act of civil disobedience.

Before the campaign began there was a final attempt at a settlement. Gandhi submitted to the viceroy a list of 'eleven points' which if conceded would avert civil disobedience. They were: (1) total prohibition; (2) reduction of the sterling : rupee ratio to 1s 4d; (3) reduction of the land revenue by at least 50 per cent, and its subjection to legislative control; (4) abolition of the salt tax; (5) reduction of military expenditure; (6) reduction of salaries in the Indian Civil Service; (7) a protective tariff on foreign cloth; (8) passage of the Coastal Traffic Reservation Bill; (9) discharge of political prisoners except those convicted of murder or attempted murder; (10) abolition of the CID or its popular control; (11) issue of licences to use firearms in self-defence.[44] Concession of these points would show the British to be in earnest – indeed, would 'mean' *swaraj*, in the sense that it would show that the Indians, having enough 'strength' to gain the eleven points, had 'strength enough to gain an Independence Constitution'. Congress would then attend the proposed Round Table conference knowing that real dominion status would be the result.[45]

The list was bizarre and it is not known how Gandhi concocted it. Prohibition was a point he would come back to again and again. Possbly its inclusion at the head of the list – and its equally prominent position in the conditions imposed on Congress at Calcutta – was part of his effort to enlist American support. (He was to make the picketing of liquor shops a special task of women workers, and this also may have been with an eye on America, where prohibition, then in full swing, had principally been the result

of agitation by women.) The demand for the issue of firearms licenses was
connected with his long-standing concern that Indians had been 'emasculated'
by being disarmed. It was probably also a bone thrown to the organizers of
the 1927 'Nagpur Satyagraha' which involved carrying arms in defiance of
the Arms Act – a campaign of civil disobedience from which Gandhi had
dissociated himself at some political cost. The points relating to currency
and tariffs must have been included to reassure the businessmen who were
among his most important supporters.

He knew, of course, that it was impossible for Irwin to agree to these
demands, and he was prepared to work out a compromise based on concession
of a few of the more important points, or even an admission of 'the justice of
all those demands'.[46] Inevitably, the government conceded nothing, confirming
the necessity of civil disobedience.

By the end of February he knew that civil disobedience would take the
form of disobeying the salt laws. Non-payment of the salt tax was not prac-
ticable because the tax was included in the price of salt. But the government monopoly of salt production could be challenged by the simple act
of picking up salt deposits on the seashore. This was Gandhi's inspiration,
and the place selected for the crime was Dandi in Gujarat. He would walk
there, with his chosen band, all the way from Sabarmati – a distance of
over 200 miles.

When Gandhi and his companions were arrested for scooping up salt,
it would be the signal for others to do the same, or set out pans of brine
to evaporate, thereby breaking the law prohibiting salt manufacture. It was
expected from the start that at some later point a government salt works would
be raided and manufactured salt removed. A retired salt officer, sympathetic
to civil disobedience, appears to have first raised the possibility in February,
though only to condemn it as theft and 'an act of First Class Hinsa', to which
the moral arguments in support of illicitly taking up sea salt did not apply.
Gandhi, however, disagreed. There was no real difference between the two
actions – why should the people not 'take possession of what belongs to them'?
After his arrest civil resisters would be at liberty to show their opposition
to the salt laws 'in a most effective manner'.[47] This seems to have been the
origin of the spectacular raid on the Dharsana salt depot in May.

On 5 March Gandhi told the ashramites that the march would start in
a week's time. Seventy-eight men were selected for the honour of offering
*satyagraha*, and at 6.30 on the dot on the morning of 12 March, in the presence

of a large crowd gathered at the ashram, they set off, each man carrying a copy of the *Gita*.

Civil disobedience could be put off no longer. But the decision was made in circumstances which should have compelled a postponement, or a reconsideration of the form it would take. Smallpox had been present in the ashram for over a month. In an article in *Young India* on 13 February Gandhi revealed that there had so far been seven cases, one of which had proved fatal. Vaccination being against his principles, the treatment being given was rest, ventilation, filtered light, no solid food, enemas and wet sheets.[48] By 9 March three ashram children had died.

Gandhi knew that isolation of smallpox patients and those in contact with them was necessary to prevent the spread of the disease. He had in fact in June of the previous year been severe with those who, disbelieving in vaccination, failed to accept an obligation to segregate themselves.[49] But in March 1930 he saw the appearance of smallpox in the ashram not as a threat to public health for which he must assume responsibility, but as a test of his resolve, arranged by God. God, he told the grieving ashramites, was putting him on 'the eve of what is to be the final test of our strength', through a preliminary ordeal. 'I may have to see not three but hundreds and thousands being done to death during the campaign I am about to launch. Shall my heart quail before that catastrophe, or will I persevere in my faith?' No, he said, he wanted everyone to understand that this epidemic was 'not a scourge but a trial and preparation, a tribulation sent to steel our hearts'.[50] So the marchers set out, taking the infection with them into the villages of Gujarat. New cases of smallpox occurred among them en route, and at least one person had to be left behind.[51]

A strict discipline was required on the march. Morning and evening prayers were compulsory, and everyone was expected to keep a diary and spin 212 rounds per day. Some people complained, but Gandhi told them that only by observing these rules could 'any massive strength be generated'. For the power of non-violence to be awakened in a man, he reminded them, for 'divine strength' to be his, he had to be 'humble like dust'.[52] These remarks represented the triumph of hope over experience, for the troubles of the ashram were not left behind on 12 March, any more than the germs of smallpox. By the third day there were beginning to be problems with the marchers demanding food from the villagers in excess of the amounts arranged.[53] They hopped into cars and casually accepted delicacies from local people. On 29 March Gandhi appealed to them not to disgrace him. It was all such a mockery, he lamented, of the ideal of *swaraj* he was trying to put before the nation.[54]

On the eve of the march, Gandhi described the form the campaign would take once he was arrested – an event he thought might occur in the next few hours, even before he set out.[55] There should be violations of the salt laws. But, 'For the rest', so long as non-violence was observed, 'everyone has a free hand'. Where there were local leaders, their decisions should be accepted. Where there were none, the people should use initiative in finding ways to court arrest. There should be picketing of liquor stores, boycotting of law courts, resignation of government servants, and refusal to pay taxes by those possessing 'the requisite strength'. There should be general withdrawal of cooperation from the government. Non-violence working 'organically, not mechanically', it was 'sufficient ... if the person who thinks out the plan and leads the people is absolutely above board and has non-violence and truth in him'.[56] Once civil disobedience became widespread, he assured a correspondent as he approached Dandi, the 'latent power of truth and non-violence' would 'act like an electric current and keep the people under control'.[57]

Entering the Kheda district on 13 March he found that local headmen were already handing in their resignations.[58] There was nothing he could do and he gave them his blessing. Despite his anxiety to be arrested and gone before the next stage of the campaign started, he was stirred by these first acts of principled resistance and discerned 'God's hand' at work. 'I have embarked on this last struggle of my life', he told the villagers of Navagam, 'because God wishes to make me His instrument for this work.' Remember, he said, that though the government believes that 'might is right ... against me, its guns and gunpowder are no more than dust or pebbles'.[59]

The crowds that greeted him on each day's halt were a confirmation that the hand of God was indeed at work.[60] Repeatedly, he marvelled at how everything seemed to be going according to a divine plan. Through this march, he told the people of Umrachi, he hoped to see God.[61]

On 6 April he broke the salt laws. All around India thousands spontaneously followed, wading into the sea with bowls and pans in one of the strangest acts of rebellion the world has seen.

Gandhi's sense of being in God's hands was now total: he was the agent of God's untrammelled will and design. 'At present', he wrote to Mahadev on

Salt March, 1930, approaching Dandi
(Sarojini Naidu at front right)

9 April, 'my very thoughts have grown wings and they seem to have effect
even when not expressed in speech or action. That is a fact. Thoughts which
are part of *tapascharya* are single-pointed, and hence their power is greater
than that of electricity or of still subtler ether.'[62] This was the state to which
he had long aspired. He reminded the readers of *Navajivan* that the struggle
was for something greater than the freedom of India. It was for 'freeing the
world from the monstrous tyranny of material greed; it is a struggle to prove
that money is not God, but that God alone is everything and that nothing
else except Him is real.'[63]

Unexpectedly still at large, he decided to use his reprieve to organize the
campaigns against liquor and foreign cloth. Principally, he wanted to see
suffering; for 'Swaraj won without sacrifice cannot last long'. The people
were instructed that being arrested for breaking the salt laws was not enough.
There must now be 'no voluntary surrender of the salt'. Let the policemen
break your fingers, he urged, rather than let go of it. Police raids on illicit

salt pans were to be resisted to the death.[64] 'The more the people are tested', he said, 'the better.'[65] Without violence there could be no non-violence.

He had not forgotten India's disgrace at Jallianwala Bagh. The people must now 'complete' their 'training in mass non-violence' by allowing themselves 'to be trampled under horses' hoofs or bruised with baton charges'. Then when the bullets flew they would 'receive them in their chests with arms folded'.[66] 'I attach no value now to jail-going', Gandhi announced to a crowd at Bulsar in Gujarat; only the breaking of innocent heads was 'worth celebrating'.[67] It remained the case that the sacrifice of the most pure was the most efficacious: 'The law of sacrifice is uniform throughout the world. To be effective it demands the sacrifice of the bravest and the most spotless.'[68] As in the past, however, the crown of martyrdom was rather indiscriminately handed out. The death of a schoolteacher who accidentally swung an axe into his leg while cutting down a toddy palm in the anti-liquor campaign was pronounced to be 'glorious' and the fulfilment of the deceased's 'life's aim'.[69]

On 14 April Jawaharlal was arrested and riots broke out in Poona, Calcutta and Karachi. 'Somehow', Gandhi wrote to Mirabehn, 'I am unmoved.'[70] But over the next two weeks the situation became more serious. On 18 April fifty young men and women raided the government armoury at Chittagong in Bengal, shooting the sentries and torching one of the buildings – a daring act of revolutionary violence which was much admired. Nineteen of the raiders later died in skirmishes with the police. Riots and strikes flared up in Madras, the crowds reacting to police *lathi* charges not with non-violent calm but with stones and brickbats, to which firing was the response. In Peshawar the government lost control of the city to the mob for ten days beginning on 24 April.

The people were certainly suffering, as casualties mounted from police firing. But only some of this suffering was arguably 'pure'. There was no sign of mass immolation by *satyagrahi*s to check the growing violence. Gandhi ceased to speak with confidence of the divine hand at work and moved to regain the initiative for active non-violence. He decided to raid the Dharsana salt works. The decision was clearly made with the Chittagong raid in mind.[71] The Dharsana raid would be its non-violent equivalent in courage and its spiritual antidote.

The point of the raid was the resistance that was sure to be offered by the authorities when an unarmed but determined body of men advanced on the salt depot in broad daylight. Bullets could be expected to fly. Gandhi envisaged himself marching to Dharsana, as he had marched to Dandi, with companions chosen for their purity of life. In a letter to the viceroy he explained that his intention was to invite British 'wrath' into 'a cleaner if more drastic channel' by inviting it upon himself. The 'science of satyagraha', he explained, required that 'the greater the repression and lawlessness on the part of authority, the greater should be the suffering courted by the victims', success being 'the certain result of suffering of the extremest character, voluntarily undergone'. He declined to accept responsibility for violent acts committed by the people: they had been warned by him many times that violence would only impede their progress. In any case, they had been provoked beyond endurance by the 'terrorism' of the government.[72]

This letter was drafted but never sent, as Gandhi was arrested on 5 May and removed once again to Yeravda jail. As usual, he seemed to enjoy his incarceration. Anxious to avoid confrontation, the authorities provided him with a goat, all the fruit he wanted, facilities for spinning, and a personal attendant.

The government had decided it would wait no longer to arrest him. The alternative, as Irwin said, was abdication of its authority to Gandhi and the Congress.[73] The need to reassert control, particularly in Peshawar, where two platoons of the Garwhal Rifles had refused riot duty, was urgent. The jails were filled under a series of emergency ordinances, the press silenced and Peshawar subdued.

Salt *satyagraha* continued until the beginning of June, when it ceased with the arrival of the monsoon. Gandhi's inspiration had proved sublime. In Bombay Congressmen boiled pots of salt water on the esplanade, surrounded by concentric rings of volunteers, standing their ground and sustaining honourable wounds as the police tried to reach the scene of the crime. Such spectacles went on day after day. Sales of contraband salt – inedible but who was eating it? – were a popular route to jail. On 21 May, at Congress initiative and with Congress planning, as Gandhi prayed and span in what he had taken to calling 'Yeravda Mandir' ('Temple'), the raid on the Dharsana salt works took place. It was the most impressive act of civil disobedience associated with Gandhi's name. About twenty-five hundred volunteers, mostly from the *patidar* villages of Kheda, under the leadership of Sarojini Naidu and the ever-underestimated Manilal Gandhi,[74] advanced on the salt works in batches of twenty-five. As one batch crumpled under the blows of police *lathi*s another, with perfect discipline, took its place. More raids followed, at Dharsana and at Wadala near Bombay. The attention of the world was riveted on them. Civil disobedience, taking various forms according to local conditions, continued throughout the year. In Gujarat, land revenue refusal took off. The foreign cloth and liquor boycotts were everywhere prosecuted with vigour. In Bihar people refused to pay the *chowkidari* (village watch-man) tax and in the Central Provinces there was mass disobedience of the forest regulations. South India, though active, was on the whole quieter, and Muslims throughout India except for the North-West Frontier remained aloof. In the North-West the disturbances followed agitation by one of Gandhi's most surprising converts, Abdul Ghaffar Khan, whose Red Shirt movement brought Congress politics, Gandhian tactics and Pathan nationalism together in an unpredictable alliance.

All this happened with remarkably little violence, probably because local Congress committees stepped in to organize the protests after Gandhi and most of the all-India leadership went to jail. The campaign was now in the hands of men for whom rivers of blood possessed no appeal. Rooted in the politics of their communities, they intended to live to rule India another day. In 1930 they showed their mettle.

In jail, Gandhi was permitted to receive newspapers, and had the satis-faction of knowing that the struggle continued and was for the most part non-violent. He discoursed impenetrably in weekly letters to Sabarmati on the ashram rules, and gently but persistently harassed the prison authorities about the type of visitors he was allowed to have and his isolation from other prisoners. His request to end this isolation was supported by a threat to 'withdraw my co-operation as to the upkeep of my body' – not a fast, but a decision to eat only those items which were part of the normal convict diet, a deprivation with which, as he delicately put it, he was not sure his system could cope.[75]

As civil disobedience continued, proving more difficult to suppress than anticipated, the viceroy began to think about negotiations with the mahatma. The Round Table conference was to begin in London in November. With most of the Congress leadership in jail, its proceedings would be farcical. Yet the viceroy himself could not be seen to parley. Two 'moderate' Indian politicians, Tej Bahadur Sapru and M.R. Jayakar, came forward in July with an offer to sound Gandhi out. With Irwin's approval they confronted him with the news that some of his supporters in Congress, including Sarojini Naidu, were looking for an end to civil disobedience, and the business community of Bombay wished to make known to him that the effect of civil disobedience on commerce was proving catastrophic, and it was time to think about an honourable settlement. Gandhi's initial response to the idea of talks was guardedly favourable but he would make no commitment without hearing from Jawaharlal, who was also in jail. The Nehrus, father and son, imprisoned together in Allahabad, took a stiffer line, and when Vallabhbhai Patel, also imprisoned, was brought into the deliberations, their position stiffened further. Gandhi backtracked and declared that until the people had suffered more, and truly melted the viceregal heart, talk of settlement was premature.[76]

Gandhi's openness to negotiations in July must nevertheless be reconciled with the bloodlust of the spring. His correspondence from jail, which was not permitted to be political, gives no clue to his thinking. The probability was that the magnificent success of the Dharsana raid, and the persistence of civil disobedience in more or less non-violent form, were convincing him that the purifying influence of actively sought suffering was at work and even greater and more irresistible *tapas* was the result. This was the force on which he could now rely for success in the next round of negotiations to decide India's future. But it appeared that the time for these negotiations was not yet.

Meanwhile the Round Table conference opened in London and was not entirely without result. Agreement in principle to an Indian federation was secured from all parties present, and the closing statement of the prime minister, Ramsay MacDonald, on 19 January 1931 appeared to offer hope of dominion status for India in the not too distant future.[77] But without Congress participation, clearly no progress was possible. Irwin decided to renew his attempt at a settlement. In a striking gesture he released Gandhi and the other Congress leaders the following week, appealing to them in a speech in the legislative assembly to accept the sincerity of his desire for peace, which he assured them was equal to their own. On 14 February Gandhi wrote requesting an interview.[78] 'I would like', he said, 'to meet not so much the Viceroy of India as the man in you.' But, he added, 'somehow or other, in the present case, I have missed the guidance of the inner voice'.

Gandhi came out of jail on 26 January in two minds about what to do next. His public and private statements over the following two and a half weeks suggest that he was at the same time anxious to fight on and open to a settlement. The question was when a settlement should be attempted. He was under conflicting pressures. Jawaharlal, Motilal and Vallabhbhai wanted to fight on. Sapru and Jayakar, back from the Round Table conference, urged negotiations. The businessmen who had made known to him in July their desire to see the end of civil disobedience also weighed in on the side of conciliation.[79] Clearly, the negotiators prevailed. But Gandhi's letter to Irwin made no concessions, was explicitly exploratory, and made it clear that he sought the meeting in deference to the wishes of others.

For Gandhi, it was always the quality of the struggle which determined the nature of the settlement, and a discovery he made on his release from jail made him reluctant to commit to negotiations right away.

A few days before, a group of ashram women, including the widow Gangabehn Vaidya whom Gandhi greatly esteemed, had been dispersed by a police *lathi* charge while holding a peaceful demonstration at Borsad in Gujarat. There had been some injuries, including a blow to Gangabehn's head, though none was serious. Gandhi described this deplorable incident (in a speech to Congress leaders) as an atrocity to which history 'offers no parallel' and (in a letter to the viceroy) as a piece of official inhumanity unparalleled 'in modern history'.[80] There could be no negotiations, he announced, until the report of a committee of inquiry was published. There were other incidents whose inclusion in the inquiry he demanded, including one in Bihar where six men were killed by police, but they were obviously not equal in horror in Gandhi's mind to the incident at Borsad.

He set great store by the suffering of women. Being the embodiment of renunciation and compassion, their suffering was bound to be especially efficacious. The day women picketing a liquor store were attacked, he had said, would be the day the liquor stores closed.[81] His letters to the ashram women revealed the kind of importance he attached to the events at Borsad. 'All people do not yet see the full significance of this incident', he wrote to Vasumati Pandit; 'Its real value will be appreciated after some time.'[82] To Gangabehn herself he wrote: 'How I would have smiled with pleasure to see your sari made beautiful with stains of blood. I got excited when I knew about this atrocity, but was not pained in the least. On the contrary, I felt happy.'[83] To Chhaganlal Joshi he wrote in a similar vein, observing that the ashram women's sacrifice had been given special merit by 'the religious spirit which inspired it'.[84] Blood sacrifice was in the air, and up to 14 February Gandhi was making clear that he hoped and expected to see more of it. 'We have only felt from afar the heat of the fire we must pass through', he told

Gangadharrao Deshpande on 10 February; 'Let us be ready for the plunge.'[85]
The postponement of negotiations until such time as a government report
appeared meant more time for suffering, more time for sacrifice, more time for
blood – preferably of the pure in heart – to flow. He intended to go himself
to Bardoli or Borsad and get arrested, evidently in connection with the day
of national work stoppages and picketing he was planning for 15 February,
in commemoration of the death on 6 February of Motilal Nehru.

Motilal's death altered the balance of forces operating on Gandhi's mind.
It 'has upset my apple cart', he wrote to Gangadharrao Deshpande.[86] The
militants were isolated politically by the loss of Motilal, and this may have
been decisive in influencing Gandhi to negotiate. Making do with whatever
*tapas* had been mustered so far, he put himself in God's hands and entrained
for Delhi on 16 February to meet the viceroy. He prayed that he might not
put his signature 'to anything which might prove a trap for the country'.[87]

Prayer no doubt also played a part in the viceroy's preparations.

Lord Irwin combined in his nature extreme Christian piety with extreme
realism about the interests of the state.[88] Of ascetic demeanour, though not
particularly ascetic habits, and possessing great charm of manner of a type
which depended on one's never forgetting that here was a great landed aristocrat speaking as if to a fellow human being, he thought himself well equipped
to deal with the Gandhis of this world. His rather undistinguished political
career before becoming viceroy had been self-consciously Disraelian. To the
extent that he had made a mark in public life, it had been as an advocate of
a Tory entente, from a position of strength as he saw it, with the untutored
apostles of Labour then emergent in parliament. He held similar views about
the empire, looking forward to its eventual transformation, without substantive
loss of British power, into a multiracial commonwealth.

He had a pronounced but carefully understated sense of humour. Exotic
forms of political life particularly entertained him: Ramsay MacDonald,
Gandhi, and, a few years later when (as Lord Halifax) he was Neville Chamberlain's foreign secretary, Hitler, Goering and Goebbels. Like Gandhi he was
often wrong but rarely doubted that he was right. He had written to a friend
as Gandhi approached Dandi of the 'silly salt stunt', which he confidently
expected to fall flat.[89] Another trait he shared with Gandhi was the ability
to convey an impression of penetration even to people who had no idea what
he meant.

He set out to meet his adversary on the basis of 'personal appeal and conviction'. But he also sought out some practical advice, concluding that he must attempt 'some play on what everybody says is characteristic, namely, vanity of power and personality'. V.S.S. Sastri, who had known Gandhi a long time, told him that the mahatma was ' "like a woman; you have got to win him; therefore before you see him, perform all your ablutions, say all your prayers and put on your deepest spiritual robes" '.[90] He seems to have taken this advice.

He was confident that in his encounter with Gandhi he would win. But he was like a Wimbledon champion defending his title against the up-and-coming opponent who is sure to return one day and defeat him. Gandhi perhaps did not in the end exercise the decisive influence on the granting of independence to India. The extent of his importance, like that of others, is in any case obscured forever by the great churning of the global ocean that was the Second World War. But the ultimate victory of Indian nationalism was certain once he passed through the portals of the building labelled with calculated informality 'Viceroy's House'. Churchill, that bundle of raw political intuitions, correctly perceived the significance of the spectacle of 'Mr. Gandhi, a seditious Middle Temple lawyer, now posing as a *fakir* of a type well-known in the East, striding half-naked up the steps of the Vice-regal palace, while he is still organising and conducting a defiant campaign of civil disobedience, to parley on equal terms with the representative of the King–Emperor.'[91] The accession of prestige to Congress was enormous, and, whatever the negotiations' immediate results, irreversible. And prestige was what the British were now relying on to rule India.

As if to underline the significance of the occasion, the meetings began only a few days after the conclusion of the festivities inaugurating New Delhi, the brilliant capital city just created for British India by Edwin Lutyens and Herbert Baker, of which the viceregal palace was the centrepiece. The thousands of guests had barely departed before Gandhi, clutching a manila folder, appeared at the viceroy's door. At stake were the terms on which civil disobedience would be called off, and on which Congress would attend the next session of the Round Table conference.

The 'two uncrucified Christs', as Sastri put it,[92] met on 17 and 18 February to explore the ground. A further meeting took place on 27 February, and meetings then continued during the first week of March. Both men reported back regularly to their advisers – in Gandhi's case, the Congress Working

Committee, which was in Delhi. On 5 March the terms of the agreement were announced: prisoners in jail for non-violent civil disobedience would be released and the relevant ordinances withdrawn; civil disobedience would be stopped; the boycott of British goods would cease, though 'peaceful picketing' aimed at buyers rather than sellers would continue; there would be no change in the salt laws, though people living by the sea could make some for personal consumption; there would be no inquiry into police conduct; property confiscated from civil resisters (this applied principally to the land revenue campaign in Gujarat) would be returned providing it had not already been sold to a third party (much of it had); and Congress was to be represented at future sessions of the Round Table conference, the agenda to be federation, 'Indian responsibility', and 'reservations or safeguards in the interests of India, for such matters as, for instance, defence; external affairs; the position of minorities; the financial credit of India, and the discharge of obligations'.[93]

Gandhi knew that the agreement to which he had put his name had secured no practical advantage to Congress. When a journalist asked him why it had been necessary to go through the turmoil of civil disobedience to obtain terms no better than had been offered in December 1929 he could offer no substantive reply. Jawaharlal wept when he saw the clause about safeguards. But Gandhi appeared to attach little importance to the constitutional position to which he had committed himself. It could all, he explained in his public statements, be re-negotiated bye and bye. It was up to Congress to establish on the basis of this agreement an inarguable claim to represent the Indian people. *Purna swaraj* would then follow.

In fact, the constitutional issue had been cleared out of the way in the earliest, exploratory phase of the talks. Irwin had presented his formulation and Gandhi had never subsequently challenged it. The talks had, however, nearly foundered on the issue of the police inquiry, on which both Irwin and Gandhi were stubborn. Irwin would not put his police force, on which he would have to rely should civil disobedience start again, under scrutiny. Gandhi wanted the innocent suffering of India to be known both to the government whose conversion he hoped to effect and to the world. Irwin thought it perverse of Gandhi to attach such importance to a minor point and called his bluff, letting the Working Committee know via Sapru, Jayakar and Sastri that on this issue there could be no compromise. Gandhi caved in, agreeing to a formula that emphasized the length to which he was going for peace. It had not, to him, been a minor point.

The reasons for Gandhi's capitulations can only be surmised. Once he committed himself to negotiations he was, as on past occasions, extremely anxious that they succeed – which was to say, that a presentable agreement, arguably moving matters forward, be produced. As he had said in *Satyagraha in South Africa*, a *satyagrahi* who failed to measure his own strength and had to accept defeat 'not only disgraces himself but also brings the matchless weapon of satyagraha into disrepute'.[94] Something, therefore, had to transpire from talks with Irwin after a year of civil disobedience on an unprecedented scale. Irwin had also created expectations of concrete results by his unconditional release of Gandhi and publicly expressed hope of a settlement.

Gandhi and Irwin met alone and informally in Irwin's study, Irwin at one point himself showing Gandhi to the bathroom. The supposedly personal nature of the encounter was thus emphasized from the start. Gandhi's reports on the meetings as they were progressing suggest that he decided early on, on the basis of his impressions of the viceroy's character, to invest some faith in him as the joint instrument of God's will. After the first meeting, he concluded that Irwin wanted peace 'because he has been touched by the struggle'.[95] At the second meeting Irwin appealed to him 'to forget about civil disobedience and to have faith' in British sincerity.[96] After this meeting Gandhi concluded that the viceroy was strong, straight, capable, firm, and 'a democrat'.[97] From this moment all hope of a stronger agreement from Congress's point of view seems to have been lost. To Jawaharlal's sour comment that the viceroy had the virtues and weaknesses of the average Englishman, Gandhi replied imperturbably 'Yes'.[98] Agreement on the police issue having been reached, he observed to Irwin: 'When you or Mr. Emerson [Irwin's Home Secretary, with whom he had had conversations] use your best arguments it does not always have much effect on me, but when you tell me that Government is in a difficulty and cannot do what I want, then I am inclined to capitulate to you.' This splendidly quixotic revelation, as from an Indian gentleman to an English gentleman, was recorded by Irwin with the observation that he now knew 'the right method of dealing with him'.[99]

Gandhi later said that he had 'succumbed not to Lord Irwin, but to the honesty in him'.[100] Perhaps he was thinking less of the viceroy's probity, to which he paid many tributes, than of intimations in him of a soul awakened, however imperfectly, to which he was bound as a matter of religion to respond – of the divine 'truth' in Lord Irwin rather than the merely human 'honesty'.

Some at the time thought Gandhi should not have been allowed to negotiate alone with the viceroy. With the death of Motilal there was no one
on the Working Committee capable of restraining or directing him. (And it
may be that Gandhi did not always see fit to put the Working Committee
fully in the picture. There are some discrepancies between his and Irwin's
reports of the meetings.) But what must ever be remembered in appraising
Gandhi's strengths and weaknesses as a negotiator in this famous encounter
is that his goal was not merely political independence but *swaraj* – a purified
and regenerate India, which his conduct on this as on every occasion would
either bring closer or postpone. The designedly personal circumstances of
the encounter threw this perennial preoccupation into relief. Irwin had no
complaints at all of Gandhi's conduct as a negotiator. He seems to have been
almost suicidally straightforward.

Yet what else could he have been? For all his celebrity, he was still a
supplicant – as was shortly to be made plain to him when Lord Willingdon
succeeded Irwin as viceroy. Once the talks began he could only play the
hand he had, and there was nothing to be gained from walking away without
an agreement, which would mean starting civil disobedience again with no
obvious prospect of a better outcome. It would mean also that the party of
violence would gain plausibility from the evident failure of his methods. A
piece of paper with smiles all round was a better option. These were the
political realities determining the extent to which the triumph of *satyagraha*
could be made visible.

Gandhi was at first defensive about his agreement in his public statements. But this ceased once it became clear that news of the settlement was
receiving overwhelming popular acclaim: *vox populi vox dei* was his rule on
such occasions. To the Working Committee, the agreement was a crushing
disappointment. But to the ordinary Indian the very fact that Gandhi had
been sitting comfortably in the viceroy's study, discussing tête-à-tête the
future of the country, was nothing short of a miracle.

Gandhi's idea had been that Congress would gain strength for its appearance
at the Round Table conference in September by seeing that his pact with
Irwin was enforced. It was soon obvious that this was not going to happen.
The radical elements in Congress immediately made known their unhappiness
with the Gandhi–Irwin pact. Jawaharlal, who was entering his most left-wing
phase, denounced it and began encouraging non-payment of rent and land

revenue in the United Provinces. He saw the agreement as a 'truce' useful for strengthening Congress's position at the grassroots. Vallabhbhai, while publicly supporting the mahatma, was making it difficult for him to abandon the resisters who had forfeited lands in Gujarat by going around the villages assuring them that Gandhi would retrieve their lost acres for them. The youth organizations of Congress accused him of betraying the heroic young by not arranging a general amnesty for all political prisoners. The execution of the terrorist Bhagat Singh, despite Gandhi's representations, on 23 March, threw fuel on this particular fire. When he arrived at the Karachi Congress, held in the last week of March, he was greeted by young men with black flags shouting 'Gandhi go back!' and 'Who got Bhagat Singh hanged?', and there were further disturbances and expressions of discontent. The agreement had to be rammed through Congress by the new president, Vallabhbhai.

There were also complaints to be dealt with from local Congress officials, who claimed that the government was not observing the terms of the agreement. These steadily increased. The government in turn accused Congress of breaches of faith. The continuance of aggressive, though technically peaceful, picketing was another problem. Here Gandhi was to some extent responsible. He loved picketing – an effective, low-risk (and consequently popular) form of non-violent agitation in support of causes that were dear to him – and was reluctant to give it up, even when it was eluding his control.

The difficulty of Gandhi's position could scarcely have been more apparent. Irwin had hoped by his largeness of approach to make him an ally of the British in moving India towards dominion status, a project to which on the metaphysical level Gandhi was not really averse. But he could not for long retain his political ascendancy in India if he were to appear to relinquish his adversarial role. When it was to be Congress against the Raj, as in light versus darkness, it had been to Gandhi that the Congress had turned. He was confronted at what should have been his moment of moral and political triumph with a host of contradictory and apparently impossible demands on him. The breakdown of the settlement, and the eclipse of his personal authority, seemed the likely result. He had to concern himself also with the strength of the Congress negotiating position – should he in the end find himself going to London – at a conference where Congress would be just one among several petitioners of the British government, past master of ruling the divided.

Congress itself was a bundle of factions. Outside Congress were the princely states (British puppets, but significant in the political equation to be worked out in London), Indian liberals (essentially at this point political entrepreneurs and men of affairs, but with the ear of the British), and – most ominously – the Muslims. Even before Karachi the communal horror had re-emerged from the crypt. Riots had broken out in Cawnpore after local Congressmen forced Muslims to close their shops in memory of Bhagat Singh. Many had died and thousands had fled the city.

In these circumstances a number of things became clear to Gandhi. They were that Congress should be accepted by both Indians and British as India's national representative, that one person alone should speak not only for Congress but also implicitly for India, and that he should be that person. He would not, he told Richard Gregg in April, go to London 'if the way is not clear for me to deliver my message'.[101] The problem was to make credible his claim to represent the whole of India within his own frame.

At the beginning of April, a new Congress Working Committee was elected, from a list of names supplied by Gandhi, and one of its first acts was to resolve that Gandhi should be the sole Congress delegate to the conference. The presumption has been that the committee was responding to Gandhi's own wish,[102] and his statements seems to bear this out. The idea was, he explained in *Young India*,[103] that what would be presented at the conference was not the concerns of individuals but only 'the Congress view'. Congress by granting him 'power of attorney' to carry out its general mandate would speak through him with one voice. It would in any case, he reminded his readers, 'not be work at the Conference that will bring swaraj' but only 'work in India': 'Not the ability of the delegation will tell at the Conference but the power behind it.'

He seemed liberated by the responsibility he was taking on. The road to *swaraj*, he knew, lay not only through the power generated by suffering but through the correct interpretation of God's will – and who better to be entrusted with that than God's servant, himself? He intended in London, when in doubt about his earthly mandate, to rely on 'God's infallible guidance and "be careful for nothing".'[104] Asked whether he would be taking advisers, he replied: 'My adviser is God. ... If I had any idea to take advisers I would have taken them as delegates.'[105]

Meanwhile, he was determined to make the settlement work. Operating as an intermediary between the government and Congress, he laboured to see that it was honoured by all parties. Success would mean acceptance 'in practice' by the government of Congress's right to speak for the people.[106]

Success proved elusive. The government availed itself of his good offices, but would not acknowledge a Congress claim to represent India as a whole. Indeed, the more Gandhi worked to show the government how responsible and how genuinely representative Congress was, the more suspicious the government became that he was trying to set up a parallel authority.

The claim to represent the whole of India could not be made good without some semblance of Hindu–Muslim unity. He therefore became active once again in the cause he had all but abandoned.

Almost his first act upon the announcement of the Gandhi–Irwin pact had been to address a mass meeting in Delhi on the topic of communal unity.[107] His settlement with Irwin, he said, would 'fail of effect without a real heart-unity between Hindus and Mussulmans'; without that, going to London would be a waste of time. He proposed to achieve it by 'voluntary surrender' – he had 'no other secret'. Either the Muslims or the Hindus – preferably the Hindus, as the majority – should give up 'all rights and privileges' and 'be content to serve' the other community. What did it matter, he asked, if Hindus gave up all their seats in parliament to Muslims or vice versa? What did parliaments matter anyway? They had only 'the shadow of power'. The 'very act of voluntary surrender' would clothe whoever embraced it 'with a power undreamt of before'. In Karachi, he told the Jamiat-ul-Ulema to 'put down whatever you want on a blank sheet of paper and I shall agree to it'. Specifically, he endorsed the Muslim League's demand that Sind be separated from Bombay to form a Muslim majority province, a move that caused consternation among Hindus.[108]

The response of the Muslims to this invocation of the Law of Sacrifice was to present Gandhi with Jinnah's '14 points', formulated in 1929 in response to the Nehru report. The leading Muslims in Congress immediately denounced the demand for separate electorates, and there was then nothing more Gandhi could do. His hands were tied by the need to keep the 'nationalist Muslims' in Congress. He announced that the opposition of Congress Muslims to separate electorates meant that the Muslim demand for them was not 'unanimous' and he could not therefore concede it.[109] Having enraged both Muslims and Hindus – to the Muslims, his backpedalling was proof he could not be trusted; to the Hindus his behaviour was beyond comprehension but obviously dangerous – he ceased his personal effort to bring about a pre-conference agreement between the communities. Negotiations continued between the Congress Muslims and the Muslim majority but broke down in June. The Working

Committee then decided that even without a communal agreement Gandhi should proceed to London to represent Congress. Despite previous statements that he would not go without a communal accord, he accepted the Working Committee's decision.

By July the Gandhi–Irwin pact was close to collapse. In the United Provinces, Gujarat, and the North-West Frontier, the struggle continued, sometimes violently. A proposal from Gandhi in June for a permanent Board of Arbitration, on which Congress would be prominently represented, was turned down by the government with the observation that all Congress had to do was obey the law. Gandhi's main hope of attending the Round Table conference as the representative of a united and transcendent Congress now lay in the success of his efforts to rescue the agreement.

The viceroy, Lord Willingdon, was as anxious as Gandhi was to see him appear (in the appropriate capacity) at the Round Table conference. Sensing the moment was right, he invited him to Simla for talks. He accepted at once.

The talks were difficult. Gandhi produced Congress's complaints against the government. The government produced evidence refuting them. Gandhi stuck to his guns on the United Provinces, justifying the no-rent and no-revenue campaigns on the grounds of economic hardship produced by a drop in agricultural prices. The government refused to address the matter in the context of discussions on enforcing the agreement. He asked for an impartial inquiry into Congress's allegations against the government, a significant dilution of his earlier proposal for a Board of Arbitration. The government, wishing to give him something to take away, promised to consider it. Willingdon undertook to send his list of allegations to local governments, and gave his personal assurance that justified complaints would be attended to. With this degree of emollience Gandhi had to be content. The question of his attendance at the conference was referred to the Working Committee, which was going to meet in August.

Events did not stand still. Government officials in Surat decided to collect forcibly all outstanding revenue from people they decided were withholding it for political reasons. Gandhi denounced the action as a breach of faith, hinted at civil disobedience, and appealed to the viceroy, who conceded only that no further coercion would be applied until the next revenue collection fell due early in the following year. The government also rejected his earlier request for an inquiry. Once again, Willingdon, under instructions to get Gandhi to London without conceding the special status he sought for Congress, softened the blow with assurances of personal concern, expressing the hope that Gandhi would not change his mind. This was on 11 August, and he was due to sail on 15 August.

The Working Committee meanwhile convened in Bombay, and on 13 August decided to withdraw Congress's participation in the conference. But it did not repudiate the Gandhi–Irwin pact. There was still some room for manoeuvre, and in his 'great eagerness'[110] to go Gandhi approached the viceroy with a hint that the inquiry issue was amenable to discussion. At the same time he braced himself to accept God's will should he be staying at home.

In the end, he sailed for London on 29 August, after a last-minute visit to Simla, from which he departed in a special train taking him to Delhi in time to board the Frontier Mail for Bombay. The government's concessions were minimal, amounting to an inquiry into whether some farmers in Bardoli had been compelled to pay more revenue than was due. Gandhi's departure came as a surprise to Willingdon, who felt vaguely outmanoeuvred. 'He may be a saint', he wrote to the secretary of state after seeing Gandhi off, 'he may be a holy man; he is, I believe, quite sincere in his principles; but of this I am perfectly certain, that he is one of the most astute politically-minded and bargaining little gentlemen I ever came across.' The mahatma, he wrote, had been 'the most difficult man to pin down'.[111]

Gandhi himself was alone and at peace as he occupied himself writing letters and articles for *Young India* on the train to Bombay. 'The horizon', he admitted, was 'as black as it possibly could be.' Yet he had no wish for companions to share his burden: 'I must go to London feeling my weakness in its fullness. I must go to London with God as my only guide. He is a jealous Lord. He will allow no one to share His authority.'[112] He 'must bear the cross', he told Rajagopalachari, 'alone and to the fullest extent'. God, whose instrument he was, would give him 'the right word at the right moment', and all would be well.[113]

# EIGHT

# The Solitary Path

It was not, then, from a position of irresistible strength that Gandhi saw himself approaching his encounter with the Raj but from a position of God-inflicted weakness: whatever strength was his at the negotiating table would come from the acceptance that he himself was nothing and God was all.

He undertook no preparation. 'Everything will come to me spontaneously when I face Mr. MacDonald and other delegates', he told a reporter at Aden.[1] 'I suppose you have thought of what you want to say', G.D. Birla observed to him on the way to his first appearance at the conference. 'I am absolutely blank', Gandhi replied; 'But perhaps God will help me in collecting my thoughts at the proper time.'[2]

He was not in fact a free agent but was bound by a resolution adopted at Karachi requiring the delegation to pursue *purna swaraj*, with control over the army, external affairs and finance, and with the right to end ties with Britain. The Karachi resolution was made more explicit by the Working Committee a week after Gandhi's departure, with the clear intention of forestalling any surprise moves by the sole delegate. Gandhi's accommodations to Irwin and to Willingdon, his abortive effort to unite the communities in an act of mutual renunciation, and his determination to take upon himself the entire burden of representation, had left his Congress colleagues feeling increasingly disquieted. It was 'voluntary surrender' to two viceroys that had got him on the boat to London. What else might he do?

In most respects Gandhi was scrupulous about observing his brief, to the point of seeming not very interested in actual negotiations. But the execution of his instructions from Congress formed only part of his objective.

He sailed from Bombay believing that God was using him as 'His instrument for the service of humanity',[3] and as he approached London God's intentions acquired a more concrete form. Might not the Round Table conference, unpromising though it appeared, be the means of bringing about the 'honourable partnership' between Britain and India which would transform the world?[4] Buoyed up by this thought, which had taken shape 'whilst I was nearing the shores of your beautiful island', he gave out upon arrival his message to the press: 'If India gains her freedom through truth and non-violence, I feel convinced it will be the largest contribution of the age to the peace of the world.'[5] More statements quickly followed asserting that the freedom of India, non-violently accomplished, would liberate all humanity not only from exploitation but from violence itself.[6]

He knew that one thing above all stood in the way of this 'dreamy hope': the conflict between Hindus and Muslims. Only an India united in acknowledgement of the sameness of all paths to God would be qualified for such a venture. Supposing, Gandhi thought to himself as he approached England's shore, 'God fires both Hindus and Mussulmans [at the conference] with a proper spirit, so that they close ranks and come to an honourable understanding' – might not the marvellous partnership be brought about?[7] On his first day in London he told the press that he was 'prepared to go the "whole hog" with the Muslims without the slightest reservation. He would sign a blank paper and leave the Muslims to write in what they considered the truth, and he would then fight for it.'[8] The stage was thus set for further adventures in renunciation.

When he arrived in London he was confronted with a Muslim delegation insisting not only on separate electorates, complete provincial autonomy, and reserved seats in the legislatures, but refusing to discuss any other constitutional issues before these demands were met. Furthermore, they had no interest in having Gandhi 'fight for' them, either on his terms or theirs. In vain Gandhi protested that it was he who was the true representative of Hindus and Muslims alike.[9] Within two weeks there was deadlock.

Departing significantly from the established Congress position, Gandhi then privately offered the Muslims separate electorates and almost everything else they wanted – with the proviso that when there was a *swaraj* government

Arriving in England for the Round Table conference, 12 September 1931

there would be a referendum for Muslim voters on the question of resuming joint electorates.[10] It was 'voluntary surrender' but it was not enough. Negotiations collapsed on 7 October over the issue of who should adjudicate the rival claims of Muslims, Hindus and Sikhs in the Punjab.

After this Gandhi's attendance at the conference seems to have been from a sense of obligation not to precipitate its shipwreck. He hoped for nothing, he said, from a gathering which, apart from himself, consisted of government nominees. But his offer of separate electorates to the Muslims had repercussions with which he had to deal. The untouchables, represented at the conference by B.R. Ambedkar, were also demanding separate electorates, and to this Gandhi was unalterably opposed, the untouchables, in his view, being Hindus, and the problem of untouchability one to be dealt with by Hindus – who furthermore, as he knew, would be enraged by the separation of the untouchables from the Hindu electorate. Trust me, was his advice to Ambedkar. 'I do not hesitate to say', he told the *Spectator*, 'that if the untouchables in all parts of India would record their votes, I should be their representative.'[11] The tone of his public remarks, and his persistence in efforts to arrive at a separate Hindu–Muslim agreement, drove Ambedkar into an alliance with the Muslims, who were taking advantage of the mistrust Gandhi was arousing among the official 'minorities' at the conference (Christians, Anglo-Indians and European businessmen as well as the 'Depressed Classes') to engineer a combination against the Hindus and Sikhs. Gandhi had anticipated neither the vehemence of Muslim demands nor the consequences of selective capitulation.

Confronted with a joint demand for separate electorates from all the groups now arrayed against him, he had nothing more to say, and there were no further developments on the communal front before the conference ended. With the Muslims now limiting their participation to matters other than communal ones, the conference staggered to a close on 1 December.

Gandhi's performance as a negotiator, admittedly in difficult circumstances, had been dismal. 'The expectation formed in many quarters here of seeing a man of commanding gifts was not fulfilled', was the verdict of *The Times* in its obituary of Gandhi in 1948.[12] Certainly his gifts did not extend to dealing directly and simultaneously with a number of stubborn opponents who were less interested in reaching an agreement than in what kind of agreement it was. His fondness for pronouncements and gestural negotiating style did not serve him well. He was undoubtedly unprepared. The result was, as *The*

*Times* put it, that he 'made no real constructive contribution to the work of the Conference'.

Nor did Gandhi make a strong impression as a speaker. His speeches at the conference were long, personal and devoid of detail, and he responded awkwardly to public questioning. He seemed unnerved by the experience of being under relatively objective scrutiny. God not only did not supply the magic words but at times permitted him to embarrass himself. He taxed MacDonald twice in plenary session with showing no consideration for his age and frailty, on the second occasion accusing him of working 'almost to exhaustion, with a pitilessness worthy of a Scotsman', an old man like himself. MacDonald meanwhile had done his homework and observed that Gandhi had the advantage of him, he being 65 to Gandhi's 62.[13]

Amid the wreckage of the conference, Gandhi made it known that what he minded most was the position taken by Ambedkar on separate electorates for the untouchables. He wished 'to say with all the emphasis that I can command that, if I was the only person to resist this thing, I would resist it with my life'[14] – a warning of the fast to come in 1932.

As the fact of failure bore in on him, and the date of his departure for India drew near, he began to think about the reason for yet another emptyhanded return from the metropolis. He was bitter about the British government's 'packing' of the conference with its own nominees. But he thought that the underlying cause was the usual one: insufficient suffering. For this there was only one remedy: more suffering. 'I came here to negotiate', he told the Commonwealth of India League in November, 'because I thought we had suffered enough. If the Conference fails, I shall know that India must suffer still more to impress the country with the justice of her demand.'[15] The conference over, he told the press: 'I never believed that we would get anything more than what our own internal strength entitled. The Round Table Conference negotiations have been a method of finding out the measure of our strength compared with those with whom power at present resides. We have evidently failed. The Congress, therefore, must refill the battery, so that it will be powerful enough to do its work.'[16] He could only operate as God's instrument in history when India produced the critical charge.

Mahadev noted in his account of the conference that 'the vision of a Ganges of self-suffering' grew upon Gandhi as the conference collapsed.[17] He spoke of 'rivers of … blood', 'a pure voluntary act of self-immolation to face the situation. It would be good for India to go through that purgatory if it must.'[18] He included himself among those who would suffer, but there was no suggestion of personal failure. It was India which had failed, and India which must now, collectively, suffer more.

In practical terms, this meant the resumption of civil disobedience, and Gandhi left the British government in no doubt that this was his intention. Indeed, the situation now existing in India left him little alternative. Relations between the government and Congress had deteriorated in his absence. In the United Provinces, as the agrarian crisis deepened, Jawaharlal had been pushing for another campaign of rent and revenue refusal. On the North-West Frontier, the Red Shirts on the Provincial Congress Committee had stepped up picketing and were encouraging non-payment of land tax. Congress politics in Bombay had taken a radical turn with the emergence of a fiery Youth League, and Vallabhbhai was promising them civil disobedience. In Bengal a series of assassinations had resulted in the government's assumption in November of emergency powers of arrest and detention without trial. If he returned from London without an agreement, Gandhi's only hope of continued leadership lay in a new campaign. So it was not constructive work which he prescribed for India's 'greater strength' but civil disobedience and rivers of blood.

He promptly downgraded the campaign for communal unity and adopted the public position that the communal question was 'of no importance before the great question of Indian freedom of which the British ministers are studiously fighting shy'. The 'disease which for the time is corroding some portions of the community' would be cured, he now said, with the advent of independence.[19]

Despite the failure of the conference, Gandhi did not consider his visit to England a waste of time. He attached much importance to the informal contacts to which he devoted himself outside the conference hall, and though these engagements were not generally, as Subhas Bose complained, of any obvious political usefulness,[20] he expected them to produce results in the future. He understood better than Bose the way the web of English political life was woven, and how small a portion of the fibre came from professional politicians. His comings and goings – attired always in his *dhoti* and shawl, a costume as immaculate and considered as the white flannels in which he had first set foot on English soil – kept him in the public eye as a superior personality who transcended politics. He sketched out to his audiences the

With textile workers on a visit to Lancashire, 26 September 1931

synergic nature of the encounter between Indian *ahimsa* and British enterprise, which, once India was free, would transform and ultimately liberate the world. Whether any of this was taken in is impossible to say. Gandhi's most literal statements of his aspirations were normally taken for verbiage.

In London he stayed at Muriel Lester's settlement house in Bow, walking the streets of the East End and meeting the neighbours. At Charlie Andrews's request he went to Lancashire to see for himself the condition of the un-employed cotton workers, for which as the author of India's foreign cloth boycott he had some personal responsibility. His defence of Indian interests was unapologetic and he advised the workers to turn their minds to better ways of making a living, such as handicrafts. Entertained by his oddity and forthrightness, they gave him a friendly reception: few of them would have disagreed that there were better ways of making a living. In a meeting with the mill owners he was equally forthright, and reminded them that Lancashire's cotton trade was bound before long to succumb to competition from Japan. One who met him 'got the impression that this man really believes he is the chosen vessel of God'. Asked what he would do if it came to a conflict between handlooms and the Bombay mills, he had replied, 'quietly, without bombast', ' "I can break the Bombay mills, if need be." '[21]

The visit to Lancashire, which produced a famous photograph taken amid a crowd of smiling millhands, was the highlight of the public relations offensive. At Eton, where he went to convert future empire-builders, his reception was polite. Oxford and Cambridge were distinctly sceptical. A meeting with members of parliament did not go well; as at the conference, he failed to convey an impression of ability. He went out of his way to cultivate the Quakers, among whom were some of his most active British supporters. But Quakers who did not like his mixing of religion with politics expressed sharp opposition during his visit. Nevertheless, he found 'many more kindred spirits than I had expected' and his faith in non-violence was 'strongly confirmed'.[22]

The plan had been to continue with a lengthy tour of Europe – a historic commitment for Gandhi, who had been reluctant to take his gospel abroad. Deeds not exhortations, 'thought-power' not 'the power of the word', he had explained in refusing an invitation to America in 1925, were what would inspire the world beyond India to make its own experiments in self-realization.[23] But God's calling him to London in 1931 seems to have been taken as permission to venture further. The plan was abandoned when he realized he could not delay his return to India. Only France, Switzerland and Italy would be visited, briefly, on the way home.

The Swiss visit was the fulfilment of Gandhi's long-standing desire to meet Romain Rolland. But the meeting of the sage of the East and the sage of the West was not a success.[24] Gandhi was a stranger to political conversation as Rolland knew it, and could muster no interest in details of the forces contending in Europe, a subject on which Rolland held forth for hours. He annoyed his host by offering unsolicited advice on his health, which was delicate. Rolland played Beethoven to his unenraptured guest. An attempt to engage Gandhi in discussion of the political dangers of his visit to Italy, which was to take place the following week, was turned aside with the assurance that all was in God's hands. Gandhi observed that God naturally spoke more clearly to him than to others, less pure. However disconcerting, his pronouncements were not inconsistent with the picture of him Rolland had presented to the world. Gandhi probably thought his host expected no less of him. But the meeting was the jolt Rolland needed to begin tearing himself away from his infatuation with the sublime.

The Italian visit, a permanent embarrassment to Gandhi, was never really explained. Pressed for his reasons by Rolland, he said he wanted to meet the pope and Mussolini. Mussolini intrigued him. After the brief audience granted him in Rome he sent Rolland his impressions. He said he was attracted by Mussolini's reforms. He seemed to 'have done much for the peasant class', and his 'care of the poor, his opposition to super-urbanization, his efforts to bring about co-ordination between capital and labour' all merited attention. Admittedly, the reforms were 'compulsory'; but this was true also, he said (evidently recalling his dislike of the majority vote), in a democracy. The Italians seemed not to mind the government's 'iron hand': violence after all was 'the basis of western society'. Mussolini's 'desire to serve his people' impressed him.[25]

He did not meet the pope, who perhaps for political reasons was unavailable. But he was given a tour of the Vatican, where he paused for a moment before a *pietà*, shedding a tear as he thought how 'nations like individuals could only be made through the agony of the Cross and in no other way'.[26]

Now began the period in Gandhi's life when, like Icarus, he flew too close to the sun.

The Round Table debacle had hardened his commitment to civil disobedience. But the experience of returning to Britain as a figure of world renown, the man everyone (except Churchill, who would not see him) seemed to want to meet, had strengthened the belief that one day the heart-unity he sought between Britain and India might come about. He returned to India at once certain of the need for *satyagraha* and optimistic about its results.

On Christmas Day, he gave a talk to a little group of fellow passengers on the ship taking him to Bombay, which was more than usually revealing about his understanding of Christianity.[27] It did not matter to him, he said, whether Jesus had ever lived. The important thing was that, 'in God's providence', the New Testament and especially the Sermon on the Mount had been 'preserved from destruction by the Christians, so-called', and through translations into many languages transmitted to the world. The fruits of the Christian gospel were yet to appear: Christianity had 'yet to be lived'; Christ was 'not yet born'. Only when there was peace on earth, and non-violence reigned supreme, would we truly be able to say that Christ was born. But peace would only come when everyone embraced the renunciation of the self

and took up the 'living Cross' of the 'Living Christ', for Christ's birth was
also 'an ever-recurring event', to be 'enacted in every life': 'destroy your whole
life, ... crucify yourself' was the universal commandment.

A week after he returned to India, Gandhi announced the resumption of
civil disobedience. If Indians remained true, he said, to 'the spirit of non-
violence' throughout the campaign, they would inaugurate 'a new era upon
earth'.[28] There is no doubt that Gandhi intended to resume civil disobedience
at the earliest opportunity. Later, many Congressmen asked themselves what
had been the hurry.

The ritual of first seeking agreement with the British came and went
with unprecedented speed. Gandhi arrived in India on 28 December, wired
Willingdon on 29 December requesting a meeting, and went into conclave
with the Working Committee later that day. The viceroy's reply, ruling out
a meeting without Gandhi's repudiation in advance of Congress activities
in the United Provinces and the Frontier, came on 31 December. On 1
January Gandhi wrote to Willingdon asking him how he could lay responsibility for recent disturbances at Congress's door, and conveying the Working
Committee's decision to revive civil disobedience should he fail to take a more
constructive approach. He proposed a meeting, but Willingdon replied the
next day declining to negotiate under threat. On 3 January Gandhi sent a
third telegram to the viceroy intimating that civil disobedience would now
have to begin.

Willingdon acted throughout in consultation with the British government,
which had already decided to forestall a resumption of civil disobedience:
Gandhi's desire to give battle was met by an equally strong desire to prevent
it. Though he knew that Willingdon was merely the instrument of government
policy, he took the viceroy's 'banging the door on my face'[29] as a personal
affront. A little more to-ing and fro-ing at this point would not have gone
amiss. His prestige had come to depend significantly on the ability to command at least an infructuous encounter.

The government then moved to bring matters to a conclusion. On 4 January,
Gandhi was arrested and jailed, and the AICC, the Working Committee and
some local Congress committees were banned, and leading Congressmen were
put in jail. There had been no advance planning for a campaign of civil disobedience, and people were left to find their way to prison as best they might.
Large numbers managed to do so, mainly through defying the emergency
ordinances restricting political activity. There were nearly 15,000 convictions

in January, and nearly 18,000 in February. But without effective direction the
campaign was fading out by March. The size of the initial response suggests
that, had it not gone off half-cocked, it could have been formidable.

Indian politics now reached an impasse: low-level disorder on the Congress
side, repression on the government side. Gandhi seemed as usual content to be
behind bars. He span, performed dietary experiments, read, studied astronomy,
composed his *Letters on the 'Gita'*, and kept up his correspondence.

By March it seemed to Mahadev, who had accompanied him to jail, that
he was longing to fast, indeed casting about for a reason.[30] On 11 March he
wrote to Hoare, the Secretary of State for India, saying he would embark
on a 'fast unto death' should the government award a separate electorate
to untouchables.[31] His letter was well on the early side, even allowing for a
desire to influence policy. The government was mulling things over and no
announcement was expected to be made soon. It was another five months
before the decision was announced to award corporate electorates to Muslims,
Sikhs, untouchables and some other minorities.

Gandhi still thought of himself, though in jail, as the leader of suffering
India. He knew only one means whereby he could bring that suffering to a
critical mass.

Gandhi had also made a spiritual discovery which encouraged a radical frame
of mind. One morning, 'all of a sudden', he asked Mahadev if he had a copy
of the *Isha Upanishad*. 'The essence of philosophy', he declared, 'is contained
in its 18 verses or perhaps in the first verse.'[32]

The *Isha Upanishad* is the shortest and one of the least penetrable of the
speculative discourses that conclude the Vedas. But even in English there is
no mistaking the metaphysical adrenaline that runs through it.

In a series of paradoxes, bluntly asserted and then rapturously embraced,
the poet presents his ideas about the nature of reality and its relation to human
consciousness. The real, he says, is the divine principle that pervades and
animates the universe. Without attributes, it just is, and knowing it involves
a hyper-awareness of the nature of things which is beyond joy and sorrow,
wisdom and foolishness, and moral judgement. The road to the real, and
implicitly to association with the divine principle, is through renunciation
conceived as mental detachment. This is the proposition announced with such
force, economy and elusiveness in the first verse. Two modern translators,
Robin Zaehner and Patrick Olivelle, offer slightly different renderings.[33]

This whole universe must be pervaded by a Lord, –
Whatever moves in this moving [world].
Abandon it, and then enjoy:
Covet not the goods of anyone at all.

(Zaehner)

This whole world is to be dwelt in by the Lord,
whatever living being there is in the world.
So you should eat what has been abandoned;
and do not covet anyone's wealth.

(Olivelle)

Gandhi made several attempts to convey his sense of the verse's meaning, of which the following is a representative one: 'It is the strict law of God that anyone who desires to be close to Him should renounce the world and yet be in it.'[34] This does not convey the spiritual excitement the poem produced in him. It threw into high relief for him the adventurous side of renunciation to which he was increasingly attracted – the ecstatic embrace of the providential, as opposed to the daily donning of the hair shirt. He saw in it something like Jesus' 'Consider the lilies'. The 'act of renunciation or dedication to God', he said in a commentary of 1937, 'will result in God taking the responsibility of feeding you, of housing and of clothing you'.[35] (He may have had his own long experience of supported living in mind.) The more he thought about it the clearer it was that the *Isha Upanishad* was the essence of all scripture, the *Gita* a commentary on its first verse.[36] Its evident advocacy of self-submission to a loving God, more actively benign the more concern for the self was abandoned, was close in spirit to the Sermon on the Mount as he apparently understood it; and yet it was indisputably 'Hindu'.

It was in a state of deliberate and holy self-abandonment that Gandhi began his fast for the maintenance of joint electorates for Hindus and untouchables on 20 September 1932 – his first fast which was explicitly 'unto death'. He believed it to be the culmination of his career in this life, the event for which he had prepared himself since his soul awakened. He was grateful to God, he said, for providing the opportunity (the Communal Award) to offer the final sacrifice. He alone, he cautioned, was fit to offer it: imitations, lacking the necessary preparation, would be 'demoniac'.[37] His inner voice was completely clear.

In spite of the political nature of its stated objective, Gandhi claimed for the fast a primarily religious character. It was a fast for the sake of the 'most downtrodden': to die for the lowliest would be the purest self-abnegation.[38] E. Stanley Jones asked him if it were not coercive. 'Yes', he replied 'the same kind of coercion which Jesus exercises upon you from the Cross.'[39]

None of Gandhi's associates, in India or abroad, really understood why he was choosing the issue of separate electorates on which to offer up his life. He himself was not consistent in his public statements about the fast's purpose. First it was to get the British government's award reversed. Then it seemed to become more about touching the heart of Hindus and getting them to open temples to untouchables. Privately, he acknowledged his fear of the Muslims, untouchables and others who had been awarded separate electorates, combining against the Hindus: he had considered fasting to secure a single joint electorate.[40]

Even before he entered the 'fiery gates' (he had written to MacDonald on 18 August communicating his decision to begin fasting on 20 September, and had made a public announcement on 18 September) moves were afoot to produce an agreement between Hindus and untouchables. These efforts failed to avert the fast. Furious at having the mahatma's life deposited in his hands, Ambedkar refused to negotiate.

Once the fast began, and the eyes of the world were on the suffering mahatma, Ambedkar realized that an agreement of some sort was unavoidable, and he acted to preserve the substance of separate representation. He drove a hard bargain. After negotiations among the parties assembled at Yeravda, an agreement was submitted to Gandhi retaining reserved seats for untouchables and proposing a system of two-stage elections in which they would vote separately in a primary election to choose candidates. With little argument Gandhi approved this agreement on the fourth day of the fast. When MacDonald's consent was given two days later he drank his glass of orange juice. Ambedkar later described the agreement, without exaggerating very much, as another way of implementing the Communal Award. It was discovered to everyone's surprise, when the details became known, that untouchables now had many more reserved seats than they had had before.[41]

Detestation of Gandhi contributed to the determination with which Ambedkar held out for his agreement. He was to describe the fast as 'a foul and filthy act'.[42] During the course of it Gandhi had told him that, of the two of them, he was the more authentic untouchable, like a captain of industry telling a striker he was the one who really knew what hard work meant.

Ambedkar thought Gandhi had been unnerved by his intransigence. This may have been so. But there were other factors in the situation moving Gandhi towards compromise. One was that the fast did not go well. After only a couple of days his condition deteriorated seriously. It was with real urgency that, in a conversation with Ambedkar, he reminded him that his life was on the line.

The other factor was the public reaction to the fast. Once Gandhi refused food temples were thrown open, and Hindus and untouchables fraternized at meetings all over the country. If the fast was about touching hearts and minds, it could be argued to have accomplished its purpose. It all proved evanescent, but naturally Gandhi hoped he was presiding over the beginning of a new era. 'The hand of God', he said, 'has been visible in the glorious manifestation throughout the length and breadth of India during the past seven days.'[43]

Had he died without an agreement being reached, his death was to have been the signal for what he thought of as stage two of his campaign against separate electorates for untouchables. Beginning with Devdas and moving on to members of the ashram, his most qualified followers would embark on a series of indefinite fasts.[44] As one died, another would take his place. These fasts were not considered imitations. Gandhi was relying on the purifying effect of his own fast to bring others already far enough along in self-purification to the point where they might attempt the supreme *yajna*. A true fast, he told Madeleine Rolland, 'generates a silent unseen force which may, if it is of requisite strength and purity, pervade all mankind'.[45] Each pure fast that followed his would generate its own 'unseen force'. As 20 September approached he directed the power of his concentrated thought towards the ashram. On the night before the fast began, he wrote to Narandas that he was trying to send everyone at Sabarmati a letter, so that he could 'feel one in my heart' with all of them. 'I am drawing the soul of the Ashram into myself', he wrote, 'and pouring my soul into the people there.'[46] 'A total fast', he reminded the ashramites, 'is the ultimate and the highest ideal of the Ashram'; the ashram had 'come into existence to help people attain' the purity required for it.[47]

The choice of Devdas to lead off is interesting. Possibly Gandhi now considered Devdas's raising of the alarm over Chauri Chaura an action meritorious in its disregard for fruits, qualifying him to be the first after himself in sacrifice. Also, Devdas was about to marry his beloved Lakshmi, for whom he had waited five years. His renunciation would have been great.

The public reaction to the 1932 fast was the strongest confirmation yet received by Gandhi that he was the agent of God's will, and he now began to make frequent references to this agency. At no stage during the fast, he told Madeleine Rolland, 'did I feel that I was doing anything.... when I said that it was God working through me, it was literally true, as far as my knowledge went.'[48] A few days later he spoke of the 'occult power' which worked through those who by subjugation of the ego had become 'worthy'.[49] All criticism of the fast received the response that it was not he but God who was responsible for what he did.

Gandhi had not done with fasting. Perhaps to free it of any taint of coercion, he spoke increasingly of it as 'prayer', and he was now inclined to offer up such prayers regularly.

Between September 1932 and August 1933 there were four fasts. In addition there was one threat to fast which was withdrawn, and a threat to put himself on the ordinary prison diet – guaranteed to bring about his decline – which was averted by the government's consent to his request for an unlimited number of visitors. After his brief fast of 3–4 December 1932 in support of the right of a fellow prisoner, a caste Hindu, to show solidarity with untouchables by cleaning latrines (thus violating the caste rules strictly maintained by the prison authorities), he wondered if he might 'have to go through a series of fasts and die by inches'.[50] Fasting, he said, had become 'a permanent and inseparable feature of my life', and 'a privilege earned by hard spiritual toil'.[51] He rejected a reminder by Malaviya of the consequences of spiritual pride. He was making, he said, 'an experiment in ahimsa on a scale perhaps unknown in history'. So long as he was not conscious of error, he would not desist. This might mean 'a fast or a series of fasts'.[52]

In December 1932 he was contemplating a fast to open the Guruvayur temple in Malabar to untouchables, which was to be the centrepiece of the campaign against untouchability he was now conducting from his prison cell. It was postponed indefinitely after two orthodox Congressmen in the central legislature blocked the enabling legislation that turned out to be required, and Malaviya had made known his disapproval. Gandhi's attempts after that to negotiate a settlement – he proposed at one point setting aside certain times of day for untouchables to enter the temple for *darshan* of the deity – came to nothing, and the matter was dropped.

But a major fast was not long in coming. On 30 April 1933 he announced his intention to undertake an 'unconditional' 21-day fast from 8 to 29 May – 'unconditional' meaning that no matter what happened he would complete it. Many were the causes, he said when announcing it, 'too sacred to mention', which 'must have precipitated' it. They were all, however, connected with the campaign against untouchability.[53] Among the precipitating factors mentioned at different times were: the realization that the practice of untouchability was more deep-rooted than he had thought (the temple openings and fraterniza- tion of September having been a nine-day wonder); the discovery of sexual lapses among his anti-untouchability workers; the desire to further purify himself in order to advance the cause; and the belief that the time was now ripe to launch the chain of fasts conceived the previous September. He did not intend to die. But regardless of whether he survived or succumbed, the human links in the chain would each undertake an 'indefinite' fast. It would be a 'great *yajna*' for the uplift of untouchables.[54]

The decision to fast was not easily arrived at; it took three sleepless nights for God's voice to come through. But peace of mind returned after the decision was made. Once the fast began, and Gandhi was existing at God's pleasure, he was in good spirits.

Two developments in Gandhi's personal life had produced a state of mental perturbation. The first was his discovery of serious, and longstanding, tur- pitude at the ashram. He found out in March that an ashramite in whom who he had taken particular pride had been involved in an affair with a young woman he considered a 'daughter'. He was aghast, not just at the immorality, but at the fact that the pair had succeeded in hiding it from him for so long. 'Falsehood cannot hide itself', he lamented, 'from one who scrupulously follows truth, non-violence and *brahmacharya*.' His failure to detect wrongdoing was 'a sure sign of the imperfection of my spiritual attain- ment'. Unknown to him, 'falsehood, violence and passion' must still be lurking within.[55] There were other troubles at the ashram. The untouchable girl he had adopted in 1920 had grown up to be a troublesome young woman with no taste for simplicity, and was making difficulties about the arrangements for her wedding. There were ashramites who treated the place as a hotel or a nursing home. It all cast doubt on the extent of his spiritual progress, so recently proclaimed.

The other development was his entanglement with Nilla Cram Cook. Cook – referred to as 'N' in the *Collected Works* – was a young American with a seriously Dionysian view of life.[56] Lovely and promiscuous, she cut a swathe through the Indian beau monde, among her lovers being the maharaja of Mysore. She was a dancer, and a student of theosophy, the *tantra* and the *shakti* cults of Bengal. While in Mysore she got involved in the anti-untouchability movement and went out to clean streets in Bangalore, which is how she came to the attention of Gandhi. He summoned her to Yeravda.

Gandhi took an intense interest in Cook's erotic career, of which she was happy to supply details, 'omitting not even a twelve-year old kiss in a high-school kissing game'.[57] He seems to have been a little flirtatious. Nevertheless, he assumed responsibility for her spiritual development. Inside the great sinner, he had decided, was potentially a great saint. He saw her as a Magdalen, which is how Anna Kingsford had seen herself (in past lives).

The trouble began when, though now under Gandhi's wing, Cook had sexual relations with workers in the anti-untouchability campaign. He was disappointed but still full of tender concern. With the young men who had fallen he was sharp. They must refrain, he instructed them, from 'consciously or unconsciously' doing anything to impede Nilla's progress. 'I feel for her deeply', he added, 'because I believe that in spite of her untruthful and immoral past she has great capacity for sacrifice and service.'[58] On the day he began his fast he acknowledged her 'large share' in bringing it about. 'If there is anything which can give her strength', he wrote, 'it will be this fast.'[59] During his convalescence he wrote to assure her of his faith that she could become perfectly pure: 'You have in you the making of such a woman.'[60] Cook left India a few months later after a breakdown. By then Gandhi had arrived at a more balanced view. But surely the impurity he had feared was within had had something to do with Nilla.

When Devdas learned of his father's intended fast he threw up his hands and wept at the thought of a fast over 'Nilla and the Ashram affairs'.[61] No doubt he was dismayed at the prospect of offering up his own life in such a cause. In preparation for the chain of fasts Gandhi started clearing the dead wood out of the ashram. Only 'those who are eager to cultivate fitness for offering themselves as sacrifice' would be allowed to stay, and no one new would be admitted. The time was come, he said, for the ashram to sacrifice itself: 'Such is the nature of my intended fast.'[62]

As the ashramites died off one by one, caste Hindus would be inspired to end untouchability. Then, through the personal acts of sacrifice required to bring this about, they too would be purified. From this, two consequences would flow. The first would be the purification of the Hindu religion, both by the removal of the blot of untouchability and by the moral improvement in its adherents. The second was that the spiritual force unleashed by a multitude of acts of renunciation and repentance would bring about 'no less than ... the Brotherhood of Man'. 'You cannot – millions of caste Hindus cannot – do reparation to several million [untouchables], whom they have suppressed for centuries', Gandhi wrote in 1934, 'without setting free a power, a force, that will envelop the whole life of the human family and knit all its members together into one.' It was because he had 'never lost sight of this goal' that he had conceived the anti-untouchability campaign as 'a deeply spiritual and exclusively religious movement'.[63] He had always emphasised the campaign's 'religious' nature but without earlier revealing how extensive were his aspirations for it.

Gandhi was ever, as a committed Hindu, anxious for Hinduism to show what he believed to be its true face to the world. Without the abolition of untouchability, Hinduism would be 'a spent bullet', and not only Hinduism but 'India' would perish.[64] His own destiny too could fall short of fulfilment if he were not as a Hindu able to present the world with a credible message of brotherly love.

To his consternation, he was released from prison on the first day of his fast. He repaired to Lady Thackersey's bungalow at Poona and there, under the supervision of a platoon of doctors, the fast was completed. The chain of fasts was indefinitely postponed. No reason was given. But it seems a fair assumption that upon his re-entry into the world Gandhi discovered there were no takers.

On 16 June Devdas married Lakshmi and settled down to 24 happy years as a husband and father, ending with his death in 1957.

On 25 July Gandhi announced the disbandment of the ashram. Though it was described as a 'sacrifice' (in solidarity with those who had 'lost their all' in the civil disobedience struggle), it was not the kind of sacrifice he had had in mind a few months before.[65]

Upon his release Gandhi immediately announced that his views on civil disobedience remained unchanged, though he advised its suspension for the duration of his fast when all thoughts would be on his state of health. He proposed the resumption of talks between himself and the government, should he survive, and appealed for the release of all civil resisters. He was under no obligation to refrain from political activity because his release could not be described as premature. As a state prisoner detained at his majesty's pleasure, there had been no expiry date for his term in jail.

The government countered right away with a statement that its policy also remained the same: there would be no negotiations until civil disobedience was dropped. Willingdon was determined to cut the ground from under Gandhi's presumption of parity with the government, reasoning that his power over Congress would thereby decline and the elements in Congress responsive to the quickening pace of constitutional reform come to the fore. After some resistance from the British Cabinet, which was reluctant to take too tough a line with Gandhi at a time when his anti-untouchability campaign was attracting favourable publicity in Britain, Willingdon's policy of keeping him at arm's length while avoiding making a martyr of him was retained.

The viceroy's calculation was correct. Gandhi's support among the leaders of Congress was at a low ebb. His current civil disobedience campaign had landed them in a blind alley and they were anxious to find some way of ridding themselves of his leadership without falling foul of popular senti-ment. His only significant supporter was Jawaharlal, who was committed to civil disobedience as a tested means of radical social protest. But Jawaharlal remained in jail until the end of August, and was entering one of his periods of disillusionment with the mahatma, during which, in the words of a biog-rapher, he 'was able to see Gandhi with a much clearer vision than at any time before or since'.[66]

It took almost a year for Congress to extricate itself from Gandhi's grip. His own miscalculations, the result principally of his now total obsession with the power of sacrifice, particularly when offered up by himself, emboldened his enemies and helped to ensure his eclipse.

Some idea of the egocentrism of Gandhi's mental state is given in two letters written in the spring of 1933. In the first, to Ramdas, he justifies his request for special facilities in jail.[67] As an 'elephant' he can hardly pretend to get by on what would sustain an 'ant': it would be to deny his true nature. He must 'humbly accept his big size and consume food weighing more than thousands of ants'. So long as he renders 'proportionate service' it can do no harm. The second letter is to Boyd Tucker, an American admirer who ventured to criticize his focus on temple entry in the anti-untouchability campaign.[68] 'I have no end to serve', Gandhi reminded him, 'but that of Truth.' He did not claim infallibility, and, 'even though I may be right in 99 cases out of 100', did not wish 'to trade upon it and assume or expect other people to assume that the 100th judgment is also right'.

His first move towards resuming civil disobedience was on 30 July, when he announced that on vacating the ashram on 1 August he would march from it with 32 companions to Ras in Gujarat, encouraging people as he went to offer individual civil disobedience. His party would carry no money and depend for food and lodging on the villages through which it passed. This was tantamount to depending on God's providence – presumably Gandhi's intention.

He and his companions were arrested on the night of 31 July and he was reinstated in Yeravda jail the next day. On 4 August he was released and served with an order to stay in Poona. He disobeyed the order, was rearrested, and was returned to prison the same day, where after a brief hearing he was sentenced to a year's imprisonment under the ordinary criminal law.

Once in jail he asked to be given the facilities for anti-untouchability work he had had before, and threatened to start fasting – he implied indefinitely – on 16 August were they not provided by them. On the 16th he started his fast, and when only limited facilities were granted declined to abandon it. The government noted that if Mr Gandhi felt that life had no interest for him were he not permitted to work without hindrance on his anti-untouchability campaign, it was prepared to release him so that he could devote all his time to it, provided he abandoned his incitements to civil disobedience. Gandhi accused the government of failing to understand the importance of 'my spiritual wants regarding untouchability'.[69]

He was soon very ill but refused the conditional release offered by the government. On 23 August, when his life was thought to be in danger, he was released unconditionally. It was soon clear that he would not be confining himself to untouchability work. Once again he sought to renew contact with the government, hoping as he explained to work for 'peace' without being expected to repudiate the principle of civil disobedience, which he regarded as having a fundamentally reconciliatory purpose through the process of conversion.

Public opinion was now beginning to turn against Gandhi: there was suspicion he had fasted to gain his release. He at first seemed delighted by his emergence from prison – was it not by God's grace? – but later expressed embarrassment. The individual civil disobedience campaign meanwhile was finding few recruits.

Congress had succeeded in July in getting Gandhi's imprimatur for the formal abandonment of mass civil disobedience. But on his insistence the obligation of individuals to offer civil disobedience had remained, and there had been no explicit challenge to his leadership. Now the old liberal politician Sastri, who had maintained close ties with Gandhi, came forward to bell the cat. On 27 August he wrote to say that the temper of the country was no longer in favour of civil disobedience but of constructive political work for *swaraj*, and urged Gandhi to withdraw from the leadership of Congress. If only he could, replied Gandhi: he was seeking light. The next to try was Jawaharlal, newly released from jail and in the mood to make a break at last. But face to face with the man he had considered a second father, himself just out of jail and getting over a punishing fast, he faltered. There was no open break. But a statement was issued saying that Gandhi would not court jail during the remainder of his unexpired one-year sentence, and would devote himself to untouchability work, holding himself ready to advise Congress as required. He told Jawaharlal in January that without him in Congress he would be 'in a wilderness'. He was aware, he had said in an earlier letter, that he stood 'thoroughly discredited as a religious maniac and predominantly a social worker'.[70]

Moves were afoot to revive the Swaraj party, increasing Gandhi's sense of isolation. But he made no attempt to retire, and on 7 November set off on a highly publicized national tour to promote the anti-untouchability cause. As usual he attracted vast crowds and collected large sums of money – but there were counter-demonstrations and public criticism by the orthodox, and open hostility from Ambedkar, whose followers were starting to ask why they should remain in the Hindu fold. Gandhi pressed on, emphasizing that the end of untouchability would not mean the end of the caste system, properly understood, and advising untouchables to take pride in their hereditary occupations and get rid of their dirty habits.

Then, on 15 January 1934, while Gandhi was still on tour, a huge earthquake took place in Bihar. Its effects were felt over 6000 square miles, and 7000 people died. Had the earthquake not taken place in the afternoon, when the peasants were in their fields, many more would have died. On 24 January, when Gandhi made his first public comments, there were still fears that the number of deaths could exceed 20,000.

Gandhi's remarks, repeated in most of his public meetings over the next few days, and given fuller expression in *Harijan* on 24 February, were a blow to many who retained some faith in his rationality, or were keeping quiet for the good of the country about his increasingly obvious irrationality. The earthquake, he explained in his mild way, was God's punishment for the sin of untouchability. Tagore as usual spoke up for common sense, aiming his most pointed criticism at the mahatma's evident exploitation of a natural catastrophe to further his current purpose. Gandhi dismissed the attack in a letter to Vallabhbhai saying that the poet had already made amends: 'He gets excited and writes, and then corrects himself. This is what he does every time.'[71] He made a courteous though unrepentant reply in *Harijan*.

Even Tagore, though he must have suspected differently, softened his public criticism by expressing surprise that Gandhi should subscribe to such views. But there was nothing surprising about them. Gandhi believed that all humanity was one, matter and spirit were one, and everything therefore ultimately affected everything else. He set out all this as if it were self-evident in defending his statements on Bihar – though, becoming perhaps aware of the egocentricity of the belief that God would kill thousands in punishment for a sin in which his servant Mohan took a personal interest, he acknowledged that the calamity might not be 'an exclusive punishment for the sin of untouchability'.[72] A few months later, in response to a letter from a science student asking 'Why Bihar?' he attempted to 'prove with the help of several illustrations' that physical events could have 'spiritual' causes. Only one illustration was offered. 'Rain', he wrote, 'is a physical phenomenon; it is no doubt related to human happiness and unhappiness; if so, how could it fail to be related to his [*sic*] good and bad deeds?'[73] He had long assumed droughts and floods to be elements of divine chastisement and purification.[74]

Bihar was on Gandhi's itinerary for his anti-untouchability tour, but he was unsure in the weeks following the earthquake whether he should go. In the end, at the urging of Rajendra Prasad, who wanted to involve him in relief work, he arrived there in March and told the Biharis to their face that they were enduring God's wrath. 'If only we had enough humility', he told 30,000 people assembled at Chapra, 'we would have no hesitation in accepting the recent earthquake as a just retribution for our sins.'[75]

It was in Bihar that Gandhi arrived at the decision that would clear the way for his resignation from Congress in October. When a group of Congressmen arrived in Patna on 4 April to confront him with the decision taken at Delhi a few days before to revive the Swaraj party, he was ready for them with the news that he was calling off all civil disobedience but his own.

Though Gandhi well understood by then how isolated he had become – the roll call of the Swarajists included some of his closest associates: Dr Ansari, Sarojini Naidu, Rajagopalachari, Rajendra Prasad – his decision was clearly not just an admission of political defeat. As on other occasions he had settled on a position which accommodated political realities as he saw them without compromising his destiny. To the consternation of the Swarajists, he announced that, as the acknowledged expert in *satyagraha*, he would be offering civil disobedience at his own discretion and in Congress's name. It took another six months for him to acknowledge that entry into the legislative councils was not just an option for individual Congressmen but the new policy of Congress.

The concerns about the spiritual fitness of his disciples which had prompted the 21-day fast had not gone away during the months of freedom. The very fact that the individual civil disobedience campaign had fizzled out suggested to Gandhi that it was spiritually underpowered.[76] Towards the end of March he summoned a group of resisters just released from jail to Bihar.[77] He perceived in them a lack of enthusiasm for sacrifice – more particularly the lack of a spontaneous, rather then a dutiful (out of love for him) commitment to it – which convinced him that he must dissociate his own vital and authentic acts of *satyagraha* from resistance offered lukewarmly and without real under-standing by others. He noted that he had 'lost' Devdas, and that other young men were 'slipping away' from him. He was perturbed by the discovery that there was slackness in observing 'the rules of satyagraha'. In a later public statement he referred to the shock of finding out that 'a valued companion of long standing' had shirked his prison duties in order to pursue his private studies. This was most likely Mahadev, who was still in jail: his passion for learning French had already earned a reprimand.

His conclusion was that the shortcomings of individual resisters were dilut-ing not only the movement's spiritual force, but his own. If rupees worth only 14 (rather than 16) annas came into circulation, he explained, the value of the real rupee declined. He was 'beginning to feel', he said, 'that I am sufficient by myself'. Without the 'adulterating' effect of the imperfect *satyagraha* of others, he believed, his own *satyagraha* would operate with greater power. 'Just as I was the only representative at the R.T.C.', he said, still unable to contemplate personal responsibility for that debacle, 'it is enough if I am the only one in the present political programme. It would be fully accomplished thereby.'

The reception he was getting on his anti-untouchability tour, which was now entering its sixth month, was an important factor in his decision.[78] The sanatanists and Ambedkar had not stopped the masses from giving him a rapturous welcome. He saw their 'spontaneous fervour' as confirmation of the power of his unmediated personal influence. It showed that 'Spiritual messages are self-propagating.' Thus he was inspired to find the solution to his political and personal disappointments in a reaffirmation of his special powers. There would be no further 'adulteration' of his message during his lifetime through its propagation by the unqualified – 'unless one arises claiming to know the science better than I do and inspires confidence'.

Mass civil disobedience was not ruled out. The same standards did not apply to it. Only unauthorized individual acts of civil disobedience were no longer allowed. His anti-untouchability tour had convinced him that there would be no shortage of recruits for mass civil disobedience when the time was ripe.[79]

The government's lifting of the ban on Congress activities on 6 June 1934 sealed Gandhi's fate. Congress was now once again a legitimate political organization after more than two years underground. The end of civil dis-obedience, the steady rise of sentiment within Congress in favour of council entry and constructive political engagement, the anticipation of expanded electoral opportunities under the Government of India Act, which was then in the final stages of gestation, let loose an unstoppable flood of political activity aimed at securing the powers of office. The Congress party in its mature form – vital, corrupt, the dispenser of patronage and sponsor of reform – came into existence.

The influence of the socialists in Congress was also on the rise. They were not averse to civil disobedience. But they had lost patience – even Jawaharlal – with the mahatma's personal and political peculiarities. His doctrine of trusteeship – that property was held in trust from God and property owners must be allowed to exercise that trust – was anathema, as was his rejection of industrialization.

Had events not conspired in September 1939 to unleash another wave of protest against the British, Gandhi's political career would have been over. There was no place for him in the new Congress, and, difficult as it was to imagine Congress without Gandhi, it was impossible to imagine Gandhi as a significant political operator without Congress. He began to acknowledge that the organization on which he had relied for so long was now alien territory.

In August he fasted for a week in penance for unruly behaviour by anti-untouchability workers. But he said that the 'unclean methods' employed in the recent Congress elections were also in his mind.[80]

The problem was how to go without accepting dismissal, an embarrassment Congress was almost as anxious to avoid as Gandhi was. The solution was found in his reassertion of his social and religious priorities. As early as April he had been thinking about a radical overhaul of the constructive programme.[81] The old institutions, their ideals now compromised, would pass away and be replaced by new ones run on the strictest principles, which, as they spread over the country, would provide new and better opportunities for service. Through them a purer generation of public workers would be born. He began to rethink the *khadi* campaign, seeing it more in the context of a revival of village life, with cloth produced for local consumption as part of the rural economy.[82] This was the germ of the All-India Village Industries Association set up later in the year.

As he travelled the country on his anti-untouchability tour, preaching the pure Hinduism of yore, he became troubled by the inconsistency between his message of simplicity and his manner of delivering it. He announced on 8 May that he would no longer use a car and would continue on foot. Like the *rishi*s of old he would 'propagate dharma' using 'natural methods of locomotion', speed being 'probably inimical to spiritual progress'.[83] He ceased to collect funds.

The walking tour ended in June with the onset of the rains, but he continued to think about a life more in keeping with his spiritual ambitions. He was drawn back to his roots as a religious visionary of rustic inclinations, and contemplated a life away from cities and all the compromises with the modern world politics had required of him

He clung to his right to offer civil disobedience in Congress's name. But in June reality began to break in. Elections to the legislative councils were coming up and Congress had to decide where it stood on the Communal Award. Communally minded Hindus in Congress were feeling betrayed by the Gandhi–Ambedkar pact. Despite Gandhi's efforts to avert a split, Malaviya and M.S. Aney rejected the Congress policy of deferring a decision on acception or rejection, and left to fight the elections on the Nationalist party ticket, with opposition to the award as the principal campaign issue. This was the long-delayed denouement of the fast of September 1932, so imperatively undertaken, so hastily concluded.

On 17 September he issued a statement[84] that he would leave Congress after the Bombay session scheduled for the last week of October – if it turned out that people really wanted him to go. He appears to have resumed his diet of uncooked food, suggesting that hopes of saving the day had not been abandoned.[85] But by the time he arrived at Bombay he had accepted the inevitable. 'I go', he said, 'with your blessing in search of greater power to discover means whereby I can give you the faith that is in me.' When called, he would return.[86]

The All-India Village Industries Association was set up under his control as an autonomous part of Congress. Rajendra Prasad, at his behest, was installed as Congress president. His retirement took place amid emotional scenes in Congress open session. He would be gone, but was clearly not intending to be forgotten.

His first move on leaving Congress was to propose a visit to the North-West Frontier Province to ascertain for himself the quality of the non-violence of Abdul Ghaffar Khan's Red Shirts. He hoped to find in them the true non-violence of the brave. He suggested he might settle down among them.

The proposed visit was not illegal but it was provocative. The Khan himself was prohibited from entering the province. Gandhi wrote to sound out the viceroy, and was told that it was 'not desirable' for him to go. He undertook to 'abide by His Excellency's wishes ... in so far as it was humanly possible' – a clear intimation that civil disobedience was under consideration.[87] On 7 December Abdul Ghaffar Khan was arrested at Wardha where he was a guest with Gandhi of Jamnalal Bajaj, and the idea was dropped. At this point, Gandhi anticipated arrest as part of a general government crackdown. But the government had him boxed in and preferred to leave him alone.

Impotence led swiftly to depression. Anger – as much anathema to Gandhi who aspired to be 'free of passion' as sexual arousal – would not go away, and he began to resort to long periods of silence to purge it. His tone with visitors was oracular, brutal and obdurate. His blood pressure periodically shot up.

He kept a foothold in politics via the Working Committee, at whose meetings he was sometimes present, and, over the next three years, through Congress presidents with whom he had a personal relationship. In August 1935, as Rajendra Prasad's term of office drew to a close, he prevailed on the government to release Jawaharlal unconditionally to join his dying wife at a

Swiss sanatorium. Within weeks he had arranged Jawaharlal's election as the next president of Congress, a position he retained through 1937. Jawaharlal was annoyed with himself for being launched into office through the Gandhian trapdoor but made no move to repudiate the old magician.

Gandhi's influence on politics during the years of his retirement can be exaggerated. For most of the time he felt isolated and insignificant. Under the Government of India Act which became law in 1935, responsible popular government was introduced in the provinces, and for the next few years almost all the political action was at the provincial level. As unofficial adviser to the Congress 'High Command' (the handful of personalities which emerged at this period as pre-eminent) his influence on the direction taken by the country was not substantial.

On one issue where he might have made a difference he remained silent. This was in 1937 when Congress triumphantly took office on the basis of a greatly expanded franchise in eight out of eleven Indian provinces. In provinces where they were the largest but not the majority party the Congress leadership refused to form coalitions. The result was to exclude Muslims from power in some areas where they had made a strong showing – an intense provocation in the United Provinces where the Muslim League had secured a significant number of seats. Congress hauteur in 1937 pushed Jinnah further down the separatist path. The responsibility was primarily Nehru's, but Gandhi did nothing to stop it. After evincing some initial sympathy with League demands in the United Provinces he did not press the matter.

His political interests at this time lay in implicitly supporting whatever was the general thrust of Congress policy. By 1937 he had convinced himself that entry to the legislatures (which it was obviously futile to oppose) was a natural stage on the road to *swaraj* – a reversal of his position in 1934 that *swaraj* would never come that way. Ignoring Nehru's opposition, he supported the inclination of the majority of the Working Committee to fight the 1937 elections.

His great interest and diversion during the period immediately after his exit from Congress and before setting up the Segaon ('Sevagram' after 1940) ashram in 1936 was the AIVIA, whose headquarters he set up at Wardha. The anti-untouchability cause was effectively dropped, with the assurance that it would now be a part of village uplift, of which untouchables would be beneficiaries.

Rural development Gandhi-style was along the lines laid down in *Hind Swaraj*. Villagers would thrive primarily through self-sufficiency, but the products of their revived handicraft tradition would provide town-dwellers as well with articles of simple beauty. Gandhi had an instinctive appreciation of the delightful imperfections of handmade objects of utility. The townspeople, he hoped, as village production revived, would see it as their duty to purchase what villages produced. All of us, he wrote to Vallabhbhai, 'should use pens, ink, knives, soap, jaggery [a coarse dark sugar] and sugar manufactured in villages and flour and rice ground or milled in villages'. Villages would then rise from poverty and take more part in the life of the country. The 'swaraj of our dreams, devoted to the welfare of villages' would become a possibility.[88] Village workers were forbidden to use fountain pens.

He saw village work as serving the cause of non-violence. Only *swaraj* built on the foundation of village life, he said, could be 'non-violent swaraj'. He looked back as in *Hind Swaraj* to the 'village republics' of pre-British India. 'I fancy', he said, 'that they were unconsciously governed by non-violence'. His aim was 'to revive them under a deliberate non-violent plan'.[89] In the process volunteers would receive a training in service and disciplined self-sacrifice. He intended to show the socialists – whose influence looked set to eclipse his own – the true remedy for the suffering of the Indian poor. 'None of them', he said, 'knows the real conditions in Indian villages or perhaps even cares to know them.'[90]

The creation of wants was no part of Gandhi's programme, and the improvement of material conditions was to be so designed as to avoid it. Seeing attachment to material things and violence as virtually synonymous, he liked to think the old Indian villages were non-violent because their inhabitants were satisfied with a dignified sufficiency in their material surroundings. This was the situation he wished to restore.

He well knew that the present condition of the rural masses for the most part ruled out a principled renunciation of the material. When he saw people starving in Orissa in 1921 – an experience he was to recall with horror for the rest of his life – he instinctively contrasted their involuntary suffering with his own purposeful denial of the appetites. They were on 'an eternal compulsory fast'.[91] His hope was to bring all the villagers of India to the point where spiritual development as he saw it was an option. There was no merit in a man without food not eating, as there was no merit in an impotent man not having sexual relations.

Experts in the appropriate fields were consulted about how the dream could be made reality, especially experts in nutrition, for the programme was also an experiment in dietary reform. The popularization of unrefined foods, such as unhusked rice, was an important aim. Dispensaries were not part of the programme and the handing out of medicine by individual workers was stopped when it came to Gandhi's attention. He saw improvements in diet and hygiene as the path to health. Village sanitation, the conversion of night-soil by simple scientific methods into usable manure, improved and humane dairy practices, non-violent beekeeping were all attempted under the aegis of the AIVIA.

Many of these efforts would meet with the approval of development agencies today. But like many who came after him Gandhi was to experience discouragement. 'The four hundred adults of Segaon', he wrote in 1937, 'can easily put ten thousand rupees annually into their pockets if only they would work as I ask them. But they won't. They lack co-operation, they do not know the art of intelligent labour, they refuse to learn anything new.'[92] Such comments became frequent. By 1938 there were few references in his writings to the AIVIA.

Now that his life was officially dedicated to the Indian poor, the issue of birth control was one with which he began to be confronted. In January 1935 two formidable women, Mrs C. Kuttan Nair from Cochin and Edith Howe-Martin from England, arrived at Wardha within weeks of each other and put to him that contraception was critical to the welfare of the Indian woman and child. Edith Howe-Martin told him plainly that sex was not dirty.[93] 'You seem', she said, 'to regard a beautiful function as something objectionable.' Were not two beings creating a new life at that moment 'nearest to the divine'? Taken by surprise at such brazenness, Gandhi's response was confused. Yes, the creation of new life was 'nearest the divine'. But only if the act was approached 'in a divine way' – that was, 'with no other desire than that of creating a new life'. Otherwise, it was 'nearest the devil'.

He had never previously entertained the idea that sex for the purpose of creating a new life had anything divine about it. Lust was lust, as in his cosmology it had to be. The previous limits of his tolerance for sexual activity had been the occasional acceptance of its necessity, as a clinical and deliberate act, when children were desired, and the recognition born of experience that it was inevitable in the unenlightened.

At first Gandhi was as implacable as ever in his opposition to any kind of birth control. When Swami Yoganand urged him to consider it as a realistic approach to bringing down India's birth and child mortality rates, he stood firm for abstinence. Asked if he believed, then, in 'many children', he said he believed in 'no children'. The human race would only 'be transformed into something better' as a result.[94] He did not abandon the view that the consequences of sex without fear of pregnancy could only be dire. Sex ad lib was like masturbation, with 'loss of manhood' (impotence) its inevitable result, 'dementia' its likely result.[95] It was better, he had told Mrs Kuttan Nair, for people to experience the effects of Nature's laws, with which contraceptives were 'an unnatural interference'. If they bred like rabbits, they could expect to die like rabbits. He did not stop believing that this would be 'a blessing in disguise'.[96]

But if it were desirable for the (male) genitalia to remain in working order, yet not be brought into contact with the female genitalia, what were they for? The startling possibility with which Gandhi had been confronted was that the practice of birth control involves a paradox: it makes sex whenever they feel like it an option for people who want to limit reproduction; but the deliberate setting aside of birth control for the sake of conception then transforms the sexual act into a solemn and sacramental one.

In December he was assailed again by the proponents of contraception. Mathuradas Trikumji of the Bombay Municipal Corporation wrote asking him to support the opening of a municipal birth-control clinic. His refusal was met with argument. Then came a visit from the most dangerous birth-control advocate of all, Margaret Sanger. There was no evading this issue which was complicating his effort to save rural India.

After going to jail for opening a birth-control clinic in 1916 Margaret Sanger had made the beauty and sanctity of married life a central theme of her campaign, gathering public support with the argument that 'planned parenthood' strengthened the institution of marriage. When they met, Gandhi said that his own marriage had been strengthened by the renunciation of sex.[97] The sexual act performed for pleasure, he said, was like eating chocolates instead of nourishing food. To Sanger this was a trivialization of the act of married love. Sexual relations, she protested, could involve both love and lust. Not being acquainted with Gandhi's ideas about 'control of the palate', she cannot have found enlightening his explanation that 'If food is taken only for pleasure it is lust.' But Gandhi had not come unprepared to this meeting and was trying to say something new. He had been given a book advocating the rhythm method and had found it 'worth pondering over'.[98] He surprised everyone at the end of his talk with Sanger by giving it his guarded approval. It at least, he said, included an element of self-control, and if accepted might put the birth-control clinics, which encouraged the abandonment of all restraint, out of business.

A few days after Sanger's visit Gandhi's blood pressure went over 200 and it was two months before he was able to take up any public duties again. The strain of rethinking some of his ideas on sex perhaps contributed to the collapse. But he had been enduring many other difficulties and disappointments, and high blood pressure had been a problem for most of the year. To list his principal troubles: he was in political eclipse; he had begun to find village work 'baffling';[99] he had once again been under fire for using young women as 'walking sticks'; Ambedkar had just made a public call for untouchables to leave Hinduism; and he had suffered greatly over the collapse of a brief reconciliation with Harilal. During his period of enforced rest and contemplation he thought about the future of India, and his conclusions involved the further revision of his views about sex.

The way civil disobedience had fizzled out had continued to weigh on his mind after his retirement from Congress, and during 1935 he pondered despairingly on the non-violence of the brave and made some strong statements about his countrymen's fearful nature. He was not inclined, he said, in 'our enfeebled circumstances', to offer them counsels of perfection.[100] Hearing that Hindu villagers in Andhra had fled from Muslim assailants, he announced it was a waste of time to preach non-violence to cowards. How could people without the guts to defend themselves ever embrace the non-violent ideal of 'self-immolation' in response to violence? Even armed resistance, he said, was better than running away.[101] Wherever he looked, he saw not only physical fear but general cravenness and futility. How little it took, he reflected, for his village workers to get discouraged: they lacked 'the Kshatriya spirit. We lose heart much too soon. We tremble to stand alone.' These defects were perceptible 'even in myself'.[102]

In the summer of 1935 the League of Nations asked him to make a statement on the Abyssinian crisis. He refused. He declined even to give newspaper interviews on the subject, having, he said, only words to offer and no force to back them up. After the Italian invasion in October he explained that had India 'as a nation imbibed the creed of non-violence, corporate or national, I should have had no hesitation in giving a lead'. Alas, India, 'whose destiny is to deliver the message of non-violence to mankind', currently fell so far short of genuine non-violence that she even had no 'capacity for offering violence'. Otherwise, her millions 'would be the greatest moral force in the world, and Italy would listen to our friendly word'.[103]

As an old man expecting, as he was given to observing at this time, only a year or two more of life, Gandhi resigned himself (for the time being) to the prospect that India's conversion to non-violence was not going to happen in his lifetime. He began to invest his hopes in the next generation. Without sex there would be no next generation, and the new idea about sex which he revealed after his recovery was that God's intended purpose for the penis was procreation.

The breakthrough had come when Vinoba, concerned about his apparent endorsement of the rhythm method, recalled a passage in the *shastras* indicating that married couples who united sexually only to have a child were true *brahamachari*s. It struck Gandhi with revelatory force that children could be produced without using up spiritual credit – for if 'a man controls his semen, except on the occasion of such a purposeful cohabitation, he is as good as an avowed *brahmachari*'. It followed that the 'function of the organs of generation is merely to generate progeny obviously of the highest type possible for a married couple'.[104]

He still had no use for recreational sex. As he put it to Premabehn Kantak, with whom at the time he was conducting a correspondence on sexual matters: 'As a man happening to see on the road the blood-stained sputum of a consumptive may take it to be a gem and long to pick it up, but will come to his senses as soon as he realizes his error, so is the case in regard to the function of the genital organs.'[105] He later refined his position on permissible sex to allow for the fact that, after one child had been produced in the approved fashion, the procreative act thereafter would be contaminated by remembered pleasure. Ideally, reproduction should be limited to one child, the offspring of virgin parents.

The article 'For the Young' written for *Harijan* in March 1936 was one of his first published statements of his new position on sex. 'Sex urge is a fine and noble thing', he declared. 'There is nothing to be ashamed of in it. But it is meant only for the act of creation.'[106] Judging from a letter of the following year, he was considering the possibility that such an act of dedicated intercourse might qualify as desireless action as expounded in the *Gita*.[107]

The eugenic factor was taken for granted in Gandhi's new thinking. Now that the begetting of children, as much as spiritual partnership, was seen to be the point of marriage, 'eugenic fitness' was declared its *sine qua non*.[108] Children were to be produced by men who brought to the moment of conception both seed of fine quality (from having been conserved) and the spiritual standing conferred by renunciation of desire up to that point.

Asked what one should do if a single act of intercourse failed to result in conception, Gandhi replied that the seed of a true *brachmachari* could not be infertile; however, as a practical matter, intercourse could be permitted 'once at the end of the monthly period till conception is established'.[109] He must not have considered the implication for conception of his long-held belief that true *bramacharis* of the female sort ceased to menstruate.

In 'For the Young' he urged 'the youth of India', who 'hold her destiny in their hands', to 'guard the treasure with which God has blessed them', and use it 'for the only purpose for which it was intended': when God had given man 'seed that has the highest potency', it was 'criminal folly' to let it 'run to waste'.[110] The dissolution of the human race was now postponed pending India's achievement of *swaraj*. Better Indians must first be born before general emancipation from the fleshly state was a possibility.

Assuming that the quality Gandhi would most have wished at this time to appear in the next generation of Indians was non-violence of the brave, the significance of a curious episode which now took place in his life becomes clear.

On 24 July 1937, 187 prisoners serving life sentences for terrorist offences in the Andamans went on hunger strike, demanding release of all political prisoners and repeal of all laws suppressing political activity. Another 30 prisoners joined the strike a week later when the demands were rejected by the Government of India. Public opinion in India was sympathetic to the prisoners and a Congress member of the central legislature requested their release and repatriation. The viceroy (Linlithgow) refused, pointing out that all of them had been convicted after trial, about a hundred had been convicted of dacoity, and over sixty had been convicted of murder, attempted murder and illegal possession of arms.[111]

Gandhi sprang into action, offering to try to get agreement to their demands if they, first, abandoned their hunger strike, and second, pledged to renounce violence and embrace non-violence.

The release of political detenus and convicts was a live issue in Congress politics, with several of the newly installed Congress provincial governments grappling with public pressure to make a grand jail delivery marking their accession to power. Gandhi's interest can be seen as one of the exploratory moves he was starting to make for an eventual return to politics. But, in the words of the editorial preface to Volume 66 of his *Collected Works*, he 'made their cause his own'. He kept up the pressure on Congress ministries, and also on the government of Bengal, visiting Calcutta in October and holding talks with prisoners formerly in the Andamans now held in the Alipur jail. In an extraordinary conversation he explained to them that he was there as 'a votary of non-violence', which he believed 'will not spread' in India 'so long as you prisoners are kept in prison'. His days, he said, were numbered, and much of the time he had left was 'going to be given in order to secure your release. I want to see you discharged before I die.'[112]

The Andamans prisoners had told him in August that they had all renounced terrorism, being 'convinced of its futility as a political weapon or creed'.[113] They did not embrace non-violence: it would not have been credible. But renunciation was enough, and Gandhi anxiously sought similar commitments from other groups for whose release he was working. He prevailed on the Bengal government in November to start releasing prisoners and was able to broker an agreement between the Congress ministries of the United Provinces and Bihar and the Government of India allowing for release of prisoners in those provinces. He offered to vet prisoners being considered for release in Bengal, ascertaining their commitment to non-violence as a condition for their return to society. His representations to the Government of India for release of prisoners remaining in the Andamans, the repository for hard cases, made no headway. But he did not give up, and continued to exert himself on behalf of political prisoners throughout India.

These efforts were a measure of how desperate he was to get some backbone into Indian politics. Not only was he willing to use his prestige to get violent revolutionaries out of jail and back into circulation, in exchange for a simple promise to reform, he made it a priority. More than once he had gone out recruiting for the empire's wars. Now he went recruiting for his non-violent army in the empire's jails.

The calling in of the military by the Congress government of the United Provinces in March to quell communal riots in Allahabad made him still more anxious to conjure up and organize the non-violence of the brave. He contemplated an organization of Congress volunteers who would go wherever required to interpose themselves between rioting communities, sacrificing themselves if necessary en masse: the time had come 'to try this experiment'.[114] Such people could only be found among the proven brave.

Gandhi's prize convert among the revolutionaries was Prithvi Singh, a highly prepossessing Rajput, who, after a spell in the Andamans and an escape from jail on the mainland in 1922, went underground until he gave himself up to Gandhi in May 1938. As Prithvi Singh was led off to prison, Gandhi said, 'visibly moved': 'It is people like these who can be the true satyagrahis.'[115] 'What do you say to my exploit about Prithvi Singh?' he asked in a letter the next day.[116] Thereafter he regularly petitioned the viceroy for Prithvi Singh's release, hesitating briefly on learning that his conviction had been for crimes of exceptional violence, but finally securing his release in September 1939.

There was a footnote to the Prithvi Singh affair. Mirabehn developed a strong attraction to him, seeing him, according to her account, as the perfect colleague for the work she was starting to do independently in the villages.[117] Gandhi proposed she abandon her vow of celibacy and marry him, and undertook to arrange the match, leaving Mirabehn (who had not arrived in India a virgin) in an emotional tumult. Prithvi Singh turned down the proposal but Gandhi pursued it. Writing to an associate to enlist his help, he affirmed that Mirabehn was 'worthy in every way', adding that she wanted a child 'and that too by Prithvi Singh'. It was thus his 'duty to persuade Prithvi Singh and if he has no religious objection it is his duty to marry her'.[118] There can have been no reason for Gandhi's matchmaking other than the desire to bring about a union of unusual eugenic promise. Mirabehn was 47, but he would have known had she stopped menstruating and conception was ruled out.

As usual he had seen his collapse in health as a fall from grace – a failure of detachment unforgivable in a follower of the *Gita*. But worse still, as he told the readers of *Harijan*, had been an experience during his convalescence of sexual arousal while fully awake, which he (and his attendants, who were immediately alerted) had been unable to divert from its natural conclusion. He could not hide such a lapse from the public which venerated him.[119] (He was not hiding either what must have been a remarkable scene, with all hands summoned in vain to detumesce the mahatma, at 66 of unimpaired virility.) After this experience, his first waking discharge in 36 years (that is, since the conception of Devdas) the effort to conserve semen was stepped up.

He moved soon afterwards from Wardha to Segaon, a village at the end of a track where he lived at first in a makeshift hut under a tree, with Mirabehn as his only companion. He was moving, *rishi*-like, deeper into India, and seems at first to have had no thought of starting an ashram. Then others made their way there. The Segaon community remained an improvised affair. Unlike Sabarmati there was no written constitution and problems were dealt with as they came up. Gandhi issued personal diktats in the form of brief notes.

The constructive programme was Segaon's *raison d'être*, but after a year or so that was fading out. With little real work to do, and no immediate prospect of political mobilization, attention shifted to the *brahmacharya* experiments, which, in the isolation of central India, became Gandhi's principal concern. The community rapidly declined into emotional disorder as devotees vied for the physical contact he permitted himself as he saw fit. Since he spent much more time there than at Sabarmati, the competition for his attention scarcely let up. He and others experienced breakdowns, and by 1938 he was finding life at Segaon intolerable. By 1939 he was observing almost complete silence there in an effort to maintain some mental equilibrium.[120]

First at Wardha, then at Segaon, he had gathered around himself a group of devoted women attendants. Some had been at Sabarmati. Others had newly entered his circle. They included the Christian Sikh princess Amrit Kaur, who would be minister of health in independent India. Gandhi had been trying since 1934, with the teasing flattery he applied to women whose association he desired, to get her involved in his work. Prabhavati Narayan, the confessedly asexual wife of the socialist leader Jayaprakash Narayan, was regularly present. Also in the inner circle were Sushila Nayar (Pyarelal's sister and Gandhi's doctor), Lilavati Asar, and the Muslim devotee Amtul Salaam. In addition, various young women came and went, Padmaja Naidu (daughter of Sarojini) and Om Bajaj (daughter of Jamnalal) among them. Mirabehn was there but detached apparently much of the time from the communal life revolving around service to the mahatma. Her long and stormy relationship with Gandhi was winding down. It was rare for all these women to be present at once, Sushila being Gandhi's closest and most constant companion in the pre-war years. (And there was Kasturbai, no longer in the sexual danger zone but with nowhere else to go but on visits to her grandchildren.)

In the first two years at Segaon the physical contact Gandhi had with these women, though unconventional by any standards, seems to have been less a matter of explicit sexual testing than of trying to demonstrate (every hour of every day) that encounters involving the danger of sexual arousal for other men had no untoward physical or mental effect on him. For the most part he rationalized this physical contact as 'accepting service'. Service ranged from being his 'walking stick' (the practice of using 'walking sticks' having been resumed after being 'renounced' again in September 1935) to rubbing his feet (a service often rendered to elderly relatives in India) to keeping him warm in bed at night. The most intimate service was a daily massage, which took up to two hours while he lay naked on a cot outdoors with a towel draped over him.

Sushila normally gave him his massage. But others, less expert, were sometimes allowed to do it for the sake of the merit they supposed was attached to it. It became a principal source of jealous rages among the residents of Segaon, Pyarelal (whose craving for physical contact with Gandhi was almost homoerotic, though he also yearned to be married) getting particularly distraught when he felt left out.

Another source of rivalry was the sleeping arrangements. Gandhi decided who slept next to him, who slept at the foot of his mat, and so forth. For a long time it was Lilavati who occupied the place next to him at night.[121] Gandhi seems never to have been alone with a sleeping companion, and everyone kept some clothes on.

One incidental but perhaps inevitable result of all this (sexual feelings once aroused usually finding an object) was that members of his entourage conceived passions for each other. Gandhi devoted much time to sorting these out. The new idea of eugenic marriage may have contributed to the lowering of inhibitions.

On 14 April 1938 he had another seminal discharge while awake. It occurred in Delhi, where he was to meet the viceroy the next day. Nothing came of this meeting, and nothing came either of a meeting with Jinnah on 28 April. It could only mean that two years of conspicuously conserving semen had gone for naught. He was not the *brahmachari* he thought he was. 'Where am I', he wrote to Amritlal Nanavati, 'where is my place, and how can a person subject to passion represent non-violence and truth?'[122]

At the urging of Mirabehn he decided, on a trial basis, to stop all the physical contact he had been permitting himself with women. But he soon decided it made no difference to his mental state. By July he had the answer: not more limitations on his contact with women, but fewer.

The decision was announced in an article in *Harijan* in which he blamed the current condition of Congress – faction-ridden and with *khadi* hardly to be seen, himself ignored – on deficiencies in his *brahmacharya*.[123] He could see no flaw in his theoretical conception, but what he had yet to work out, he said, was 'the nature of the limitations' that a *brahmachari* should impose on himself in his contact with the opposite sex. He was 'experimenting' to find out what they should be. Despite the self-criticism, the article left no doubt that Gandhi's achievement of *brahmacharya* was still the pivot on which Indian politics turned. He had thought himself to be God's instrument, he said, 'for presenting non-violence to India for dealing with her many ills'. 'The progress already made', he claimed, 'is great. But much more remains to be done.'

'And so', says Pyarelal, 'he set out to discover' these limitations for himself.[124] Alas, he does not say how. Rumours about goings-on at Segaon were soon current. Gandhi was compelled to deny them in 1939, acknowledging only that Sushila gave him massage and 'medicated baths'.[125] Nothing is known for a fact about the means by which he began more purposefully to test the physical and mental limits of his chastity.

Full *brahmacharya*, Gandhi said in the *Harijan* article, could only be attained 'by the grace of God'. Only when God, by his grace, was seen 'face to face' did 'complete control over all the senses' become irreversible, and the vital power built up through unexpended semen become permanent. Power acquired by mere human effort was always at risk of dissipation by sexual lapses, or even by 'evil, or even rambling, disorderly, unwanted thoughts' – like 'steam kept in a leaky pipe'.

He saw that he had never achieved the 'full control' necessary 'to organize vast masses of mankind for non-violent action', which only came when God at last revealed his face. Understanding his past backsliding, he felt hope for the future. In 'the darkness that seems to have enveloped me', God's grace, in its absence, became vivid to him. Might God not yet show grace to his servant, and share with him his unopposable power?

# NINE

# Götterdämmerung

O nce again Gandhi bounced back from gloom and discouragement. By the
end of September he was feeling 'wonderfully well', blood pressure never
'so steady and low as now'.[1] There are no obvious reasons – no developments
on the political front or in his personal life – for the improvement in spirits.
Prithvi Singh's accession to the non-violent cause continued to hearten him.
But the renewal must have come from within.

He chose to attempt his re-entry into public life in the way he had begun:
through a personal intervention in a local dispute, sidestepping Congress but
riveting its attention on him. It was a quarrel in a princely state – his home
state of Rajkot – that was the occasion.

Before 1938 Congress had avoided getting involved in the affairs of princely
India. But after the 1937 elections there was a change of direction. The
Government of India Act envisaged a federal government for independent
India, and it became important to ensure that representatives from the states
in the federal parliament would support Congress policy. Congress began
actively to support local movements demanding a dilution of princely au-
tocracy. Such movements were implicitly anti-British, for it was the British
political agents in the states who, though they sought to curb princely excess,
propped up princely rule.

Gandhi had been firm in rejecting involvement in the affairs of the states,
regarding it as a diversion of energy. In addition, he preferred to see a gradual,

internal evolution of good government in them along the lines of 'trusteeship'. He was also realistic about his ability to take on the iniquities of princely rule. 'In British territory', he wrote in 1929, 'I know we can exert some influence on the happenings, big and small'; but in the native states it would be a different story.[2] When he began to give his blessing in 1938 to some of the pro-democracy agitations developing in the states, it was on the understanding that progress would have to come from suffering by the people themselves. His decision to go to Rajkot in February 1939 was a surprise.

The movement in Rajkot was aimed at getting its dissolute young ruler, Dharmendrasinhji, to restore the elected popular assembly created by his father.[3] Things came to a head in August 1938 when a protest meeting was dispersed by a *lathi* charge. Under the direction of Sardar Patel, a highly effective campaign – which included, in classic Patel style, strikes, withholding of land revenue, boycotts of goods produced in the state-run cotton mills, boycott of electricity produced at the state power station, and even a run on the state bank – then began in September. In December Dharmendrasinhji and his *diwan*, Durbar Virawala, the effective ruler of Rajkot, offered to reconstitute the assembly. This should have been the happy ending of the Rajkot campaign, but instead an intense struggle ensued over the composition of the committee charged with reconstituting the assembly, with the British authorities instructing Dharmendrasinhji and Virawala to block Patel's nominees. Emboldened, Virawala clamped down on political activities and started throwing people in jail. Kasturbai Gandhi went to Rajkot to protest – apparently at her own wish, through many assumed the mahatma was guiding her – and was also put in jail. On 25 February Gandhi announced he was going to Rajkot.

He was going, he said, at God's abrupt and unexplained command. 'Why am I going, whither am I going? What for? I have thought nothing about those things. And if God guides me, what should I think? Even thought may be an obstacle in the way of His guidance.'[4] Even so, he was calculating that a brief visit by him would set things straight. His relations with the Rajkot ruling family were such that either Dharmendrasinhji 'will restore the pact or he will refer me to the Resident and I shall settle it up with him in no time'.[5]

In the context of Congress politics, the timing of his move was advantageous. Subhas Bose had been elected president in January 1938, and re-elected over Gandhi's candidate Pattabhi Sitaramayya in January 1939. Now itching to stage a mass civil disobedience campaign, and equivocal in his attitude to violence, he was set to preside at the Tripuri Congress beginning on 10 March. A showdown was anticipated between the Gandhian wing and the supporters of Subhas.

With Gandhi's encouragement and almost certainly at his suggestion, the Gandhians on the Working Committee had resigned on 22 February, with the intention of embarrassing Bose at Tripuri and perhaps forcing his resignation.[6] It was a good time to leave the sordid scene of battle and repair to the moral high ground wherever it might be. If things got sorted out quickly in Rajkot, Gandhi could proceed to Tripuri in the glow of victory. If not, he could leave Bose's destruction to his proxies as he strove for the public weal elsewhere. He let it be known that his attendance at Tripuri was not likely.

Scarcely had he arrived in Rajkot than he experienced the urge to fast. Two days of getting nowhere with the imperturbable Virawala exhausted his patience and after the usual sleepless night God spoke to him. On the third day of the fast he wrote to the resident, in an oddly diffident fashion prefiguring his later remorse, asking that the viceroy intervene against Dharmendrasinhji.

Gandhi had lost none of his power to inspire public emotion. Almost five years had passed since his last fast, it was a fast unto death, and he was 69 years old. There was an outpouring of support, mass meetings and a *hartal* in Bombay, and reports that the provincial ministries of the United Provinces, the Central Provinces, Bihar and Bombay were about to resign. (Virawala, however, was heard to remark that it would be a good thing for Rajkot if the mahatma died there: it could become a pilgrimage centre.) The viceroy proposed the arbitration of the chief justice of India, whereupon Gandhi broke his fast on 7 March. On 3 April the chief justice ruled that Patel's nominations to the committee must be upheld.

But Virawala's resources were not exhausted and he turned the tables on his unwelcome visitor. Noting that Gandhi had asked that Muslims and Rajputs be included on the committee, he now proposed that they be added to the nominees, with an untouchable thrown in for good measure, thus depriving the group selected by Patel (and the Rajkot Praja Parishad which he represented) of its majority. Rajputs and Muslims staged demonstrations accusing Gandhi of bad faith, and Jinnah and Ambedkar weighed in. Triumph turned to farce. It was time to resort to 'compromise', and Gandhi offered on his own authority to let Virawala nominate the entire committee, with the Parishad retaining the right to object. Virawala refused, and on 24 April Gandhi left Rajkot.

Absorbing the shock of defeat, Gandhi asked himself how he could have failed to win the heart of Virawala. Obviously, it was some defect in his *ahimsa*. It dawned on him that he had resorted to coercion in bringing government pressure to bear through his appeal to the viceroy – something that, for all his expertise in *satyagraha*, he had not noticed at the time. The solution revealed itself: renunciation of all the fruits of the misconceived appeal. On 17 May he publicly voided his acceptance of the chief justice's award and apologized to all his opponents, assuring the Parishad that 'every act of purification, every accession of courage, adds to the strength of the cause of a people affected by a movement of satyagraha'.[7] Fortunately for the people of Rajkot, Dharmendrasinhji died in a hunting accident the following year, Virawala died of venereal disease shortly after, and Dharmendrasinhji's successor proved more amenable to their aspirations.

Gandhi felt pleased and invigorated by the conclusion to the Rajkot affair. He had made spiritual progress, he thought, by accepting error and renouncing its fruits. His spirits rose. He rejected Jawaharlal's complaint that Rajkot had been set back a hundred years; he was certain he had 'rendered great service'.[8]

Having discerned and purged the 'hidden violence' in himself, he began to perceive that everything that had gone wrong in India since his advent to power was caused by such unconscious violence, mainly in others, though he blamed himself for allowing agitation to go forward without first ensuring its perfect peacefulness.[9] Since violence 'recoiled upon itself', creating more violence, the result had been the ever-worsening communal riots, and the current state of Congress, full of dissension and ill will. All this must change. But he reminded Indians that cowardice remained the worst sin of all. The renewed emphasis on *ahimsa* left his conception of non-violence in a state of fragile equilibrium between the manly capacity for violence and the repudiation of it.

Meanwhile the despatch of Bose was accomplished. Bose's undoing at Tripuri was brought about by a motion from the veteran Congress politician G.B. Pant expressing confidence in the old Working Committee and proposing that the president be guided in selecting a new Committee by 'the wishes of Mahatma Gandhi'. Gandhi claimed to have been aware in advance only of the first part of the motion. He expressed disapproval of the second part and refused to supply names. It was up to him, he told Bose, to select a new Committee and put it to the AICC; if it was rejected he should resign. Knowing his only hope lay in getting a list for which he could claim Gandhi's approval, Bose pleaded with him for nominations. On 29 April Gandhi delivered the *coup de grâce*. Given that he and Bose were so far apart on fundamentals, he said, 'if I give you names, it would be an imposition on you'.[10] Bose resigned the same day and was replaced by Rajendra Prasad.

Though all preserved the convention that the mahatma was above the fray, no one seems to have been under any illusion as to who was responsible for Bose's demise. When the Gandhi Seva Sangh met on 5 May there were awkward questions. Coercion was violence, Gandhi protested: 'How can I resort to it?'[11] In August he was instrumental in getting Bose removed from the presidency of the Bengal Congress Committee, and debarred from being an elected member of any Congress committee for the next three years.

Bose and the Rajkot *satyagraha* faded from public view as attention turned more and more to the coming war. On 23 July Gandhi wrote a letter to Hitler, which the government did not allow him to send, apologizing for bothering him and making a personal appeal to him not to plunge the world into war. 'Must you pay that price', he asked, 'for an object however worthy it may appear to you to be?'[12]

It was never entirely clear which side Gandhi was on in the war. He acknowledged that the Allies had some claim to represent democracy against authoritarianism – but his attitude towards democracy had always been ambivalent. He admired Hitler for his 'dash, energy, resourcefulness and capacity', his bravery, dedication, powers of concentration and organization, and unclouded intellect[13] – many of the same qualities for which he admired the British. He noted that Hitler was said to be a vegetarian and to live 'a life of self-sacrifice': 'He has no vices. He has not married. His character is said to be clean. He is always alert.'[14] The thought cannot have escaped him that Hitler, like the demon Ravana, must have done much *tapascharya*.

He had a fundamental incomprehension of how bad Hitler really was. His advice to the Czechs and the Jews to offer non-violent resistance, though not without its tantalizing grain of truth, failed to come to grips with the realities of either Nazi ideology or Nazi power. He was to cite as confirmation of his belief in the ultimate futility of violence that armed resistance had not saved either Poland or Czechoslovakia from its fate.[15] In May 1940 he proposed to Linlithgow that Britain sue for peace. He received an icy reply but nonetheless appealed in *Harijan* to Britons to lay down their arms and 'invite Herr Hitler and Signor Mussolini to take what they want of the countries you call your possessions', to 'take possession of your beautiful island', let them 'occupy your homes', and if 'they do not give you free passage out', let themselves be slaughtered. It would work out better in the end than if they sullied themselves with all-out war.[16]

Ultimately his attitude to the war was determined by what he thought God's purpose was in unleashing Hitler on the world. There was 'no question', he explained to a correspondent in October 1939, 'of violence or non-violence on the part of God'. God used even violent, God-hating men for his purposes. 'How do we know for whose destruction Hitler was born?'[17] The answer to this question, formulated in 1942, was surely in Gandhi's mind when he asked it. It was that 'the Nazi power had risen as a nemesis to punish Britain for her sins of exploitation and enslavement of the Asiatic and African races'.[18] Hitler was the human equivalent of the Bihar earthquake.

He settled on a view of the war as a kind of court case proceeding before a divine tribunal, the party with the most moral credit to be awarded the victory. He had, he told Birla, 'hardened my heart' to the horrors in Europe.[19] God would decide who won, and if the British fought cleanly and did right by India it would be them. When the British bombed Berlin on 24 September 1940 he considered that they had done grave damage to their claim for justice 'before the imperial court of God'.[20]

The question was: what role was he – and India – meant to play in this cataclysm visited on Britain by the Almighty? His views on this developed in the context of the Congress reaction to the outbreak of war.

From the start, Congress suspicion of British motives in declaring war on Germany was the determining factor in its response. Indian politicians perceived the hypocrisy of the British claim that they were fighting to save democracy. To a subject people, the claim could hardly ring true. The years of appeasement in Europe further deprived it of credibility. It was obvious that Britain was fighting to avoid conquest and preserve its empire. So clearly did Congress perceive this that, though it had routinely placed on record its condemnation of Nazism for years, it failed to concede any objective value to Britain's stand against Germany, and declared that its priority would be to secure the freedom of India.

It was understood that when Britain was at war, India would be also. But Linlithgow's 'failure' to consult Indian opinion before making the official announcement was made the occasion for putting the government on notice to expect trouble. A week after the outbreak of war, the Working Committee demanded that the British government state its intention to liberate India and 'give immediate effect to it, to the largest possible extent'. The possibility was left open that a free India would support the British war effort.[21]

Gandhi's first reaction when war broke out had been a rush of emotional sympathy for Britain. The thought of the destruction of London, when it suddenly seemed possible, shocked him. He said that though he wished India to remain non-violent, Britain would have his moral support, and India's deliverance could wait. When the Working Committee met he discovered that no one shared these views. He abandoned them and supported the Congress demands. This meant persuading himself that any eventual wartime alliance between an independent India and Britain might still remain non-violent, or would involve a departure from non-violence that was 'temporary' and 'confined to the narrowest field'. He would not be serving the cause of non-violence, he wrote, if he 'deserted my best co-workers because they could not follow me in an extended application of non-violence'.[22] He saw that to separate himself from Congress now would be to condemn himself to irrelevance.

His support of the Working Committee's position hardened as he began to see it as presenting a legitimate challenge to the British government. When Samuel Stokes wrote to him to tax him with not understanding the necessity of defeating Nazi Germany, he replied that when in doubt about 'a matter involving no immorality either way', it was his habit to 'toss' and read divine guidance in the result. In this case the Congress demand was the coin that had been tossed. If the British response showed that their intentions toward India were 'pure', it would mean that 'God wants the Congress to throw its whole weight on the side of Britain, so that ultimately the victory may go not to the strongest arms but to the strongest cause'.[23]

This being his position, when the British announced in October that they were not prepared to depart from the plans for India's constitutional advance embodied in the 1935 Act, he took it to be God's will that India should withhold its support. His focus now shifted to further non-violent resistance to British rule. He came to see this as India's contribution to world peace. 'If India can win swaraj non-violently even while this conflagration is going on', he wrote in September 1940, 'the latter is bound to be extinguished by that one event.'[24] Such would be the spiritual force unleashed by India's suffering and Britain's acknowledgement of it in the form of independence.

On 18 October he called for Congress to 'go into the wilderness' and strengthen itself to attain its legitimate objectives.[25] On the same day, he wrote the letter asking for whose destruction Hitler might have been born. Four days later the Working Committee directed the Congress provincial ministries to resign. It was assumed that civil disobedience would follow.

By inspiration or calculation, Gandhi had chosen a good moment to ask Congress to abandon elected office. Congress rule in the provinces was beset by problems, inherent for the most part in the assumption of responsibility, which were eroding its claim to represent the Indian nation. The wilderness, where unity might be retrieved in opposition, had its attraction.

The situation was now hospitable to a return to power by Gandhi, as leader of a new campaign. Leadership he was happy to resume, but the idea of a mass campaign disturbed him. The country was not truly non-violent – and how would Muslims react to a Congress campaign, now that Congress and the League were open enemies? The country was instructed to 'await and obey your general's word'.[26] Delay was wise and convenient. Congress could organize itself for opposition while it observed the course of the war in Europe, and waited to see if the British made a better offer.

The German victories of April 1940 produced consternation in the Congress leadership. A somewhat firmer offer of support for Britain was made, in return for a declaration of Indian independence and the immediate creation of a National Government. In view of the anticipated need to prepare for the defence of India, Gandhi was asked to step down from his generalship. But he was almost immediately reinstated when the British offered only an expanded executive council, and a War Advisory Council which Indians would be invited to join. Churchill was now prime minister, the Battle of Britain was on, and he would not be trifled with by the naked fakir and his friends. Congress moved to outright opposition to the war effort, and Gandhi began to work out what to do next.

He decided on a campaign of individual civil disobedience – in this case, civil disobedience offered by a series of selected individuals – based on a demand whose acceptance he believed would mean the substance of *swaraj*. It was to be a campaign for free speech on the subject of the war, specifically the right to disseminate the statement: 'It is wrong to help the British war effort with men or money. The only worthy effort is to resist all war with non-violent resistance.'[27] The aim of world peace was embodied in the illicit statement, which stopped short, in the name of *ahimsa*, of confronting the British at bay with a direct demand for independence.

Only the pure would be selected for sacrifice. But *brahmacharya* in the narrow sense of 'conservation of the vital energy brought about by sexual restraint' would be acceptable.[28] Gandhi himself would not offer civil disobedience but would remain at Sevagram, where he had 'built up ... an atmosphere for my growth'.[29] The first offering was Vinoba Bhave, who stood high in Gandhi's esteem but was unknown to the public, and not even a member of Congress. The next was Jawaharlal, Congress's knight *'sans peur et sans reproche'* in Gandhi's words of 1937,[30] now a widower and presumed to be conserving his vital fluid. Having agreed to selection before the exact nature of the programme was disclosed he then found it unconvincing, but was prevailed on to continue. The intention was, Gandhi explained, to rely on 'regulated thought producing its own effect'; he must 'suspend judgement and watch results'.[31]

Gandhi's hopes for the campaign were high. So pure was Vinoba that he at first thought it might not be necessary to call another volunteer. So powerful would be the effect of the thought expressed in the illicit statement, when recited by someone of such uncommon quality, that British resistance would crumble. Vinoba's arrest having had no visible result, nor Jawaharlal's either, he invested his hopes in the cumulative effect of the action being repeated by many others. Volunteers were expected to court arrest through a public recitation of the statement, leaving others to pass it on, the act to be performed ceremonially but preferably in some obscure village. Gandhi wanted thought alone, which 'is more effective than speech and writing',[32] to do its work. Publicity might even diminish its effect. This least remembered of Gandhi's campaigns was also his most ambitious. He saw it at the time as his last and best.

Jawaharlal was arrested on 31 October before he could even utter the magic words, and government censorship meant that most of the arrests that eventually took place were not even reported in the newspapers. Gandhi began to contemplate a fast. It would 'certainly be tainted with attachment for the fruit'; but 'all beginnings are tainted'.[33]

When Jawaharlal was sentenced to four years' imprisonment – which even Churchill thought severe – the fast was shelved and the campaign immediately broadened. It would remain 'individual' but not sequential, and strict purity would no longer be required, commitment to the constructive programme being sufficient. The first to go would be members of the Working Committee, and then of the AICC, followed by office holders in local Congress organizations. Gandhi scrutinized the lists of volunteers, and Subhas Bose was told his services were not required. Pyarelal and Mahadev were offered up in December; but the government had not made a single concession.

Congress leaders still at large recognized the futility of Gandhi's approach. But they had neither the strength nor the courage to set him aside. Certain he was on the right track, Gandhi was anticipating a long campaign, perhaps five years. The thousands in jail were mute but (literally) powerful testimony to India's opposition to the war. And Congress in opposition and out of office was where he liked it to be.

On 3 December 1941 the government, observing the weakening of Gandhi's position and hoping Congress might be ready to cooperate in the face of danger from Japan, released all *satyagrahi* prisoners. On 7 December, before the reconstituted Working Committee could meet, the Japanese bombed Pearl Harbor and began their advance across the Far East towards India. When the Working Committee met at the end of the month there was one thing on which it was in broad agreement: that non-violence was no longer a priority. But the prospect of a Japanese invasion produced in the end only a slight softening of its earlier position. Congress would cooperate in national defence if the British met its earlier demand for a National Government, understood as signifying the independence of India. Otherwise, they would have no truck with 'an arrogant imperialism, which is indistinguishable from Fascist authoritarianism'.[34]

The element of unreality in the political debate must here be noted. Congress opposition to the war effort had not prevented the mobilization of the Indian Army. The question was whether Congress would give its blessing to what had already happened.

Gandhi had allowed himself to believe that Congress acceptance of his leadership of the campaign meant that it supported the anti-war sentiments he had placed at the heart of it. This notion, which had permitted his return to power, now had to be abandoned. He resigned his leadership and repaired to Sevagram, stating his resistance to any deal with the British which involved Congress in hostilities.

By the time Sir Stafford Cripps, the Labour leader of the House of Commons, arrived in India in March 1942 with a new offer from the British

government – independence after the war in exchange for Congress participation in the war effort – nothing could have persuaded him to accept any
proposal involving support for the British military campaign. He let it be
known that he would never approve acceptance of the Cripps offer.

Yet it was not Gandhi who sabotaged the Cripps mission. It was Churchill.
Having permitted the offer to be made in order to convince the Americans
that Britain meant to do right by her colonies, he stepped in when it appeared Cripps might be approaching success to persuade the cabinet that
their envoy was exceeding his brief. Cripps had to pull back and the talks
broke down.

With the collapse of the Cripps mission amid general demoralization in
Congress, there was once again a space in Indian politics that Gandhi could
fill. It is necessary to understand the frame of mind in which he did so.

His interpretation of the war had continued to develop, always in an
apocalyptic direction. Events confused him; confusion pushed him towards
the ever bigger picture. The German invasion of Russia, the Anglo-Russian
alliance, American support for Britain, and the American declaration of war
after Pearl Harbor were developments he could only put down to the general
insanity. Like the great final battle of the *Mahabharata*, which was ever in his
mind, the war appeared to him a conflict in which none of the participants
in the end could be victorious. But his belief in God's benign design ruled
out despair.[35]

He thought increasingly in terms of a visitation of divine wrath not just
on imperialism but on materialism. The London Blitz, and the devastation
of other cities from the air, powerfully affected his thinking. He expected
India's cities to experience the same fate. 'The age of cities', he announced,
'is thus coming to an end. The slogan of 'Back to the villages' was never so
true as today.'[36] It was as if God were putting *Hind Swaraj* into operation.
Out of ruin would arise a new world. As early as February he was urging
city dwellers in the danger zone to migrate 'in an orderly manner' to the
villages, carrying the constructive programme with them.[37]

He was gripped by a desire to bring things to a head. The death-like calm,
the 'falsity' of the Indian political atmosphere, in which, as he perceived it,
people hated the British but were afraid to say so, irritated and depressed him.
The only events of note were communal riots, with which he felt impotent
to deal.

Though not abandoning in principle the view that Britain could redeem itself by turning over India to the Indians, he now saw no prospect of eliciting the great act of renunciation. Political action had produced no result, and his personal standing with the British was at a low ebb. Some of his closest British friends had parted company with him over the war, and there was a torrent of criticism of him in the British press; Henry Polak, in an angry letter, had summed up the general disgust.[38] Most unusually, Gandhi permitted himself some expressions of distress at what was being said about him. Closer to home, his efforts to get on terms with Linlithgow had failed. The viceroy's jail delivery of December 1941, which ended his campaign of regulated thought, he knew for the insult it was.

Mitigating these reverses was the conviction, formed during the early months of 1942 as the British fled before the Japanese advance, that the sun was setting on the British power in Asia. Gandhi did not expect the British to mount an effective defence against a Japanese attack on India. And like many other Indians he noted the manner in which the British looked after their own – and no one else – during the retreats from Burma and Malaya, and saw in it a portent for India: 'One route for the whites, another for the blacks! Provision of food and shelter for the whites, none for the blacks!'[39]

It came to him ten days after Cripps left India that the British should just be told to go. 'The presence of the British', he decided, 'blocks our way';[40] and he put aside the effort pursued over so many years to bring about in them a change of heart. The failure of the Cripps mission made everything clear. Knowing nothing of Churchill's backstage operations, he presumed that a Labour politician, on terms of personal friendship with Indian leaders, had turned out to be just another imperialist. Could there be a better demonstration of the strength and impersonality of the system itself? The British would never voluntarily relinquish power: 'They are what they are and nothing will change them.'[41] He could now see 'no difference between the Fascist or Nazi powers and the Allies'.[42] Better, then, that the British 'leave India to her fate': 'I feel somehow that India will not do badly then.'[43]

It seems unlikely that he really thought the British, who 'are what they are and nothing will change them', might up and leave at this point. Given India's strategic importance and value as a source of military manpower, there was certainly no prospect of it. Nevertheless, Burma and Malaya had been abandoned: possibly Gandhi thought the British would be tempted by pre-emptive capitulation in the case of India. He anticipated negotiations with the Japanese after the British left, thinking it likely that once the British were gone there would be no Japanese ill will towards India, the British departure having removed the chief incentive for a Japanese attack. He himself, he emphasized, harboured no ill will towards Japan. Should the Japanese embark on conquest, non-violent non-cooperation would be offered, principally by special cadres.

The immediate question was, what would happen if the British declined to depart? Gandhi in that case saw only one way forward: civil disobedience on an unprecedented scale. In the 'Draft Instructions for Civil Resisters' presented to the Working Committee on 4 August he envisaged: a one-day *hartal* (not to include government employees); resignation of all Congress members of public bodies from the central assembly on down; resignation of any civil servant 'called upon to perpetrate excesses or injustice'; departure of all students from educational institutions associated with the government; refusal of orders from the military authorities to vacate land or houses; illegal manufacture of salt; refusal to pay land tax.[44] Strikes and universal withdrawal of cooperation by government workers were also contemplated, though they did not appear in the final draft approved by the Committee. Gandhi assumed they would happen once the movement, which was to be an 'open rebellion of a non-violent character',[45] without central direction, took flight.

He accepted – embraced – the risk of chaos in the hope of making all things new. He wanted the British, he said, 'to leave India in God's hands, but in modern parlance to anarchy', so that 'a true India will rise in the place of the false one we see'.[46] Anarchy, he said to a group of Congressmen, was 'the only way': 'give us chaos', meaning 'leave India to God', was his message to the British government. (He noted that this was putting it in his own language, 'a language that the masses will not understand'.[47])

He was thinking of an act of such perfect abandonment to God's will that even violence ceased to be a consideration. In this campaign God would truly be in command and violence would occur or not according to his design. 'Supposing', he said to Vinoba at the end of July, 'a non-violent struggle has been started at my behest and later on there is an outbreak of violence, I will put up with that too, because eventually it is God who is inspiring me and things will shape as He wills. If He wants to destroy the world through violence using me as his instrument, how can I prevent it?'[48]

He despatched Mirabehn to Delhi to inform the government of his intention not to call off the campaign if violence broke out. But he also took the precaution of blaming the government in advance for whatever violence might occur[49] – a theme returned to once widespread violence took place.

He was increasingly agitated by the thought of Indian 'cowardice', which he felt the war was bringing into sharper relief. The British had now shown they never meant it when they talked of Indian independence. But while the nations of the world were pouring out their blood 'like water' to defend their liberty, Indians, to their shame, just silently seethed. It would thus be 'a good thing if a million people were shot in a brave and non-violent rebellion against British rule'. After that, India could 'face the world'.[50]

He had thirsted for blood before, and the willing embrace of chaos in the cause of freedom was not entirely new. 'I would accept chaos in exchange for it', he had announced in 1928.[51] From 1940 he was challenging the British to get out and leave India to manage its own affairs. But it was only in 1942 that he made a demand for their immediate departure and linked it to a massive campaign. 'The sands of time', he later wrote, 'were running out. Rivers of blood were flowing fast among the warring nations, and politically-minded India was looking on helplessly – the masses were inert. Hence the cry "Quit India". It gave body to the freedom movement.'[52]

He seems to have feared that at this critical moment in history India might lose its claim to lead the world in suffering and sacrifice, with adverse consequences for the global spread of non-violence. He saw no alternative but to plunge India into non-violent war because 'If non-violence be the greatest force in the world, it must prove itself during the crisis.'[53] 'What is *our* record?' he asked as he contemplated the world's battlefields.[54]

The movement's successful outcome would mean that the power of non-violence would be 'firmly established' – 'Empire idea dissolves and world State takes its place', all nations being free and equal, disarmed except possibly for a 'world police to keep order in the absence of universal belief in non-violence'.[55]

The greater including the less, the Indian communal problem would be solved, antagonism vanishing 'like the mist before the morning sun of liberty', once the Indian millions, relieved of 'the paralysing British arms' had become 'an undefined but one mass of humanity'.[56] This might, he acknowledged, involve a period of violent struggle – though a curious light is shed on his acceptance of the possibility of civil war between the communities by his as-surance to Evelyn Wrench in 1941 that such a conflict would be a brief affair, fought with 'sticks, stones and soda-water bottles', of which the combatants would soon tire, leaving wiser men 'to bring about an honourable peace'.[57] To add the weight of his own renunciation to the process he made a proposal to Jinnah on the eve of Quit India: if the Muslim League took part, it could form the government of free India.

It was not at all a foregone conclusion that Congress would sign on to Gandhi's extraordinary new plan. It took three months for it do so. Raja-gopalachari held out against the demand for British withdrawal, and urged cooperation with the British war effort. There was 'no ahimsa', he told Gandhi, in his plan: it was 'politics, pure and simple', and the manufacture of hate.[58] But Nehru, unable to come up with anything else, eventually was persuaded, and this was decisive. Nehru's acquiescence was assured when Gandhi reversed himself and agreed to let British troops remain in free India to fight the Japanese. This would not, he assured the readers of *Harijan*, diminish the 'virtue and the value' of Britain's renunciation of power.[59]

Exhorting Indians to 'do or die', Gandhi launched his campaign on 8 August. The attempt to convert the British was not entirely abandoned. He envisioned a few weeks of conversations before the real action began. One of his miscalculations was that the government would permit this to happen. Plans to arrest him and other Congress leaders had been made long ago and on 9 August were carried out. Gandhi was locked up in the Aga Khan's palace at Poona, with Mahadev, Mirabehn, Sushila Nayar and Kasturbai, who went voluntarily. Pyarelal joined them later.

Rebellion instantly broke out, but it was not non-violent.[60] By the end of August the viceroy was informing London that 'I am engaged here in meeting by far the most serious rebellion since that of 1857, the gravity and extent of which we have so far concealed from the world for reasons of military security'.[61] The secretary of state, Leopold Amery, inadvertently provided many with their marching orders on 10 August when, in a speech justifying the arrests, he referred to plans – not actually authorized by the Congress leadership – for strikes, sabotage of transport and utility systems, and cutting of telegraph wires, all of which then proceeded to happen. Hundreds of police stations were attacked, and in parts of north India government disappeared.

The movement spread so quickly the British authorities took for granted the existence of a conspiracy, but its existence has never been proved. What is known is that the radical wing of Congress, apparently demolished at Tripuri, stepped into the gap created by the arrest of the leaders. To this extent there was substance in Gandhi's later claims that had he not been arrested the movement might have remained non-violent. But there seems to have been little possibility that he could have effectively provided restraint. Nor is it clear, given his apocalyptic state of mind, that he would have made a serious attempt at it. He had wanted a showdown, had kept up pressure on Congress to endorse it, and had made public his expectation that the movement would develop spontaneously in ways for which he would not hold himself responsible. Nor could his countrymen have failed to notice the simple heartfelt rage with which he denounced the ruling power: it lent plausibility to all the manifestos, secret instructions, and exhortations to violent rebellion which began to circulate in his name. Yet he probably meant it when at the end of September he expressed shock at the 'calamity' that had overtaken the country.[62]

The rebellion was crushed by the British authorities – another miscalculation by Gandhi, who seems to have had hopes of a swift capitulation, perhaps after 'three or four days' of widespread non-cooperation and disobedience.[63] There were about 1,000 Indian deaths, mostly from police firing, though crowds were also machine-gunned from the air. It was not necessary to shoot a million people. By the end of September the British had regained control.

Gandhi meanwhile had settled into his jail routine and was bombarding the jail authorities with the usual complaints. He revised, from memory, his *General Knowledge about Health*, updating the section on *brahmacharya* to include his views that a true *brahmachari*, for whom 'the distinction between men and women almost disappears', need not avoid the opposite sex, and that a single act of married intercourse dedicated to reproduction was consistent with the *brahmachari* state.[64] He steadfastly maintained in letters to Linlithgow that it was government repression that was responsible for the violence, and on receiving no satisfactory reply announced at the end of January that he would fast for 21 days to soothe his pain. The fast was an ordeal, but he survived, to the government's relief. 'I do not know', he remarked, 'why Providence has saved me on this occasion. Possibly, it is because He has some more mission for me to fulfil.'[65]

It was a time of loss. Mahadev died suddenly on 15 August 1942, and Kasturbai died after a difficult illness on 22 February 1944. Gandhi himself fell ill with malaria in April 1944. Assuming his political career was over and not wanting him to die in jail, the government released him on 6 May. He emerged to find the Axis in retreat. Rome was captured by the Americans on 4 June, the Normandy landings began on 6 June, the Germans were falling back in Russia, the Americans were advancing through the Pacific, and the British reconquest of Burma had begun. He had backed the wrong horse.

Gandhi's mood was sober. The Working Committee was still in jail, Congress was banned, and he had no experience of acting as an all-India leader without his customary instruments. He steered a careful course between conciliation of the British, who could no longer be assumed to be on the way out, and conciliation of the revolutionary nationalists who had emerged as the heroes of Quit India, some of whom were still underground. He deplored their 'secrecy' but was restrained in his condemnation of their violence, and emphatic in praise of their courage. The popular violence of 1942 he characterized as a 'molehill' compared to the 'Himalayan violence of the authorities'.[66] Privately he confessed that non-violence had been compromised and that he was once again groping towards a modus operandi based on 'perfection, as far as may be, of individuals', which 'acts as the leaven raising the whole mass'.[67]

In interviews during the first week of July with a British journalist, intended to effect an opening to Wavell, the new viceroy, he announced that he did not intend to offer civil disobedience, and would be satisfied for the duration of the war with a National Government having control over the civil administration; he would offer no resistance to the government's cooperation with the military authorities. On Churchill's instructions, the overture received a studied rebuff. Gandhi made no further moves until the release of the Working Committee in June 1945. He declined even to make political capital out of the Bengal famine, which he saw clearly was 'man-made'.[68]

He maintained his position that communal differences would fade away once India was free. But he was forced by developments during his internment to seek a political accommodation with Jinnah. The League had stood aside from Quit India, and, with the Congress leadership in jail, had raised its profile. The demand for Pakistan was now on the table, the product of distrust of the 'Hindu' Congress and desperate dreams of a return to the days of Muslim glory. The secular Jinnah was now obliged to talk of a Muslim 'nation' – an ethnographic absurdity given that many Muslims were converts from Hinduism – and though he had not yet ruled out the creation of 'Pakistan' within an all-India federation, the League's very success in making itself the representative of Muslim opinion meant that the increasing popular fervour for Pakistan defined his options. Anything short of a demand for complete separation could now look like weakness.

Everything in Gandhi revolted against partition, and he was not willing to consider the devolution of power to two separate states. His term for it was 'vivisection': the disciple of Anna Kingsford could hardly have more strongly expressed his repugnance. To avoid it he was prepared to give his support to a formula proposed by Rajagopalachari: that the League and Congress would cooperate in an independent government while a plebiscite was organized in the Muslim majority areas on the issue of separation from India. On this basis he sought a meeting with Jinnah a few weeks after his release.

In the weeks leading up to the meeting it became apparent that Gandhi thought of the Rajaji formula as the opportunity for a transforming encounter. He meant to attempt the conquest of Jinnah 'with trust and love', believing that Jinnah, knowing 'I have no axe to grind', had 'complete faith' in him.[69] The paradox of renunciation exercised its usual influence. He believed he might 'maintain the unity of India' by accepting 'the freedom of every part' – that is, the freedom of the Muslim majority areas to vote for separation after independence.[70] The Rajaji formula, which Jinnah had already declared unsatisfactory, represented the limit of concession to which he was prepared to go. But he believed that goodwill would be generated by the fact of the concession having been made. His aim was then to prove to Jinnah 'from his own mouth that the whole of the Pakistan proposition is absurd'.[71]

Jinnah, however, wanted an agreement on Pakistan before the British left. He did not budge from the position that Congress could not be trusted to negotiate once it was in power. Gandhi's insistence that he came not as a representative of the Hindus but as himself cut no ice. If he represented only himself, Jinnah wanted to know, what was the use of talking to him. The Rajaji formula proved a non-starter, the talks collapsed, but were not without result. Pakistan was now inarguably the issue, and Jinnah indisputably the man to talk to about it.

Gandhi now more or less retreated into private life, directing his thoughts to the pursuit of perfection, even if it could only be the perfection of the few.

Even before the Jinnah debacle Gandhi had begun to concentrate again on the cultivation of inner strength. His interest in nature cure revived, and the *brahmacharya* experiments at Sevagram sailed into uncharted waters.

Kasturbai's death had removed a major obstacle to testing the limits of his purity, and gathering up of strength from purity maintained. Now, alone, and fearful of political futility, he set out to test himself to the very limit by asking female associates to sleep with him naked. They seem to have been the usual crowd, with the addition of Abha, the 16-year-old wife of his great-nephew, Kanu Gandhi. The practice was referred to as 'the experiment'.

The first indication of the new programme appears to be a letter to Munnalal Shah early in September (shortly before his first meeting with Jinnah and his seventy-fifth birthday), responding to alarm over the form taken by the experiment, of which word had leaked out. Shah would probably have been one of the first to know: his wife was at some point conscripted into it (and then dropped out). He had begun, Gandhi said (according to the English translation) to 'plough in fresh fields'. He acknowledged 'that this experiment is a very dangerous one indeed', but thought it was 'capable of yielding very great results'.[72] Possibly he was expecting it to give strength to his effort to convert Jinnah. In spite of many remonstrances he was never to agree to give it up – though now and then it was 'suspended'.[73]

Sleeping naked with naked women inevitably has 'tantric' connotations in India, and it cannot be said for sure that tantric ideas played no part in Gandhi's taking this ultimate step. He did acknowledge eventually, in a conversation with Swami Anand and Kedar Nath in March 1947, the similarity between tantric rituals involving the pursuit of spiritual power through feats of sexual self-control and his own belief that *brahmacharya* meant not avoiding temptation but actively resisting it. But in the same conversation he spoke of a debt to Western writers like Havelock Ellis and Bertrand Russell, who were 'firm believers in the possibility and desirability of purity of life' independently of social conventions.[74]

His new sleeping arrangements were the culmination of a long-standing practice of testing his sexual resolve, which seems from the beginning to have involved intimate relations with women. 'Sleeping together came with my taking up of *brahmacharya* or even before that', he told a correspondent in March 1945; he said he had experimented with his wife but 'that was not enough'.[75] In a letter to Munnalal at the same time he wrote: 'You can say that ever since I went to England I have been pursuing the idea of *brahmacharya*.'[76] It was certainly very 'tantric' to believe that to get control of his sexual impulses he needed a partner. But the question of influence remains unresolved. He may have become more open to explicitly tantric ideas – with

which he was familiar from Sir John Woodroffe's books, first encountered in
Yeravda jail in 1924[77] – as he realized how close his experiments of the 1930s
were taking him to them in practice.

The resumption of sexual experimentation was bound up with the attachment recently formed to his young great-niece, Manu Gandhi.[78]

Manu had been one of his 'walking sticks' briefly at Sevagram before his
internment, and when Kasturbai became ill in 1944 went to Poona to help care
for her. After Kasturbai died she remained there with the tacit consent of the
authorities. At this point Gandhi seems to have been resisting the fondness
– referred to as 'ignorant attachment', meaning a failure of non-attachment
– he had begun to feel for her. When they went their separate ways after
his release he struggled for some time against the desire to have her at his
side. But he was convincing himself that she possessed qualities which made
association with her potentially significant for his spiritual growth. 'The
virtues that I have seen in you', he wrote to her, 'are not found in all girls.
Having regard to them, when I see the smallest drawback in you it seems to
me a mountain and something unbearable.'[79] The virtues he discerned were
a capacity for service, demonstrated in her devoted nursing of Kasturbai, and
an apparent absence of sexual feeling. To Gandhi these were the defining
attributes of the developed female soul.

By October Manu had joined Gandhi at Sevagram. By January 1945 she
had begun to share his bed: Gandhi wrote to Jaisukhlal Gandhi, her father
(Manu was not an orphan as some accounts have it), that this was in order
'to correct her sleeping posture'.[80] When the experiment was 'suspended' in
March, the suspension explicitly excluded Manu. In May, ill and unable to
bear what Gandhi described as her 'fear of the surrounding atmosphere'[81]
– meaning the mounting criticism of the experiment, though Manu clearly
also suffered from the displeasure of Gandhi's former sleeping partner, Sushila
– she returned home. She was soon back, but in August ran away and stayed
for a while with her sister in Bombay. Gandhi was unwilling to live without
her; Manu was unwilling to live with him as the object of his experimentation. He released her for a year to pursue her studies, but summoned her
to Bengal in October 1946. It was not until December that she joined him
in Srirampur in Noakhali. This time she promised that she would stay with
him to the end.

What were Gandhi's feelings for Manu? They obviously involved more
than a regard for her character: without the element of the erotic there would

have been no point in their association. Sweet-faced, nubile, innocent and (as it first appeared) biddable, she seems to have been irresistible to the ageing mahatma, who wanted to maintain his prowess in renunciation and retain it as a national asset. She was very young – her age in 1944 is given as 19 in some sources, 16 in others – and presumably this was part of her attraction. The 16-year-old Abha was the other recruit of this period. Together they seem eventually to have replaced his partners of the 1930s, with respect to whom physical familiarity and the end of youth's bloom (they had all been older than Manu and Abha to start with) may have dulled the edge of temptation.

As always, it was important to Gandhi for someone's involvement with him to be 'voluntary'. This complicated his courtship of Manu, whom he sometimes peremptorily summoned and sometimes told to come only if she wanted. He also had to contend with the reluctance of Jaisukhlal to cede her to his care. The objections of Kanu Gandhi, Abha's husband, had been over-ruled, and those of Jaisukhal were also overruled in due course. How much Jaisukhlal knew before December 1946 of his daughter's relationship with his uncle is not known. He expressed concern before allowing her to go to Bengal that the atmosphere around Gandhi was 'impure' and that Pyarelal might misbehave:[82] Pyarelal indeed had fallen in love with Manu and wanted to marry her.[83] Jaisukhlal was at a disadvantage in challenging the mahatma's morals. In 1944 Gandhi had written to him suggesting he had embezzled money, either through his work promoting *khadi* or from a private employer.[84]

On 19 December 1946 Manu – possibly with her father (accounts differ) – arrived in Srirampur. On 20 December she joined Gandhi in bed and he explained to her that together they would embark on a new experiment, whose ' "heat [i.e. *tapas*] will be great" '.[85] By 30 December, still in Srirampur, the experiment had begun: Gandhi wrote to Pyarelal that Manu was sleeping naked in his bed.[86] In what respect this was a new departure from their previous relations is not known. Perhaps Manu had not taken all her clothes off before. Perhaps the novelty was in the privacy in which their encounters would take place.

Manu's volumes of reminiscence – *The Lonely Pilgrim, The Miracle of Calcutta, Bapu – My Mother, The End of an Epoch, Last Glimpses of Bapu* – are discreet about her physical relations with Gandhi, though they contain much other material relating to the final stage of his life. They cannot be presumed to be a reliable source. Inconsistencies, obvious later interpolations in supposed diary entries, and statements irreconcilable with known facts or

material in the *Collected Works* are all problems. They are the only source
of many of the documents quoted extensively in them – letters, Manu's and
Gandhi's diaries – and the originals have never been produced. They often
read like popular devotional literature: much is made of Gandhi's resemblance
in 1947 to Rama wandering in exile in the forest (a resemblance which indeed
seems to have occurred to Gandhi). Possibly they were written not by Manu
at all but by someone with whom she collaborated.

With the release of the Working Committee in June 1945 the exclusion of
Gandhi from Congress politics began.

Labour's victory in the general election of July brought with it the prospect
of independence for India, and in March of the following year a delegation
from the British Cabinet arrived in Delhi to discuss the transfer of power.
There was no question of entrusting Gandhi with negotiations. The talks with
Jinnah had not pleased the Working Committee, and with victory in sight it
was no longer necessary to accommodate his unpredictable bargaining style
and eccentric notions of *swaraj*. He was now the person everyone wanted to
keep friendly – he still drew huge and adoring crowds – but no one wanted
to elevate above consultative status. Nehru upset him by revealing his plans
for the industrialization of India. Patel brutally set him aside.

Continuing its habits of diplomacy, the Government of India under both
Wavell and Mountbatten displayed if anything more consideration for Gandhi's
feelings than the Congress leadership. But the cynical Wavell thought him
ruthless, too vague and slippery to deal with; and Mountbatten, cosmopolitan
in his tastes and prepared to be entertained by Gandhi's discourses, incurious
about religion and happy to take his holiness for granted, was taken aback by
the audacity of his manoeuvres against the League and Pakistan.

Wavell was careful to ensure Gandhi was present at Simla with other
leaders at the end of June 1945 to consider his proposals for the formation of
a new executive council, conceived as the first step towards an independent
government. But Gandhi was conscious all the time of being on the sidelines.
He was advocating as usual giving the Muslims what they wanted, so long as
it was not Pakistan, but made no attempt to impose his views on Congress.
'If I tried to override them', he told an American reporter, 'I might succeed
for once. But the moment I try to cling to power, I fall, never to rise again.'[87]
The conference ended when Jinnah's insistence on the sole right to nominate
Muslims proved unshakeable.

Conferring with Nehru, July 1946

Gandhi kept his distance from the elections held in 1946. They confirmed that the League was now without question the representative of the Muslims, winning 439 of the 494 designated Muslim seats. He emerged from political seclusion, however, when the Cabinet Mission arrived in March. Stafford Cripps was a member of the mission, and he was determined this time to have Gandhi involved in the negotiations, not, as in 1942, exuding intransigence from afar. Cripps's cultivation of him gave Gandhi the chance to play a significant role, and it was he who precipitated the final breakdown of the negotiations by threatening to walk out unless the Working Committee insisted that the proposed new Interim Government include a Congress Muslim – anathema to Jinnah, who at the time Congress produced the demand was still talking.[88] The move reflected Gandhi's increasing distaste for and impatience with the negotiations, which, in concentrating on delineating 'groupings' of provinces along communal lines, seemed close to conceding the principle of Pakistan. For some time before he made his stand – meant to affirm Congress's claim to be a national and not a communal organization – he was urging the government to cease trying to put together an artificial and unstable coalition and hand over to either Congress or the League. This was naturally construed by the government as an invitation to install the majority party in power.

He fought partition to the end. When the Working Committee, amid rising communal violence, decided in March 1947 to accept the partition of the Punjab, he began to press for an immediate devolution of power to the Muslim League. Jinnah, he proposed, should be asked to form the Interim Government and take his Pakistan plan to the country. There was method in this: the League could never hope to govern while it was subject to a Congress majority in the central assembly. Its Pakistan proposal would be dead on arrival, and the League itself would fall from power. As Gandhi explained when he aired his proposal to Mountbatten, a minority government would have to depend for its survival on (in the words of Mountbatten's report) 'able advocacy of the measures they wished to introduce'. Mountbatten, always attracted by the boldly unconventional in politics and in war, was stunned but intrigued. When the Working Committee declined to endorse the proposal, Gandhi asked him to enact it on his own initiative. But the viceroy had by then recovered his balance. The proposal was set aside.[89]

When the decision to divide India was announced in June, Gandhi advised people to accept it and bring about concord through love. But independence did not bring to an end his campaign against Pakistan. In September, amid the prospect of war between the two new dominions over Kashmir, he asked Mountbatten, who had remained as governor-general, to cable Attlee in his 'personal capacity as an Englishman' proposing that any member intending to make war on another be expelled from the Commonwealth. He denied having Pakistan in mind but it was obvious to Mountbatten that he did. Mountbatten countered with the reminder that Nehru, now prime minister of India, must first be consulted – and Gandhi replied that he already had been, and had turned the suggestion down! Whereupon Mountbatten, feeling 'we were in such deep water, and the point was so very unclear', and it was getting late, decided to end the meeting with a request that the proposal be put in writing.[90]

For a man of non-violence, Gandhi's attitude to the prospect of war with Pakistan was notably unresisting. 'What must be must be' appears to have been his position, as it had been when he contemplated the prospect of civil war within an undivided independent India.

Gandhi was the only Congress politician to hold out against partition. The rest of the Congress leadership accepted it to avoid a bloodbath. In the end there was a bloodbath anyway, and, after a fashion, Gandhi's long-anticipated civil war came about. But it solved nothing. The killing went on until it stopped, leaving India divided and half a million dead.

Gandhi and many others shared the blame for these horrors. Despite his unorthodoxy, despite his friendships and alliances with Muslims, he was a 'Hindu' politician, incessantly invoking Rama and publicly embracing the ascetic practices associated with Hindu holiness. The message he wanted India, as a nation, to broadcast to the world was a mixture of Hinduism and Christianity, philosophically alien to Islam. He never dissociated himself sufficiently from the Hindu communalist wing of Congress. He always seemed ready to blame the Muslims for communal disorders. He demurred at being treated as an *avatar* by the masses, but left no doubt that his spiritual aspirations might as well be so understood by the ignorant. In the early months of 1946, as communal hatred smouldered in India, he was touring the country holding the vast prayer meetings, complete with mass chanting of the *Ramdhun*, which were now his preferred means of exposing himself to the crowd. He saw the chanting as a form of synchronized spiritual experience, evoking the power of silent thought and connecting the mob to God. He saw it as a form of crowd control. But there was no denying its association with popular Hindu piety. When he began to include readings from the Koran, fanatical Hindus turned up to heckle. Communal feeling, however high-mindedly invoked, was a tiger he could not ride.

All the same, his opposition to Pakistan really had nothing to do with communalism. The division of India into two hostile states put an end to his dream of offering to the world, with the achievement of Indian freedom, a perfect example of the power of non-violence. Some people sarcastically asked him on the eve of independence if the departure of the British was going to lead to *Ramarajya*. How could it, he said, with India thus divided.

The collapse of order and abandonment to murder which accompanied the population movements of 1947 seemed to deal the last blow to any prospect of India leading the world to a better state. Even then he did not give in to despair. He wrote to Yvonne Privat in November 1947 that the hope lingered with him 'that India shall survive the death dance and occupy the moral height that should belong to her after the training, however imperfect, in non-violence, for an unbroken period of 32 years since 1915'.[91] But by then he had given up hope that it would be in his lifetime.

Naturally, he supposed there must be 'some shortcoming in me' that was responsible for the present state of affairs.[92] He concluded that his own campaigns had liberated energy which was now being misdirected. 'The internecine feud that is going on today in India', he wrote to a German correspondent a month before his death, 'is the direct outcome of the energy that was set free during the thirty years' action of the weak'.[93] As to why during all those years he had failed to perceive that 'what we practised during the fight with the British under the name of non-violence, was not really non-violence', the explanation was now clear: 'God had purposely sealed my eyes, as He wanted to accomplish His great purpose through me. That purpose [presumably the eviction of the British] being accomplished, He has restored to me my sight.'[94]

The collapse of the Cabinet Mission marked the final disintegration of Gandhi's influence over the Congress leadership. Disregarding his own advice about clinging to power, he had forced Patel and Nehru to choose between publicly repudiating him over the Congress Muslim issue and keeping negotiations open with Jinnah. They meant never to find themselves in such a position on any future occasion. Gandhi fell, never to rise again.

In the wilderness, he occupied himself with the constructive programme, including a new initiative on untouchability. It had shocked him to learn that in his own province of Gujarat there was currently only one town in which temples were open to untouchables, and nowhere where they could use the public wells. Henceforth he made a point of staying in untouchable quarters. He even announced that at Sevagram he would only solemnize marriages in which one party was an untouchable. He briefly revived the idea of a chain of fasts. But he did not alter his view that a man's *dharma* lay in following his ancestral occupation. The contradictions in his thinking remained unresolved. Gandhi's life might thus quietly have come to a close, had the bloodletting of 1947 not provided it with a tragic finale.

Jinnah's reaction to the breakdown of the Cabinet Mission negotiations was to announce that the League would now abandon constitutional methods. 16 August 1946 was named as 'Direct Action Day'. It passed off peacefully in most of India with processions and *hartal*s. But in Calcutta the mob took control, beginning with Muslims attacking Hindus, continuing with Hindus retaliating, and ending with general murder in which the majority community (Muslim or Hindu depending on the area of the city) slaughtered the minority. Five thousand people, mostly Muslims, died during the four days of the 'Great Calcutta Killing'.

The violence spread to Noakhali in east Bengal, where Muslims killed Hindus, and then in early November to Bihar, where Hindus killed Muslims in retaliation.

When the news arrived of violence in Noakhali on 15 October Gandhi decided to go to Bengal. When he got to Calcutta news came of the slaughter in Bihar. Noakhali was now relatively peaceful, though many Hindus were still afraid to return to their homes. But he did not alter his plan. He hoped that the milkless diet he had taken up on arrival in Bengal would mean he could exert some influence, at long distance, on Bihar. Eventually, in March, under pressure from Muslims, he went to Bihar, suspecting that Hindu misdeeds were exaggerated. When he got there he found that the situation was worse than in Noakhali.

On 6 November he left Calcutta for Noakhali and on 20 November took up residence in the predominantly Muslim village of Srirampur. Here he settled down to try to improve the atmosphere, including encouraging the Hindus by his example to cast out fear and stay put, or to return. Throughout the period of partition he adjured Indians in the affected areas to stand and die rather than run away.

He had begun to think not of fasting, but of an unsought yet sacrificial death. 'I do not want to retire from Bengal as a defeated coward', he told some visitors to Srirampur on 26 November; 'I would like to die here, if need be, at the hands of an assassin. But I do not want to court such death.'[95] Meanwhile he awaited the arrival of Manu, who had been summoned from Calcutta.

He was in a state of spiritual depletion when he left for Bengal, with no particular plan and knowing only that 'I won't be at peace with myself unless I go there'.[96] The Cabinet Mission negotiations had filled him with foreboding. He spoke repeatedly of the 'darkness' around. Was the carnage of Calcutta the beginning of the 'necessary' bloodbath he had expected for so long? He shocked Wavell by suggesting that it was.[97] He found himself giving way to 'anger' – a sign that he was far from the state of equalmindedness enjoined in the *Gita*. He 'flared up madly' at Rajendra Prasad for handing out nuts and raisins to some well-nourished children at a ceremony honouring his birthday.[98] He was reconsidering his desire, first expressed on the day he launched Quit India and frequently restated, to continue to live and serve until he was 125.

It was not until he got to Noakhali that a positive conception of what he was doing there started to take shape, and with it an intermittent lightening of the gloom. As always, the recovery of a sense of purpose buoyed him up. But his mood for the rest of his life remained predominantly one of despondency, becoming at times despair. He was rarely to experience again the feeling of being in command of events: all was improvisatory, responsive and uncertain. The blessed state in which 'Mere thoughts act' despite seeming physical inaction eluded him.[99]

It came to him that his purpose in Noakhali must be truly to test the power of his *ahimsa*, which had not seemed 'to answer in the matter of Hindu–Muslim relations'.[100] To do this required depriving himself of his usual entourage and, as far as possible, living alone in hostile surroundings. Accordingly, when he settled at Srirampur, he dispersed most of the group which had accompanied him to Bengal – Pyarelal, Sushila, Abha and others – to villages nearby, and kept with him only two companions: the Bengali scholar Nirmal Kumar Bose, who had taken leave from his post at Calcutta University, and a shorthand typist, Parasuram. If under these circumstances, he reasoned, he could bring peace to Noakhali, he might yet bring peace to India. It might be that his seclusion in this Bengali village, full of hate and misery and ignorance, would be 'the crowning act of my life', his mission to Noakhali 'the biggest that has fallen to my lot'.[101] He would discover what was the fault in his *ahimsa*, and, God willing, there put it right. If in the event he failed in his representation of truth and non–violence, he hoped God would take him away 'and work through some other agent'.[102]

Before even leaving Delhi an anticipation of what might be possible in Noakhali seems to have passed through Gandhi's mind. One 'pure, active thought', he told a friend trying to dissuade him from going, 'proceeding from the depth and endowed with all the undivided intensity of one's being, becomes dynamic and works like a fertilized ovum'.[103] If peace between Hindus and Muslims were to come to India via Noakhali it would be through the power of thought.

He knew that it was necessary in order to accomplish the goal he was now setting for himself for complete purity to be achieved at last. This must involve the perfection of his *brahmacharya*, and this was where Manu came in. On her arrival in Srirampur, he enlisted her cooperation, emphasizing – according to her account – the purity, fearlessness and confidence in his good intentions that would be required of her.

Above all, she was to experience no trace of sexual arousal, for the under-taking would fail if either of them lusted after the other. He wanted to be so pure, he told Nirmal Kumar Bose, who had asked him what was 'so special about hugging an old man of seventy-seven', that it would be impossible for impure thoughts to arise in his presence.[104] He subscribed to the traditional Indian view that a *brahmachari* was physically attractive; perhaps this was why he saw nothing strange in a man of his age concerning himself with whether he aroused desire in a young girl. (And indeed in his late seventies, deep-chested, taut-muscled, smooth-skinned from years of daily massage, and, we can assume from his willingness to appear naked, with genitals of at least normal size, Gandhi was not an entirely implausible sex object.)

His 'present venture', he said, was 'a *yajna* – a sacrifice, a penance',[105] and he referred to his relations with Manu as part of this *yajna*, distinguishing it from the exercise in self-control known as 'the experiment', in which vari-ous women had taken part. He was hoping his relations with Manu would make efficacious a great act of self-abandonment to God through suffering and service – his putting himself in harm's way to serve the cause of peace in Noakhali. The 'penance' involved was for the defects responsible for the 'failures' of his *ahimsa*, necessitating the same act of self-abandonment. The sexual self-restraint involved in sleeping with a young girl was also in itself an element in the *yajna*. A sacrifice to be accepted must be perfect. Hence the solemnity and frequency with which Gandhi appears to have reminded Manu that 'Not a trace of impurity can pass muster here.'[106]

Defending his relations with Manu to Manilal in July, Gandhi wrote that 'even if only one *brahmachari* of my conception comes into being, the world will be redeemed'.[107] His aims as always were larger than the condition of India. Was he daring to hope that he had embarked on the final sacrifice of his lower to his higher nature, which if accomplished would destroy the last vestiges of fleshly attachment and mean the perfect abandonment of his soul to God? Whether this was the ultimate significance of the great *yajna*, no one can say.

There is a story – the source appears to be a conversation Erik Erikson had with Bose – that Gandhi was overheard saying in connection with his relations with Manu in Noakhali: 'If I can master this, I can still beat Jinnah.'[108] In the context of the achievement of perfect *brahmacharya*, averting partition would have been a natural objective.

An aspect of the *yajna* emphasized in Manu's accounts, though not in Gandhi's, was his assumption of the maternal role. According to Pyarelal (though not Manu), Kasturbai on her deathbed had asked Gandhi to take the place of a mother to Manu, whose own mother had died. Judging from *The Lonely Pilgrim* and *Bapu – My Mother*, this mothering principally took the forms of advising Manu on her deportment and worrying that she might wear herself out in his upkeep. It seems not to have been an aspect of their relationship that was salient to others. Nevertheless, private efforts to 'serve' Manu in the manner of a mother, thereby attaching to himself some of the qualities of selfless service peculiar to the female domain, would have been in keeping with the *yajna*'s ambitions. Woman, Gandhi had always maintained, was 'the embodiment of sacrifice and suffering'.[109] In this spirit *The Perfect Way* had taught that the Christ must, through experience and knowledge, become 'both man and woman'.[110] Bapuji, Manu recorded, had often said to her 'that he wants to cultivate and present to the world an ideal of the perfect man who is a perfect mother as well'. 'Though a male in physical form', he told her one night in the little village of Daspada, 'I have become your mother in essence.'[111]

Gandhi stayed in Srirampur for six weeks until 7 January 1947, when he set off on his seven-week 'pilgrimage' through Noakhali, walking barefoot from village to village and taking shelter where he found it. It was an extraordinary undertaking for an old man. The road went through forest tracks and over rickety wooden bridges: Gandhi practised negotiating these before he left. His party was not small. In addition to himself, Manu and Bose (Parasuram had left because he objected to Gandhi sleeping with Manu), there was an armed escort of 20 policemen, provided by the Bengal government, a group of reporters, and two Sikhs, former officers of the Indian National Army, the rebel force recruited by Subhas Bose from Indian soldiers taken prisoner by the Japanese. The Sikhs had volunteered themselves for Gandhi's protection but went unarmed. Local volunteers helped to carry the baggage, which included as always Gandhi's commode. The usual routine of bath, massage and scrupulously measured intake of food, continued on the march. There was a prayer meeting each evening to which local people were invited.

Muted hostility, turning to open hostility as news of atrocities in Bihar continued to come in, was the general response to Gandhi's presence from the Muslim population. The paths Gandhi had to follow were strewn at times with brambles and human turds. In some places Hindus returned to their homes, and there were no violent outbreaks while he was on the scene. But communal harmony was still far distant when he left for Bihar in March.

Scandal broke out over his relations with Manu shortly after the pilgrimage began. Word leaked out to his colleagues on the political scene, but got around locally as well. On 1, 2 and 3 February he defended himself in public prayer meetings: in the circumstances of the tour, the fact that he and his female companion slept naked together had been impossible to keep quiet. Possibly he did not try to hide it. But his comments at the prayer meetings do not give that impression. Knowledge of his improprieties may have contributed to the build-up of resistance to his presence in Noakhali. If so, his hopes for his *yajna* were doomed from the start by the means he chose to pursue it.

Letters flew in from a wide range of acquaintance, and from Devdas, Manilal and Ramdas. Almost everyone was horrified, even people who might be presumed to have some knowledge of what had been taking place at Sevagram. Manu's kinship to him, her youth and innocence, thrown into high relief by her sequestration in murderous Bengal, may all have helped to precipitate the explosion. Outrage at Gandhi's recklessness in thus comporting himself in village huts, and fear that he would take the scandal with him to Bihar, appear to have been factors. Gandhi stood firm. What was the opinion of the less enlightened compared with what he hoped to accomplish? It was his *dharma*: he would not forsake it. Nevertheless, his isolation was horrible. Old and valued colleagues broke with him; the editors of *Harijan* resigned. Amritlal Thakkar arrived to remonstrate with him, and other colleagues confronted him in Bihar. They taxed him with secrecy – for Gandhi, who had claimed his life was an open book, the unkindest cut. He acknowledged its justice. And it was all in vain. He arrived in Bihar the day before the Working Committee convened in Delhi and resolved to accept the partition of the Punjab. Letters to Nehru and Patel brought unconsoling replies. Nehru explained with his usual courtesy that the time for realism was here. Patel said that he was entitled to his opinion.

Manu, who was by now buckling under the strain, took herself out of Gandhi's bed after getting a letter from Thakkar asking her to end the arrangement for the sake of his public work in Bihar. But the relationship was resumed in Delhi and, according to Pyarelal, continued to the end.

Nirmal Kumar Bose left Gandhi's service over Manu on 18 March, though he joined up with him again later in Calcutta. He appears to have been less shocked than some others by the sexual impropriety of the relationship. But he was severe with Gandhi over his unconcern with the effect of his behaviour on Manu, whom he regarded as incapable of mature consent. He had observed also the emotional unbalance of the women in Gandhi's entourage, and their ceaseless competition for his time and favour. (His critics in Bihar had observed the same thing, asking why if his experiments were of such benefit to humanity, his companions were 'emotionally unhinged'.[112]) Gandhi said little in his defence, other than that some of his companions had been unbalanced to begin with. With the observation that, for him, *brahmacharya* was 'that thought and practice which puts you in touch with the Infinite and takes you to His presence', he rested his case.[113]

Except for a brief visit to Delhi to meet the newly arrived Mountbatten, Gandhi remained in Bihar for two months. Confronted by evidence that Congressmen had been involved in the massacres, and that murders had been committed with his own name on the murderers' lips, he strove to recall his fellow Hindus to their sacred traditions of non-violence. He reminded them that India's reputation was in their hands. Some penitence was shown. But his efforts on behalf of the Muslims attracted hostility. Angry letters arrived accusing him of betraying the Hindus.

After a spell in Delhi doing what he could to influence events in the realm of high policy, and a brief visit to Kashmir, he hastened to Bengal in May. Trouble had recrudesced in Noakhali.

Arriving in Calcutta on 9 August, Gandhi found the city in the grip of disturbances as the Hindu and Muslim populations disentangled themselves and moved into separate localities. A delegation from the local Muslim League entreated him to stay and save their community from the massacre they anticipated on 15 August – independence day. He agreed, on condition that orders were sent to Muslims in Noakhali to keep the peace.

For two weeks it looked as though Gandhi's message of non-violence might achieve an extraordinary triumph. He lived with H.S. Suhrawardy, the Muslim chief minister blamed by many Hindus for the Great Calcutta Killing, in an abandoned house in a Muslim district, without any police protection, and together they worked to bring about harmony between the two communities. It was one of his most brilliant inspirations – and, in its combination of public drama and quiet but genuinely selfless dedication, perhaps the best thing (in the opinion of the present writer) Gandhi ever did.

He was asleep when India embraced its 'tryst with destiny' – Nehru's words – at midnight on 14 August, and observed independence day with a one-day fast. But something amazing was happening on the streets of

Calcutta. Hindus were embracing Muslims, and Muslims were embracing Hindus. The Punjab was going up in flames but in Bengal and Bihar the situation approached tranquillity.

The truce held and on 26 August Mountbatten wired to 'My dear Gandhiji' congratulations on his service as a 'One Man Boundary Force'. Euphoric, Gandhi wondered 'whether the dream of my youth is to be realized in the evening of my life', and almost reconciled himself to Pakistan.[114] When Nehru wired to him that the Punjab needed his 'healing presence', it was with some of the old spirit that he told him he could not be spared from Bengal.[115] Soon he was anticipating almost with enthusiasm trying 'the same thing for the Punjab'.[116] But he knew enough to wonder if it was all 'just a momentary enthusiasm'.[117]

He planned to leave with Suhrawardy for Noakhali on 2 September, but on the evening of 31 August, after he had gone to bed and Suhrawardy had gone to his own house to prepare for the journey, a crowd of Hindu youths turned up. They had with them a heavily bandaged man they claimed had been stabbed by a Muslim. A later examination of the man by a government doctor supposedly revealed no stab wounds, and in a letter to Patel the following day Gandhi aired suspicions that the whole thing had been set up by the Hindu Mahasabha. It hardly matters.

Gandhi's accounts of what happened next that night,[118] in the letter to Patel and a statement released to the press, show that courage abandoned him when the angry crowd started smashing the windows and trying to gain entry to the house. It was Manu and Abha, who were lying on either side of him, who, 'without my knowledge, for my eyes were closed', got up and went to deal with the intruders. He lay there, listening to people roaming the house and banging on the doors, until he decided he had to do something and got up. He then appealed to the crowd from a doorway, where 'friendly faces surrounded me and would not let me move forward'. Bricks were thrown, a *lathi* blow aimed in his direction. Two policemen by now present did nothing, but a superintendent who arrived with reinforcements persuaded him to leave the scene and the crowd was eventually dispersed. Both accounts suggest that he would in some way have engaged physically with the crowd had not others restrained him.

The following afternoon word came in of violent outbreaks in several parts of the city. A truck full of Muslims was attacked with grenades not far from where Gandhi was staying. He went to the scene and saw the bodies lying on the street. During evening prayers a group of businessmen came to see him, wanting advice about how to deal with the violence. 'Go in the midst of the rioters and prevent them from indulging in madness or get killed in the attempt', were Gandhi's instructions. 'The situation', he added, 'calls for sacrifice on the part of top-rankers.'[119]

It seems to have struck him at this point that his advice was at odds with his behaviour of the previous night. He went on to say, according to an unreferenced footnote in the *Collected Works*, apparently based on accounts by Pyarelal and Manu (both present), that he himself would of course never be permitted by those devoted to him thus to sacrifice himself. Pyarelal has him thinking: 'Have I the right to give vicarious advice to others so long as I have not set the example myself?'; and Manu has him saying aloud, 'As long as I myself do not take any step, I have no right to tender any sort of advice to others.'[120]

After this visit Gandhi took the decision to fast. It was the 'step' which gave him the right to urge others on to sacrifice. And indeed on the second day of the fast he was calling for volunteers, preferably 'top-ranking', to go out and get killed. He would not mind, he said, if 'the whole of Calcutta swims in blood'; for it would be 'willing offering of innocent blood'. Then he would 'rush barefoot in the midst of the flames' until peace was restored or he died: 'That is my conception of a peace mission – not a mealy-mouthed, milk-and-water business.'[121]

Rajagopalachari, now governor of West Bengal, fearing that if Gandhi died things would get worse, came later in the evening to ask him to delay the fast until it became clearer in what direction events were moving. The fast was 'preventive', Gandhi explained: 'I know I shall be able to tackle the Punjab too if I can control Calcutta. But if I falter now, the conflagration may spread' – leading, he feared, to intervention by outside powers and the end of India's brief independence.[122] In a letter to Patel early the next morning he said he was fasting to see if God had any further use for him. If he had, he would calm people down and 'preserve my body', presumably for use in the Punjab: 'If I lack even the power to pacify the people, what else is left for me to do?'[123] Unable to manage himself the self-immolation at the hands of the mob urged on others, Gandhi chose public slow starvation instead – to many perhaps a greater horror.

Of his power to pacify the people there was in the event no doubt. On the first day of the fast leaders of the Hindu Mahasabha, Subhas Bose's Forward

Bloc, and the Muslim League, came and offered their services to restore order. On 4 September a deputation of 'about fifty people reported to be controlling the turbulent elements in Calcutta'[124] arrived and undertook to arrange the surrender of the ringleaders. Soon rioters made their way to Gandhi's room to implore his forgiveness. Amid these remarkable scenes his Calcutta fast came to an end. The next day truckloads of weapons were driven to his door and formally surrendered. The city remained quiet.

Violence had been nipped in the bud. It had been organized violence, led and coordinated by the Hindu extremist organization Rashtriya Swayamsevak Sangh (RSS), and had not yet reached the point at which mass retaliation would have given it a life of its own. Gandhi's decision to fast galvanized the more responsible elements in the city's political leadership to act to avert the next stage of confrontation. Within 24 hours of his decision joint patrols recruited from the paramilitary wing of the Hindu Mahasabha and the Muslim League were on the streets. In another 24 hours order was restored. Only Gandhi could have set such a train of events in motion.

He himself naturally saw the operation of the fast in spiritual terms. 'My fast', he said, 'isolates the forces of evil; the moment they are isolated they die, for evil by itself has no legs to stand upon.'[125] Whatever this meant to the thugs to whom he happened to be speaking, it meant to him that by surrendering his life to God, on whose sufferance alone evil existed, he had caused God's purpose to operate through him.

He announced at once that he was leaving for the Punjab. Suhrawardy and Rajaji begged him to stay to be sure the peace held, but he left on the 7th, heading first for Delhi. The peace held, not only in Calcutta but in Noakhali – now part of Pakistan – where Gandhi's volunteers remained for the next few months.

He arrived to find that on 3 September, as he was fasting in Calcutta, the violence of the Punjab had spilled over into Delhi. Sikh and Hindu refugees, discovering the extent to which the capital of the Mughals was still a Muslim city, were exacting retribution. Muslim shops were looted, their owners butchered, the buildings torched. The houses of Muslims, and people suspected of harbouring Muslims, were attacked. On the first day a thousand people died. Mountbatten had to be called back to take control: at the request of Nehru and Patel he secretly assumed emergency powers. Nehru himself was seen swinging a *lathi* at a murderous crowd. It took two weeks for the violence in Delhi to subside.

The state of affairs in Delhi, a city which throughout a long history of communal tension had preserved its urbanity, came as a shock to Gandhi. Probably his closest friend in politics had been Dr Ansari, the Muslim physician whose house in Delhi had been his second home and on many occasions the unofficial Congress headquarters. Now Ansari's daughter and son-in-law were staying at a hotel because they feared for their lives in the house. The extent of the refugee problem also came as a surprise. The authorities were trying to cope with an influx now approaching a quarter of a million, and in addition having to find quarters for almost as many Delhi Muslims who had lost their homes and were awaiting shipment to Pakistan; they were housed principally in Humayun's tomb and the Purana Qila, two of Delhi's finest monuments to Muslim glory. Gandhi's plan was to stay at the sweepers' colony. But it was now a refugee camp, and on Patel's orders he found himself being driven to Birla House, to whose comforts he had to reconcile himself.

He stayed in Delhi but there was little he could do. The conditions that had made possible the miracle of Calcutta did not exist. His Hindu political associates in Delhi were national leaders without local roots, unlike the Bengali politicians who had put themselves at his disposal. His Muslim associates were Congress Muslims with no influence over the Muslim majority. He knew no one who could enforce his wishes on the leaderless tide of refugees flowing into the city. 'I find no one in Delhi', he told the new rulers of India on his arrival, 'who can accompany me and control the Muslims. There is no such person among the Sikhs or among the Rashtriya Swayam-sevak Sangh either. I do not know what I shall be able to do here.'[126] He contacted the RSS, even courted it a little, but got nothing from it but a disavowal of involvement in the violence.

On 18 September, when wholesale murder had ceased but the atmosphere remained tense, he was joined at Birla House by Suhrawardy. But Suhrawardy soon found that in Delhi his writ did not run and he was just another Muslim taking a chance whenever he appeared on the streets. In November Gandhi was still lamenting the lack of intermediaries through whom to work. As he had in Noakhali he had vowed to 'do or die'. Now he felt more than ever doubtful of what he could do: 'But my other vow, that of dying, will certainly be fulfilled. For that I have not the least worry.'[127]

He postponed his departure for the Punjab, and in the end never went, though he continued to express his wish to go. It was obvious there was nothing he could do. Also, the longer he remained in Delhi, the clearer it became to him that he should stay. The disturbed state of the city put him into closer contact with Nehru and Patel than he had been for some time. Their desire to involve him in keeping the peace meant constant visits to Birla House. There were many matters in which he wished to involve himself and in Delhi he could not be ignored. He wanted prohibition to be adopted and Hindustani made the language of government business; he also found much to dislike and oppose. He criticized government extravagance and corruption. He opposed the setting up of more Western-style universities, the importation of food, and government controls on the sale of food and cloth. In November he made something of a comeback at the AICC meetings, successfully sponsoring several resolutions. Now, he told Pyarelal, he must see to their implementation: 'I see my battle has to be fought and won in Delhi itself.'[128]

Even after order was restored Delhi was not a city at peace. Muslims were still being frightened out of their houses, there were stabbings, ugly demonstrations took place, there was a Hindu boycott of Muslim fruit and vegetable sellers. There had been nothing like the expressions of fraternity witnessed in Calcutta.

Gandhi went about the city with no evident care for his safety, doing whatever he could. He held daily prayer meetings at Birla House, which were open to all. He well understood that he was in danger, and that the danger came from his own people, to whom his association with Muslims was traitorous, his preaching of non-violence a means of disarming them before the enemy. People came to him and naively set him straight about these things. At this defining moment, they could not imagine why he was not a good Hindu.

Death weighed on him. He expected it, sometimes wanted it. Devoted since Noakhali to the practice of *Ramanama* – the mantric repetition of Rama's name – he said he hoped to die with 'Rama' on his lips. *Moksha* was not mentioned in his last months of life, presumably being deemed remote. But he strained incessantly for self-forgetfulness in God so that death when it came would befit him.

He began to feel that unless hearts were unlocked and minds liberated in Delhi he could not claim to be doing his appointed work. He could take no credit, he told Devdas, referring to the restoration of order, for what had been achieved since his arrival.[129] Conflagrations in other places were claiming his attention: in Sind, Hindus were being pushed out; in his own Kathiawar, Muslim businessmen, the very group he had allied himself with in South Africa, were being attacked and driven away. He could do nothing, he decided, about any of this, until Delhi had been transformed. With 'what face', he asked, could he go to Sind? But if he could achieve something in Delhi, it would 'have an impact on the whole of India.'[130]

Gandhi began his last fast on 13 January 1948. Its aims were peace in Delhi, peace in India and peace in the world. 'I flatter myself', he said, 'with the belief that the loss of her soul by India will mean the loss of the hope of the aching, storm-tossed and hungry world.' The 'reward' of the fast would be 'the regaining of India's dwindling prestige and her fast-fading sovereignty over the heart of Asia and throughout the world'.[131] Its targets were the malefactors of all communities, but especially the Hindus and Sikhs in Delhi, the government of Pakistan which was denying equality to Sikhs and non-Muslims, the United Nations which was about to begin its debate on the crisis in Kashmir, and implicitly it appears the Indian government for its decision to withhold from Pakistan, pending resolution of the crisis, its remaining share of the cash balances of undivided India. Pyarelal suggests that it was the question of the cash balances which tipped Gandhi towards fasting rather than waiting for the assassin's knife.[132]

Gandhi's position on Kashmir as events unfolded had become straight-forwardly pro-Indian. He supported the airlift of Indian troops to Srinagar and opposed the involvement of the United Nations. Nevertheless, the diversion of resources to war disturbed him. What was God's purpose? Could this be the conflagration from which India would be born anew? When the Indian government decided to stop payment of the 550 million rupees owed to Pakistan he asked Mountbatten for his opinion. Mountbatten's reply was that it would be the 'first dishonourable act' of the Indian government.

This set Gandhi 'furiously thinking', in Pyarelal's words, and he realized that he must do something to retrieve India's honour. The final push towards fasting came when a delegation of Delhi Muslims came to Birla House and castigated him for not being able to guarantee their safety.

Once the fast had started, it became apparent that there was no obvious way for it to end. The government announced on the third day that the cash balances would be paid. But Gandhi's other concerns were so large and the criteria for assuaging them so vague that he could, had he chosen, have gone on until he died. He may have wished to reserve the possibility. After the government's announcement he said that he would end his fast only when 'the Hindus, Muslims and Sikhs of Delhi bring about a union, which not even a conflagration around them in all the other parts of India or Pakistan will be strong enough to break'.[133]

Responses to the fast were mixed. There were the usual entreaties and expressions of concern. Telegrams of support arrived from around the world, including Pakistan, where government ministers commended his concern for communal harmony. Visitors, Indian and foreign, filed past his cot. But shouts of 'Let Gandhi die!' were heard on the streets of Delhi and at the gates of Birla House.

On 17 January there were several developments. The maharajah of Patiala arrived in Delhi and told the Sikhs to desist from attacking Muslims, hastening afterwards to Gandhi's bedside to inform him personally. The Mountbattens came on a visit of solidarity. Processions, one over a mile long, in which the communities mixed together, converged on Birla House.

While all this was going on, Gandhi's health was taking a turn for the worse. In the afternoon he gave Maulana Azad a list of conditions for ending the fast, with an indication that he would accept a guarantee from responsible persons that they would be met. They were highly specific. Muslims should be free to hold their annual Urs festival; Hindus living in mosques should leave them; Muslims should be allowed to move about freely in their old localities; they should not be subject to economic boycott; they should be able to travel safely on the trains; they should be allowed to return to their homes if they wished. When on the following day a hundred or so of the city's notables, including representatives of the RSS, came to assure him that these conditions – with the exception of safety on the trains, which was not mentioned – would be met, he broke his fast. He had decided to live.

At his evening prayers he said he could not resist the urgings of those who had gathered at his bedside that morning, or the telegrams both from India and Pakistan which had continued to pour in, and he could not disbelieve the pledge of friendship among the communities which had been given. Were the pledge fulfilled, it would revive his hopes 'to live the full span of life doing service of humanity till the last moment'. Some said that span was 125 years, he added; some said it was 133.[134]

He had settled for far less than he asked for. But he appears to have taken the outpouring of public emotion as an expression of God's will that he should preserve himself for further service. The outcome of his fast, he said, 'could not be otherwise when I find that thousands of refugees and others have been fasting since yesterday. Signed assurances of heart-friendship have been pouring in upon me from thousands. Telegraphic blessings have come from all over the world. Can there be a better sign of God's hand in this act of mine?'[135] The next day he wrote to a Muslim correspondent that his fast had been broken 'as a result of worldwide co-operation'.[136] He announced that he would go to Pakistan, where he would 'try to make Muslims understand their folly'.[137] Pyarelal was despatched to the Pakistan high commissioner to enquire about a visit. The answer came back: not yet.

On 20 January a bomb exploded about 75 feet from where Gandhi was sitting, a botched attempt at assassination. One of the conspirators was arrested; the others made off in a taxi. All were Hindu militants from Maharashtra, members of the Hindu Mahasabha or RSS. On 30 January one of them, Nathuram Godse, approached Gandhi as he walked to his prayer meeting in the Birla House garden, folded his hands in greeting, and shot him three times in the chest. As he fell to the ground, it is reported, the word 'Rama' passed his lips.

So ended the life of a religious man caught up in the coils of the snake that was politics. He had wanted the power to make people good. To this inherently worldly purpose his actions had inevitably aligned themselves.

# Glossary

| | |
|---|---|
| *ahimsa* | Non-violence, non-destruction of life |
| *atman* | The eternal self or soul |
| *avatar* | Incarnation of the god Vishnu (e.g. Rama), come to restore moral order to the world; Gandhi used the term to mean a man who became one with God |
| Bania | Merchant |
| *bapu* | Father; Gandhi was called 'Bapu' by some of his associates |
| *bodhisattva* | One who has attained enlightenment but who remains in the body in order to help others attain that state |
| *brahmacharya* | The first of the four stages of life, before marriage and the assumption of family responsibilities; the term denotes chastity and was used by Gandhi to mean control not only of the sexual appetite but control of all the senses |
| *brahman* | The absolute, the eternal ground of all existence |
| Brahmin | Priest, member of the highest caste |
| *charkha* | Spinning wheel |
| *darshan* | Blessed sight of a holy person |
| *dharma* | Generally, the righteous performance of one's duty in life; specifically, one's duty as determined by membership of a caste |
| *dhoti* | Loincloth |
| *diwan* | Prime minister of an Indian state |

| | |
|---|---|
| *harijan* | 'Child of God'; Gandhi's term for an untouchable, a member of the lowest group in Indian society, believed to defile caste Hindus on contact |
| *hartal* | Voluntary closure of shops or businesses as a form of protest |
| *karma* | Literally, action; specifically, the law of retribution by which one's past actions determine one's future fate, in particular the form of one's rebirth |
| *khadi* | Hand-spun, hand-woven cloth |
| Kshatriya | Warrior, member of the second highest caste |
| *lathi* | Long wooden stave, used by Indian police |
| *mahatma* | 'Great soul', outstanding spiritual personality |
| *moksha* | The state of the liberated soul, freed from rebirth |
| *panchayat* | Village council, with customary legal authority |
| *pandit* | Learned man, religious expert |
| Patidar | Member of a farming caste in Gujarat active in Gandhi's campaigns |
| *punya* | Accumulated merit |
| Ramarajya | Literally, 'rule of Rama'; loosely, the golden age to come, when righteousness prevails |
| *rishi* | Hindu sage |
| *sadhu* | A holy ascetic |
| *sanatani* | Orthodox |
| *satyagraha* | 'Truth-force', 'soul-force'; Gandhi's philosophy and practice of peaceful disobedience to unjust laws |
| *satyagrahi* | Practitioner of *satyagraha* |
| *shakti* | Term used in connection with various aspects of spiritual power which are conceptualized as feminine |
| *shastra* | Exposition of sacred law |
| *shuddhi* | Reconversion of Indian Muslims to Hinduism |
| Sudra | Member of the lowest of the four castes, performer of physical labour |
| *swadeshi* | Made in India |
| *swaraj* | 'Self-rule'; used by Indian nationalists to denote independence from Britain (*purna swaraj* denoted full independence); used by Gandhi to mean both political independence and self-discipline in pursuit of his ideal of purity |
| *tantra* | Ritual worship of and identification with the source of life |
| *tapas* | The 'heat' (power) generated by ascetic practices |
| *tapasya/tapascharya* | Austerity, penance, in pursuit of *tapas* |

| | |
|---|---|
| Vaisya | Member of the third highest caste, traditionally a landowner or merchant |
| *varna* | One of the four principal castes (*Brahmin, Kshatriya, Vaisya, Sudra*) |
| *veda* | One of the sacred books of the ancient Indians |
| *yajna* | Sacrifice |
| *yoga* | Indian philosophical system prescribing mental and physical exercises for the purpose of spiritual progress |

# A Note on Sources

The source most frequently cited, by far, is *The Collected Works of Mahatma Gandhi* (*CWMG*), published by the Government of India through the Navajivan Trust in 100 volumes beginning in 1958. (Volume 1 had shortly to be enlarged and reformatted. References are to the revised edition.) Volumes 1–90 follow a chronological sequence, ending with Gandhi's death on 30 January 1948. Volumes 91–97 contain papers collected later on and are chronologically arranged only within each volume. Volumes 98 and 99 are subject and title indexes. Volume 100 is a collection of the editorial prefaces that appear at the beginning of each volume of the *Collected Works*. (NB: In 2000 the Government of India began issuing a new edition of the *Collected Works* with all papers in chronological order.)

References by me to Gandhi's letters published in the *Collected Works* (*CW*) are given with the date of their composition. References to articles, interviews, speeches, and so on are given with the date of actual production, wherever possible, rather than the date of publication.

The English translations from material originally in Gujarati and Hindi in the *Collected Works* present problems of interpretation with which I am not able to deal. For an idea of what they are, see Bhikhu Parekh, 'Gandhi and his Translators' (*Gandhi Marg* 87, 1986). In acknowledgement of these problems I have indicated references to translated material by a 'T' in parentheses.

Gandhi's two published memoirs, *Satyagraha in South Africa* and *An Autobiography, or The Story of My Experiments with Truth*, can be found in the *Collected Works* in Volumes 29 and 39 respectively. They are pioneering works in a most un-Indian literary form. They contain every conceivable pitfall for the biographer. I have tried to use them rigorously and fairly. Both were originally written and published in Gujarati – *Satyagraha in South Africa* in 1923–24 and the *Autobiography* in 1925–29. The history of their composition, serial publication, translation into English, and publication in book form is given in the *Collected Works*. References to the *Autobiography* are to the Penguin edition of 1982, which is readily available.

Biographies of Gandhi that I have found useful are: David Arnold, *Gandhi* (London, 2001); Geoffrey Ashe, *Gandhi: A Study in Revolution* (New York, 1968); Judith Brown, *Gandhi: Prisoner of Hope* (Delhi, 1990); Antony Copley, *Gandhi* (Oxford, 1987); Erik Erikson, *Gandhi's Truth: On the Origins of Militant Non-violence* (New York, 1969); Louis Fischer, *The Life of Mahatma Gandhi* (London, 1951); Martin Green, *Gandhi: Voice of a New Age Revolution* (New York, 1993); B. R. Nanda, *Mahatma Gandhi* (Oxford, 1958); Robert Payne, *The Life and Death of Mahatma Gandhi* (New York, 1969); Stanley Wolpert, *Gandhi's Passion (Oxford, 2001)*; and George Woodcock, *Gandhi* (London, 1972). The official multi-volume biographies are in a class by themselves – immensely useful, immensely frustrating, immensely impressive, immensely touching. These are D.G. Tendulkar's *Mahatma* (Delhi, 1951–54; revised 1960–63) and *Mahatma Gandhi* (Ahmedabad, Bombay and Delhi, 1956–97) by, first, Pyarelal Nayar, Gandhi's devoted secretary, who died after completing four volumes, and, second, his sister, Sushila Nayar, Gandhi's doctor, who wrote an additional five volumes. Mahadev Desai, Gandhi's other secretary, equally devoted, died in 1942 and produced only a few short but interesting accounts of episodes in Gandhi's career: his diaries, published intermittently and selectively in English translation (*The Diary of Mahadev Desai*, Ahmedabad, 1953; and *Day-to-Day with Gandhi*, Varanasi, 1968–74) repay careful reading. (The same problems of English translation apply as to the *Collected Works*.)

The principal scholarly sources for Gandhi's background and early life are Chandran S. Devanesen's *The Making of the Mahatma* (Madras, 1969) and Stephen Hay's 'Between Two Worlds: Gandhi's First Impressions of British Culture' *(Modern Asian Studies* 3, 1969). For Gandhi's political career in South Africa I have relied principally on Maureen Swan's *Gandhi: The South African Experience* (Johannesburg, 1985). James Hunt's *Gandhi in London* (Delhi, 1978) and *Gandhi and the Nonconformists* (Delhi, 1986) deal, respectively, with those periods of Gandhi's life spent in London and with his Christian contacts in South Africa. Judith Brown's two detailed studies of Gandhi's political career in India, *Gandhi's Rise to Power: Indian Politics 1915–1922* (Cambridge, 1972) and *Gandhi and Civil Disobedience: The Mahatma in Indian Politics 1928–34* (Cambridge, 1977) are essential reading. Unfortunately, they take the story only up to 1934. The remainder of Gandhi's career receives sketchier treatment in her *Gandhi* and *Modern India: The Origins of an Asian Democracy* (Oxford, 1994). The twelve volumes of *The Transfer of Power 1942–7*, edited by Nicholas Mansergh and E.W.R. Lumby (London, 1970–83), document the last years of British rule and the final stage of Gandhi's career seen through British eyes.

There are numerous pious exegeses of Gandhi's thought, of interest only to those concerned with the nature of his influence on people. Some serious and useful studies are: Margaret Chatterjee, *Gandhi's Religious Thought* (Notre Dame, 1983); Raghavan Iyer, *The Moral and Political Thought of Mahatma Gandhi* (New York, 1973); Bhikhu Parekh, *Colonialism, Tradition and Reform* (Delhi, 1989); and Gene Sharp, *Gandhi as a Political Strategist* (Boston, 1979). Geoffrey Ostergaard's 'Gandhian Non-Violence: Moral Principle or Political Technique' (in V.T. Patil, ed., *New Dimensions and Perspectives in Gandhism*, Delhi, 1989) briskly makes the case that *satyagraha* is 'a closed system of thought, incapable of proof, unfalsifiable'.

George Orwell's 1949 essay 'Reflections on Gandhi' (in Sonia Orwell and Ian Angus, eds, *Collected Essays, Journalism and Letters of George Orwell*, Volume 4, London , 1968) should be read for its inimitable 'fairmindedness' and élan. Ved Mehta's *Mahatma Gandhi and his Apostles* (New York, 1977) opens a window on the strange world of 'Gandhism'.

Other works are cited as required and full references to them given with their first citation in the endnotes. The conclusions stated or implied in this book about Gandhi as a historical actor on the Indian scene are obviously based on more reading than can be accommodated in such citations. Sunil Khilnani's 'Bibliographical Essay' in his *The Idea of India* (New York, 1998) should be consulted by those wanting to know more about the historical context.

# Notes

## 1. Kathiawar and London

1. *Autobiography*, 19–21.
2. *CW* [*Collected Works*] 12: 381, 11 March 1914 (T). See also *CW* 10: 373, 26 November 1910 (T); *CW* 24: 170, 1 June 1924 (T); *CW* 26: 151, 15 February 1925.
3. *Autobiography*, 23; *CW* 1: 44, 13 June 1891. Pyarelal (*Mahatma Gandhi – The Early Phase*, Ahmedabad, 1965, 203) says Gandhi was married 'in his thirteenth year'; Gandhi's earliest biographer, Joseph Doke (*M.K. Gandhi: An Indian Patriot in South Africa*, London, 1909, 21) says he was married at 'the age of twelve'. The marriage may have taken place even earlier. The chronology at the end of the 1958 edition of *CW* 1 has 'Married Kasturbai' under the year 1881, and Martin Green (*Gandhi: Voice of a New Age Revolution*, New York, 1993, 60) gives the date as 'May 1881', which would have made Gandhi 11. See also Stanley Wolpert, *Gandhi's Passion* (Oxford, 2001), 13, 270.
4. *CW* 1: 42, 13 June 1891; *Autobiography*, 50.
5. *Autobiography*, 26–8, 38–9; *CW* 72: 127, 'After June 3, 1940' (T).
6. *CW* 1: 44, 13 June 1891; *Autobiography*, 72–3.
7. *Autobiography*, 42–4.
8. Ibid., 61–3.
9. Warren Sylvester Smith gives a general picture of the scene in *The London Heretics, 1870–1914* (New York, 1969). Peter Washington's *Madame Blavatsky's Baboon* (New York, 1995) while concentrating on the Theosophical Society and its offshoots has information and many pointed observations on the milieu in which the Society flourished. And see also Stephen Hay, 'The Making of a Late-Victorian Hindu' (*Victorian Studies* 33, 1969).
10. *CW* 48: 326–7, 20 November 1931.

11. *CW* 33: 378–9, 27 May 1927.
12. Colin Spencer, *The Heretic's Feast* (Hanover, 1996), 170. Spencer's book seems to be the only serious attempt so far to write an intellectual history of vegetarianism.
13. A.F. Hills, *Essays on Vegetarianism* (London, n.d.), 32. *Essays on Vegetarianism* was a collection of Hills's articles from *The Vegetarian*, which ceased publication in 1897. Gandhi subscribed to and contributed to *The Vegetarian* while in South Africa. It can be consulted at the offices of the Vegetarian Society in Altrincham, Cheshire.
14. Hills, *Essays on Vegetarianism*, 66, 68, 164.
15. Ibid., 85.
16. Ibid., 200.
17. Ibid., 9–10.
18. Ibid., 80.
19. Ibid., 67–9.
20. *CW* 1: 121–4, 24 March 1894.
21. Hills, *Essays on Vegetarianism*, 57, 74–5.
22. *Autobiography*, 69–70, 195.
23. Ibid., 77. On Edwin Arnold and his writings, see Brooks Wright, *Interpreter of Buddhism to the West: Sir Edwin Arnold* (New York, 1957).
24. Edwin Arnold, *The Light of Asia* (Twickenham, 1998 [1879]), 80; *Autobiography*, 157; and (e.g.) *CW* 24: 85, 18 May 1924.
25. Arnold, Preface to *The Light of Asia*, x.
26. Hills, *Essays on Vegetarianism*, 14–15.
27. Pyarelal, *Mahatma Gandhi – The Early Phase*, 259.
28. *Autobiography*, 77–8. (Gandhi remembers *Why I Became a Theosophist* as *How I Became a Theosophist*.)
29. Peter Washington's *Madame Blavatsky's Baboon* is a source for such facts as there are about Blavatsky's life before she founded the Theosophical Society. Her life deserves serious biographical study but no one seems yet to have taken up the challenge. Frederick Crews has made an attempt, in a two-part article in the *New York Review of Books* ('The Consolation of Theosophy', 19 September and 3 October 1996), to assess her influence on strains of twentieth-century European thought not directly connected with the theosophical movement. Theosophy was not invented but revived by Madame Blavastsky. In the West, its roots are in Neoplatonism; in the east, in the Upanishads. These seem to have been largely independent developments, but there may have been some Eastern influence on Neoplatonism; see J.F. Staal, *Advaita and Neoplatonism* (Madras, 1961); and R.T. Wallis, *Neoplatonism* (New York, 1972). The long article on 'Theosophy' by Paul Oltramare in *The Encyclopaedia of Religion and Ethics* (New York, n.d), Vol. 12, forms a useful introduction. Oltramare identifies the three principal features of classical theosophical systems as: 'desire for deliverance from suffering and death, hope to succeed by personal effort, confidence in the saving efficacy of knowledge' (305).
30. It seems likely that he read or at least glanced at it at some point, given his involvement with theosophy in South Africa. See Pyarelal, *Mahatma Gandhi – The Early Phase*, 491.
31. H.P. Blavatsky, *The Secret Doctrine* (Point Loma, 1909 [1888]), Vol. 2, 268.

32. H.P. Blavatsky, *The Key to Theosophy* (Los Angeles, 1930; reprint of 1899 edn), 1–3. The book's organization is diffuse: the summary attempted in the following paragraphs brings together scattered material.
33. Blavatsky, *The Key to Theosophy*, 68.
34. For Besant, see Arthur H. Nethercot, *The First Five Lives of Annie Besant* (Chicago, 1960) and *The Last Four Lives of Annie Besant* (London, 1963); Anne Taylor, *Annie Besant* (Oxford, 1992); and the aptly titled *Annie Besant and Progressive Messianism* by Catherine Wessinger (New York, 1988).
35. H.P. Blavatsky, *The Voice of the Silence* (Wheaton, 1992 [1889]), 2, 9.
36. Annie Besant, *Why I Became a Theosophist* (London 1891), 30.
37. *Autobiography*, 77–8.
38. *CW* 27: 62, 7 May 1925.
39. Doke, *M.K. Gandhi*, 32. Bishop Fred B. Fisher reported 'very strong gossip' that Gandhi had considered joining the City Temple. (Fisher, *That Strange Little Brown Man, Gandhi*, New York, 1932, 97–8.) Parker was a celebrated preacher whose sermons were collected for publication. See, for instance, *The Inner Life of Christ* (Chattanooga, 1998), a collection still in print. In South Africa, Gandhi read 'the Commentary of Dr. Parker of the City Temple' (*Autobiography*, 123). This most likely refers to some part of what became the multi-volume *The People's Bible* (London, 1896–1907) which consists of 'commentaries' (often delivered as sermons) on all the books of the Bible. Gandhi found it 'morally stimulating' but of no use 'to one who had no faith in the prevalent Christian beliefs' – which may be a fair description also of his reaction to the sermons he heard in London.
40. *Autobiography*, 78. For a more exact translation from Gandhi's original Gujarati see *CW* 39: 481.
41. *CW* 35: 248, 15 November 1927; *CW* 51: 21, 4 September 1932.
42. *Autobiography*, 78.
43. Thomas Carlyle, 'The Hero as Prophet', in *On Heroes and Hero-Worship* (London, 1974 [1841]), 74.
44. Ibid., 74–91, 99. For an appreciation of Mohammed by Gandhi which closely echoes that of Carlyle, see *CW* 25: 127, 11 September 1924.
45. Thomas Carlyle, 'The Hero as Prophet', 60. For a glimpse of what appealed to Gandhi in Carlyle, see *CW* 96: 303, 311, n.d.

## 2. South Africa: Beginnings

1. Pyarelal, *Mahatma Gandhi – The Early Phase* (Ahmedabad, 1965), 280; *CW* 32: 2, 9–10, 5 November 1926 (T).
2. *Autobiography*, 101–2.
3. *CW* 35: 293, 22 November 1927.
4. *Autobiography*, 146.
5. See, e.g., *CW* 14: 477–8, 6 July 1918; *CW*: 9: 106, 9 November 1908 (T).
6. Prabhudas Gandhi, *My Childhood with Gandhiji* (Ahmedabad, 1957), 45; *Autobiography*, 279.
7. Prabhudas Gandhi, *My Childhood with Gandhiji*, 119.

8. *Autobiography*, 108.

9. *Autobiography*, 109–11; but see also *CW* 1: 57–8, 26 May 1893. On being enrolled as an advocate before the Natal Supreme Court the following year Gandhi put aside his turban when requested by the Chief Justice to adopt the same costume as other barristers (*Autobiography*, 145–6).

10. *Autobiography*, 114; *Satyagraha in South Africa* (*CW* 29), 38–9. See also *CW* 68: 171, c. 4 December 1938; and Joseph Doke, *M.K. Gandhi: An Indian Patriot in South Africa* (London, 1909), 35–6. Doke's book was written with Gandhi's cooperation and circulated by Gandhi in London in 1909.

11. *Autobiography*, 126.

12. This account of Gandhi's involvement with the South Africa General Mission is put together from ch. 2 of James Hunt's *Gandhi and the Nonconformists* (Delhi, 1986) and pp. 122–5 and 134–7 of the *Autobiography*.

13. E.H. Johnson, *The Highest Life; a Story of Shortcomings and a Goal, Including a Friendly Analysis of the Keswick Movement* (New York, 1901), 46.

14. Ibid., 45. Johnson's book is critical of the theurgical tendencies in the Keswick Movement.

15. *Autobiography*, 135; Hunt, *Gandhi and the Nonconformists*, 34.

16. Dudley Kidd, quoted in Hunt, *Gandhi and the Nonconformists*, 28. See also 31.

17. *Autobiography*, 124–5.

18. *Autobiography*, 135.

19. *Autobiography*, 137.

20. Pyarelal, *Mahatma Gandhi – The Early Phase*, 269, 321.

21. Gandhi destroyed the correspondence with Maitland, and there appear to be no letters from Gandhi surviving in Maitland's papers (personal communications from Stephen Hay and James Hunt). Gandhi told Pyarelal that the correspondence with Maitland was the only one he regretted having destroyed. See Pyarelal, *Mahatma Gandhi – The Early Phase*, 326; and *Satyagraha in South Africa* (*CW* 29), 194.

22. *CW* 1: 127–8, 'Before June, 1894' (T); *CW* 32: 593–602 (Appendix 1) (T), Raychandbhai's letter to Gandhi. See also the editorial preface to *CW* 32: v–vi.

23. Maitland and Carpenter were co-authors of a pamphlet (*Vivisection*, London, 1893).

24. Anna Kingsford also wrote *The Perfect Way in Diet* (London, 1881), a treatise on vegetarianism based on the thesis she submitted for a medical degree at the Sorbonne in 1880. Writers on Gandhi have sometimes confused *The Perfect Way in Diet* with *The Perfect Way; or, the Finding of Christ* (London, 1923 [1882]). Gandhi read *The Perfect Way in Diet* while in London (*Autobiography*, 60).

25. Information about Kingsford and Maitland comes from Maitland's devotional *Anna Kingsford: Her Life, Letters, Diary and Work* (London, 1896, 2 vols); *The Story of the New Gospel of Interpretation* by Edward Maitland (London, 1894 [1893]); Maitland's editorial preface to *'Clothed with the Sun'* by Anna Kingsford (New York, 1889; first published in London in the same year); the prefaces to *The Perfect Way; or the Finding of Christ*, by Anna Kingsford and Edward Maitland in 1881 and 1886, and the preface by Samuel Hopgood Hart in 1922; also references scattered through the text of *'Clothed with the Sun'* and *The Perfect Way*. The fashionable world of the spiritually and spiritualistically minded in which

Kingsford and Maitland moved – *The Perfect Way* was first presented to the public as a series of lectures given in the Mayfair drawing rooms of friends – is described in Yeats's unfinished autobiographical novel *The Speckled Bird* (Toronto, 1976) in which Anna Kingsford appears as the woman who remembers all her luridly amorous previous lives but has never been known to flirt. Kingsford's and Maitland's patron and financial angel was Lady Caithness, who went around the Riviera dressed as Mary, Queen of Scots, of whom she believed herself to be a reincarnation. Gandhi's knowledge of this world, if any, would have come from the monochromatic version of it in Maitland's *Anna Kingsford*. See also Washington, *Madame Blavatsky's Baboon* (New York, 1995), 70–78.

26. Martin Green, *The Origins of Nonviolence* (University Park, PA, 1986), 72.

27. Letter from Pyarelal to Hunt, 3 June 1978, quoted in James Hunt, *Gandhi and the Nonconformists*, 49. See also Pyarelal, *Mahatma Gandhi – The Last Phase*, Vol. 1, Book 2 (Ahmedabad, 1966 [1956]), 223–4.

28. Pyarelal, *Mahatma Gandhi – The Early Phase*, 259, 770; *CW* 41: 383–4, 12 September 1929; *CW* 64: 6, 6 November 1936.

29. Mahadev Desai, *Day-to-Day with Gandhi* (Varanasi, 1968–74), Vol. 7, 128 (July 1925).

30. *CW* 91: 10, 18 August 1894.

31. Mary Alling Aber, *Souls...* (Chicago, 1893), vii. Aber also wrote *An Experiment in Education* (New York, 1897), an account of her school in Boston.

32. Aber, *Souls...*, 154.

33. *CW* 1: 161, 3 August 1894.

34. Kingsford and Maitland, *The Perfect Way*, 15–16, 126.

35. Ibid., 41.

36. Ibid., 162.

37. Ibid., 69.

38. Ibid., 4.

39. Ibid., 9.

40. Ibid., 336.

41. Ibid., 229.

42. Ibid., 44.

43. Ibid., lxix. The term 'Gnosis' has always been associated with belief in an emanationist theology, glorification of the God within, the desire to transcend the material state, the assumption that religious utterances have hidden meanings not apparent to the populace, the belief that 'reason' (which includes enlightened individual exercise of the intuition) is fundamental to religious understanding, and a distrust of ecclesiasticism. All these beliefs, assumptions and attitudes were features of Esoteric Christianity, but the progenitors of Esoteric Christianity were careful not to describe it as a form of 'gnosticism', a term they appear to have thought referred too narrowly to the multiplicity of gnostic sects (both pagan and Christian and all claiming versions of the *gnosis*) which flourished in the early Christian era. Kingsford and Maitland preferred to associate themselves with the broader concept of 'esotericism'. The documents discovered at Nag Hammadi in 1945 have reopened the whole question of the 'gnostic' element in Christianity. Elaine Pagels, in *The Gnostic Gospels* (New York, 1989), 133–4, gives a quotation from the Gospel of Philip in which the concept of 'seeing God' is used much as

Kingsford and Maitland use it.

44. Maitland, *Anna Kingsford*, Vol. 2, 243–8; also Maitland, *The Story of the New Gospel of Interpretation*, 168–72.

45. Kingsford and Maitland, *The Perfect Way*, 237–8.

46. Kingsford, 'Clothed with the Sun', 95–8. See also *The Perfect Way*, 223–4.

47. Kingsford and Maitland, *The Perfect Way*, 108–9, 200–201, and passim.

48. Preface by Maitland to Kingsford, 'Clothed with the Sun', xix. See also 'Clothed with the Sun', 119–20; and *The Perfect Way*, 115.

49. Kingsford and Maitland, *The Perfect Way*, 44; and also 211, 248.

50. Ibid., 224.

51. Ibid., 218.

52. Ibid., 112–3.

53. Ibid., 61.

54. Maitland, *The Story of the New Gospel of Interpretation*, 154–5.

55. Kingsford, 'Clothed with the Sun', 91.

56. Kingsford and Maitland, *The Perfect Way*, 252–7.

57. Ibid., 256–7.

58. Maitland, *The Story of the New Gospel of Interpretation*, 165–8.

59. Quoted in Washington, *Madame Blavatsky's Baboon*, 77.

60. *CW* 1: 160, 4 August 1894 ('Letter to Mrs A. M. Lewis').

61. In 1893, at the request of the Vegetarian Society, Edward Maitland wrote a paper to be read at the Vegetarian Congress in Chicago. This paper, 'The Highest Aspect of Vegetarianism' (in Kingsford and Maitland, *Addresses and Essays on Vegetarianism*, London, 1912, 181–94), was a recapitulation of the doctrines of Esoteric Christianity.

62. Raychandbhai's letter (*CW* 32: 593–602), which contains both Gandhi's questions and his answers, was of course written in Gujarati, and I have not attempted to deal with the obvious difficulties raised by translation. Nor have I attempted to come to grips with the subtleties of Raychandbhai's arguments, which I am not qualified to assess. Raychandbhai is usually referred to as a Jain, but his thought was very eclectic (from within the Indian tradition), as Gandhi himself acknowledged in his preface to a collection of Raychandbhai's writings (*CW* 32: 1–13, 5 November 1926 (T)). My own sense of the nature of his influence on Gandhi is that it was Raychandbhai's saintly, searching life, and competence in disputation, which principally impressed him.

63. *CW* 32: 13, 5 November 1926 (T).

64. *CW* 1: 169–70, 26 November 1894.

65. The quotation was actually from a letter written to Kingsford and Maitland by their friend Baron Spedalieri, and reproduced with a confusing attribution in the preface to the second edition of *The Perfect Way* (xxviii–xxx).

66. *Natal Mercury*, 19 December 1894. Quoted in Pyarelal, *Mahatma Gandhi – The Early Phase*, 549–50.

67. *CW* 1: 189–91, 21 January 1895; *CW* 1: 192–3, 2 February 1895.

68. *Autobiography*, 136.

69. Report of the Esoteric Christian Union, 1894, quoted in Pyarelal, *Mahatma Gandhi – The Early Phase*, 325.

70. Gandhi was made aware of this (*Autobiography*, 137–8).

71. Margaret Chatterjee (*Gandhi's Religious Thought*, Notre Dame, 1983), Raghavan Iyer (*The Moral and Political Thought of Mahatma Gandhi*, New York, 1973), and Bhikhu Parekh (*Colonialism, Tradition and Reform*, Delhi, 1989) have documented and sought explanations for the oddities of Gandhi's 'Hinduism'. Parekh is particularly sensitive to Gandhi's use of language. Some other writers have treated Gandhi more straightforwardly as a 'reformer' of Hinduism, in the context of earlier reform movements – notably R.C. Zaehner in his *Hinduism* (London, 1962).

72. Bhikhu Parekh, *Colonialism, Tradition and Reform*, 194.

73. Millie Polak, *Mr. Gandhi: The Man* (Bombay, 1950 [1931]), 151.

74. *CW* 50: 211, 'History of the Satyagraha Ashram', 1932 (T).

75. *CW* 54: 471, 21 April 1933 (T).

76. See, e.g., *CW* 22: 188, 15 January 1922 (T).

77. *CW* 27: 449, 29 July 1925; *CW* 31: 69, 29 June 1926 (T).

78. *Autobiography*, 125; Kingsford and Maitland, *The Perfect Way*, 44.

79. *CW* 55: 286, 22 July 1933; *CW* 68: 172, *c.* 4 December 1938.

80. [Romain Rolland,] *Romain Rolland and Gandhi Correspondence* (Delhi, 1976), 189; also *CW* 48: 405–6, 8 December 1931.

81. *CW* 19: 179, 29 December 1920 (T).

82. *CW* 23: 349, 3 April 1924.

83. *CW* 57: 327, 30 March 1934.

84. J.C. Kumarappa, *Practice and Precepts of Jesus* (Ahmedabad, 1945), 102; *CW* 79: 279–80, 21 March 1945. It is clear from the context that 'used to believe' implies no repudiation.

85. *CW* 21: 14, 25 August 1921.

86. Mahadev Desai, *Day-to-Day with Gandhi*, Vol. 1, 139 (May 1918).

87. *Autobiography*, 136.

88. James Hunt, in *Gandhi in London* (Delhi, 1978), 152, says Maitland sent him the book. Pyarelal (*Mahatma Gandhi – The Early Phase*, 627) says the sender was 'a well-wisher in England'.

89. *Autobiography*, 136.

90. *CW* 10: 249, 10 May 1910.

91. *CW* 37: 262, 10 September 1928 (T).

92. Leo Tolstoy, *The Kingdom of God is Within You* (Lincoln, 1984 [1894]), 221.

93. Ibid., 101.

94. Ibid., 105.

95. *CW* 9: 444, 1 October 1909.

96. *CW* 48: 407–8, 8 December 1931.

97. *CW* 37: 262–8, 10 September 1928 (T).

## 3. South Africa: *Satyagraha*

1. *Autobiography*, 131.

2. Ibid., 137–9.

3. Maureen Swan, *Gandhi: The South African Experience* (Johannesburg, 1985), 45–9.

4. *CW* 1: 63–5, 29 September 1893.

5. *CW* 1: 154, 'Before July 14, 1894'.

6. *CW* 1: 177, 'Before December 19, 1894'.

7. *CW* 1: 174, 183, 'Before December 19, 1894'.

8. *CW* 1: 187, 'Before December 19, 1894'; Pyarelal, *Mahatma Gandhi – The Early Phase* (Ahmedabad, 1956), 478. See also *CW* 13: 277, 4 June 1916 (T) and *CW* 13: 278, 5 June 1916 (T).

9. *CW* 1: 63, 29 September 1893.

10. *Autobiography*, 206.

11. *CW* 2: 29, 14 August 1896.

12. *Autobiography*, 203–5; Swan, *Gandhi: The South African Experience*, 89–90.

13. *Autobiography*, 192.

14. Ibid., 242.

15. Ibid., 194–5. See also *CW* 10: 296, 25 July 1910 (T), which suggests that the effort to be celibate had begun by 1896.

16. Louis Kuhne, *The New Science of Healing; or, The Doctrine of the Unity of Disease* (Butler, NJ, 1893). Kuhne wrote prolifically and Gandhi does not specify which works he read. For an interesting discussion of the influence of Kuhne and Just on the development of modern Indian yoga, see Joseph Alter, *Gandhi's Body: Sex, Diet and the Politics of Nationalism* (Philadelphia, 2000), ch. 3.

17. *Autobiography*, 232.

18. Adolf Just, *Return to Nature!* (New York, 1903 [1896]), 23.

19. Ibid., 49.

20. Ibid., 52.

21. *Autobiography*, 249–50.

22. *CW* 65: 78, 13 April 1937 (T).

23. *Autobiography*, 249.

24. *CW* 11: 442, 18 January 1913 (T).

25. *CW* 32: 69, 19 November 1926 (T).

26. *Autobiography*, 233.

27. Chandrashanker Shukla, ed., *Reminiscences of Gandhiji* (Bombay, 1951), 102.

28. *CW* 79: 17, 9 January 1945 (T).

29. Joseph Doke, *M.K. Gandhi: An Indian Patriot in South Africa* (London, 1909), 5; Millie Polak, *Mr Gandhi: The Man* (Bombay, 1950 [1931]), 30; Pyarelal, *Mahatma Gandhi – The Birth of Satyagraha* (Ahmedabad, 1986), 25.

30. Sushila Nayar, *Mahatma Gandhi – Satyagraha at Work* (Ahmedabad, 1989), 458; Chandrashanker Shukla, ed., *Incidents of Gandhi's Life* (Bombay, 1949), 287. Nayar dates their meeting as 1893; Ritch recalls it as 'somewhere about 1895'.

31. *Autobiography*, 259; S. Nayar, *Mahatma Gandhi – Satyagraha at Work*, 457.

32. *CW* 4: 429, 13 May 1905.

33. Annie Besant, *In the Outer Court* (London, 1906; based on lectures given in 1895), 128–9.

34. Anne Besant, *Esoteric Christianity, or, The Lesser Mysteries* (New York, 1902), 184–93, 200–201.

35. Ibid., 190–91.

36. Ibid., 221.

37. Ibid., 227.

38. See Ronald Neufeldt, 'A Lesson in Allegory: Theosophical Interpretations of the *Bhagavadgita*', in Robert N. Minor, ed., *Modern Indian Interpreters of the Bhagavadgita* (Albany, 1986), 11–33; and Eric Sharpe, *The Universal Gita: Western Images of the Bhagavad Gita* (La Salle, IL, 1985), 88–96.

39. *CW* 32: 152–8, 11 and 13 April 1926 (T).

40. *CW* 4: 103–5, 14 January 1904.

41. *CW* 4: 112–3, 21 January 1904; *CW* 4: 115–7, 21 January 1904 (T); *CW* 4: 121–2, 28 January 1904 (T).

42. *CW* 4: 368–70, 4 March 1905; *CW* 4: 375–7, 11 March 1905; *CW* 4: 405–9, 15 April 1905 (T); *CW* 91: 40–41, 25 March 1905. These are not verbatim accounts, but summaries that appeared in *The Star* newspaper and *Indian Opinion*; the latter appears to be a summary provided by Gandhi himself.

43. *CW* 19: 571, 13 April 1921.

44. *CW* 11: 65, 8 May 1911 (T). On the Johannesburg Lodge of the Theosophical Society, see Phyllis Lean, *Fifty Years of Theosophy: A Brief History of the Johannesburg Lodge* (Johannesburg, 1949).

45. See, e.g., *CW* 96: 33, 14 November 1909. *CW* 96 contains Gandhi's correspondence with Herman Kallenbach and the Polaks. It shows very clearly Gandhi's consciousness of the effect he had on some of his admirers.

46. *Autobiography*, 244–5.

47. Ibid., 245.

48. Pyarelal, *Mahatma Gandhi – The Birth of Satyagraha*, 349–50.

49. *Autobiography*, 259.

50. Ibid., 274.

51. Ibid., 277; Polak, *Mr. Gandhi: The Man*, 41.

52. *Autobiography*, 274–5.

53. Geoffrey Ashe, *Gandhi* (New York, 1980 [1968]), 82–3; Louis Fischer, *The Life of Mahatma Gandhi* (London, 1982), 91–2; George Woodcock, *Gandhi* (London, 1972), 25.

54. These articles are in *CW* 8: 239–42, 269–71, 281–3, 289–90, 303–5, 324–6, 337–9, 371–5. They came out between 16 May and 18 July 1908 and were written originally in Gujarati with the title 'Sarvodaya – The Advancement of All'.

55. *CW* 7: 122, 27 July 1907 (T).

56. John Ruskin, *Unto This Last* (London, 1909 [1862]), 120.

57. Ibid., 126–31.

58. *CW* 8: 282, 6 June 1908 (T).

59. *CW* 8: 373–5, 18 July 1908 (T).

60. *CW* 96: 109, 31 January 1913.

61. Sources for Phoenix, in addition to correspondence in the *Collected Works*, are Prabhudas Gandhi, *My Childhood with Gandhiji* (Ahmedabad, 1957); Pyarelal, *Mahatma Gandhi – The Birth of Satyagraha*; Nayar, *Mahatma Gandhi – Satyagraha at Work*; Ravjibhai Patel, *The Making of the Mahatma*, trans. and ed. Abid Shamsi (Ahmedadbad, 1990); Polak, *Mr. Gandhi: The Man*.

62. Polak, *Mr. Gandhi: The Man*, 31–2, 49–51, 67, 68, 72, 77–8, 89, 91, 113–4, 124–5.

63. *CW* 8: 139, 9 January 1909 (T).

64. *Autobiography*, 197, 291; and see also *CW* 95: 184, n.d.

65. *Autobiography*, 197.

66. *CW* 44: 220, 14 October 1930 (T). See also the correspondence with J.C. Kumarappa on the subject of vows (*CW* 44: 264–5 and 312; and *Gandhi Marg*, 1st Series, Vol. 3, 1959). C.F. Andrews was critical of Gandhi's practice of taking vows: Hugh Tinker, *The Ordeal of Love* (Delhi, 1979), 17. Other statements of interest on vows are *CW* 24: 278, 22 June 1924 (T); *CW* 41: 272–4, 22 August 1929; *CW* 42: 413, 23 January 1930; *CW* 46: 254, 18 June 1931.

67. *Autobiography*, 289.

68. *CW* 77: 50, 31 December 1942.

69. *CW* 65: 111, 18 April 1937.

70. *Autobiography*, 286–9. See also Shula Marks, *Reluctant Rebellion: The 1906–8 Disturbances in Natal* (Oxford, 1970).

71. *CW* 5: 266–7, 7 April 1906 (T); *CW* 5: 281–2, 14 April 1906 (T).

72. *CW* 5: 134, 18 November 1905; *CW* 5: 233–4, 17 March 1906; *CW* 5: 251–2, 31 March 1906.

73. *CW* 5: 117, 28 October 1905 (T).

74. *CW* 25: 89–90, 14 September 1924 (T); *CW* 3: 113–14, 19 October 1899.

75. *CW* 5: 57–8, 2 September 1905 (T).

76. *CW* 50: 326, 3 August 1932 (T).

77. Swan, *Gandhi: The South African Experience*, 100–103.

78. *CW* 5: 413–4, 8 September 1906 (T).

79. See, e.g., *CW* 5: 410, 3 September 1906 (T); and *Satyagraha in South Africa* (*CW* 29), 85.

80. *Satyagraha in South Africa* (*CW* 29), 83–5.

81. *CW* 5: 400–403, 25 August 1906.

82. Pyarelal, *Mahatma Gandhi – The Birth of Satyagraha*, 490–91. The account of this meeting appeared in the Gujarati section of *Indian Opinion* on 8 September.

83. *CW* 5: 442, 22 September 1906 (T); Maureen Swan, *Gandhi: The South African Experience*, 88, 126, gives the context.

84. *CW* 5: 404–5, 1 September 1906.

85. *CW* 5: 405, 1 September 1906.

86. *Satyagraha in South Africa* (*CW* 29), 83–4.

87. *CW* 5: 401, 3 September 1906 (T).

88. *CW* 5: 408–9, 1 September 1906.

89. *CW* 5: 414, 8 September 1906 (T).

90. *CW* 5: 418, 9 September 1906 (T); also Pyarelal, *Mahatma Gandhi – The Birth of Satyagraha*, 494–6 James Hunt (*Gandhi in London*, Delhi, 1978, 51) connects the Hamidia Islamic Society with the Ahmadiya movement, the militant proselytizing Muslim movement which remains particularly active in Africa.

91. *CW* 5: 460, 6 October 1906; *CW* 5: 439, 22 September 1906 (T).

92. *Satyagraha in South Africa* (*CW* 29), 88–90.

93. *CW* 5: 457, 29 September 1906 (T); *CW* 5: 462, 6 October 1906 (T).

94. *CW* 5: 474, 20 October 1906 (T).

95. Hunt, *Gandhi in London*, ch. 3; Nayar, *Mahatma Gandhi – Satyagraha at Work*, ch. 1.

96. *CW* 6: 407–8, 6 April 1907 (T).

97. *CW* 6: 273–6, 280–81, 284–7, 298–300, 312–13, 316–18, 330–32, 340–42 (5 January–

23 February 1907) (T); William Salter, *Ethical Religion* (Boston, 1889).

98. *CW* 6: 422, 20 April 1907 (T).

99. *CW* 8: 114, 29 February 1908 (T).

100. *CW* 8: 49–51, 1 February 1908.

101. *CW* 8: 42, 30 January 1908; *CW* 8: 44, 30 January 1908.

102. *CW* 8: 94, 22 February 1908 (T). In May, however, he asked Smuts to deport the man he thought was the instigator (*CW* 8: 253–4, 21 May 1908).

103. Swan, *Gandhi: The South African Experience*, 163, quoting account in the *Rand Daily Mail*, 7 March 1908.

104. *CW* 7: 455, 28 December 1907 (T).

105. *CW* 8: 23, 'Before January 19, 1908' (T); *CW* 8: 131–2, 7 March 1908 (T); *Satyagraha in South Africa* (*CW* 29), 92; *Autobiography*, 292.

106. *CW* 8: 61, 8 February 1908 (T).

107. *CW* 9: 243, 7 June 1909.

108. *CW* 19: 466, 23 February 1921. And see also *CW* 21: 472–5, 20 November 1921 (T).

109. *CW* 12: 461, 'Before July 11, 1914'.

110. *CW* 4: 392–4, 1 April 1905.

111. Bhikhu Parekh, *Colonialism, Tradition and Reform* (Delhi, 1989), 16–17.

112. Including, it appears, Henry Drummond, whose *Natural Law in the Spiritual World* (New York, 1886) he recalled in 1928 having read thirty years ago (*CW* 35: 445, 7 January 1928 (T). See also *CW* 35: 83, 19 August 1925.

113. See e.g. *CW* 22: 399, 18 July 1944.

114. *CW* 44: 220, 14 October 1930.

115. *CW* 54: 56, 11 March 1933. Gandhi's ideas bear some resemblance to the Hindu concept of *rita* (cosmic order) but he did not discuss them in that context.

116. *CW* 44: 281, 7 November 1930 (T); *CW* 49: 478–9, 25 May 1932.

117. [Romain Rolland,] *Romain Rolland and Gandhi Correspondence* (Delhi, 1976), 189–90; also *CW* 48: 405–6, 8 December 1931.

118. *CW* 55: 345, 5 August 1933.

119. *CW* 5: 460–61, 6 October 1906 (T). An even earlier example of this kind of thinking is in *CW* 3: 414–5, 20 August 1903, in an article about a terrible fire in the Paris metro.

120. *CW* 6: 443, 22 April 1907 (T).

121. *CW* 7: 455–7, 28 December 1907 (T); and see also *CW* 8: 156–8, 28 March 1908 (T), for a related article on famine in India.

122. *CW* 57: 164–6, 16 February 1934.

123. *CW* 8: 91–2, 22 February 1908 (T); *Satyagraha in South Africa* (*CW* 29), 130.

124. *Satyagraha in South Africa* (*CW* 29), 166–7.

125. *CW* 8: 86, 15 February 1908 (T); *CW* 9: 260, 'Before June 21, 1909' (T).

126. *CW* 8: 85–6, 15 February 1908 (T).

127. *CW* 8: 159, 28 March 1908 (T); and see Chapter 1, 22.

128. *CW* 9: 216, 24 May 1909 (T).

129. *CW* 9: 271, 'After June 23, 1909' (T).

130. *CW* 9: 283, 'After July 10, 1909' (T).

131. *CW* 9: 240, 5 June 1909 (T).

132. *CW* 9: 209, 25 June 1909.

133. *CW* 96: 11, 22 June 1909.

134. For the New Thought movement and Trine's place in it, see Charles Braden, *Spirits in Rebellion; the Rise and Development of New Thought* (Dallas, 1963) and Beryl Satter, *Each Mind a Kingdom: American Women, Sexual Purity and the New Thought Movement* (Berkeley, 1999). William James was intrigued by New Thought and its offshoots and wrote of them in *Varieties of Religious Experience* (New York, 1902), which Gandhi read in jail in 1923 (*CW* 23: 184, 26 August 1923).

135. R.W. Trine, *What All The World's A-Seeking* (Boston 1897 [1896]), 109.

136. *CW* 23: 178, 3 January 1923; *CW* 25: 84, 4 September 1924; *CW* 55: 257, 8 July 1933.

137. Doke, *M.K. Gandhi*, 7, 97.

138. Ibid., 89–93.

139. This is consistent with the 'esoteric' interpretation of St. John's gospel.

140. Quoted in Hunt, *Gandhi in London*, 134.

141. Ibid., 134–7.

142. *CW* 10: 42–53 (*Hind Swaraj*). *Hind Swaraj* is in *CW* 10: 6–68.

143. *CW* 10: 37.

144. *CW* 10: 54.

145. *CW* 10: 19.

146. *CW* 9: 396, 8 September 1909.

147. Edward Carpenter, *From Adam's Peak to Elephanta* (New York, 1892), 176–82.

148. Edward Carpenter, *Civilization: Its Cause and Cure*, (New York, 1891 [1889]), 15.

149. *CW* 96: 80, 23 September 1911.

150. *CW* 9: 425–7 'After October 26, 1909' (T). See also G.K. Chesterton, 'What is Indian Nationalism?', *Illustrated London News*, 18 September 1909.

151. Arthur H. Nethercot, *The Last Four Lives of Annie Besant* (London, 1963), 127–34. These lectures were collected and published in book form by the Theosophical Society in 1909 as *The Changing World*.

152. *CW* 10: 151, 'About February 5, 1910' (T). See also, e.g., *CW* 96: 109, 31 January 1913.

153. See *CW* 12: passim and *CW* 96: for the period 1913–14; also Prabhudas Gandhi, *My Childhood with Gandhiji*; Patel, *The Making of the Mahatma*; Polak, *Mr. Gandhi: The Man*; and Gandhi's *Autobiography*, 312–14.

154. *CW* 12: 45–52, 26 April 1913 (T). Gandhi's ideas about controlling sexual impulses, and the benefit therefrom, could sound very 'Victorian'. See *CW* 12: 52, where he advises those who 'feel passion rising in them' to take a cold bath. Steven Marcus's *The Other Victorians* (London, 1964) and Dr. William Acton's *Functions and Disorders of the Reproductive Organs* (London, 1857) make interesting comparative reading. Gandhi read Paul Bureau's *Towards Moral Bankruptcy* (London, 1925) in 1926 and was impressed by it (see summaries in *CW* 31: 77–9, 103–5, 135–40, 183–6, 218–22, 259–62, 286–9, 309–12). Bureau's ideas were similar to Acton's – basically that chastity produced health and vigour. He was inspired to write the book by the decline in the French birth rate due to the use of contraception. As to Indian influences, Gandhi read Patanjali's *Yogadarshan* at some point in South Africa (*CW* 9: 117, 28 December 1908 (T); Pyarelal, *Mahatma Gandhi – The Early Phase*, 709).

155. *CW* 25: 252, 21 or 22 October 1924. See also *CW* 61: 394, 'Before September 7, 1935'.

156. *CW* 23: 102, 17 March 1922 (T).

157. *CW* 96: 107, 11 January 1913.

158. *CW* 12: 126, 2 July 1913 (T).

159. *CW* 96: 94, 27 November 1911; *CW* 96: 98, 4 December 1911; *CW* 96: 99, 8 December 1911; *CW* 96: 101, 22 December 1911.

160. *CW* 10: 138–9, 27 January 1910 (T).

161. Chandran S. Devanesen, *The Making of the Mahatma* (Madras, 1969), 374.

162. I have followed Maureen Swan's reconstruction of events (*Gandhi: The South African Experience*, 244–5).

163. *CW* 10 275, 18 June 1910 (T).

164. *CW* 9: 417, 'After September 16, 1909' (T).

165. *Satyagraha in South Africa* (*CW 29*), 227–8.

166. *CW* 9: 106, 9 November 1908 (T). See also *CW* 9: 105, 9 November 1908; *CW* 9: 417–18, 17 September 1909 (T); and *Autobiography*, 294–7.

167. *CW* 96: 167, 27 February 1914.

168. *CW* 96: 181–2, 12 April 1914.

169. *CW* 12: 410, 22 April 1914. (T).

170. *CW* 10: 447, 9 March 1911 (T).

171. Ravjibhai Patel, *The Making of the Mahatma*, 179.

172. *CW* 12: 414, 6 May 1914.

173. *CW* 77: 98, 21 May 1943.

174. Quoted in Nayar, *Mahatma Gandhi – Satyagraha at Work*, 746.

175. *CW* 12: 460–62, 'Before July 11, 1914'.

## 4. Return to India

1. *CW* 12: 527, 13 August 1914.

2. *CW* 12: 554–5, 15 November (T); and *CW* 12: 531–2, 18 September 1914 (T).

3. *Autobiography*, 316–7, 319.

4. *CW* 12: 538, 13 October 1914.

5. James Hunt, *Gandhi in London* (Delhi, 1978), 186–7; *CW* 12: 556, 20 November 1914.

6. Bal Gangadhar Tilak, *Gita-Rahasya* [*The Esoteric Import of the Gita*] (Poona, 1965 [1915]), xviii and *passim*.

7. *CW* 13: 11, 17 January 1915 (T).

8. Jivaram Kalidas Shastri, *Epithet 'Mahatma' and Address Offered to Mahatma Gandhi* (Gondal, 1975); *CW* 13: 15–16, 27 January 1915 (T).

9. *CW* 96: 201, 12 February 1915; also *CW 96* 212, 21 May 1915.

10. *CW* 13: 54, 22 April 1915.

11. This seems to be the sense of *CW* 13: 39, 'After 14 March 1915' (T).

12. Extracts from the letter are given in English translation in Sushila Nayar, *Mahatma Gandhi – India Awakened* (Ahmedabad, 1994), 242–4.

13. *CW* 13: 62–3, 25 April 1915 (T).

14. These are found in the *Autobiography*, 350–53. Gandhi's train of thought is hard to follow, but again, I give what seems to be the sense of it.

15. *CW* 96: 207, 21 March 1915.

16. *Autobiography*, 353.

17. *CW* 13: 91–4, 'Before May 20, 1915' (T).

18. *CW* 96: 227, 23 October 1915.

19. *CW* 18: 338–9, 9 October 1920 (T).

20. Balvantsinha, *Under the Shelter of Bapu* (Ahmedabad, 1962), 183–4, 192–3; *CW* 67: 110, 6 June 1938 (T).

21. See *CW* 10: 228–9, 23 April 1910 (T). A remark critical of untouchability in a letter to Chhaganlal of 21 April 1907 (*CW* 6: 435 (T)) seems to refer not to the existence of 'untouchable' people but to temporary states of 'untouchability' in caste Hindus. A brief address to a group of untouchable admirers on 9 July 1914 (*CW* 12: 459 (T)) advocates treating untouchables, who 'are our own brethren', with respect. Gandhi was clearly stung by South African taunts about the Indian practice of untouchability (see *CW* 13: 277, 4 June 1916 (T) and *CW* 13: 278, 5 June 1916 (T)) but it was not one of the Indian 'defects' on which he chose to dwell. Most likely he favoured abolition but felt unable to risk Indian support by saying so.

22. *Autobiography*, 255–6; *CW* 19: 289, 29 January 1921.

23. *CW* 59: 461, 'On or before December 15, 1934'.

24. *CW* 44: 134–5, 9 September 1930 (T). Gandhi's rationale for opposing untouchability differed from that of Christian missionaries in India who, in the light of their own beliefs, condemned it (and frequently the caste system itself) as violating the equality of all men before God. See Duncan B. Forrester, *Caste and Christianity: Attitudes and Policies on Caste of Anglo-Saxon Protestant Missions in India* (London, 1980).

25. *CW* 54: 349, 9 April 1933 (T).

26. *CW* 54: 186, 25 March 1933.

27. *CW* 13: 301, October 1916 (T).

28. Quoted in Edward Maitland, *Anna Kingsford* (London, 1896), Vol. 2, 5.

29. *CW* 13: 94, 'Before May 20, 1915' (T).

30. *CW* 21: 187, 23 September 1921.

31. *CW* 13: 301–2, October 1916 (T).

32. *CW* 60: 45, 2 January 1935; *CW* 56: 289–90, 27 November 1933.

33. *CW* 13: 219–25, 14 February 1916.

34. *Autobiography*, 254.

35. *CW* 70: 202, 25 September 1939. Geoffrey Ostergaard, 'Gandhian Non-Violence: Moral Principle or Political Technique', in V.T. Patil, ed., *New Dimensions and Perspectives in Gandhism* (Delhi, 1989), is good on the way *ahimsa* tends to blend with other key concepts in Gandhi's writings. *Ahimsa* and 'Truth' are sometimes explicitly equated. Gandhi's mind was a convergent one.

36. *CW* 13: 228–9, 16 February 1916.

37. *CW* 13: 566–9 (Appendix 2), July 1916.

38. *CW* 13: 294–7, October 1916.

39. *CW* 20: 513, 14 August 1921 (T).

40. *CW* 37: 314, 4 October 1928.

41. *CW* 12: 412, 29 April 1914 (T).

42. *CW* 37: 310–13, 4 October 1928. Issues related to the death of the calf are aired at length in *CW* 37.

43. *CW* 37: 312, 4 October 1928.

44. *CW* 59: 461, 'On or before December 15, 1934' (Appendix).

45. *CW* 13: 262, 20 March 1916.

46. *CW* 20: 49, 1 May 1921 (T).

47. *CW* 13: 260, 20 March 1916.

48. *CW* 13: 210–16, 6 February 1916.

49. *Autobiography*, 342–4.

50. My sources for the Champaran *satyagraha*, in addition to the *Collected Works* and Nayar, *Mahatma Gandhi – India Awakened*, ch. 6, are the *Autobiography*, 365–84; Judith Brown, *Gandhi's Rise to Power: Indian Politics, 1915–1922* (Cambridge, 1972), 52–82; Stephen Henningham, 'The Social Setting of the Champaran Satyagraha: The Challenge to an Alien Elite', *Indian Economic and Social History Review* 13, 1976; and Jacques Pouchpedass, 'Local Leaders and the Intelligentsia in the Champaran Satyagraha (1917): A Study in Peasant Mobilization', *Contributions to Indian Sociology* 8, 1974.

51. *CW* 13: 408–9, 21 May 1917.

52. *CW* 13: 365, 16 April 1917 (T).

53. *CW* 13: 525 'About September 2, 1917' (T).

54. See Peter Robb, 'The Government of India and Annie Besant', *Modern Asian Studies* 10, 1976.

55. Quoted in Anne Taylor, *Annie Besant* (Oxford, 1992), 312.

56. My sources for the Kheda *satyagraha*, in addition to the *Collected Works* and Nayar, *Mahatma Gandhi – India Awakened*, ch. 7, are the *Autobiography*, 391–7; Crispin Bates, 'The Nature of Social Change in Rural Gujarat: The Kheda District, 1818–1918', *Modern Asian Studies* 15, 1981; Brown, *Gandhi's Rise to Power*, 83–111; and David Hardiman, *Peasant Nationalists of Gujarat: Kheda District 1917–1934* (Delhi, 1981), principally chs 1–6.

57. *CW* 14: 144, 'After January 11, 1918' (T).

58. Hardiman, *Peasant Nationalists of Gujarat*, 107.

59. *CW* 14: 212–13, 26 February 1918.

60. *CW* 14: 115, 21 December 1917 (T).

61. Mahadev Desai, *A Righteous Struggle* (Ahmedabad, 1951), 4.

62. *CW* 14: 233, 3 March 1918 (T).

63. *CW* 14: 229–30, 1 March 1918 (T).

64. *CW* 14: 256–7, 15 March 1918 (T); *CW* 14: 258–9, 16 March 1918 (T); *CW* 14: 260–63, 17 March 1918 (T).

65. *CW* 14: 256–7, 13 March 1918 (T); and Desai, *A Righteous Struggle*, 24.

66. *CW* 14: 267–8, 18 March 1918 (T).

67. *CW* 14: 270, 19 March 1918 (T).

68. *CW* 14: 264–5, 17 March 1918 (T).

69. *CW* 14: 475, 6 July 1918.

70. *CW* 13: 485–6, 3 August 1917.

71. *CW* 13: 499, 12 August 1917.

72. *CW* 14: 474–8, 6 July 1918.

73. *CW* 14: 504–5, 25 July 1918 (T).
74. *CW* 14: 463, 30 June 1918.
75. *CW* 14: 321, 10 April 1918; Brown, *Gandhi's Rise to Power*, 146.
76. *CW* 14: 377–8, 29 April 1918.
77. *CW* 14: 380–81, 30 April 1918.
78. *CW* 14: 374, 27 April 1918.
79. *CW* 14: 376, 29 April 1918.
80. Gandhi told Esther Faering on 30 June 1918 (*CW* 14: 462–3) that it was at the war conference that he had been forced to confront the practical implications of his views on Indian cowardice.
81. *CW* 14: 477, 6 July 1918.
82. *CW* 14: 397, 15 May 1918 (T).
83. *CW* 14: 443, 22 June 1918 (T).
84. *CW* 14: 440, 22 June 1918 (T).
85. *CW* 14: 438, 21 June 1918 (T); see also *CW* 14: 469–70, 4 July 1918, and Mahadev Desai, *Day-to-Day with Gandhi* (Varanasi, 1968–74), Vol. 1, 118.
86. Indulal Yajnik, *Gandhi As I Know Him* (Delhi, 1943), 62.
87. *CW* 14: 502, 24 July 1918 (T).
88. *CW* 14: 510, 29 July 1918.
89. *CW* 13: 471, 'Before July 11, 1917' (T).
90. *CW* 14: 448, 23 June 1918 (T); *CW* 14: 469, 4 July 1918 (T).
91. *CW* 14: 459, 29 June 1918 (T); *CW* 14: 518, 31 July 1918 (T).
92. *CW* 15: 47, 20 September 1918.
93. Rajendra Prasad, *Autobiography* (Bombay, 1957), 104–5.
94. *CW* 15: 65, 26 November 1918 (T).
95. *CW* 14: 146, 13 January 1918; *CW* 15: 54, 1 October 1918 (T); *CW* 91: 171, 2 October 1918 (T); Millie Polak, *Mr. Gandhi: The Man* (Bombay, 1950 [1931]), 151.
96. *CW* 15: 25–6, 17 August 1918 (T).
97. *Autobiography*, 409. See also *CW* 15: 70–71, 10 January 1919 (T); *CW* 15: 74–5, 21 January 1919 (T); *CW* 15: 81–2, 30 January 1919; *CW* 15: 83, 'Before February 2, 1919'.
98. *CW* 15: 71, 10 January 1919 (T).
99. Brown, *Gandhi's Rise to Power*, 153–4.
100. *CW* 15: 88, 9 February 1919 (T).
101. *CW* 14: 477–8, 6 July 1918.

## 5. The Battle Joined

1. *CW* 15: 119, 26 February 1919.
2. *CW* 15: 218–20, 14 April 1919.
3. *CW* 15: 243–4, 18 April 1919; *CW* 15: 236, 16 April 1919; *CW* 15: 238–40, 17 April 1919.
4. *CW* 15: 364–5, 12 June 1919.
5. *CW* 15: 437, 6 July 1919.

6. *CW* 15: 468–71, 21 July 1919; Peter Robb, *The Government of India and Reform: Policies Towards Politics and the Constitution 1916–1921* (Oxford, 1976), 135.

7. Judith Brown, *Gandhi's Rise to Power: Indian Politics, 1915–1922* (Cambridge, 1972), 180–85; David Hardiman, *Peasant Nationalists of Gujarat: Kheda District 1917–1934* (Delhi, 1981), 138; Robb, *The Government of India and Reform*, 134–5.

8. See Mahadev Desai, *Day-to-Day with Gandhi* (Varanasi, 1968–74), Vol. 2.

9. *CW* 86: 230, 15 December 1946.

10. *CW* 15: 86–7, 9 February 1919. Also *CW* 15: 67, 2 December 1918; *CW* 15: 104, 25 February 1919; *CW* 15: 154, 25 March 1919; *CW* 15: 166–9, 30 March 1919.

11. *CW* 17: 406–7, 12 May 1920.

12. *CW* 15: 120, 26 February 1919.

13. *CW* 15: 104, 25 February 1919.

14. *CW* 15: 179, 5 April 1919.

15. *CW* 15: 186, 6 April 1919.

16. *CW* 15: 226–7, 15 April 1919; *CW* 15: 229–30, 15 April 1919; *CW* 15: 243–4, 18 April 1919; *CW* 15: 259–60, 29 April 1919.

17. *CW* 15: 168–9, 30 March 1919.

18. Brown, *Gandhi's Rise to Power*, 232–3; *CW* 15: 334, 30 May 1919.

19. *CW* 15: 246, 21 April 1919.

20. *CW* 18: 334, 6 October 1920 (T).

21. *Autobiography*, 424.

22. *CW* 15: 332–3, 30 May 1919.

23. Brown, *Gandhi's Rise to Power*, 195–6.

24. *CW* 15: 197, 8 April 1919.

25. *CW* 15: 288–9, 8 May 1919.

26. *CW* 15: 312–13, 19 May 1919.

27. *CW* 19: 173, 29 December 1920.

28. *CW* 45: 121, 25 January 1931.

29. *CW* 30: 538, 6 June 1926 (T).

30. *CW* 15: 315, 20 May 1919 (T).

31. For background see Gail Minault, *The Khilafat Movement* (New York, 1982); Philip Hardy, *The Muslims of British India* (Cambridge, 1972); B.R. Nanda, *Gandhi: Pan-Islamism, Imperialism and Nationalism* (Bombay, 1989).

32. Nirad C. Chaudhuri, *Thy Hand, Great Anarch!* (n.p., n.d.), 19. See also Brown, *Gandhi's Rise to Power*, 316–7.

33. Brown, *Gandhi's Rise to Power*, 207–16; Nanda, *Gandhi: Pan-Islamism, Imperialism and Nationalism*, 207–8, 218–19. For Gandhi's equivocal response to Bari, see *CW* 18: 425–8, 3 November 1920; *CW* 18: 431–4, 3 November 1920 (T).

34. Nanda, *Gandhi: Pan-Islamism, Imperialism and Nationalism*, 219.

35. *CW* 17: 498–501, 20 June 1920; *CW* 96: 273, 27 March 1920; *CW* 96: 274, 17 June 1920. See also Hugh Tinker, *The Ordeal of Love* (Delhi, 1979), 164.

36. Indulal Yajnik, *Gandhi As I Know Him* (Delhi, 1943), 130–31.

37. *CW* 17: 458, 26 May 1920; *CW* 17: 475, 2 June 1920.

38. *CW* 17: 386–7, 4 May 1920 (T). Compare *CW* 17: 391, 5 May 1920.

39. Desai, *Day-to-Day with Gandhi*, Vol. 2, 154–5.

40. *CW* 17: 391, 5 May 1920.

41. *CW* 17: 477–8, 2 June 1920.

42. *CW* 17: 503, 22 June 1920.

43. *CW* 17: 521–2, 30 June 1920.

44. *CW* 17: 45, 25 February 1920.

45. *CW* 30: 229, 3 April 1926 (T).

46. *CW* 97: 32, 18 March 1920 (T).

47. *CW* 17: 503, 22 June 1920.

48. *CW* 17: 488–90, 16 June 1920. See also *CW* 18: 385, 27 October 1920 (T).

49. *CW* 17: 493–5, 20 June 1920 (T).

50. *CW* 17: 500, 20 June 1920.

51. Quoted in Brown, *Gandhi's Rise to Power*, 198.

52. *CW* 17: 489, 16 June 1920.

53. *CW* 15: 332–3, 30 May 1919.

54. Brown, *Gandhi's Rise to Power*, 236, citing H.F. Owen, 'The Leadership of the Indian National Movement, 1914–20' (Ph.D. thesis, Australian National University 1965). Gary Wills (*Cincinnatus: George Washington and the Enlightenment*, New York, 1984) has called George Washington a 'virtuoso of resignations'. The term applies to Gandhi. See also Brown, *Gandhi's Rise to Power*, 203, for another effective deployment at this time of the threat of resignation.

55. *CW* 16: 378–460, 9 January 1920.

56. *CW* 16: 410, 9 January 1920.

57. *CW* 17: 482, 9 June 1920.

58. *CW* 17: 521–2, 30 June 1920.

59. *CW* 19: 79–80, 8 December 1920; *CW* 19: 103, 13 December 1920; *CW* 19: 277–8, 26 January 1921.

60. *CW* 18: 235–6, 8 September 1920. See also, e.g., *CW* 18: 188, 21 August 1920.

61. *CW* 26: 19, 18 January 1925.

62. *CW* 17: 468, 30 May 1920 (T).

63. *CW* 92: 33, 1 July 1929.

64. *CW* 5: 469–70, 11 October 1906.

65. *CW* 14: 403, 23 May 1918. See also *CW* 32: 341–2, 26 October 1926; *CW* 73: 12, 15 September 1940 (T).

66. James Hunt, *Gandhi in London* (Delhi, 1978), 59, has noted the similarity between Gandhi's description of the English character in 1906 and the ideal man of the *Gita*.

67. *CW* 16: 491, 'After January 18, 1920'.

68. *CW* 7: 122, 27 July 1907 (T).

69. *CW* 13: 65, 27 April 1915.

70. *CW* 48: 147, 13 October 1931.

71. *CW* 22: 140, 5 January 1922.

72. *CW* 22: 460–63, 23 February 1922. For the adventures of Paul Richard, see Michel Richard, *Without Passport: The Life and Work of Paul Richard* (New York, *c.* 1987).

73. *CW* 35: 457, 12 January 1928.

74. Lionel Curtis, *Civitas Dei* (London, 1934–7), Vol. 1, p, 164.

75. Anna Kingsford and Edward Maitland, *The Perfect Way; or, the Finding of Christ* (London, 1923 [1882]), 252–7; and see Chapter 2, 41.

76. Annie Besant, *Avatâras* (London, 1900), 122–4.

77. Catherine Wessinger, *Annie Besant and Progressive Messianism* (New York, 1988), ch. 6.
78. *CW* 17: 107, 21 March 1920 (T); also *CW* 22: 289, 29 January 1922 (T).
79. *CW* 20: 157, 1 June 1921. See also *CW* 15: 126, 'On or after March 5, 1919' (T); *CW* 43: 52, 12 March 1930.
80. *CW* 18: 387, 27 October 1920 (T).
81. *CW* 17: 535–40, 'Before July 1920' (T).
82. *CW* 13: 34, 4 March 1915 (T).
83. *CW* 18: 345–8, 13 October 1920.
84. *CW* 18: 347, 13 October 1920.
85. Esther Faering, *'My Dear Child'* (Ahmedabad, 1956). See also *CW* 16 and 17.
86. *CW* 16: 506, 25 January 1920.
87. *CW* 17: 95, 18 March 1920.
88. *CW* 17: 43, 22 February 1920.
89. *CW* 17: 436, 20 May 1920 (T). See also Stanley Wolpert, *Gandhi's Passion* (Oxford, 2001), 104–6.
90. *CW* 17: 532–3, 15 May 1920 (T).
91. For Saraladevi, see Martin Green, *Gandhi: Voice of a New Age Revolution* (New York, 1993), 273–85.
92. *CW* 18: 130, 10 August 1920.
93. *CW* 17: 359, 30 April 1920.
94. *CW* 17: 375, 2 May 1920.
95. *CW* 17: 384, 3 May 1920.
96. *CW* 18: 191, 23 August 1920.
97. *CW* 19: 138, 17 December 1920.
98. *CW* 19: 137, 17 December 1920.
99. *CW* 18: 92, 28 July 1920.
100. *CW* 18: 117, 4 August 1920.
101. *CW* 19: 257, 19 January 1921 (T).
102. *CW* 21: 439, 17 November 1921.
103. *CW* 21: 474, 20 November 1921 (T).
104. *CW* 21: 484, 24 November 1921.
105. *CW* 20: 381–2, 17 July 1921 (T).
106. *CW* 54: 399, 13 April 1933 (T).
107. *CW* 19: 180–81.
108. *CW* 95: 214, n.d. (T).
109. *CW* 16: 283, 3 November 1919 (T).
110. *CW* 21: 325–6, 20 October 1921 (T).
111. *CW* 18: 209, 29 August 1920 (T).
112. *CW* 18: 361, 20 October 1920.
113. *CW* 18: 242, 8 September 1920.
114. *CW* 18: 361, 20 October 1920. See also, on the general topic of Gandhi's organization of protest, Ranajit Guha, 'Discipline and Mobilize' in *Subaltern Studies VII* (Delhi, 1992).
115. *CW* 18: 243, 8 September 1920; *CW* 18: 244–5, 8 September 1920.
116. *CW* 18: 241–2, 8 September 1920.
117. Shahid Amin, 'Gandhi as Mahatma: Gorakhpur District, Eastern UP, 1921–2',

in Ranajit Guha and Gayatri Spivak, eds, *Selected Subaltern Studies* (New York and Oxford, 1988).

118. Ghanshyam Shah, 'Traditional Society and Political Mobilization: The Experience of Bardoli Satyagraha (1920–1928)', *Contributions to Indian Sociology* 8, 1974, 96.

119. Ved Mehta, *Mahatma Gandhi and His Apostles* (New Haven, 1993 [1977]), 204.

120. Desai, *Day-to-Day with Gandhi*, Vol. 5, 313.

121. *CW* 21: 73, 8 September 1921.

122. See W.F. Crawley, 'Kisan Sabhas and Agrarian Revolt in the United Provinces', *Modern Asian Studies* 5, 1971; Gyanendra Pandey, 'Peasant Revolt and Indian Nationalism: The Peasant Movement in Awadh, 1919–22', Guha and Spivak, eds, *Selected Subaltern Studies*.

123. Brown, *Gandhi's Rise to Power*, 321.

124. David Hardiman, 'Adivasi Assertion in South Gujarat: The Devi Movement of 1922–3', in *Subaltern Studies III* (Delhi, 1984), 226.

125. See 'The Moplah Rebellion (1921)' in Parshotam Mehra, *A Dictionary of Modern Indian History, 1707–1947* (Oxford, 1985), which summarizes the conflicting views, with references. Stephen F. Dale, *Islamic Society on the South Asian Frontier: The Mappilas of Malabar 1498–1922* (Oxford, 1980), gives a comprehensive history of the Moplahs.

126. See *CW* 21: 47–9, 4 September 1921 (T); *CW* 21: 70–72, 8 September 1921; *CW* 21: 112–3, 16 September 1921; *CW* 21: 204–5, 25 September 1921 (T); *CW* 21: 320–22, 20 October 1921; *CW* 21: 345, 27 October 1921; *CW* 21: 542–4, 8 December 1921.

127. *CW* 19: 91, 8 December 1920 (T).

128. *CW* 19: 230, 13 January 1921 (T).

129. *CW* 19: 574–5, 13 April 1921.

130. *CW* 20: 70–72, 8 May 1921 (T).

131. *CW* 20: 513–14, 14 August 1921 (T).

132. *CW* 19: 572, 13 April 1921.

133. *CW* 21: 148–9, 19 September 1921.

134. *CW* 21: 235–6, 4 October 1921.

135. *CW* 21: 331–2, 23 October 1921 (T). See also Yajnik, *Gandhi As I Know Him*, 254.

136. *CW* 21: 455–7, 17 November 1921.

137. *CW* 21: 459–61, 17 November 1921.

138. *CW* 21: 461–2, 17 November 1921 (T).

139. *CW* 21: 480–81, 24 November 1921.

140. See the talks Gandhi gave to the Gandhi Seva Sangh in March 1938 (*CW* 66: 424–33, 26 March 1938 (T); *CW* 66: 444–50, 28 March 1938 (T)).

141. *CW* 21: 491, 27 November 1921 (T).

142. Yajnik, *Gandhi As I Know Him*, 252–5; Krishnadas, *Seven Months with Mahatma Gandhi* (Ahmedabad, 1951), ch. 27.

143. *CW* 21: 539, 8 December 1921.

144. *CW* 22: 64, 67, 18 December 1921; *CW* 22: 89, 24 December 1921.

145. *CW* 22: 68, 19 December 1921.

146. *CW* 21: 560–63, 11 December 1921 (T).

147. *CW* 22: 299, 31 January 1922 (T).

148. *CW* 22: 302–5, 1 February 1922. (The ultimatum was in the form of a letter to the viceroy, dated 1 February 1922, and presumably sent on that date. It was published in the newspapers on 4 February, before a response had been received.)

149. *CW* 22: 344–50, 7 February 1922.

150. *Bombay Chronicle*, 7 February 1922, 5. Shahid Amin's *Event, Metaphor, Memory: Chauri Chaura 1922–1992* (Berkeley, 1995), has much of interest to say about the events of 4 February and their persistence in folk memory and nationalist historiography.

151. *CW* 22: 350–51, 8 February 1922.

152. *CW* 22: 345, 348, 7 February 1922.

153. *CW* 22: 351, 8 February 1922.

154. *CW* 22: 416, 16 February 1922.

155. *CW* 22: 374, 9 February 1922; M.R. Jayakar, *The Story of My Life* (Bombay, 1958), Vol. I, 555.

156. *CW* 22: 377–81, 12 February 1922.

157. [Romain Rolland,] *Romain Rolland and Gandhi Correspondence* (Delhi, 1976), 19.

158. The following account is based on these sources: the Allahabad *Leader* and the *Bombay Chronicle* for the first half of February 1922; Gandhi's incoming correspondence for the same period, held at the Gandhi Library, Sabarmati Ashram, with photocopies available at the National Gandhi Museum and Library, New Delhi; Krishnadas, *Seven Months with Mahatma Gandhi*, ch. 34; Pyarelal and Sushila Nayar, *In Gandhiji's Mirror* (Delhi, 1991), 113–15.

159. *Leader*, 15 February 1922, 6.

160. *CW* 22: 425, 19 February 1922 (T). See also Sushila Nayar, *Mahatma Gandhi – India Awakened* (Ahmedabad, 1994), 391, and Yajnik, *Gandhi as I Know Him*, 281. Yajnik says Gandhi called off the campaign 'Because his pet youngest son, Devidas, telegraphed to him "Grave news of serious riots"' at Chauri Chaura. He gives no date but seems to suggest 8 February.

161. *CW* 22: 435–7, 18 February 1922.

162. *CW* 22: 255, 26 January 1922.

163. Romain Rolland, *Mahatma Gandhi: The Man Who Became One with the Universal Being* (New York, 1973; first published in French in 1923 and English in 1924), 200.

164. *CW* 22: 387, 12 February 1922 (T).

165. *CW* 22: 425, 19 February 1922 (T).

166. *CW* 22: 417,419, 16 February 1922; *CW* 22: 425–6, 19 February 1922 (T).

167. *CW* 22: 404–8, 15 February 1922.

168. *CW* 22: 413, 16 February 1922.

169. *CW* 22: 468–9, 25 February 1922. Gandhi at this time was distinguishing between 'defensive' individual civil disobedience (law-breaking for the purpose of conducting a normal activity) and 'aggressive' or 'offensive' individual civil disobedience (law-breaking for the purpose of breaking the law). Both were permitted in the 25 February resolution. It was 'offensive' individual civil disobedience whose postponement had been envisaged 'for some time' on 16 February (*CW* 22: 413).

170. *CW* 22: 500–504, 2 March 1922.

171. *CW* 23: 20, 6 March 1922 (T).
172. *CW* 22: 415–21, 16 February 1922.
173. Quoted in Judith Brown, *Gandhi and Civil Disobedience: The Mahatma in Indian Politics 1928–34* (Cambridge, 1977) xvii–xviii. See also Nanda, *Gandhi: Pan-Islamism, Imperialism and Nationalism*, 356.
174. *CW* 22: 406, 15 February 1922.
175. *CW* 23: 21, 7 March 1922.
176. *CW* 17: 406, 12 May 1920.
177. Kingsford and Maitland, *The Perfect Way*, 44, 60.

# 6. In the Wings

1. *CW* 23: 100, 17 March 1922 (T).
2. *CW* 17: 405, 12 May 1922.
3. Sabyasachi Bhattacharya, ed., *The Mahatma and the Poet: Letters and Debates Between Gandhi and Tagore 1915–1941* (Delhi, 1997), 59.
4. *CW* 20: 163, 1 June 1921.
5. Bhattacharya, ed., *The Mahatma and the Poet*, 68–87; *CW* 21: 287–91, 13 October 1921.
6. Sankaran Nair, *Gandhi and Anarchy* (Madras, 1922); Sushila Nayar, *Mahatma Gandhi – India Awakened* (Ahmedabad, 1994), 298; Geoffrey Ashe, *Gandhi* (New York, 1968), 243.
7. *CW* 21: 474, 20 November 1921 (T).
8. *CW* 47: 307, 18 August 1931.
9. *CW* 59: 308, 9 November 1934.
10. See especially *CW* 96, Appendix 4, 23 November 1939.
11. Quoted in James Hunt, *Gandhi and the Nonconformists* (Delhi, 1986), 105. The Transvaal Chinese Association allied itself with Gandhi on the registration issue and took part in the *satyagraha* campaign.
12. C.F. Andrews, *India and the Simon Report* (London, 1930), 120–21.
13. *CW* 60: 23, 22 December 1934 (T).
14. Andrews's Gandhi 'trilogy' comprised: *Mahatma Gandhi's Ideas* (London, 1929), *Mahatma Gandhi: His Own Story* (London, 1930), *Mahatma Gandhi at Work* (London, 1931).
15. C.F. Andrews, *What I Owe to Christ* (London, 1932), 73.
16. Hugh Tinker, *The Ordeal of Love* (Delhi, 1979), 88. I rely for what follows on Tinker, *The Ordeal of Love*, ch. 5; Andrews, *What I Owe to Christ*; and the three articles contributed by Andrews to the Calcutta publication *The Modern Review* in 1922 ('Buddhism and Christianity', July 1922; 'Buddhism and Christianity (Continued)', August 1922; 'Buddhism and Christianity: A Postscript', September 1922).
17. Andrews, *What I Owe to Christ*, 156.
18. Ibid., 214.
19. Ibid., 247.

20. Ibid., 214, 231. See also 85–6 on the Kingdom of God as the earthly manifestation of divine love.

21. E. Stanley Jones. *The Christ of the Indian Road* (London, 1926 [1925]); S.K. George, *Gandhi's Challenge to Christianity* (London, 1939).

22. John Haynes Holmes and Donald S. Harrington, *The Enduring Greatness of Gandhi: An American Estimate*, ed. Haridas T. Mazumdar (Ahmedabad, 1982), 3–25. For more on Holmes, see C. Seshachari, *Gandhi and the American Scene: An Intellectual History and Inquiry* (Bombay, 1969), 109–14.

23. John Haynes Holmes, 'Introduction' to C.F. Andrews, *Mahatma Gandhi: His Own Story* (New York, 1930), 31–2.

24. Holmes, 'Introduction', 20; John Haynes Holmes, *My Gandhi* (London 1954), 180.

25. Romain Rolland, *Mahatma Gandhi: The Man Who Became One with the Universal Being* (New York, 1973 [1923]), 247.

26. Romain Rolland, *Above the Battle* (London, 1916).

27. Romain Rolland, *Beethoven* (Paris, 1903).

28. Rolland, *Mahatma Gandhi*, 206, 248.

29. David James Fisher, *Romain Rolland and the Politics of Intellectual Engagement* (Berkeley, 1988), 8–12.

30. Romain Rolland, *Prophets of the New India* (London, 1930). The studies of Ramakrishna and Vivekanda were combined in one volume in the English edition.

31. [Romain Rolland,] *Romain Rolland and Gandhi Correspondence* (Delhi, 1976), 111–14.

32. See, e.g., Robert Graves, *Lawrence and the Arabs* (London, 1927) and Basil Liddell Hart, '*T.E. Lawrence' in Arabia and After* (London, 1934).

33. K.M. Munshi, *I Follow the Mahatma* (Bombay, 1940), 153–4.

34. Mahadev Desai, *Day-to-Day with Gandhi* (Varanasi, 1968–74), Vol. 3, 312.

35. *CW* 31: 540–41, 'Before October 29, 1926'.

36. Paul Richard, *The Scourge of Christ* (New York, 1929), 216. This long poem was begun during the First World War. The French original seems never to have been published. Richard's *Dawn Over Asia*, translated into English by Aurobindo Ghose, was published in Madras in 1920. His *To the Nations* was published in New York in 1917 with an introduction by Tagore. The same themes appear in them all.

37. *CW* 48: 281–2, 11 November 1931; Holmes and Harrington, *The Enduring Greatness of Mahatma Gandhi*, 111–12.

38. *CW* 25: 116–17, 11 September 1924.

39. P.V. George, *The Unique Christ and the Mystic Gandhi* (Tiruvalla, 1933).

40. *CW* 28: 431, 5 November 1925.

41. See e.g., *CW* 42: 435, 30 January 1930.

42. *CW* 29: 382, 7 January 1926.

43. *CW* 28: 303, 8 October 1925.

44. *CW* 25: 536, 11 January 1925 (T).

45. *CW* 23: 348, 3 April 1924.

46. *CW* 24: 323, 29 June 1924 (T).

47. Swami Paramahansa Yogananda, *Autobiography of a Yogi* (Los Angeles, 1981 [1946]), 421.

48. *CW* 23: 200–201, 7 February 1924.

49. *CW* 24: 268–9, 19 June 1924; *CW* 24: 310, 17 July 1924 (T).

50. This is clear from his account in *CW* 24: 334–40, 3 July 1924, entitled 'Defeated and Humbled'.

51. *CW* 24: 307, 28 June 1924 (T).

52. *CW* 24: 311, 28 June 1924 (T).

53. *CW* 24: 337, 3 July 1924.

54. *CW* 24: 334, 3 July 1924.

55. *CW* 25: 97, 6 September 1924.

56. *CW* 25: 99, 6 September 1924.

57. *CW* 25: 129–30, 11 September 1924; *CW* 25: 140, 14 September 1924 (T). See also *CW* 25: 258–60, 23 October 1924, 'The Law of Love'.

58. *CW* 25: 111, 10 September 1924 (T).

59. *CW* 25: 149, 15 September 1924.

60. *CW* 25: 139–40, 15 September 1924 (T). See also *CW* 25: 229, 19 October 1924 (T) and *CW* 25: 235, 15 October 1924.

61. *CW* 25: 171, 18 September 1924.

62. *CW* 25: 174–6, 18 September 1924; *CW* 25: 181–4, 19 September 1924. See also Desai, *Day-to-Day with Gandhi*, Vol. 4, 190–211.

63. *CW* 25: 175, 18 September 1924.

64. *CW* 25: 225, 8 October 1924 (T).

65. *CW* 25: 381, 1 December 1924 (T).

66. *CW* 25: 448, 21 December 1924.

67. Aurobindo Ghose, *The Doctrine of Passive Resistance* (Pondicherry, 1952; first published as a series of articles in *Bande Mataram* in April 1907).

68. *CW* 27: 400–401, 'On or before July 22, 1925'. See also *CW* 23: 13–14, 5 March 1922 (T); *CW* 33: 88–9, 16 February 1927; *CW* 78: 64, 1 September 1944 (T).

69. *CW* 25: 316, 14 November 1924; Samuel E. [Satyanand] Stokes, *National Self-Realization and Other Essays* (Delhi, 1977), ch. 21.

70. *CW* 25: 231, 15 October 1924; *CW* 25: 237, 16 October 1924; *CW* 25: 587, 15 January 1925.

71. *CW* 21: 291, 13 October 1921; *CW* 21: 307–8, 20 October 1921.

72. Annie Besant, *In the Outer Court* (London, 1906, based on lectures given in 1895), 124–8.

73. *CW* 10: 356, 'After November 16, 1910' (T).

74. *CW* 15: 340, 1 June 1919 (T).

75. *CW* 96: 278, 29 August 1921.

76. *CW* 19: 241, 19 January 1921.

77. *CW* 23: 134, 14 April 1922.

78. *CW* 30: 452, 27 May 1926. Compare *Huckleberry Finn*: 'When I got a little ways I heard the dim hum of a spinning wheel wailing along up and sinking down again; and then I knowed for certain I wished I was dead – for that is the lonesomest sound in the whole world.'

79. *CW* 21: 179, 22 September 1921.

80. *CW* 32: 163, 15 April 1925 (T).

81. *CW* 46: 254–7. 18 June 1931.
82. Bhattacharya, ed., *The Mahatma and the Poet*, 109.
83. See, e.g., *CW* 95: 181, n.d. (T).
84. After three years at Sabarmati Slade decided to leave and work independently in Bihar (*CW* 38: 43, 12 November 1928; *CW* 38: 77, 19 November 1928). Books by foreigners giving accounts of ashram life include Nilla Cram Cook, *My Road to India* (New York, 1939); Verrier Elwin, *The Tribal World of Verrier Elwin* (Oxford, 1964); and Reginald Reynolds, *A Quest for Gandhi* (New York, 1952). Two books by Indians which contain much interesting material are Balvantsinha, *Under the Shelter of Bapu* (Ahmedabad, 1956) and Narayan Desai, *Blessed was it to be Young – with Gandhi* (Bombay, 1967). Narayan Desai was Mahadev's son.
85. Desai, *Day-to-Day with Gandhi*, Volume 7, 272.
86. *CW* 54: 13, 8 March 1933 (T).
87. *CW* 60: 399, 8 April 1935 (T). See also *CW* 71: 278, 22 February 1940 (T).
88. *CW* 50: 353–4, 11 August 1932 (T); Pyarelal and Sushila Nayar, *In Gandhiji's Mirror* (Delhi, 1991), 88, 90.
89. Pyarelal, *Mahatma Gandhi – The Early Phase* (Ahmedabad, 1966 [1956]), 15.
90. *CW* 30: 229–30, 3 April 1926 (T).
91. *CW* 27: 259–62, 18 June 1925.
92. *CW* 91: 315, 27 July 1925 (T).
93. *CW* 30: 512, 30 May 1926 (T).
94. *CW* 34: 19, 17 June 1927 (T).
95. *CW* 49: 374–5, 27 April 1932 (T).
96. *CW* 36: 261–3, 26 April 1928.
97. *CW* 36: 270, 26 April 1928; *CW* 36: 307, 11 May 1928.
98. *CW* 36: 342, 26 May 1928.
99. The *Discourses on the 'Gita'* are in *CW* 32: 94–376; *Anasaktiyoga* is in *CW* 41 90–133; *Letters on the 'Gita'* is in *CW* 49 111–49. Gandhi summarized his approach to interpreting the *Gita* in the article 'Meaning of the "Gita"' (*CW* 28: 315–21, 11 October 1925 (T)).
100. *CW* 41: 96. J.T.F. Jordens, 'Gandhi and the *Bhagavadgita*', in Robert N. Minor, ed., *Modern Indian Interpreters of the Bhagavadgita* (Albany, 1986), takes the measure of Gandhi's unorthodoxy and notes the correspondence between some of his ideas and those of Edward Maitland (pp. 90, 106).
101. See Chapter 3, 97–8, and Chapter 5, 167.
102. *CW* 32: 188–93.
103. *CW* 41: 109.
104. Mahadev Desai, 'My Submission', in *The Gita According to Gandhi* (Ahmedabad, 1984), 48.
105. *CW* 32: 270.
106. *CW* 32: 194.
107. *CW* 32: 270.
108. *CW* 32: 209.
109. *CW* 32: 327.
110. *CW* 31: 350–51, 2 September 1926.
111. Desai, *Day-to-Day with Gandhi*, Vol. 8, 216, 226–32, 234–5, 242–3, 259–62, 284–9, 298–300, 304–9.

112. See Gyanendra Pandey, *The Ascendancy of the Congress in Uttar Pradesh 1926–34: A Study in Imperfect Mobilization* (Delhi, 1978), ch. 5, for a close study of the process in the United Provinces.

113. *CW* 31: 368, 9 September 1926.

114. *CW* 25: 178–9, 19 September 1924.

115. See Tinker, *The Ordeal of Love, passim.*

116. *CW* 32: 458–62, 26 December 1926.

117. *CW* 31: 318, 20 August 1926.

118. *CW* 32: 387, 4 December 1926 (T); also *CW* 32: 440–41, 20 December 1926 (T).

119. *CW* 32: 466, 27 December 1926.

120. *CW* 32: 470, 28 December 1926.

121. *CW* 33: 163–7, 17 March 1927. For extracts from Saklatvala's open letter see *CW* 33: Appendix 1.

122. *CW* 33: 189, 24 March 1927.

123. *CW* 33: 168–9, 19 March 1927. For more, see Desai, *Day-to-Day with Gandhi*, Vol. 9, 281–99.

124. *CW* 33: 201, 28 March 1927 (T).

125. *CW* 24: 116, 25 May 1924 (T).

126. *CW* 33: 215–16, 6 April 1927 (T); *CW* 33: 229, 11 April 1927 (T); *CW* 33: 236–7, 14 April 1927 (T); *CW* 33: 429–303, June 1927 (T).

127. See, e.g., *CW* 33: 338, 19 May 1927; *CW* 34: 94, 2 July 1927 (T); *CW* 91: 420, 'Before May 10, 1927' (T).

128. *CW* 33: 261, 26 April 1927.

129. *CW* 33: 263–4, 27 April 1927 (T).

130. *CW* 34: 334, 12 August 1927 (T); *CW* 34: 505, 10 September 1927.

131. *CW* 33: 322, 14 May 1927; *CW* 34: 2–4, 16 June 1927. See also *CW* 34: 22–4, 19 June 1927 (T) on the Jains.

132. See *CW* 33: 298–9, 8 May 1927; and *CW* 33: 301–3, 10 May 1927.

133. *CW* 34: 539–47, 15 September 1927; see also *CW* 40, 21 March 1929.

# 7. Salt

1. *CW* 34: 31, 19 June 1927; *CW* 34: 304–6, 10 August 1927.

2. *CW* 35: 432–4, 4 January 1928; *CW* 35: 469–70, 17 January 1928; Sarvepalli Gopal, *Jawaharlal Nehru: A Biography* (Delhi, 1993), 60.

3. *CW* 36: 49, 24 February 1928; also *CW* 36: 15, 9 February 1928; *CW* 36: 77, 3 March 1928; *CW* 36: 171, 1 April 1928 (T).

4. *CW* 36: 22–3, 'Before February 12, 1928'.

5. *CW* 37: 85, 22 July 1928 (T).

6. *CW* 36: 35–6, 19 February 1928 (T).

7. *CW* 65: 129, 20 April 1928 (T).

8. Ghanshyam Shah, 'Traditional Society and Political Mobilization: The Experience of Bardoli Satyagraha (1920–1928)', *Contributions to Indian Sociology* 8, 1974: 98. The official version of the Bardoli campaign can be found in Mahadev Desai, *The Story of Bardoli* (Ahmedabad, 1929).

9. Shah, 'Traditional Society and Political Mobilization', 96.
10. Jugatram Dave, quoted in Jan Breman, *Of Peasants, Migrants and Paupers: Rural Labour Circulation and Capitalist Production in West India* (Delhi, 1985), 137.
11. *CW* 37: 152, 11 August 1928.
12. A veteran proponent of *swadeshi*, Rai had remained a supporter of Indian mill production and ideologically uncommitted to *khadi*. In the early months of 1928 Gandhi had been angling inconclusively for his support of a foreign cloth boycott anchored in the *khadi* movement. (See *CW* 36: 207–8, 8 April 1928; *CW* 36: 283, 29 April 1928; *CW* 36: 311–2, 12 May 1928.) He had been a late convert to non-cooperation.
13. *CW* 38: 65, 17 November 1928.
14. *CW* 38: 129–32, 30 November 1928. For extracts from Shaukat Ali's letter, to which Gandhi was replying, see *CW* 38, Appendix 2.
15. *CW* 38: 136–8, 6 December 1928.
16. *CW* 36: 76, 3 March 1928.
17. *CW* 37: 374, 18 October 1928.
18. *CW* 38: 267–73, 26 December 1928; *CW* 38: 283–96, 28 December 1928.
19. *CW* 36: 282, 29 April 1928.
20. For early examples of this view, see *CW* 43: 306–8, 24 April 1930; *CW* 45: 376–7, 1 April 1931.
21. *CW* 38: 5, 1 November 1928.
22. *CW* 36: 90, 8 March 1928.
23. *CW* 38: 4, 1 November 1928; *CW* 38: 29–30, 8 November 1928.
24. *CW* 37: 58–9, 15 July 1928 (T).
25. *CW* 38: 292–3, 28 December 1928.
26. *CW* 38: 313–14, 1 January 1929.
27. *CW* 40: 209–12, 8 April 1929.
28. *CW* 40: 311, 'Before April 30, 1929' (T).
29. *CW* 41: 211, 21 July 1929 (T).
30. See Kathryn Tidrick, *Empire and the English Character* (London, 1990), 244–5.
31. *CW* 42: 235, 2 December 1929 (T); *CW* 42: 251, 8 December 1929 (T); *CW* 42: 392–3, 12 January 1930.
32. *CW* 42: 382–3, 10 January 1930.
33. *CW* 42: 419, 22 January 1930; see also *CW* 42: 414, 18 January 1930 (T).
34. *CW* 42: 455, 6 February 1930.
35. *CW* 42: 444, 2 February 1930.
36. *CW* 42: 511, 16 February 1930.
37. *CW* 43: 39, 'On or before March 11, 1930'; see also *CW* 43: 126, 26 March 1930 (T).
38. *CW* 42: 497, 27 February 1930.
39. *CW* 42: 480, 20 February 1930.
40. *CW* 42: 481, 20 February 1930.
41. *CW* 42: 389, 11 January 1930.
42. *CW* 42: 444, 2 February 1930; see also *CW* 42: 483, 20 February 1930.
43. *CW* 42: 497, 27 February 1930.
44. *CW* 42: 434, 30 January 1930.
45. *CW* 42: 469–70, 13 February 1930; *CW* 43: 57–9, 12 March 1930.

46. *CW* 43: 45, 'On or before March 11, 1930'.
47. *CW* 42: 500–501, 27 February 1930.
48. *CW* 42: 470–71, 13 February 1930; also *CW* 92: 171, 3 March 1930.
49. *CW* 41 140–41, 30 June 1929 (T).
50. *CW* 43: 30–31, 'Before March 9, 1930'.
51. *New York Evening Post*, 5 April 1930, 2; *New York Times*, 6 April 1930, 1, 2; Katherine Mayo, 'Gandhi's March Past', *Atlantic Monthly*, September 1930, 327–8; Prema Kantak, 'At Sabarmati', in Chandrashanker Shukla, ed., *Reminiscences of Gandhiji* (Bombay, 1951), 149–50; *CW* 43: 91–2, 17 March 1930 (T); *CW* 43: 97–8, 'After March 17, 1930' (T).
52. *CW* 43: 97–8, 'After March 17, 1930' (T).
53. *CW* 43: 73, 14 March 1930.
54. *CW* 43: 146–9, 29 March 1930.
55. *CW* 43: 46–8, 11 March 1930.
56. *CW* 43: 41, 'On or before March 11, 1930'.
57. *CW* 95: 80, 2 April 1930 (T).
58. Sardar Patel had been in the villages of Gujarat in the first months of 1930 making arrangements for the mass campaign. David Hardiman, *Peasant Nationalists of Gujarat: Kheda District 1917–1934* (Delhi, 1981), 190–91, suggests that Patel organized a land revenue refusal campaign in defiance of Gandhi's orders. It is not clear where Gandhi stood on the land revenue question. His apparent hesitations may have reflected a concern with timing. See Sushila Nayar, *Mahatma Gandhi – Salt Satyagraha: The Watershed* (Ahmedabad, 1995), 243–4; *CW* 43: 217, 9 April 1930 (T); *CW* 43: 340–41, 27 April 1930 (T).
59. *CW* 43: 70–72, 13 March 1930 (T).
60. *CW* 43: 125, 26 March 1930 (T).
61. *CW* 43: 145, 28 March 1930 (T).
62. *CW* 43: 216, 9 April 1930 (T).
63. *CW* 43: 343, 27 April 1930 (T).
64. *CW* 43: 213, 8 April 1930 (T); *CW* 43: 214–5, 9 April 1930; *CW* 43: 262, 15 April 1930.
65. *CW* 43: 261, 15 April 1930 (T).
66. *CW* 43: 268–70, 17 April 1930.
67. *CW* 43: 327–8, 26 April 1930 (T).
68. *CW* 43: 297, 21 April 1930.
69. *CW* 43: 339, 27 April 1930 (T).
70. *CW* 43: 280, 17 April 1930.
71. *CW* 43: 329–30, 26 April 1930 (T).
72. *CW* 43: 389–93, 4 May 1930.
73. Irwin to Secretary of State, 29 April 1930, quoted in Brown, *Gandhi and Civil Disobedience*, 110–11.
74. An earlier, smaller 'raid' took place under Sarojini Naidu's leadership on 16 May. The volunteers advanced towards the salt works and sat down when they reached the police cordon; 220 were arrested. On 21 May the volunteers kept on advancing. Manilal returned to South Africa in 1931 and was active in the non-violent opposition to apartheid until his death in 1956.
75. *CW* 44: 184, 30 September 1930.

76. *CW* 44: 117–21, 5 September 1930. See Judith Brown, *Gandhi and Civil Disobedience: The Mahatma in Indian Politics 1928–34* (Cambridge, 1977), 157–68, for an account of the negotiations.

77. Appearances were deceiving. See R.J. Moore, *Endgames of Empire: Studies of Britain's Indian Problem* (Delhi, 1988), 46–8.

78. *CW* 45: 175–6, 14 February 1931.

79. See Sumit Sarkar, 'The Logic of Gandhian Nationalism: Civil Disobedience and the Gandhi–Irwin Pact (1930–1931)', *Indian Historical Review* 3, 1976.

80. *CW* 45: 132–3, 31 January 1931 (T); *CW* 45: 136–7, 1 February 1931.

81. *CW* 43: 252, 13 April 1930 (T).

82. *CW* 45: 142, 2 February 1931 (T).

83. *CW* 45: 145, 2 February 1931 (T).

84. *CW* 45: 142, 2 February 1931 (T).

85. *CW* 45: 169, 10 February 1931.

86. *CW* 45: 169, 10 February 1931.

87. *CW* 45: 180–81, 16 February 1931 (T).

88. See Tidrick, *Empire and the English Character*, 240–49.

89. Irwin to G.R. Lane-Fox, 31 March 1930, quoted in S.R. Bakshi, *Gandhi and Salt Satyagraha* (Kerala, 1981), 61.

90. Irwin to Secretary of State, 16 February 1931, quoted in Lord Birkenhead, *Halifax: The Life of Lord Halifax* (Boston, 1966), 296.

91. In Robert Rhodes James (ed.), *Winston S. Churchill: His Complete Speeches* (New York, 1974), Vol. 5, 4985.

92. Quoted in Brown, *Gandhi and Civil Disobedience*, 178.

93. The text of the agreement is in *CW* 45: Appendix 6. For the talks, see *CW* 45: 185–268.

94. *Satyagraha in South Africa* (*CW* 29), 166–7.

95. *CW* 45: 188, 17 February 1931 (T).

96. *CW* 45: 200, 18 February 1931 (T).

97. *CW* 45: 201, 18 February 1931 (T).

98. *CW* 45: 201, 18 February 1931 (T).

99. *CW* 45: 244, 4 March 1931.

100. K.P. Thomas, *B.C. Roy, the Congressman from Bengal* (Calcutta, 1955) 164–5.

101. *CW* 46: 52, 20 April 1931.

102. Brown, *Gandhi and Civil Disobedience*, 204–5.

103. *CW* 45: 403, 9 April 1931.

104. *CW* 45: 404, 9 April 1931.

105. *CW* 47: 133, 'Before July 15, 1931'.

106. *CW* 47: 319–22, 20 August 1931.

107. *CW* 45: 269–74, 7 March 1931.

108. *CW* 45: 380–84, 1 April 1931 (T).

109. *CW* 45: 394, 6 April 1931.

110. *CW* 47: 284, 'After August 12, 1931' (T).

111. Willingdon to Secretary of State, 28 August 1931, quoted in Brown, *Gandhi and Civil Disobedience*, 239.

112. *CW* 47: 367–9, 28 August 1931.

113. *CW* 47: 372, 28 August 1931.

# 8. The Solitary Path

1. *CW* 47: 391, 4 September 1931.
2. Chandrashanker Shukla, ed., *Incidents of Gandhi's Life* (Bombay, 1949), 24.
3. *CW* 47: 384, 29 August 1931.
4. *CW* 48: 19, 15 September 1931.
5. *CW* 48: 1, 12 September 1931.
6. *CW* 48: 3–4, 12 September 1931; *CW* 48: 8–9, 13 September 1931; *CW* 48: 45, 20 September 1931.
7. *CW* 48: 19, 15 September 1931.
8. *CW* 48: 5, 12 September 1931 (from the report in the *Sunday Times*).
9. See, e.g., *CW* 48: 96, 30 September 1931 (the British note on Gandhi's conversation with MacDonald).
10. See Judith Brown, *Gandhi and Civil Disobedience: The Mahatma in Indian Politics 1928–34* (Cambridge, 1977), 248; R.J. Moore, *The Crisis of Indian Unity 1912–1940* (Oxford, 1974), 220–21.
11. *CW* 48: 179, 'On or after October 17, 1931'.
12. *The Times*, 31 January 1948, quoted in James Hunt, *Gandhi in London* (Delhi, 1978) 201.
13. *CW* 48: 365, 1 December 1931; *CW* 48: 372–4, 1 December 1931.
14. *CW* 48: 298, 13 November 1931.
15. *CW* 48: 289, 12 November 1931.
16. *CW* 48: 381, 3 December 1931.
17. Mahadev Desai, *The Nation's Voice* (Ahmedabad, 1932), 149.
18. *CW* 48: 263, 1 November 1931.
19. *CW* 48: 221, 23 October 1931.
20. Subhas Chandra Bose, *The Indian Struggle 1920–1942* (Bombay, 1964), 227–8.
21. *CW* 48: Appendix 1, 496–7.
22. *CW* 48: 434, 23 December 1931.
23. *CW* 28: 186–9, 17 September 1925.
24. Rolland's account of the visit is in [Romain Rolland,] *Romain Rolland and Gandhi Correspondence* (Delhi, 1976), 163–224; Mahadev Desai's account is in *CW* 48: 395–8; 6 December 1931; *CW* 48: 401–22, 8 December 1931 to 'On or after December 10, 1931'.
25. *CW* 48: 429–30, 20 December 1931.
26. *CW* 48: 434, 23 December 1931; Sushila Nayar, *Mahatma Gandhi – Salt Satyagraha: The Watershed* (Ahmedabad, 1995), 401.
27. *CW* 48: 437–9, 25 December 1931.
28. *CW* 48: 492, 3 January 1932.
29. *CW* 48: 479, 2 January 1932.
30. Mahadev Desai, *The Diary of Mahadev Desai* (Ahmedabad, 1953), 26.
31. *CW* 49: 191, 11 March 1932.
32. Desai, *The Diary of Mahadev Desai*, 29.
33. R.C. Zaehner (ed.), *Hindu Scriptures* (London, 1966) 165; Patrick Olivelle, *Upanishads* (Oxford, 1996), 248.
34. *CW* 58: 183, 13 July 1934 (T).
35. *CW* 64: 294, 20 January 1937.

36. *CW* 64: 259, 16 January 1937.

37. See, e.g., *CW* 51: 50, 13 September 1932 (T).

38. *CW* 51: 55, 15 September 1932; *CW* 51: 65, 16 September 1932.

39. Quoted in B.R. Nanda, *Gandhi and His Critics* (Delhi, 1993 [1985]), 21. See also *CW* 53: 229, 5 February 1933; *CW* 53: 259, 11 February 1933.

40. *CW* 50, 466–7, 18 August 1932 (Appendix). See also Brown, *Gandhi and Civil Disobedience*, 313, 315.

41. For Ambedkar's account of the fast, see his *What Congress and Gandhi Have Done to the Untouchables* (Bombay, 1946), 270–71. See also Sushila Nayar, *Mahatma Gandhi – Preparing for Swaraj* (Ahmedabad, 1996), 78–9; D.G. Tendulkar, *Mahatma* (Delhi, 1951–54; revised 1960–63), Vol. 3, 167–75; and *CW* 51: Appendix 1B (from Mahadev Desai's diary).

42. Ambedkar, *What Congress and Gandhi Have Done to the Untouchables*, 270.

43. *CW* 51: 143, 26 September 1932.

44. *CW* 51: 96–7, 19 September 1932 (T); *CW* 51: 119, 20 September 1932; *CW* 51: 460 (Appendix 1B) (T). That there would be a 'chain' of fasts – as opposed to simply a large number of fasts by individuals – was not spelled out in September 1932. It was only in the following year – in connection with the 21-day fast of May 1933 – that Gandhi made it clear that the mass fasting he had in mind in order to bring about the end of untouchability would take place, at least initially, in sequence. (See n54 below).

45. *CW* 52: 326, 6 January 1933.

46. *CW* 51: 84, 19 September 1932 (T).

47. *CW* 51: 53, 13 September 1932 (T); *CW* 51: 96–7, 19 September 1932 (T).

48. *CW* 52: 376, 6 January 1933.

49. *CW* 53: 483 (Appendix 2), 13 January 1933 (T).

50. *CW* 52: 114, 4 December 1932.

51. *CW* 52: 161, 9 December 1932; *CW* 52: 175, 12 December 1932.

52. *CW* 53: 332–3, 18 February 1933.

53. *CW* 55: 74, 30 April 1933.

54. *CW* 55: 93, 2 May 1933 (T). On the chain of fasts, see *CW* 55: 87–91, 1/2 May 1933 (T); *CW* 55: 131, 6 May 1933 (T); *CW* 55: 136, 7 May 1933 (T); *CW* 55: 143–4, 7 May 1933 (T); *CW* 55: 145, 7 May 1933 (T); *CW* 55: 146, 7 May 1933 (T); *CW* 55: 163, 9 May 1933 (T).

55. *CW* 54: 159, 22 March 1933 (T). See also *CW* 55: 442 (Appendix 4), 4 May 1933.

56. 'Parvati, Dionysus. I loved nothing in the world as those names.' Nilla Cram Cook, *My Road to India* (New York, 1939), 68. For more on Cook see Martin Green, *Gandhi: Voice of a New Age Revolution* (New York, 1993), 329–36, and Madeleine Slade, *The Spirit's Pilgrimage* (New York, 1960), 179–80.

57. Cook, *My Road to India*, 349.

58. *CW* 54: 121–2, 18 March 1933.

59. *CW* 55: 153, 8 May 1933 (T).

60. *CW* 55, 191 9 June 1933 (T).

61. Nayar, *Mahatma Gandhi – Preparing for Swaraj*, 113.

62. *CW* 55: 90, 2 May 1933 (T). On Gandhi's efforts to 'purify' the ashram before it sacrificed itself, see also *CW* 55: 154, 8 May 1933 (T); *CW* 55: 163, 9 May 1933 (T); *CW* 55: 185, 6 June 1933 (T).

63. *CW* 57: 194, 21 February 1934.

64. *CW* 64: 33–4, 13/14 November 1936.

65. *CW* 55: 294–5, 25 July 1933. But see *CW* 55: 288, 22 July 1933 (T), for the statement that the disbandment was also intended to pre-empt a government takeover following non-payment of land revenue.

66. Sarvepalli Gopal, *Jawaharlal Nehru: A Biography* (Delhi, 1993), 94.

67. *CW* 53: 417–19, 25 February 1933 (T).

68. *CW* 53: 465–6, 4 March 1933. Extracts from Tucker's letter were published by Gandhi in an article in *Harijan* on 11 March 1933 (*CW* 54: 49).

69. *CW* 55: 361–2, 19 August 1933; *CW* 55: 453–4 (Appendix 12), 18 August 1933.

70. *CW* 57: 30, 21 January 1934; *CW* 56: 167, 1 November 1933.

71. *CW* 57: 155, 13 February 1934 (T). Tagore's statement is in *CW* 57, Appendix 1.

72. *CW* 57: 87, 2 February 1934.

73. *CW* 57: 392, 15 April 1934 (T).

74. See, e.g., his (more guarded) comments on the 1927 floods in Gujarat (*CW* 34: 358, 15 August 1927 (T); *CW* 34: 397–8, 25 August 1927).

75. *CW* 57: 318, 27 March 1934.

76. *CW* 97: 187, 23 April 1934 (T).

77. Some record of these conversations can be found in *CW* 57: 299–305, 22 March 1934 (T). What follows on Gandhi's thinking regarding individual *satyagraha* is also based on *CW* 57: 348–9, 2 April 1934 and *CW* 57, Appendix 3, 'On or after April 4, 1934'.

78. For how impressed Gandhi was by the reception he got on this tour, see *CW* 57: 84–5, 1 February 1934, and *CW* 57: 304, 22 March 1934 (T).

79. *CW* 57: Appendix 3, 'On or after 4 April, 1934'.

80. *CW* 58: 158–60, 10 July 1934; *CW* 58: 297–8, 6 August 1934.

81. See *CW* 57: 510 (Appendix 3), 'On or after 4 April 1934'.

82. *CW* 57: 441–2, 27 April 1934.

83. *CW* 57: 466, 8 May 1934; *CW* 57: 473, 9 May 1934; *CW* 57: 474, 10 May 1934 (T); *CW* 57: 485, 'Before May 12, 1934'.

84. *CW* 59: 3–12, 17 September 1934.

85. *CW* 60: 229, 15 February 1935; *CW* 59: 199, 19 October 1934 (T).

86. *CW* 59: 229, 26 October 1934.

87. *CW* 59: 406, 28 November 1934. See also *CW* 59: 276, 31 October/2 November 1934; *CW* 59: 348–9, 15 November 1934.

88. *CW* 59: 371, 18 November 1934 (T).

89. *CW* 72: 338, 31 July 1940.

90. *CW* 61: 403, 10 September 1935 (T).

91. *CW* 25: 273–4, 31 October 1924; also *CW* 19: 563, 13 April 1921.

92. *CW* 65: 433, 24 July 1937.

93. *CW* 60: 95–7, 'Before January 21, 1935'.

94. *CW* 61: 393–4, 'Before September 7, 1935'.

95. *CW* 63: 273, 12 September 1936.

96. *CW* 60: 66–9, 8 January 1935.

97. For the meeting with Sanger, see *CW* 62: 156–60, 3/4 December 1935; and Margaret Sanger, *An Autobiography* (New York, 1938), 470–71.

98. *CW* 62: 154, 2 December 1935 (T).

99. *CW* 61: 369, 26 August 1935.

100. *CW* 61: 291, 28 July 1935 (T).

101. *CW* 61: 264–7, 20 July 1935.

102. *CW* 61: 450, 26 September 1935 (T).

103. *CW* 62: 28–30, 12 October 1935.

104. *CW* 62: 247, 6 March 1936 (T); *CW* 62: 261–3, 14 March 1936.

105. *CW* 62: 372, 6 May 1936 (T).

106. *CW* 62: 297, 28 March 1936.

107. *CW* 65: 315–16, 18 June 1937 (T).

108. *CW* 65: 202, 5 June 1937.

109. *CW* 64: 443–5, 20 March 1937.

110. *CW* 62: 297, 28 March 1936. See also *CW* 62: 279, 21 March 1936.

111. Nayar, *Mahatma Gandhi – Preparing for Swaraj*, 420–21.

112. *CW* 66: 281, 30 October 1937.

113. *CW* 66: 90, n1, 30 August 1937.

114. *CW* 66: 432–3, 26 March 1938 (T).

115. *CW* 67: 89, n1, 28 May 1938.

116. *CW* 67: 92, 22 May 1938.

117. Slade, *The Spirit's Pilgrimage*, 216–17.

118. *CW* 72: 371–2, 9 August 1940 (T).

119. *CW* 62: 210–12, 29 February 1936; *CW* 62: 372–3, 6 May 1936 (T).

120. *CW* 70: 285–6, 22 October 1939.

121. The interested reader is referred to the *Collected Works* from 1936 on, including *CW* 93, 94 and 95, which provide much information. A letter to Pyarelal of 11 November 1940 (*CW* 95: 111–113 (T)) gives a vivid picture of the situation at Segaon. See also Mehta, *Mahatma Gandhi and His Apostles*.

122. *CW* 67: 58, 2 May 1938 (T).

123. *CW* 67: 194–8, 23 July 1938.

124. Pyarelal, *Mahatma Gandhi – The Last Phase*, Vol. 1, Book 2 (Ahmedabad, 1966 [1956]), 213.

125. *CW* 70: 312–15, 30 October 1939.

## 9. Götterdämmerung

1. *CW* 67: 382, 29 September 1938.

2. *CW* 92: 64, 21 August 1929 (T).

3. For the Rajkot *satyagraha*, see John Wood, 'Rajkot: Indian Nationalism in the Princely Context', in Robin Jeffrey, ed., *People, Princes and Paramount Power* (Delhi, 1978).

4. *CW* 68: 461, 27 February 1939 (see also n1).

5. *CW* 68: 446, 24 February 1939.

6. The sequence of events is laid out in B.K. Ahluwalia and Shashi Ahluwalia, *Netaji and Gandhi* (Delhi, 1982), chs 6, 7 and 8.

7. *CW* 69: 271, 17 May 1939.

8. *CW* 69: 369, 23 June 1939.

9. For Gandhi's first major statement of this point of view, see *CW* 69: 389–92, 4 July 1939.
10. *CW* 69: 180, 29 April 1939.
11. *CW* 69: 208, 5 May 1939 (T).
12. *CW* 70: 20–21, 23 July 1939.
13. *CW* 70: 227, 2 October 1939. See also *CW* 72: 188, 18 June 1940; *CW* 72: 193, 22 June 1940.
14. *CW* 75: 177, 17 December 1941 (T).
15. *CW* 75: 205, 8 January 1942 (T).
16. *CW* 72: 229–31, 2 July 1940.
17. *CW* 70: 271, 18 October 1939 (T).
18. *CW* 76: 50, 19 April 1942.
19. *CW* 72: 88, 21 May 1940 (T).
20. *CW* 73: 52–4, 25 September 1940.
21. The Working Committee's statement is given in the appendix to Sushila Nayar, *Mahatma Gandhi – Preparing for Swaraj* (Ahmedabad, 1996).
22. *CW* 70: 203–6, 25 September 1939.
23. *CW* 71: 36–8, 15 December 1939.
24. *CW* 72: 437, 2 September 1940.
25. *CW* 70: 267–8, 18 October 1939.
26. *CW* 70: 375, 23 November 1939.
27. D.G. Tendulkar, *Mahatma* (Delhi, 1951–54; revised, 1960–63), Vol. 6, 3.
28. *CW* 73: 69, 29 September 1940.
29. *CW* 73: 21, 15 September 1940.
30. *CW* 65: 380, 10 July 1937.
31. *CW* 73: 127, 24 October 1940. See also *CW* 73: 126, 24 October 1940 (Gandhi's statement to the press on the new campaign) for more on 'thought-power' and its anticipated effect.
32. *CW* 74: 117, 16 June 1941 (T). Gandhi was here writing of his decision in October 1940 to suspend publication of *Harijan* rather than accept government censorship.
33. *CW* 73: 142, 31 October 1940 (T).
34. The CWC resolution of 30 December 1941 is in *CW* 75, Appendix 2.
35. On the Cripps mission, see R.J. Moore, *Churchill, Cripps and India, 1939–1945* (Oxford, 1979). The observation attributed to Gandhi that the Cripps offer was a post-dated cheque on a failing bank does not appear in *CWMG*. See Sushila Nayar, *Mahatma Gandhi – Final Fight for Freedom* (Ahmedabad, 1997), 234.
36. *CW* 75: 205, 8 January 1942 (T).
37. *CW* 75: 326, 17 February 1942; *CW* 75: 401–2, 10 March 1942. See also *CW* 76: 27, 13 April 1942.
38. *CW* 96, Appendix 4.
39. *CW* 76: 195–6, 6 June 1942.
40. *CW* 76: 449, in Appendix 5, consisting of extracts from Louis Fischer's *A Week with Gandhi* (New York, 1942). The interviews given to Fischer in June 1942 were some of the most illuminating Gandhi gave.
41. *CW* 76: 108, 15 May 1942.
42. *CW* 76: 187, 6 June 1942.

43. *CW* 76: 60–61, 22 April 1942.

44. *CW* 76: 364–7, 4 August 1942.

45. *CW* 76: 297, 14 July 1942.

46. *CW* 76: 105, 14 May 1942; also *CW* 76: 197, 6 June 1942 .

47. *CW* 76: 109, 15 May 1942. The only source for this meeting is a document in British official archives, purportedly an intercepted report. Sushila Nayar (*Mahatma Gandhi – Final Fight for Freedom*, 269–70) accepts its authenticity.

48. *CW* 76: 334, 26 July 1942 (T); also *CW* 76: 160, 28 May 1942 (T).

49. *CW* 76: 220, 14 June 1942 (T).

50. *CW* 76: 328–9, 'Before July 25, 1942'; also *CW* 76: 273, 5 July 1942.

51. *CW* 35: 456, 12 January 1928.

52. *CW* 77: 157, 15 July 1943.

53. *CW* 77: 145–6, 15 July 1943.

54. *CW* 76: 329, 'Before July 25, 1942'.

55. *CW* 76: 341, 28 July 1942; also *CW* 76: 381, 7 August 1942.

56. *CW* 76: 50, 19 April 1942.

57. *CW* 95: 121, 'Before December 9, 1941'.

58. *CW* 76: 463, 8 August 1942 (in Appendix 11).

59. *CW* 76: 254, 27 June 1942.

60. Principal sources for Quit India are Francis G. Hutchins, *India's Revolution: Gandhi and the Quit India Movement* (Cambridge MA, 1973), and Gyanendra Pandey, ed., *The Indian Nation in 1942* (Calcutta, 1988).

61. Quoted in Nayar, *Mahatma Gandhi – Final Fight for Freedom*, 349.

62. *CW* 76: 414, 23 September 1942.

63. *CW* 76: 334, 26 July 1942 (T).

64. *CW* 77: 19–25, 11 October 1942. Compare *CW* 12: 45–52, 26 April 1913 (T).

65. *CW* 77: 71, 3 March 1943.

66. *CW* 77: 405, 19 July 1944.

67. *CW* 77: 407, 20 July 1944.

68. *CW* 77: 439, 30 July 1944.

69. *CW* 78: 24, 'On or before August 12, 1944'.

70. *CW* 78: 25, 12 August 1944 (T).

71. *CW* 78: 97, 12 September 1944.

72. *CW* 78: 82, 'On or after September 5, 1944'; also *CW* 78: 81, 'On or after September 4, 1944', and *CW* 78: 83, 'On or after September 5, 1944.' *CW* 79: 212–3, 6 March 1945 (T) contains both information and disclaimers regarding the 'experiment'. Ved Mehta's interviews with Abha Gandhi and Sushila Nayar (in *Mahatma Gandhi and His Apostles*, New Haven, 1993 [1977]), 198–204) give some information.

73. *CW* 79: contains much correspondence on the topic.

74. *CW* 87: 90–91, 15/16 March 1947.

75. *CW* 79: 222, 7 March 1945 (T); *CW* 79: 192, 1 March 1945 (T).

76. *CW* 79: 215, 6 March 1945 (T).

77. Sir John Woodroffe, aka 'Arthur Avalon', was a British judge in Calcutta who wrote extensively on the *tantra*. His best known works were *The Serpent Power* (1914) and *Shakti and Shakta* (1918). He was anxious to demonstrate the philosophical respectability of tantrism as a spiritual discipline connecting its practitioners to

cosmic energy, and downplayed the sexual practices associated with it. Gandhi read Woodroffe's books during his jail sentences of 1922–4 and 1930–31. In 1932 he told Mahadev Desai he had found one of Woodroffe's books, recently lent to him by Indulal Yajnik, disgusting (Mahadev Desai, *The Diary of Mahadev Desai*, Ahmedabad, 1953, 144). But his reference to Woodroffe in the conversation of 15/16 March 1947 (*CW* 87: 91; see n74 above) with Swami Anand and Kedar Nath was respectful. Woodroffe approached tantrism as an esoteric system. But in practice it is not easy to say where the distinction lies between explicitly 'tantric' ideas and ideas about sex generally held in India. Some scholars now see tantrism as the ritualized expression of an Indian folk conception of sexuality. Beliefs about the benefits of conserving semen, with which Gandhi had long been familiar, fall into this category (see Chapter 3, 96, and Chapter 3, n154).

78. My account of this relationship is based as far as possible on the contemporary documentation in *CWMG*.
79. *CW* 77: 331, 23 June 1944 (T).
80. *CW* 79: 45, 19 January 1945 (T); see also *CW* 79: 96, 5 February 1945 (T).
81. *CW* 80: 163, 22 May 1945 (T).
82. *CW* 86: 220–21, 12 December 1946 (T).
83. See the letters from Gandhi to Pyarelal in *CW* 94, beginning 2 October 1946, 304.
84. *CW* 77: 311–2, 12 June 1944 (T).
85. Nirmal Kimar Bose, *My Days with Gandhi* (Delhi, 1974), 101.
86. *CW* 94 333, 30 December 1946 (T).
87. *CW* 80: 384, 29 June 1945.
88. *CW* 84: 347, 19 June 1946; Judith Brown, *Gandhi: Prisoner of Hope* (Delhi, 1990), 368, 429 n38.
89. *CW* 87: 539–40, Appendix 7. See also Appendices 8 through 15; and *CW* 87: 179–80, 1 April 1947; *CW* 87: 199–200, 4 April 1947; *CW* 87: 246–7, 10 April 1947; *CW* 87: 254–5, 11 April 1947; and Pyarelal, *Mahatma Gandhi – The Last Phase* (Ahmedabad, 1958), Vol. 2, 78–86.
90. *CW* 89: 523 (Appendix 2).
91. *CW* 90: 130, 29 November 1947.
92. *CW* 88: 116–7, 9 June 1947 (T).
93. *CW* 90: 337, 1 January 1948.
94. *CW* 90: 217, 11/12 December 1947; also *CW* 89: 62, 'Before August 20, 1947'.
95. *CW* 86: 164, 26 November 1946.
96. *CW* 86: 52, 'On or before October 28, 1946'.
97. *CW* 85: 516 (Appendix 2).
98. *CW* 86: 11, 21 October 1946.
99. *CW* 89: 341, 16 October 1947; also *CW* 89: 216, 22 September 1947.
100. *CW* 86: 183, 2 December 1946.
101. *CW* 86: 193, 4 December 1946; *CW* 86: 288, 30 December 1946 (T).
102. *CW* 86: 262–3, 25 December 1946 (T).
103. *CW* 86: 52, 'On or before October 28, 1946'.
104. Quoted in Ved Mehta, *Mahatma Gandhi and His Apostles*, 194.
105. *CW* 87: 15, 24 February 1947.
106. Manu Gandhi, *The Lonely Pilgrim* (Ahmedabad, 1964), 9.

107. *CW* 88: 348, 16 July 1947 (T).
108. Erik Erikson, *Gandhi's Truth: On the Origins of Militant Non-violence* (New York, 1969), 403–4. See also Pyarelal, *Mahatma Gandhi – The Last Phase*, Vol, 1, Book 2 (Ahmedabad, 1956), 219.
109. *CW* 42: 5, 17 October 1929.
110. Anna Kingsford and Edward Maitland, *The Perfect Way* (London, 1923 [1882]), 262. See also Pyarelal, *Mahatma Gandhi – The Last Phase*, Volume 1, Book 2, 223.
111. Manu Gandhi, *The Lonely Pilgrim*, 93, 111.
112. *CW* 87: 92, 15/16 March 1947.
113. *CW* 87: 103, 17 March 1947.
114. *CW* 89: 49, 16 August 1947.
115. *CW* 89: 75, 22 August 1947.
116. *CW* 89: 116, 30 August 1947.
117. *CW* 89: 55, 17 August 1947 (T).
118. *CW* 89: 126–7, 1 September 1947 (T) (letter to Vallabhbhai Patel); *CW* 89: 129–32, 1 September 1947 (press statement). Manu's accounts are in *The Miracle of Calcutta* (Ahmedabad, 1959), 65–7, and *The End of an Epoch* (Ahmedabad, 1959), 16–17.
119. *CW* 89: 129, 1 September 1947 ('Talk with Marwari Deputation').
120. Pyarelal, *Mahatma Gandhi – The Last Phase*, Vol. 2, 407; Manu Gandhi, *The Miracle of Calcutta*, 70.
121. *CW* 89: 138, 2 September 1947.
122. *CW* 89: 132–3, 1 September 1947.
123. *CW* 89: 134, 1/2 September 1947 (T).
124. The description given in *CW* 89: 150 n1, 4 September 1947.
125. *CW* 89: 150, 4 September 1947. See also *CW* 89: 266, 1 October 1947 (T).
126. Pyarelal, *Mahatma Gandhi – The Last Phase*, Vol. 2, 433.
127. *CW* 90: 23–4, 13 November 1947 (T).
128. *CW* 90: 145, 1 December 1947.
129. *CW* 90: 421, 14 January 1948 (T).
130. *CW* 90: 375, 7 January 1948 (T); *CW* 90: 384, 8 January 1948 (T).
131. *CW* 90: 409, 12 January 1948; also Pyarelal, *Mahatma Gandhi – The Last Phase*, Vol. 2, 701.
132. Pyarelal, *Mahatma Gandhi – The Last Phase*, Vol. 2, 700–701.
133. *CW* 90: 437, 16 January 1948.
134. *CW* 90: 453, 18 January 1948.
135. *CW* 90: 453, 18 January 1948.
136. *CW* 90: 455, 19 January 1948.
137. *CW* 90: 447, 18 January 1948.

# Index